The Arab Table

The Arab Table

RECIPES AND CULINARY TRADITIONS

May S. Bsisu

WM
WILLIAM MORROW
An Imprint of HarperCollins*Publishers*

HarperCollins books may be purchased for educational, business, or sales promotional use. For information, please write: Special Markets Department, HarperCollins Publishers, 10 East 53rd Street, New York, NY 10022.

Designed by Ralph Fowler

Photographs by Anna Williams

Printed on acid-free paper

Library of Congress Cataloging-in-Publication Data

Bsisu, May S.
    The Arab table: recipes and culinary traditions/May S. Bsisu.
        p.   cm.
    ISBN 978-0-06-058614-0
    1. Cookery, Arab.   I. Title.

  TX725.A7B75   2005
  641.59'2927—dc22   2005046045

13 14 15 16 SCP 10 9 8 7 6

In memory of my grandmother

Nazleh (1910–2003)

and my sister Ikram (1948–1990).

For my children,

Wasfi, Basil, and Naji,

my pride and joy,

and for all of my nieces and nephews.

Contents

Acknowledgments

This book is the realization of a long-held dream. Like all dreams, it passed through many stages, each one guided by family and friends who gave me their unconditional support and love.

My husband, best friend, and wise counselor, Aref, who has never hesitated to go out of his way to do what's best for our family, was with me every step of the way during the creation of this book. Not only did he handle all of the business dealings associated with it, but he read every word, tasted every dish again and again, and offered advice. I reserve my deepest gratitude for you, Aref, for keeping the promise you made to my parents thirty years ago.

Wasfi, Basil, and Naji, you are the most joyful achievements of my life. What greater reward is there for a mother than to watch her boys grow into healthy, successful, and happy young men? I am filled with pride at the mere mention of you. May you remember the wonderful times we've spent around our own kitchen table and the tables of our extended family and friends. Stay close and gather your future families together often, always around good food blessed with love and happiness.

A special thank you to my father and mother,

Abdul Aziz and Lamice Shakhashir, who are and always will be my greatest source of comfort. No matter how geographically far apart we are, your love is always here with my family and me. You have stood by me throughout my life, during the bright moments as well as the difficulties, and for this I am eternally grateful. I am blessed to have siblings I can count on, too. Thank you, Maha, Akram, and Haifa.

I would like to express my deep appreciation and gratitude to my editor, Harriet Bell, who showed a rare brand of patience and understanding to this first-time author. Thank you for believing in the importance of this book. The support and help I received from Kathleen Hackett was unparalleled and invaluable in the creation of this book. Kathleen spent long hours cooking with me in my kitchen in order to translate the swirl of activity into lucid recipes and headnotes. Thank you, Kathleen, for capturing my voice in these pages. I am grateful, too, to David Nussbaum for translating my personal stories into the essays interspersed throughout the book. I would not have had the great opportunity to work with Harriet Bell were it not for my agent, Lisa Ekus.

A very special thanks to the recipe-testing team, who spent untold numbers of hours meticulously measuring, chopping, weighing, timing—and talking and eating—their way through every single recipe in this book. Chef Jack Rouse shared his cooking expertise—and his good humor. Chef Leonard Hollander, always eager and enthusiastic, did a great job of taking detailed notes. Many thanks to my friend Sharon Roeder, an artist and accomplished home cook, who tested recipes alongside me and documented every measure and method along the way. Amanda Stout was an invaluable assistant throughout the testing of the recipes. Many thanks to my friend Karen Fazzio, who lent a hand in the kitchen. I am also grateful to Chef Nathan Jolly, from Tellers Restaurant in Cincinnati.

Authoring a cookbook is an enormous undertaking, and translating the recipes into visually stunning photographs requires special expertise and collaboration. I thank Anna Williams for taking such beautiful photographs. And many thanks to food stylist Alison Attenborough for doing an excellent job of making my food look so delicious and true to the way I present it. Stylist Helen Crowther's flawless eye for shape, form, and composition comes through in every photograph.

There are several special friends who assisted me without hesitation. Maha Sabbagh, my dearest friend, offered valuable information and insight. She tested recipes, researched ingredients, and pushed me along when the road seemed too long. Omar Sabbagh came through when I needed help organizing my thoughts. Melissa Zimmer spent many weekends putting my scattered recipes in order. I also wish to thank those who helped me launch my food and cooking career in the United States: Susan Shertzer devoted an enormous amount of time and energy organizing and scheduling my cooking classes. Marilyn Harris graciously introduced me to the city's food community when I first arrived and continues to offer tremendous support and friendship. A simple thank you to Marilyn does not seem enough.

My appreciation goes to my many friends and colleagues, including Jeni Lee, Mike and Tammy Palmer, Julie Dukens, portrait photographer Ron Rack, and Rocco dal Vera—from the bottom of my heart. I also want to thank my dear childhood friend Najwa Al Qattan, professor of Middle Eastern history at Loyola University, for her help in writing and explaining the history of the Arab world and its effect on the culture and food. Thank you, Najwa, for the past thirty years of friendship.

Finally, many thanks to the great team at William Morrow, including the always delightful Lucy Baker, publicist Carrie Bachman, copyeditor Kathie Ness, and jacket art director Roberto de Vicq de Cumptich.

x *Acknowledgments*

Introduction

"Tafadalo! *Please, come to the table!*"

WHEN I ASK MY FAMILY, friends, business associates, and others to join me at my table, this phrase has much more meaning than a mere "Come and get it." The Arabic *tafadalo* literally means "do me the honor"; it is an offering and an invitation. In Arab and Arab-American homes, giving to others and sharing a meal, especially with guests, is a time-honored tradition and an expression of hospitality. When you join me at my table, you do me the honor of sampling the bounty of the Arab table.

My guests are often surprised by the abundance, diversity, and fresh flavors of the Arab table when dining in my home. With this cookbook you also do me the honor of learning about the culinary and related social customs of Arab people. Too little is understood about the Arab world, and it is my hope that through these recipes, along with the explanations of customs and holy days, you will become more familiar with Arab traditions and discover the pleasures of the Arab table.

My Many Homelands

I was born in Amman, Jordan, into a Muslim family. My father, Abdul Aziz Shakhashir, is Palestinian, originally from the city of Nablus in the West Bank. My mother, Lamice Said Sabbagh, was born into a Lebanese family from Sidon, in southern Lebanon. We lived in Jordan for a few years until my father's business took us to Kuwait. When I was eleven, my parents sent me and my younger sister, Maha, to the Beirut Evangelical School for Girls, a Christian boarding school. Although it was difficult to be so far from my mother and father, our maternal grandparents lived in Beirut, and Maha and I spent every weekend with them. In the kitchen of my grandmother, whom I called *tata* Nazleh, and who was one of the finest cooks I have ever met, I learned priceless lessons about the foods of our people—and much about life.

After graduating from high school, I began my studies at Beirut University College and soon met Aref Wasfi Bsisu, a young man from a Palestinian family. College work was not as much fun as he was, I admit, and a year later we were married. Sadly, the Lebanese civil war started at that

1

time, so we moved to Kuwait City, where Aref established himself in business. In 1976 we moved to London, where our first son, Wasfi, was born. My parents and brother, Akram, soon followed us, and for a number of years we divided our time between Kuwait and England. Our younger boys, Basil and Naji, were born in London as well.

Our own destiny lay elsewhere, however. Both of us wanted to find the best place to raise our children, and we decided to pursue immigrating to the United States. The invasion of Kuwait and the first conflict in the Gulf confirmed the wisdom of our decision. In 1990 we settled near Cincinnati, Ohio, and started our new lives.

In the many places that I've called home—and the many more that I've visited—the one constant in our lives has been food. What I have learned as well, in these far-flung places, is that there is both a great similarity in all Arab cuisine—a common store of basic ingredients, closely related dishes, and familiar food customs—and a marvelous diversity, with distinctive flavors, unique preparations, and endless variations. And although my travels, curiosity, and years of cooking have given me expertise in Arab foods, it would take several lifetimes to learn it all (and would fill a library of cookbooks too). In my grandmother's kitchen in Beirut, in desert villages in Jordan, in hotel kitchens in Kuwait, and in friends' homes and fine restaurants and from street vendors in Baghdad, Cairo, and Damascus—and even in North London and Cincinnati—I've found new dishes to add to to my Arab table.

This is not surprising, if you consider the breadth of the Arab world. Looking at a map, you'll see that it lies across nearly a quarter of the globe: starting on the west at the Atlantic shores of North Africa, across the eastern shore of the Mediterranean, and then farther eastward across the vast Arabian Peninsula to the Arabian Sea. In all these lands, the majority of the population shares the Arabic language, a historical and cultural heritage, and (except for the important minority of Christian Arabs) the Muslim faith.

The Arab World: A Brief History

The Arab world comprises several nation-states in the Middle East and North Africa. The inhabitants of this area, which extends from "the Atlantic Ocean to the Arabian Gulf," as many Arabs are fond of noting, share linguistic and cultural traditions. At the same time, the region is rich in religious, ethnic, and cultural diversity. On its western flank, the Arab world melds with Africa, and to the north and east it shades into Turkey and Iran, respectively. Along the Eastern Mediterranean, the Syrians, Lebanese, Palestinians, and Egyptians belong to a world also inhabited by non-Arabs. Hence, although much connects cities such as Alexandria and Baghdad, for example, each also has a history of its own. It is this history that explains some of the great varieties in the foods of the Arab world.

Local and regional histories are woven out of political, economic, and cultural networks; these networks are the stuff of place, of home. The networks are themselves circumscribed by agricultural and geographical realities. In some cases, locale is paramount, as in the production of olive oil and other olive-related foodstuffs in Lebanon and Palestine. In other instances, and particularly in more recent centuries, the forces of international trade and the colonial experience overshadow local realities.

Food, like all human inventions, has a story to tell. And as a growing body of food histories and commodity studies suggest, food packs a mighty good tale. First, of course, there is the question of natural availability: what grows well in a particular native habitat. Then perhaps more dramatically, there is the introduction of certain ingredients through trade—spices, tomatoes, potatoes, and chocolate, for example. In addition, cultural practices and religious taboos often regulate, and at times prohibit, the consumption of one food or another (such as pork, beef, or alcohol). Politics plays a great role as well; just consider the history of tea.

The Arab world has had a tumultuous history in the past century, a history that has had an impact on its food as well. At the end of the nineteenth century, the Ottoman Empire, which had controlled the Arabic-speaking world since the early sixteenth century, still exerted control from the borders of Iran (then Persia) in the east to the Arabian Peninsula in the south. But in Egypt and farther west along the North African coast, Britain and France had already established a colonial presence that would grow over the coming decades. The Empire's entanglements with France and Britain (and with Russia) came to an end at the close of World War I in 1918, when the Ottomans—along with their European allies, the German and Austro-Hungarian empires—lost the war as well as the peace. The Empire was dismembered and its various parts emerged as nation-states. Yet the reassembly process—the manner in which borders were drawn and made real—was complicated and bloody. And it was a process that in large measure ignored the regional identities and political desires of the inhabitants, serving instead the interests of Britain and France. The victors of the Great War took political and economic control over the area, using a number of means both direct and indirect. Although the majority of the Arab States had gained at least nominal sovereignty by the middle of the

twentieth century, violence did not end. Today, more than half a century later, much of the region is still torn by war.

In the decades following the end of World War I, the Arab world found its history and politics at the intersection of new local and international realities. Present-day Arabs find themselves belonging to countries that are politically autonomous but have much in common with neighboring states—ties that exceed that of a common language, extending to social behavior and culinary traditions.

The geographical diversity of the Arab world also contributed to the creation of different cuisines. The Eastern Mediterranean region, for example, is rich in olive oil, vegetables, and wheat—foods we see in Lebanese, Syrian, and Palestinian cuisine. On the other hand, typical dishes in the Arab Gulf States, where the climate is less hospitable, rely more on imported foods.

History and geography provide a backdrop against which the varieties of foods and palates in the Arab world can be understood. The preparation of food represents one of humanity's most original ways of creatively transforming the products of nature into a life-sustaining enterprise, one that has its own story, its own history. This history is on full display in the recipes in *The Arab Table*.

Similarities and Differences

The waves of conquest and migration that brought the Arab language and Islam to this immense territory, starting some 1,400 years ago, naturally carried along the foods and culinary customs of the homelands of the Arab people. Out of the Arabian Peninsula came the spices, meats, and transportable foods that were the staples of the nomadic Bedouin tribes. From the Fertile Crescent and the lush lands nearer the Mediterranean came fresh fruits, vegetables, and grains. These flavorful and versatile ingredients became the foundation of the distinctive cookery of the Arab table, with myriad variations developing in the different geographic regions.

So what are the common elements of Arab cookery? Here's an overview of some of the most important. More details about ingredients and food products can be found in the Arab Pantry (page 12), with information on where to purchase them in Sources (page 347).

Bread: Bread is so highly valued in the Arab world that if a scrap is thrown into the street, someone will quickly pick it up and utter the name of god, then put it on a ledge or other safe place so no one can step on it. Bread is a primary ingredient in salads and in fateh, a layered dish made with bread, rice, and meat or chicken.

Dairy and meat products: Yogurt, made from sheep's, cow's, or goat's milk, is used in many ways: thin as a refreshing drink, drained and thickened as a condiment, and even dried. In the Gulf States, camel's and goat's milk is used as a beverage and as a cooking ingredient. Almost everywhere in the Arab world, lamb is the principal meat, with stuffed baby lamb being the most prized dish an Arab can serve to his guests. In Bedouin cultures, sheep and camel meat is cooked as well.

Fresh and dried fruits, fruit products, and nuts: Pomegranates, lemons, dates, *loumi* (dried limes), apricot juice, pomegranate drink, almonds, and pistachios are all staples in the Arab kitchen, along with oranges, figs, and apples.

Grains: Rice is eaten throughout the Arab world. It is cooked in countless ways, both savory and sweet. Rice is sometimes served by itself, alongside meat, fish, or vegetables, and it is often incorporated into main dishes and mezza. Wheat—whole, cracked, and as flour for bread and pastries—is a staple grain. Grains such as bulgur are eaten for breakfast in North African countries.

Oil: Olive oil—produced in Lebanon, Jordan, Syria, Palestine, and parts of North Africa—is the most common cooking fat and dressing oil. In some regions where olives are scarce, other oils predominate, such as sesame oil in Iraq.

Salads: Always available at lunch and dinner, salads are typically eaten at the beginning of a meal. Salads, made with a wide variety of fresh vegetables, always have a simple fresh dressing of lemon juice, salt and pepper, and olive oil.

Spices: Cinnamon, allspice, anise seeds, nutmeg, sumac, cardamom, cloves, cumin, caraway, black pepper, saffron, and turmeric are the essence of the Arab table. The use and history of spices is one of the most fascinating aspects of the Arab table. The Arabian Peninsula, where our food traditions originated, has been connected to the spice trade throughout its history. In fact, before the Qur'an was revealed to the prophet Mohammad (peace be upon him), he accompanied caravans carrying spices for trade across the peninsula to Syria and Egypt.

Vegetables: Raw or cooked, vegetables such as eggplant, zucchini, cauliflower, okra, and spinach are favorite ingredients. Both fresh and dried beans and legumes, such as peas and lentils, are also essential.

Finally, a word about how meals are served in Arab homes. Lunch and dinner always start with mezza, an assortment of little tidbits served on small plates. Mezza sometimes accompany other dishes or together make a whole meal. Typical mezza include salads, pulses, grains, and vegetables.

Usually all the dishes are placed on the table at once rather than in different courses. It is customary to eat certain foods first or in combination with others, and I've written about those traditions throughout the book.

For Muslims everywhere, pork and alcohol are prohibited. However, the degree to which the prohibitions are followed is a matter of individual choice. Wines and liquors are available and enjoyed by many in Arab societies. Christian Arabs consume pork, so it is available in those communities in Jordan, Lebanon, and Egypt. In Islam, meats must be ritually slaughtered in order to be *halal,* or "allowed," a process much like the Jewish kosher slaughtering traditions.

Of course the dishes of the Arab table vary from region to region, as well as from house to house and cook to cook! Natural factors such as geography, climate, terrain, and agriculture play a huge role, determining the native food resources in each area. Many trade routes brought different foods to the various regions as well.

Arab cooking has also been influenced by the mingling of Arab and non-Arab peoples, often over many centuries of coexistence. In North Africa, Arab and Berber cultures have melded. In the Mediterranean and Middle East, Arabs and Jews have lived side by side for generations. A host of European cultures—including Spanish, Italian, French, and Greek—have had an impact on Arab cooking. The Turkish influence has been felt not only in the Arab lands bordering Turkey but all across the Arab world, which was subsumed within the Ottoman Empire for so long. In the easternmost Arab lands, Persian and Indian cultures made their mark. One can also easily find the influence of the colonial powers—especially England and France—that dominated Arab territories when Ottoman rule ended.

While my cooking is primarily grounded in the cuisines of Lebanon, Jordan, Kuwait, Palestine, Syria, Iraq, and Morocco, the recipes in this book derive from the methods, preparations, and ingredient combinations of all the countries in the Arab world. Because the territories and identities of many Arab nation-states were established relatively recently—just since World War I and even later—flavors and dishes do not always stay within a particular country's borders. Good food travels without a passport.

MOROCCO

Morocco's food is marvelously varied. The south of the country, where sugarcane and dates grow, is famous for its sweets. The mountain areas are rich with nuts and fruits, including apples, figs, lemons, apricots, and pomegranates. Preserved lemons are a staple flavoring in the Moroccan kitchen.

Lamb and mutton are the preferred meats. In the south, the meat is marinated in mint, olive oil, lemon juice, and orange juice; in the north, cooks prefer coriander and garlic.

The classic dishes of Morocco include *harira,* a chicken soup that is thickened with flour and eggs and flavored with saffron and cinnamon. There are as many recipes for harira as there are families in Morocco. Shorabat Adas Wa Hummus is my version of this delicious soup.

Couscous was originally made at home from semolina flour, salt, and water. Today every supermarket in the U.S. offers couscous that cooks almost instantly with the addition of broth or water. *Couscous* is also the name of Morocco's national dish, a luscious combination of spiced turnips, squash, potatoes, and chicken nestled on a bed of fluffy semolina.

A *tajine* is a lamb or chicken stew with sweet and sour flavorings, such as honey and vinegar or fruits and nuts. Tajines are spiced with ginger and saffron. The stews in this book are closely related to Moroccan tajines but are distinguished by the addition of *taqliya,* a mixture of sautéed cilantro and garlic, which is more typical of Egyptian and Eastern Mediterranean cuisines. (*Tagine* also refers to the traditional two-piece conical cooking vessel in which these stews are prepared.)

Bistilla is a pie consisting of flaky pastry filled with chopped meat, chicken, or fish, parsley, and ground almonds, all seasoned with ginger, nutmeg, cinnamon, saffron, and cardamom.

Moroccan *mint tea,* green tea flavored with fresh peppermint leaves and sugar, is enjoyed at breakfast, after meals, when guests arrive, and at all gatherings.

TUNISIA

Tunisia, the smallest country in North Africa, lies on the Mediterranean between Libya and Algeria. The cuisine of this coastal land is known as the "food of the sun," and it has a reputation for being the spiciest among the North African countries. *Harissa,* a condiment made from pounded hot peppers, garlic, olive oil, caraway seeds, coriander seeds, and salt, is found on every table at every meal. Favored ingredients in Tunisia include apricots, oranges, almonds, prunes, and cherries as well as barley, wheat, fava beans, and chickpeas. A wide variety of seafood, including shrimp, tuna, sardines, red mullet, and octopus, is enjoyed year-round, and lamb and couscous are often found on the Tunisian table.

Most dishes are seasoned with combinations of cumin, caraway, cinnamon, and rosebuds. The Tunisians adore long, leisurely meals featuring multiple courses.

IRAQ

Iraq's cuisine is noted for its refinement and sophistication, and perhaps more than any other Middle Eastern country, it is recognized as the most varied. The extensive Iraqi pantry includes eggplant, okra, chard, fava beans, wheat, barley, rice, bulgur and flavorings like vinegar, tamarind, dried lime (*loumi*), dill, dates, apricots, quince, and pomegranates. Iraqi food is distinguished by the use of sesame oil rather than olive oil. Among the most popular dishes in Iraq are *masgoof,* a simple dish of grilled *shabout* fish from the Tigris River, served with lemon slices and eaten with bread. *Dolma* is the name given to vegetables—including onions, tomatoes, eggplant, peppers, grape leaves, and cabbage leaves—that are stuffed with a mixture of rice, onions, chickpeas, raisins, fresh dill, mint, and parsley. Iraqi cooks take pride in the many varieties of *kibeh* that their country is known for, in particular the version from Mousel, in the north, which is made from *jereesh,* a coarsely cracked wheat that is similar to bulgur. In *arouck,* another popular dish, ground meat, scallions, and celery are fried and then kneaded into leavened dough, which is then rolled flat and baked—similar to the Meat Pies on page 81. *Threed* is a braised lamb stew that is served over broth-soaked pieces of *tanour,* a round whole-wheat flatbread.

SYRIA

Home to Damascus, the capital and arguably the oldest continuously inhabited city in the world, Syria has food traditions that are rich and varied—and as old as the city itself. In general, Syrian cooking is a cuisine of details and precision. For example, vegetables for salads are cut precisely—especially the tomatoes, which must be diced perfectly. Syrian cooks peel open their cardamom pods and grind the tiny seeds inside to season their coffee, rather than throwing the whole pod in the grinder as the Lebanese do. The flatbread in Fattah Dajaj (Chicken with Rice and Yogurt) is cut in precise pieces with a knife and then fried, rather than being torn and then toasted as it is in other Middle Eastern countries. Another mark of a Syrian dish is in its garnishes—they are treated with the utmost delicacy.

Syrian dishes often go by the same name as many Arab dishes, but the preparation of them can be quite different in different parts of the country, as a similar dish can be prepared in different ways throughout the country. For example, in Damascus, fresh coriander (cilantro) is pounded with garlic and swirled into stews to finish them, while in the rest of Syria, dried coriander is mashed with the garlic.

Eggplant is found in every garden and on every table for breakfast, lunch, and dinner. Syrian cooks have elevated the preparation of eggplant to an art form. It is diced and cooked with eggs, marinated and tossed into Fattoush Betinjan (Eggplant Salad), deep-fried for Maklobit Betinjan (Eggplant Upside Down), and grilled for Betinjan Mutabal (Eggplant Spread).

Though it is Lebanese in origin, *kibeh,* a mix of pounded lamb and bulgur, is prepared in countless ways in Syria. It is fried; cooked in a sauce flavored with pomegranate syrup; mixed with chopped onions, walnut, sumac, and lots of butter and grilled; and shaped into a dome, grilled, and served with a spicy walnut dip called Muhmmara. Aleppo, in the north bordering Turkey, is recognized in the Middle East as a temple of haute cuisine and is known throughout the Arab world for making the finest sweets.

Halawet al Jibin (Semolina Rolls), the finger-length pirouettes of semolina dough filled with sweetened cheese and soaked in sugar syrup, and *maamouniyeh,* a semolina desert layered with kashta and flavored with rose water, similar to Lebanese *bohsalini,* are among the most famous.

EGYPT

Egyptian food today is influenced by the cuisines of Syria, Lebanon, Turkey, Greece, and Italy. Mezza dishes, stuffed vegetables, *kibeh,* and pasta have all made their way onto Egyptian tables, both in restaurants and in homes. Accomplished farmers, Egyptians have long grown a cornucopia of fruits and vegetables. The fertile soil of the Nile River area allows farmers to grow figs, dates, sugarcane, strawberries, watermelon, mangoes, pomegranates, black and white grapes, artichokes, leeks, onions, okra, garlic, lettuce, cucumbers, radishes, cabbage, fava beans, and turnips.

Some of Egypt's traditional dishes include slow-cooked fava beans, or *ful,* and Fatteh Dajaj (Chicken and Rice with Creamy Yogurt Sauce), a popular Ramadan dish. Kushari, a warming combination of lentils and pasta served with a spicy sauce, is also a common home-cooked Egyptian dish. And of course there is *Ta'mia* (Falafel).

JORDAN

The food of Jordan is very much influenced by neighboring Lebanon, Syria, Iraq, and Palestine as well as its own geography. In the mountainous regions, lentils, chickpeas, bulgur, olives, olive oil, and grapes are pantry staples, while in the valleys, citrus fruits and vegetables are more abundant, as is sumac, which grows wild.

Jordanian food is also influenced by Bedouin food. One of the most distinctive and famous of these foods is *jameed,* sheep's milk which is put into a bag made from the animal's skin and shaken until it dries. It is then shaped into a ball about double the size of a golf ball and covered with salt to preserve it.

Mansaf, often made for a large gathering to mark an occasion, is made by layering cooked rice on top of large breads known as *tanour,* covering the rice with cooked *jameed* and then topping everything with lamb and nuts. The grand presentation is placed in the middle of the dining table.

Labneh, or yogurt cheese, is found on every breakfast table in Jordan, either for spreading like cream cheese or shaped into balls that have been rolled in crushed oregano or *zaatar,* a thyme and sesame seed seasoning.

Kahwa, or Arab coffee, is beloved in Jordan, where it is often poured, just a few drops at a time, from a long-handled copper pot, called a *dallah,* into a small handle-less cup.

LEBANON

Lebanese cooks are some of the most sophisticated in the Middle East, partially due to the cooking techniques taught to them by the French, who occupied the country in the 1940s. However, it is primarily the huge variety of fresh fruits and vegetables found in this small country of many microclimates that has shaped Lebanon's culinary traditions. The coastal plain is abundant with dates, bananas, citrus fruits, and sugarcane, while olives, grapes, figs, and almonds thrive slightly higher up. At even higher elevations, apricots, cherries, peaches, plums, hazelnuts, and walnuts are plentiful. Wheat grows in the valleys.

The Lebanese are recognized throughout the Arab world for their elaborate feasts of small dishes, or mezza, served before the main course or as a meal in themselves. Lebanese cooking is noted for its use of fresh fruits, vegetables, and seafood. Garlic and olive oil are staples. Vegetables are usually eaten fresh or cooked in olive oil. While fresh ingredients are the basis of the cuisine, so too are preserved foods, which come from the mountainous regions of the country, where harsh winters require villagers to preserve cheeses such as *shankleesh,* and to make fruit leathers from apricots, figs, and apples. Lebanese make a syrup from the juice of pomegranate seeds, and pickle everything from cucumbers to cauliflower and grape leaves.

Some of the most beloved dishes in Lebanon (and on my table here in Kentucky) include *kibeh,* a paste made from ground lamb and bulgur. The national dish of Lebanon, it is eaten in a variety of ways, including raw, as in the addictive Kibeh Nayeh. *Tabouleh,* a salad of chopped parsley, tomatoes, and bulgur, is a typical lunch salad or side dish in Lebanon, where fresh herbs are a vital part of the cuisine.

Tripoli is famous for *Boza bi Haleeb,* the mastic-flavored milk that is hand-pounded into an elastic ice cream that is found in sweetshops all over Lebanon.

PALESTINE

The food of the holy land of Christians, Jews, and Muslims is perhaps more heavily influenced by the history of the land and its people than any other country in the Middle East. In the last 2,000 years, Palestine has been a destination for millions of pilgrims, visitors, conquerors, and settlers, each of whom arrived with their own foods, cooking methods, and customs. Along with their tumultuous history, Palestinians have grown accustomed to adapting their cuisine to whatever is available to them. Palestinian cooks are known for creating several different dishes based on one ingredient and for using every last bit of it, from the pulp of the zucchini to every part of the chicken and lamb, including the gizzards and livers. On a Palestinian table you will find *zaatar,* the thyme-sesame mix that is eaten with bread and olives for breakfast; and *mujadara,* a side dish of brown lentils with rice and caramelized onions. *Kunafa,* a dessert made with shredded pastry and akawi cheese, marks most festive occasions in Palestine. Sage tea is a favorite drink at breakfast, after lunch and dinner, and whenever guests arrive.

YEMEN

Yemen is one of the most geographically varied of the Middle Eastern countries. A coastal plain lies along its southern rim, while highlands mark the interior and a desert stretches across the eastern region. The food of Yemen often includes *hawajat,* a vibrant yellow spice mixture that contains turmeric, black pepper, cumin, coriander, and cardamom. It is used in all kinds of dishes, from chicken soup to poached fish to broiled meat, and is where most of a dish's flavor is derived, since this is a cuisine based on little fat, sugar, lamb, beef, or dairy. In fact, most main dishes are cooked with a bit of animal fat seasoned with hawajat. A typical Yemeni meal features bread, rice, and broiled chicken, and potatoes, tomatoes, and cabbage cooked into a stew similar to Batata Yakhni. Two condiments are found on every Yemeni table: *z'houg,* a hot paste made from ground green chiles mixed with parsley, cilantro, garlic, cardamom, cumin, and olive oil, and *hilbeh,* a relish made from tomato sauce and ground fenugreek seeds.

Favorite Yemeni dishes include *sayadiah,* a golden fish and rice dish fragrant with cardamom, cinnamon, cloves, and coriander (distinguished from the Saudi version, which doesn't include turmeric). *Kabsa,* a succulent dish of lamb slow-cooked in a seasoned broth, is prepared the same way the Saudis make it, but with a blend of peppercorns, cardamom, saffron, caraway, and turmeric flavoring and coloring the broth. *Tibsi samak* is a flavorful dish of red snapper baked in a tomato and pomegranate sauce and seasoned with black pepper, garlic, cumin, cloves, and cardamom.

Basbousa, one of the most popular desserts in Yemen, is a semolina cake similar to Namoura, but made richer with the addition of eggs and yogurt.

Coffee is a specialty of Yemen. The best coffee beans are grown inland on the high mountain terraces, where the plants thrive in the fertile ground. *Mokha* takes its name from the port city from which Yemeni coffee is shipped. Coffeehouses are plentiful in Yemen, and many restaurants have a lounge on the upper floor where people enjoy sharing stories over coffee and tea.

The customary way to end a banquet in Yemen is with *Mohalabia,* the delicate pudding of ground rice and milk. In the Levant, it is made of milk and corn flour.

THE GULF STATES: SAUDI ARABIA, KUWAIT, BAHRAIN, QATAR, UNITED ARAB EMIRATES, AND OMAN

The cuisines of the Gulf States are very much connected because of their shared geography and history.

The Arabian Gulf swarms with fish, the most prized being *hamour,* a fat-fleshed grouper. *Kan'ad,* or king mackerel, is used in daily cooking, such as fish stews. *Zubaydi,* similar to trout but found only in the Gulf, are fried or stuffed with spicy sautéed onions. Crab, lobster, and shrimp are also widely available.

Much of the cooking in the Gulf States reflects the impact of the ancient spice traders, who brought spices from the Indian subcontinent as they crossed the Arabian Peninsula on their way to the Mediterranean. Kuwaiti cuisine, in particular, is very much influenced by Indian and Pakistani food.

Dates—a staple of Bedouins on the move—are also an important food in this region, and several varieties are cultivated.

One of the basic foodstuffs of Gulf cooking is *jereesh*—wheat kernels that are soaked, dried, and crushed. Often used as a substitute for rice, it is boiled and served with a topping of onions and hot pepper. *Harees* is jereesh cooked with chunks of meat, chopped onions, and tomatoes—very popular during Ramadan and religious holidays. Jereesh is the Gulf cook's equivalent of the bulgur that is used in Syria and Lebanon.

Food for Every Special Occasion

In the Arab world, food plays an important role in most social interactions. Misunderstandings are cleared up, contracts are sealed, and love is revealed during meals.

But nowhere is food more significant than in the observance of religious traditions. All the major holidays of the Muslim year are marked with particular food customs: feasts, fasting, and special dishes for special days. Because so many people ask me about the month of Ramadan, I've devoted a special section (page 258) to the reasons and rituals of the daily fast.

Throughout the book there are explanations of other Muslim holidays along with traditional foods that are served: the Eid that marks the end of Ramadan, the big Eid (or feast) associated with the pilgrimage of Muslims to Mecca, and the unique "white" meal with which we welcome the New Year. Christmas and Easter (and the Lenten season that precedes it) are also observed with special foods and festive meals, not only by Christian Arabs but also by many Muslim families, like ours, who enjoy these holidays with our neighbors and friends.

As in all cultures, important life events in Arab society—such as the birth of a child, a marriage, or a death—bring people together for celebration, to honor an individual, or to enjoy shared connections. We prepare special foods for these occasions, and I offer some menu ideas and explanations of these customs.

The Spirit of the Arab Table

There is one essential ingredient in every Arab meal, in whatever country, whether it is a big holiday feast or a simple dinner with just a guest or two: This is our cherished tradition of hospitality and generosity. These principles of honor and respect are deeply rooted in our home and family life and are passed on from generation to generation. Here is a simple introduction to the customs that make every place at an Arab table a comfortable one, whether you are the host or a guest:

- Always entertain warmly and joyously. Don't worry about having too many at the table; to entertain many together is to honor them all mutually.

- Great hospitality is not a luxury—it is a must! Whether a person is a dear friend or merely an acquaintance, whether invited or just someone who dropped by, the host should be generous in every way. The Arabic rule is *Karam:* the guest is king.

- If you are the cook, it is your responsibility to prepare the food to the taste of your guests, assuming you know what they like and what they can and cannot eat.

- If you are invited to an Arab home for lunch or dinner, no gift is expected, although flowers or chocolate is always appreciated. You are expected, however, to return the invitation and entertain your hosts in your home.

- An Arab host may also invite her guests to try each dish. Since usually all the food is on the table, it is the guest's choice as to where to start. If you are the host, do encourage your guests to put a couple of things on the plate and enjoy the various flavors. And if you are a guest, don't feel you have to fill your plate with everything all at once!

- In an Arab home, it is customary to say *"Al Hamdu lil lah"*—"Thanks to God"—after finishing a meal. Some Arabs say a prayer before a meal, similar to the custom of saying grace, but most just say *"Bis mil lah"*—"In the name of God"—before eating.

- If you are the host, remember to say *"Tafadalo"* when you are ready for your guests to come to the table.

- Whether you are the host or guest, courtesy demands that you wash your hands before and after a meal.

- When a guest leaves the home of a host after a meal, he or she says *"Daymah"* or *"Amer,"* which means "May the blessing stay with your home."

The Arab Pantry

Aish

This whole-wheat pocketless flat bread is typically found on the Egyptian table. It is about 5 inches in diameter and ½ inch thick. The Moroccan version is flavored with anise seeds.

Allspice (**bahar helo**)

The complex flavor of this berry of the evergreen pimiento is sweet, with hints of cinnamon, nutmeg, and cloves—hence its name. Allspice, also called Jamaican pepper, is often used in combination with other spices in meat, poultry, and fish dishes. It is also used in some soups and vegetable dishes. Allspice is rarely used when preparing cold or appetizer dishes.

Almonds (**luz**)

In the Arab world, the green almonds that are harvested in late spring are a popular snack. Wrapped in a fuzzy green peel, they are tender enough to eat raw and are typically served as part of a mezza spread, with a small bowl of salt for dipping. Look for fresh green almonds

at Middle Eastern or Italian grocery stores. In early autumn, the kernels of these almonds, which are similar to the heart-shaped, meaty Spanish Marcona variety available here, are brought to market. The best way to buy almonds is skin-on—it protects them from becoming rancid and also prevents them from drying out. For most of the recipes in this book, including fried almonds, they must be peeled.

To peel almonds, put them in a small saucepan with enough cold water to cover, bring to a boil, and then remove from the heat. Pour the almonds, with the water, into a bowl and set aside. When the nuts are cool enough to handle, peel them by squeezing one at a time between your thumb and forefinger—the skin will come off right away. Put the peeled almonds on a paper towel to dry. (Alternatively, you can blanch the almonds in a microwave oven by spreading the nuts in a single layer on a microwave-safe dish and heating them on high power in 30-second intervals, checking after each interval to ensure that the nuts do not cook. When the skins feel loose, pinch the nuts as described to remove the peel.

Peeled almonds are used in sweets such as Namoura and Mughli.

Anise seeds (yansoon)

Anise seeds are small, shiny brown seeds that come from anise pods. With their sweet licorice taste, ground anise seeds are a wonderful flavoring in cookies and breads. Whole anise seeds are used in Anise Seed Tea, often prescribed for relaxing. Anise seeds can be added to any tea, in fact, for a subtle licorice flavor. They are also an ingredient in *arak,* the Lebanese drink made from fermented grapes, which has a distinct licorice flavor. Another common use of anise seeds is to ease the teething pains of small babies; the boiled seeds are wrapped in cheesecloth and used as a pacifier.

Apricots (mishmish)

Apricots, both fresh and dried, are very popular in the Middle East and are used in both savory and sweet dishes, in jams and preserves, and to make fruit leather. The best apricots come from the Bekaa valley in Lebanon, Aleppo and Damascus in Syria, and all over Tunisia and Morocco. I find that the best apricots here in the U.S. are to be found at farmer's markets because the growers let the fruit ripen on the tree.

As for dried apricots, buy them at a Middle Eastern grocery whenever possible; they are invariably fresher than the packaged versions in the supermarket. Look for Turkish or Syrian apricots that are dark in color, which is an indication that they have ripened on the tree. If you do buy them packaged, look for Blenheim or Patterson brands from California; I have found them to be consistently fresh. Dried apricots are used in dessert recipes, especially during the month of Ramadan, because they are believed to satisfy both hunger and thirst. They can be stored in a tightly sealed plastic bag or jar in the refrigerator for 6 months, or frozen for up to 1 year.

Apricots are also pureed, spread on a long wooden board, and dried in the sun, to make apricot leather. Once dry, the sheets are brushed with sesame oil to give them an appetizing sheen. The leather is then folded like a towel and wrapped in plastic; it is often sold in golden cellophane wrapping. It can be eaten as is (much like the fruit roll-ups so popular among children in the U.S.) or dissolved in water to make a refreshing Apricot Juice. Fruit leather should be refrigerated after the package is opened. It can be frozen for up to 1 year.

Arab coffee (bin)

Arab coffee is made from beans grown in Aden, Yemen, which are considered among the best in the world. Throughout the Arab world, the beans are roasted differently from country to country and often from family to family. In Lebanon, the beans are dark-roasted and brewed plain, while in Palestine and Jordan, cardamom is added to the mix. Some families prefer all of the beans to be light-roasted; others mix them the way my family does— one third light and two thirds dark. In the Gulf States, where they drink unsweetened coffee at all occasions, the beans are medium-roast and the coffee contains lots of cardamom. Buy your coffee beans from a Middle Eastern store where they will grind the beans—and even add the cardamom—for you while you wait. Vacuum-packed varieties are available, too, at Middle Eastern groceries.

Arab flatbread (khoubez araby)

All Arab bread is "flat." Some—widely available in the U.S. as "pita" bread—has a pocket; other types do not. Arab bread is available in different sizes and thicknesses, from ⅛ inch to ¼ inch, and is made from whole-wheat or white flour, and sometimes a combination of both. The smallest versions (1½ inches wide) are excellent for accompanying mezza and can also be split open, seasoned, and baked to make chips. The midsize breads, which can be anywhere from 4 to 7 inches wide, are also used to make chips, and are served for scooping up olives, zaatar, and various dips and salads. The largest Arab bread is about 10 to 12 inches wide and is also known as Lebanese bread. The medium and large sizes are the ones most often called for in this book.

Arab bread is called *kmaj* in Jordan and Palestine, where it is made in only 5- to 6-inch-wide rounds and is ½ inch thick. I have found that the Farahat company (see Sources) makes the finest example of this bread in America.

Arab bread freezes very well as long as it is wrapped tightly. Defrost it at room temperature for a couple of hours and then warm it in a preheated 300°F oven for 5 minutes. Wrap it in a napkin or kitchen towel immediately to keep it soft and warm.

See also Markouk; Tanour.

Arak

A clear alcohol made from distilled grapes and flavored with anise seeds, arak is the Lebanese version of ouzo and pastis. It is traditional to drink arak with mezza. It is available in fine liquor stores or by mail (see Sources).

Artichokes (ardi-shoukeh)

The recipes in this book call for artichoke bottoms, which are used liberally in Arab cooking. They are available in bags in the freezer at Middle Eastern groceries and at gourmet food shops. Frozen artichoke bottoms require little preparation—a quick trimming is all. I find the Egyptian brands, such as Givrex, are the most tender.

Arugula (jarjeer)

This tender green, which is sometimes also called "rocket," has a bitter, peppery, mustard-like flavor. The leaves should be bright green and dry. Arugula is very perishable and should be stored, wrapped in a paper towel inside a plastic bag, in the refrigerator. In Middle Eastern shops it is sold in small bunches with the roots attached, and must be trimmed and thoroughly washed (see page 46 on washing greens and herbs). I prefer to buy organic arugula whenever possible.

Bay leaf (warak gar)

Also called bay laurel or laurel leaves, bay leaves are used to flavor soups, stews, and lamb dishes. Of the two kinds on the market—Californian and Turkish—I prefer the sweeter, more subtle oval Turkish variety. California bay leaves are long and thin and impart a slightly bitter flavor to foods. Dried bay leaves should not crumble or be broken in the package. Discard them if they are bland or brittle when you rub one between your hands. To ensure freshness, buy them from a source where the turnover is high. Store bay leaves in a tightly sealed container in a cool, dark place.

Beans (hobob)

Fresh and dried beans are staples in Arab cooking. They are most common in Egyptian cuisine, where they are depended upon for basic nourishment. Fava beans, chickpeas, and white beans are among the most frequently used beans in the Arab world. Dried beans are sold prepackaged or in bulk, and are best purchased from a store with a high turnover because, although beans can be stored for a long time, they can get tough if kept too long. Before they are cooked, dried beans must be soaked in water overnight; use a ratio of 3 parts water to 1 part beans.

Beets (shamandar)

Buy small fresh beets with their leaves intact. To store beets, cut off the root end, place them in a plastic bag, and store in the refrigerator.

Bulgur (burghul)

Bulgur is cooked hulled wheat that is dried and then cracked into coarse, medium, or fine grain. There are two varieties, white and brown bulgur, and either one can be used in most of these recipes. The brown bulgur has a rich, nutty flavor that is wonderful in hearty soups and stews, while the white variety is a better choice for delicate salads like Tabouleh. Use fine or medium bulgur in raw preparations such as Kibeh and Tabouleh, and coarse bulgur for cooking side dishes such as Spiced Bulgur with Tomatoes. A good Middle Eastern grocery store will carry all the varieties of bulgur; the supermarket may carry only medium-grain. Coarse bulgur should be soaked for 10 minutes in cold water before cooking.

Cabbage (malfoof)

Arabs use two kinds of cabbage: The round compact green cabbage is used raw, shredded for salads and garnishes. The slightly flat foot-wide white cabbage with loose leaves is used for stuffing and can be found in Middle Eastern shops.

Caraway seeds (carawya)

These seeds have a nutty, warm taste. They are used ground in savory and sweet dishes, including Caraway and Anise Seed Pudding, which is traditionally prepared to celebrate the birth of a child. They are also used whole, boiled in water to make a stomach-soothing tea. Caraway seeds should be stored in a tightly sealed container in the refrigerator.

Cardamom (hab hal)

Cardamom, both whole pods and ground, are in plentiful supply on the Arab spice shelf. The pods may be green or (bleached) white. The seeds inside the pods are small and black, and lend dishes a pungent, somewhat camphor-like flavor. Ground cardamom is made by grinding the pod and seeds together into a fine powder; make it this way unless otherwise indicated in a recipe. When the pods are called for in the recipes in this book, they are always cracked to release their distinctive flavor. Cardamom is not often used in Lebanese dishes, but it is quite popular in the rest of the Arab world. Fresh cardamom pods are often chewed to mask the scent of garlic.

Carob molasses (dibis kharoub)

This thick syrup, made in southern Lebanon from the carob pod, is mixed with a little tahini and spread on Arab bread for breakfast or dessert, especially for the Suhur meal during the month of Ramadan. It can be found at Middle Eastern groceries.

Cayenne pepper

The powdered version of small dried chile peppers, *Capsicum frutescens,* cayenne is used with a light touch in Arab cuisine, subtly seasoning Falafel and Spicy Tomato Sauce. It is more often used to decorate a dish and lend it just a bit of heat at the same time, as in Dressed Chickpeas and Hummus.

Chat Masala

Masala is an Indian term for "spice mixture." The term derives from an Arab word for "necessity." These spice mixtures are used in salads, sauces, stews, and curry dishes. Garam masala typically includes cinnamon, fennel, rose petals, and other ingredients. Chat masala is a combination of four spices, often cardamom, black pepper, cumin, and cinnamon. Xacutti masala is another blend that includes fenugreek, chiles, and coconut. Chat masala combines ground pomegranate seeds, dried mango, dried mint, ground ginger, cayenne pepper, black pepper, cumin, and coriander. It imparts a lemony flavor and is used in the Saudi Spice Mixture.

Cheeses (ajban)

Most Arab cheese is made from goat's or sheep's milk. They are typically found only in Middle Eastern shops. In Lebanon, fresh goat cheese, *jibneh khadra*, is available in limited quantities for a short time in the spring. It is served with mezza and after meals, and is used as a filling for Kibeh bi Seniyah.

Shankleesh is a hard fermented version of *qarisheh,* a whey cheese similar to ricotta. Golf-ball-shaped shankleesh are lightly coated

in thyme and sold packed in olive oil in jars or in vacuum-pack bags, which you will find in the frozen food section of any Middle Eastern grocery store. The cheese is served with mezza or as an appetizer (see Shankleesh Mutabal).

Akawi is a hard, salty white cow's-milk cheese that is native to Syria and Lebanon. It is used in both sweet and savory dishes. When used in desserts, such as Kunafa, it must be desalted. When cooked, akawi has an elastic texture similar to melted mozzarella.

Jibneh majdooleh is a chewy white sheep's-milk cheese flavored with nigella seeds; it is typically formed into a tight braid. It is exceedingly salty and must be soaked in fresh water before eating or using in any recipe. Serve it with Arab Chips, or for breakfast with Arab flatbread.

Halloumi is a sheep's-milk cheese that is hard and rather salty. It is an excellent cooking and table cheese, and is popular cut in thick slices and grilled, fried, or tucked into Arab bread, seasoned with zaatar and warmed in the oven for breakfast. Halloumi is available in Middle Eastern shops in 10-ounce packages or in bulk, set in brine. It can be frozen for up to 6 months.

Jibneh Nabulsy is made only in Palestine and Jordan, but it is popular in Syria and Lebanon, too. Nabulsy is often found in 3-inch chunks packed in brine in glass jars. It must be desalted in fresh water (see page 310) before eating or cooking with it. Leave nabulsy in the brine until ready to use. It will keep for up to 1 year in the refrigerator.

Kashkawan, often called Kashkaval in the U.S., is similar to Greek kasseri and Spanish manchego. It is a firm yellow sheep's-milk cheese that is often eaten after a meal or offered on a mezza spread.

Chickpeas (hummus)

Chickpeas are the main ingredient of Hummus, the popular Middle Eastern dip. They are available dried or precooked in cans. Dried chickpeas should be soaked overnight before using. Once soaked, they can be stored in the freezer in resealable plastic bags or rigid containers. Canned chickpeas should be drained, rinsed, and boiled for a couple of minutes to remove the characteristic tinny taste. (See page 52 for information on preparing canned and dried chickpeas.) Chickpeas are used in salads, dips, and spreads as well as in meat and chicken dishes like Kidra (a dish of saffron rice and lamb cooked in yogurt) and Fatteh Hummus bi Laban (cooked chickpeas with bread and yogurt). Both dried and canned chickpeas can be found in supermarkets, health food stores, and Middle Eastern shops. Dried chickpeas will keep for up to 1 year in a container with a tight-fitting lid.

Cilantro (kuzbarah)

The whole leaves of cilantro are used to garnish dishes. A mixture of chopped garlic and cilantro, called *taqliya,* is a popular flavoring in fish dishes, soups, and stews in the Gulf States. Buy fresh cilantro in bunches at your grocery store, and store them, wrapped in a paper towel inside a plastic bag, in the refrigerator. (See Cilantro and Parsley, page 46.)

Cinnamon (kirfa)

Both whole cinnamon sticks and ground cinnamon are called for in these recipes. I prefer Ceylon cinnamon, which can be purchased by mail order (see Sources).

Clarified butter (samna)

Clarified butter is butter from which the milk solids have been removed. You can make clarified butter yourself (see page 45), or you can purchase it in glass jars or tins, where it is often labeled *ghee,* the Indian term for clarified butter. I prefer the Ziyad brand, which is available in Middle Eastern and Indian specialty food shops and has recently begun to show up in large supermarket chains. There are two kinds of clarified butter, *samna* (ghee) and *samna baladi.* Samna baladi is never available at the market; it is made by Bedouin sheepherders and consists of clarified butter boiled with cracked wheat, nutmeg, and turmeric, which gives it its bright yellow color. Today cooks in the Levant region shy away from using samna because it is high in cholesterol. It is a must, however, in some recipes, especially rice dishes.

Cloves (kibsh kuronful)

Whole and ground cloves season both main courses and desserts on the Arab table. They are especially prominent in Kuwaiti and Saudi Arabian dishes and are an essential ingredient in the spice mixes from these two countries. They also flavor quince and date preserves.

Coriander seeds (Kuzbarah)

Coriander is dried seed of the cilantro plant, which is sometimes called Chinese parsley. While cilantro has a strong pungent smell, the seeds have a delicate lemony flavor.

Cornstarch (nasha)

Cornstarch is used in desserts, especially puddings, as a thickening agent.

Cucumbers (khiyar)

In the Middle East, cucumbers are small, slender, and firm, unlike the standard variety you find in U.S. supermarkets. Look for them in Middle Eastern stores, or substitute small Kirby (pickling) cucumbers or English cucumbers. Store cucumbers in the refrigerator, in a drawer lined with paper towels to absorb any moisture; they should last for 1 week.

Cumin seeds (camoon)

Arab cooks believe that cumin aids the digestion. Though it is not as common in Arab cooking as say, coriander, it is sometimes ground to a fine powder and added to lentil and fish dishes, especially in the Gulf States and the Levant (Jordan, Syria, Lebanon, Palestine).

Dandelion (Hindba)

A leafy green with a taste similar to spinach, dandelion leaves should be bright green and tender when you buy them. The best season for dandelion greens is in the spring, when they are young. Wrap the leaves in paper towels, place them in a resealable plastic bag, and store them in the refrigerator for up to 1 week. Before using, cut off the stems and wash the leaves thoroughly (see page 46). You can find dandelion greens in some supermarkets, and in Italian and Middle Eastern groceries. Dandelion greens can be substituted for chicory in Sautéed Greens with Crispy Onions.

Dates (tamr)

There are countless varieties of dates, but regardless of the type, they should be shiny and plump when you buy them. Avoid those that are dull and have a dry, floury coating,

which means they are old. Store dates in a resealable plastic bag in the refrigerator; they will keep for up to 2 weeks.

Dates are grouped in three varieties: soft, semi-soft, and dry. Soft dates have a high moisture content and a low sugar content. They are the most perishable of all dates. Some typical varieties include Burhi, Halawy, Khadrawy, and Medjool. Semi-soft dates have firm flesh, are low in moisture, and have a high sugar content. Some of the varieties that grow in the U.S. include Deglet Noor, Dayri, and Zahidi. Dry dates are hard, with a very low moisture content and a high sugar content. The most common dry dates are Thoory and Kinta.

Dates ripen in three stages: In the rutab stage, the fruit begins to soften. In the khalal stage, they reach maximum size and achieve their identifying color. In the tamr stage, the fruit is fully cured or dried.

Berhi: These are the only dates that are available on the branch. They are yellow in the khalal stage, turning golden amber in the rutab stage and mahogany in the tamr stage. Berhis have a solid, smooth clear skin. The flesh is firm and tender, with a soft syrupy texture. They are available from July to August. It is better to buy these when they are on the branch. Buy them when they are hard and yellow. They will ripen within a couple of days, and are delicious at the three stages of ripening. Berhi dates freeze well.

Deglet Noor: Originally from Algeria, these have a delicate flavor, a firm texture, and range in color from light red to amber. Deglet Noors are best eaten fresh. They are the kind most Arabs present as gifts.

Halawy: These Iraqi dates have thick, wrinkled flesh and range from yellow to golden brown in color as they ripen. Halawys are best eaten fresh.

Khadrawy: Another Iraqi variety, these sweet dates have a caramel-like texture. They ripen to amber and then cure to a reddish brown. They are used in the rutab stage for making date preserves.

Medjool: These large reddish brown dates have thin skin that is deeply wrinkled and creased. The flesh is deliciously meaty. Medjool is my favorite variety to eat fresh out of hand. They are great given as gifts and to use in Date Cake and in some pastries. Medjool dates can become sour as a result of long inadequate storage; it's best to taste one before buying.

Thoory: Often referred to as "bread dates," these dry, firm, chewy dates are used in baking, as in *maamoul*, and can also be used to make Kuwaiti Grilled Snapper.

Zahidi: Egg-shaped Zahidis hail from Iraq. Their tough skin (during the khalal stage) makes them excellent for making Kuwaiti Grilled Snapper.

Dill (shabbat)

Dill is essential to making authentic Ful Mudamas, the popular fava bean breakfast dish. Fresh dill must be used soon after it is purchased; it will keep in the refrigerator for up to 3 days.

Dried limes (loumi)

These rock-hard, brownish black globes are a staple flavoring in the cuisine of the Gulf States. The limes are left on the trees until they are dry and are then picked to sell at the market. Buy loumi from Middle Eastern or Indian grocery stores. They are typically sold in small plastic bags or in bulk; store them for up to a week in the refrigerator, or freeze them.

Dukka

Dukka means "to pound" in Arabic, which is the way this blend of chickpea flour, coriander, caraway, dill, sumac, and sesame is made: in a mortar and pestle. A jar of dukka is found in every kitchen cupboard from Palestine to Syria to Egypt. Dukka is used as often and is served in the same way as its Lebanese equivalent, zaatar—by sprinkling it on Arab Yogurt Cheese and spreading the cheese on olive oil–coated bread. In Egypt dukka is made with chickpea flour, cumin, black pepper, and cinnamon. Like zaatar, the mix of spices used to make dukka varies from home to home and village to village. Some people like to use crushed Brazil nuts, hazelnuts, or pumpkin seeds instead of the chickpea flour. See the recipe on page 39.

Eggplant (betinjan)

Several types of eggplant are used in Arab cooking. Large, firm, dark purple eggplants are used for frying, or are roasted and then pureed to make spreads like Mutabal. Small baby eggplants, also called Japanese or Italian eggplants, are used for stuffing or pickling; they can be found in Middle Eastern or farmer's markets. Choose the smallest ones, as they will be most tender.

Male eggplants have fewer seeds and more flesh. To determine the gender of an eggplant, look at its base. The male will have a well-rounded bottom while the female's will be smaller, narrow, and often indented. Store eggplants in a cool dry place and use them within 2 days of purchase.

Fava beans (ful akhdar)

Fresh fava beans, also known as broad beans, English beans, and Windsor beans, are usually available for only a short time in late spring, when they can be found in Italian, Middle Eastern, and gourmet markets. The pods are large and thick, and vary from 2 to 12 inches in length. Look for beans that are young and tender, and not bulging in their pods. Stem the pods with a knife, and then pry them open to reveal the beans. If the beans are not young and tender, you will have to blanch them to remove the skins—a process that can be avoided if the beans are very small and fresh. For this reason, many Arab dishes featuring fava beans are prepared only in the spring. If you want to cook fava beans off-season, use the frozen beans, which are available year-round at Middle Eastern groceries; one popular brand is Shahia, imported from Egypt. Peel the skins before cooking.

Dried fava beans are available in two different varieties: the larger split beans called *habas*, used to make Falafel, and the small brown variety known as *ful*, used in the breakfast and mezza known as Ful Mudamas. *Habas* are already peeled, but they must be soaked and then cooked for a long time, which is why I often use the canned variety. *Habas* are available in the ethnic section of any large supermarket and of course at Middle Eastern grocery stores. Both canned and dried *ful* will keep for a year if stored in a cool dry place.

Flour (taheen)

Unbleached all-purpose flour is the type that is used most often in this book. An exception is bread flour, which is called for in the bread recipes. I use the dip-and-level method for measuring flour: dip the measuring cup into a canister or sack, then level the flour in the cup with the flat side of a knife.

Freka (Green Wheat)

Freka is the roasted grains of green wheat stalks. There are two types: whole green kernels and shelled kernels. Whole green freka can be purchased in Middle Eastern stores. Although this freka might be labeled "clean," you should always pick it over very thoroughly because stones and other debris may remain from the harvesting process. Shelled freka is often sold in bulk and is more likely to have broken kernels, which should be picked over as well. As with bulgur, freka should be soaked in cold water for 10 minutes before cooking. Store freka in a resealable plastic bag in the refrigerator for up to 1 year, or in a tightly sealed container in a cool dry place for up to 6 months.

Garlic (toum)

Buy the large white-skinned garlic that is most widely available in supermarkets. The garlic bulbs should be firm and plump and covered in tight, dry skin. Garlic should be stored in an open bin. As long as it's kept pefectly dry, it can last for up to 2 months.

Grape leaves (warak enab)

Grape leaves are available both fresh and packed in brine. Fresh grape leaves are far less common in the U.S., but if you can find them, by all means use them. They must be soaked in boiling water for a few minutes until they soften, then rinsed under cold water. Blanched fresh grape leaves can be used immediately or can be tightly wrapped and frozen for up to 1 year. Brine-cured grape leaves are far more common here, and are always available at Middle Eastern grocery stores. I prefer the Afaia and Orlando brands because the leaves are just the right size for making authentic stuffed grape leaves.

Green beans (fasoulia khadra)

Also called "snap" beans because of the crisp noise these fresh beans make when broken in half, green beans should always be "topped and tailed"—trimmed on both ends—in my recipes. I prefer flat Italian green beans (*badria*) because they most closely resemble the buttery variety I grew up eating. Also called Romano beans, they are available fresh in Italian markets and gourmet food shops and frozen at any large supermarket. Fresh green beans will last in the refrigerator for about 4 days.

Halvah (halawa)

Halvah is a candy made of sesame paste, egg whites, and sugar. Sometimes pistachios and almonds stud this sweet treat, or it is flavored with chocolate. Halvah is traditionally eaten during Lent and for breakfast during the month of Ramadan. You can find halvah in Middle Eastern, Greek, and health food stores.

Harissa

Harissa is a hot red sauce from Morocco and Tunisia, used as a condiment in many North African dishes. There are several variations of the sauce, but my favorite is the simple blend of sun-dried chiles, garlic, and olive oil. Some other combinations include cumin, coriander, mint, and caraway. Harissa paste comes in tubes or jars and is available in gourmet stores and Middle Eastern groceries. It is used in many North African dishes, such as the Moroccan Chicken Soup.

Jameed

Liquid jameed is essential to making Mansaf, the Jordanian national dish. This dried sour sheep's milk is sold in fist-size balls, or reconstituted and packaged in liquid form; it can be found in Middle Eastern grocery stores. *See also* page 206.

Jereesh

Wheat kernels that are soaked, dried, and crushed, jereesh is used primarily in dishes from the Gulf region. (Bulgur, by comparison, is boiled, then dried and cracked.)

Kataifi (kunafa)

Kataifi is paper-thin shredded wheat dough; it resembles shredded wheat cereal. It is used to make the specialty dessert known as *Kunafa bi Jibin* (page 307) and can be found in Middle Eastern markets.

Labneh

Labneh is simply yogurt that has been drained of its whey to create a thickened, soft spread with the consistency of cream cheese. The best labneh is the kind you make yourself (see page 110), although it can be purchased in Middle Eastern stores in blocks in plastic containers. Small balls of labneh (*tabat labneh*), marinated in olive oil and packed in glass jars, are also available.

Lamb (kharouf)

Buy fresh lamb if at all possible for the recipes in this book. Arab cooks use only freshly butchered meat, and although it was difficult to find when I first moved to the U.S., I now know several local butchers who carry excellent fresh lamb. Seek one out in your area. I often order fresh lamb from Jamison Farm in Missouri (see Sources). If I am going to make Kibeh Nayeh, which is eaten raw, I buy halal or kosher lamb from my favorite local Middle Eastern butcher. I do not recommend using the frozen lamb from Australia or New Zealand.

Lemons (hamod)

Lemon juice is used liberally in the Arab kitchen; I always use fresh-squeezed. If you are making fresh lemonade, use a thin-skinned variety such as the Meyer lemon.

Lentils (adas)

Two kinds of lentils are used in these recipes. Brown lentils, the most widely available, are available in most supermarkets. The smaller orange split lentils are available at health food stores and Middle Eastern markets. Lentils do not need to be soaked before they are cooked.

Lettuce (khass)

Romaine lettuce, widely used in the Arab world, is what is recommended for the salads in this book. Look for full leaves that are bright green, fresh, crisp, and show no signs of wilting. To wash lettuce leaves, plunge them in a bowl of cold water, then gently lift them out with your hands. Dry the leaves thoroughly with paper towels or use a salad spinner. Wrap the clean dry leaves in paper towels, place them in a resealable plastic bag, and store in the refrigerator for up to 3 days.

Mahlab

This fragrant spice is made from the kernels inside the pits of black cherries. It can be purchased in coarse powder or in kernel form, which can be pounded to a powder with a mortar and pestle. Mahlab is used to flavor sweet breads, cookies, and pastries. It can be stored in a jar with a tight-fitting lid for up to 1 year.

Markouk

This unleavened whole-wheat bread is baked on a *saj,* a convex iron plate heated by a wood fire, and is as thin as a handkerchief. It is also folded like one, and sold six loaves to a package in Middle Eastern stores. This bread is widely used in the mountains of Lebanon and is, in fact, labeled "mountain bread" in some gourmet food shops and high-quality supermarkets. Authentic markouk, however, is available only in Middle Eastern shops. Markouk is used to line the serving platter for many dishes, including Lamb Kebabs and Lamb in Creamy Sheep's Milk Yogurt.

Mastic (miskeh)

Mastic is the resin collected from the native Greek *Pistacia lentiscus* tree. It comes packaged as small pebbles, which are sometimes translucent or pale yellow. Mastic is used in judicious amounts to lend an exotic, subtle licorice flavor to milk puddings and ice creams as well as chicken and meat marinades. Mastic needs to be ground before it is used. To grind it, place a few pebbles on a spoon and add a dash of salt or sugar, depending on whether the recipe is savory or sweet. Set another spoon on top of the mastic, with the handle pointing in the opposite direction. Grip one spoon in each hand, close to the neck of the handle, and press them together to crush the grains between them. You can also grind it by moving a pestle in a circular motion inside a mortar. Because mastic is sticky once it's crushed, it is not suitable for grinding in an electric spice grinder. In the old days, before packaged gum was available, mastic was mixed with a bit of wax to soften it and make chewing gum. Store mastic in a glass jar with a tight-fitting lid in a dry place. It is carried in Middle Eastern stores.

Milk (haleeb)

Use whole milk whenever milk is indicated in these recipes, except in making yogurt, when low-fat or nonfat varieties are acceptable.

Mint (naana)

Mint is very much loved in the Arab world and is used liberally—in salads, to brighten cooked dishes, in drinks, and as a garnish. I suggest using spearmint, which is closest in flavor to the variety of mint I used in the Middle East. Of course the best mint is that which you grow yourself; it grows very easily and robustly in nothing more than a pot on a window ledge. Buy your fresh or dried mint from a health food store or farmer's market; or look for organic brands of dried mint at the grocery store. I do not recommend the dried variety in the herb and spice aisle at the supermarket; it lacks the assertive flavor these dishes need.

Mixed spices (baharat)

These blends vary from country to country and, when they are made at home, from house to house. Several baharat recipes can be found in the Basics chapter. Middle Eastern stores carry mixed spices, either made by the store

owners themselves or prepackaged by companies like Abedo.

Nigella (habit al barakeh)

Tiny, black, aromatic nigella seeds are often mistaken for onion or black caraway seeds, but they are not related to either. Nigella is a member of the buttercup family, and in Arabic the name means "the seed of blessing"—an indication of its powerful healing qualities. It is usually used in both sweet and savory pastries. When chewed, the seeds taste a bit like oregano, with a nutty flavor. Nigella is available at Middle Eastern and Indian markets.

Nutmeg (joz el teeb)

Nutmeg is used primarily in chicken, meat, and rice dishes in the Middle East and is found predominantly in the recipes of the Gulf region. Always buy whole nutmeg and grate it as you need it—it's far more flavorful than any commercially ground nutmeg.

Nuts (mukasarat)

Nuts are widely used by Arab cooks in both sweet and savory dishes, as well as in rice dishes and for garnishes. The most popular nuts are pine nuts and almonds, which are often fried and used as garnishes. Store nuts in a resealable plastic bag in the refrigerator or freezer for up to 1 year. *See also* Pine nuts, Pistachios, Walnuts.

Okra (bamyeh)

Okra is very popular in the Arab kitchen— especially the small okra, which is the best choice for these recipes. It is not easy to find small fresh okra—you will rarely find it in a supermarket—but I have found 1-inch-long pods at farmer's markets. If you can't find baby okra, opt for the frozen variety available at Middle Eastern groceries and some supermarkets. Never use precut okra in these dishes; it will give the food a slimy texture. When trimming the pods, remove the cap with a sharp knife without actually cutting into the pod itself.

Olive oil (zeit zeitoun)

An Arab cook cannot cook without olive oil. It is used to dress salads, to drizzle over food just before serving, for dipping, and to cook vegetables. Because I cook every day, I buy my extra virgin olive oil from Middle Eastern shops, where it is decanted in large cans that are well priced. My favorite brand is Jordan's Treasure. It comes bottled in three different sizes and in 2-gallon tins. If stored properly, well away from light and heat, olive oil will last for a year. Buy the best olive oil you can afford to drizzle over finished dishes or to dress salads. On the other hand, for a cooking oil, any variety, such as corn or safflower oil, will do. Note that you cannot deep-fry in extra virgin olive oil because it will burn.

Olives (zeitoun)

Green or black olives are found on every Arab table. Packed in brine, they are always available, often in bulk, in Middle Eastern stores and in the deli department of your supermarket. Unfortunately, most stores don't label them by their varietal name; instead they label them Palestinian, Jordanian, Lebanese, or Moroccan. Imported Greek olives are a fine substitute. Olives in brine can be stored in a sealed container in a cool, dry place for up to 1 year.

Orange-Blossom Water (mazaher)

Also known as orange-flower water, this fragrant liquid is made from the essence of bitter-orange blossoms and is used in both savory and sweet dishes, as well as in refreshing and soothing drinks. Often used together with rose water, *mazaher* is the subtler of the two, though a little goes a long way to perfume a dish. Orange-blossom water is sold in bottles in gourmet food shops, where it is likely to be more expensive than if purchased at a Middle Eastern grocery store. Orange-blossom water can be kept in your pantry for a year, even after opening the bottle.

Oregano (zaatar akhdar)

Oregano is used both fresh and dried in Arab cooking. A salad made solely of fresh oregano leaves is among the most beloved in the Middle East, while pastries liberally studded with it are common on the mezza table. I prefer to use organic oregano whenever possible; it can be stored, wrapped in paper towels and tucked into a resealable plastic bag, for up to 5 days in the refrigerator. To ensure its freshness buy dried oregano in bulk from a busy purveyor.

Osfour

Sometimes incorrectly referred to as saffron, these orange-yellow strands are the stigmas of the safflower plant. Osfour has a mild flavor and gives a yellow tint to meat and rice dishes. Unlike saffron, which transmits flavor, osfour is used mainly as a coloring rather than to enhance the taste of the dish. Osfour threads are always soaked in a little boiling water for 1 minute before being used. They are used mainly in chicken and meat dishes from Lebanon, Syria, and Palestine, and very rarely used in the cooking of the Gulf States. The threads are sold either ground or whole and can be found in Middle Eastern shops.

Parsley (bakdonis)

Fresh (never dried) flat-leaf or Italian parsley is used in these recipes. Although small packages of prewashed parsley are available, they tend to be rather expensive. I prefer to buy parsley in large bunches, which are fresher. See page 46 for tips on washing parsley.

Pepper (filfell)

Although there are several different types of peppercorns, black pepper and white pepper are the ones most often used in the Arab kitchen. White pepper is rarely used in recipes from the Gulf States. Whole peppercorns are used in making stocks and stews. I use white peppercorns with chicken, black with beef and lamb. It's always best to use freshly ground pepper, rather than the preground.

Phyllo

This paper-thin pastry is used in several recipes, such as Baklava. Buy frozen phyllo from a store with a high turnover (older phyllo won't bake to the flaky consistency you want). Store unopened phyllo in the refrigerator for up to 2 weeks. Opened phyllo can be refrigerated, well wrapped in a damp towel inside a plastic bag, for up to 2 days. Frozen unopened phyllo can be stored in the freezer for a year. Phyllo must be thawed overnight in the refrigerator before use and cannot be refrozen. I prefer the Athens brand, which comes in two sealed pouches, each containing twenty sheets of dough.

Pine nuts (snoober)

Pine nuts are used both raw and fried in Arab cooking. There are several types of pine nuts on the market. Arabs use the long, thin oval nuts (pignoli), which are tastier than the rounder, shorter nuts that come from Asia. Your best bet is to buy them (they will be labeled Mediterranean) from a Middle Eastern shop, where they are less expensive and generally fresher than those found at a supermarket.

Pistachios (fostuk halabi)

The best pistachios come from Iran; they are pale green and about ½ inch long. Unfortunately they are not readily available in the U.S. I have found the best alternative to be those grown in California. In the Arab kitchen, pistachios are used whole, ground, as in Shredded Pastry with Cheese and Baklava, or soaked to soften them to garnish certain desserts. You can find shelled unsalted pistachios in Middle Eastern grocery shops. Shell-on salted pistachios are among the simplest mezzas.

Pomegranate (ruman)

There are two types of pomegranates, one sweet and the other sour. The sweet pomegranate is the one that is most widely available in the U.S. The seeds are eaten fresh, used to garnish desserts, or crushed to make a juice drink. The sour fruit is the source of pomegranate syrup (see below), a staple of the Arab pantry.

Pomegranate syrup (dibis al ruman)

Used as a flavoring for vegetables and meat, tart, robust pomegranate syrup is made from sour-pomegranate juice that is boiled until it is reduced to a thick, dark burgundy liquid with the consistency of melted chocolate. Use this intensely flavored syrup carefully, as it can overwhelm a dish. *Dibis al ruman* comes in bottles imported from Lebanon or Syria. You do not need to refrigerate pomegranate syrup after it is opened; it will keep for a year, but can last even longer if refrigerated after opening. My two favorite brands, Cortas and Indo European, are readily available at Middle Eastern markets.

Potato (batata)

Although a New World vegetable, the potato has become a common ingredient in Arab cooking. Any type of boiling potato will work in these recipes unless otherwise specified.

Purslane (bakli)

This sprawling plant grows wild in the Middle East. The leaves are small, round, and a vibrant green and have spicy, slightly bitter flavor. Purslane is used in mixed vegetable salads and can be substituted for any green in most salads. Purslane will keep in the refrigerator for up to 3 days. It can be found at farmer's markets and specialty markets.

Quince (safarjal)

Quince, a very bitter fruit, is only eaten cooked in the Arab world. It is popular in Moroccan cuisine and is also made into preserves in Lebanon. You can find quince in your supermarket, usually only in the spring. Cooked, preserved, or dried candied quince is used in desserts or eaten for breakfast or brunch. Perhaps the most popular way to eat quince is in preserves, which you can find in Middle Eastern or Greek shops.

Raisins (zebeeb)

I almost always use golden, or sultana, raisins in my cooking. In the Gulf States, raisins are used primarily in cooked food, especially with rice and meat, while in the Levant they are found in sweets and are eaten out of hand as a snack. Raisins should be stored in a jar with a tight-fitting lid in a cool place or in the refrigerator.

Rice (ruz)

Rice is an essential and beloved ingredient in the Arab kitchen. It is served with almost every meal, either in a stuffing, on the side, or mounded on a serving plate to serve as a bed for succulent chunks of meat. Two different types of rice are used in these recipes: The most common and popular is basmati, a long-grain rice that is the Arab cook's white rice. I prefer the Tilda and Royal brands. The other is short-grain Egyptian rice *(masri),* which is used primarily to make stuffings for vegetables. In Egypt, however, it is used with stews. If you can't find Egyptian rice, sushi rice is a fine substitute. It is essential to rinse rice three times in fresh water before cooking.

Rose petals

Rose petals from the south of Lebanon are used to make preserves and are also candied for garnishing desserts. You might be able to find them in Middle Eastern shops, but your best bet is to look in Arab pastry shops or to order them by mail (see Sources).

Rose spices (kamouneh)

A popular addition to kafta and kibeh dishes in southern Lebanon, where roses grow abundantly, *kamouneh* is a fragrant mixture of dried red pepper, basil seeds, coarse salt, dried oregano, cloves, cinnamon, cumin seeds, white and black peppercorns, and baby roses. It is rarely sold in shops, but you can find it in some Middle Eastern stores or by mail order (see Sources).

Rose water (**maward**)

This fragrant water distilled from rose petals is used in both savory and sweet dishes. Just a few drops will transform a cup of tea. Use rose water carefully—add too much to a dish and it will infuse it with a bitter taste. All Middle Eastern shops carry bottles of rose water and many shelve several brands; they are all essentially the same.

Saffron (**zafaran**)

Saffron is indispensable to the cooking in the Gulf States, where its spicy, somewhat bitter flavor is used in Lamb Beryani, Rose Water–Scented Chicken with Saffron Rice, and Moroccan Couscous. If you peek inside any common crocus plant, you will see the deep orange threads that constitute saffron. To use saffron in these recipes, crush the threads and soak them in a little rose water (the time will be specified with each recipe), or boiling water if you prefer, to give added aroma and color to rice. Saffron is expensive—about $1,000 per pound—mainly because the stamens must be picked by hand, and tens of thousands of flowers must be picked to make 1 pound of saffron. Several grades of saffron are widely available; I use the highest grade of Spanish saffron I can find. Turmeric is often used as an inexpensive alternative to saffron.

Salep (**sahlap**)

A fine powder extracted from a variety of dried orchid tubers, salep is used as a thickening agent in ice cream. Salep is also boiled with milk to make a thin, sweet porridge that is served like soup. I make it for members of my family when they have a sore throat. Like Cream of Wheat or rolled oats, salep porridge is delicious with a little butter and cinnamon. You can find it in paper cartons in Middle Eastern shops. Store salep in a glass jar in the refrigerator, where it will keep for up to 1 year.

Semolina (**smeed**)

Semolina is another name for hard wheat flour. It is ground either coarse or fine and is sold prepackaged in bags, which I recommend, or loose in bulk. Coarse semolina is used to make Namoura (Semolina Cake), and fine semolina is used for Semolina Rolls. It is available in Middle Eastern and Greek grocery stores and in health food shops. Store semolina in a cool, dry place for up to 3 months or in the refrigerator for up to 1 year.

Sesame paste (**tahini**)

A thick paste made from ground raw sesame seeds, sesame paste is a key ingredient in many Arab sauces, dips, and even desserts. Though an essential member of the Middle Eastern pantry, tahini is also used in Greece, India, and parts of Africa. It is available in various grades and qualities, and the flavor can vary dramatically from brand to brand (just like peanut butter). As a general rule, Greek tahini has the richest, nuttiest flavor. I prefer the Ziyad brand. The ideal consistency of tahini for Arab cooking is that of a creamy puree. It is most often mixed with lemon juice for savory preparations, forming a firm white paste; the whiter the tahini becomes, the better its quality. Tahini will keep in the pantry for a year, and up to 6 months after it is opened. The oil in the tahini separates, so either store your container upside down or stir the oil back into the paste before using it.

Note that in the U.S., "tahini" refers both to the unadorned sesame paste and to the sauce made with sesame paste, lemon juice, garlic, and salt (see page 32).

Sesame seeds (sumsum)

Sesame seeds, raw or toasted, are used in pastries and are an essential ingredient in *zaatar*. They are also used in making tahini and halvah: You can find small jars of sesame seeds in the spice section of your local supermarket, but it is more economical to buy them in bulk from a Middle Eastern grocery or a health food shop. Because they have a high oil content, sesame seeds can quickly turn rancid, so it's best to buy them in small amounts and use them relatively quickly. If kept in an airtight container in a cool, dry place, they will last for up to 3 months; if refrigerated, they will last up to 6 months; and they will keep for up to 1 year in the freezer.

Shrak. See *Tanour*.

Spices

Spices should be kept in airtight containers in a cool, dark place since heat and light can quickly diminish their potency. I like to clean out my spice cabinet in the first week of the new year to ensure that they are fresh.

When judging the quality of spices, use your nose and your taste buds. If the spice does not have a strong flavor or a fragrant smell, throw it away. Bottled dried spices generally have a 6-month shelf life from the time they are opened. Mark the first-use date on the bottom of your spice container to help you keep track of its age.

Fresh-ground: The best way to grind your own spices is with an electric coffee grinder that is used specifically for that purpose—do not use the same grinder for coffee. To clean the grinder after each use, tap it gently on the edge of the sink to remove any loose bits and then grind a piece of bread in it—the bread will absorb the residual spices and their aroma.

Store the grinder with its cover off to allow it to breathe.

Whole spices: Whole spices stay fresh longer than ground, so if you can, buy them whole and grind as needed. To intensify the flavors of whole spices, roast them in a nonstick skillet over high heat or in a preheated 350°F oven for a few minutes, or until the aroma is released. Let the spice cool completely before grinding it.

If you don't have access to a reputable spice purveyor, you can always purchase them through the mail. I am a big fan of Penzey's (see Sources). Because of their high turnover, their spices are always fresh.

Spinach (sabanekh)

This leafy dark green vegetable is very common in the Middle East, where it is the basis for delicious stews and is seasoned and stuffed into savory pastries. Try to find the young smooth leaves, which are a little more tender than the larger curly leaves. Spinach has a lot of grit, so wash it thoroughly. I always use baby spinach in salads, the larger leaves in soups and stews. Frozen spinach can be substituted for fresh spinach in many recipes (it will be noted in the recipe).

Sumac

Cherry-red sumac powder is a popular seasoning throughout the Middle East (especially in Turkey, Syria, and Jordan), lending a pleasant sourness and rosy color to sauces, poultry, fish, and salads. Its flavor is on the order of lemon juice or vinegar, but milder and less acidic. The ancient Romans used sumac for its sour flavor before the arrival of lemons in Europe. Sumac is also mixed with thyme leaves and sesame seeds to make *zaatar*. Picked from a common shrub, sumac berries are ground to make the seasoning, with a small amount of salt added to facilitate processing. Since inferior brands contain too much salt, always taste sumac before buying it if possible, or buy only from reputable merchants. Whenever seasoning with sumac, always taste the dish before adding additional salt.

Tahini. See *Sesame Paste.*

Tamarind (tamer hindi)

Tamarind is the pod fruit of the tree by the same name. Picked fresh, tamarind pods contain tiny beans surrounded by a somewhat sour pulp, which is compressed into a moist, dense paste and sold in vacuum-sealed packages. Tamarind paste must be soaked in hot water for about an hour to reconstitute it and is used to make a refreshing drink (much the same way Apricot Juice is made from fruit leather) to break the fast during Ramadan. You can also find tamarind in concentrated liquid form—labeled "tamarind syrup"—in Middle Eastern and Indian stores. Tamarind will keep, tightly sealed, in the pantry, for a year.

Tanour

Also known as *shrak,* tanour is the preferred bread in the Gulf States, where it is called *khoubez tanour.* Baked in a *taboun,* a small vessel set into a hole in the ground, tanour is leavened whole-wheat bread that is about 13 inches in diameter and about ¼ inch thick. It looks like a baked pizza without the topping.

In Iraq this bread is called *arouck,* and it is distinguished by the thinly sliced spiced lamb and onions in the dough. It is served for breakfast and with cheese for a snack.

Thyme (zaatar)

Thyme is an evergreen herb that grows wild in the Middle East. Dried thyme is mixed with oregano, sesame seeds, and sumac to make the *zaatar* mixture that is eaten with Arab bread and olive oil.

Turmeric (kurkum)

The yellow color of this ground dried root is similar to ground ginger, but the flavor is pungent and slightly bitter. Turmeric is used to color and flavor cakes and rice. In the old days it was used to make perfumes. Turmeric is also used in coloring mustard. It can be found in supermarkets and Middle Eastern stores.

Turnip (lifit)

Young, tender turnips are pickled and packed in a brine of salt, vinegar, and beet juice, which turns them mellow. Several brands of bottled pickled turnips can be found in Middle Eastern stores. Look for turnip pickles packed in deep red beet juice—the darker the liquid, the higher the quality. After opening the jar, store it in the refrigerator.

Verjus (husrum)

French for "green juice," verjus is called *husrum* juice in the Arab world. It is named for the unripe green grapes from which the juice is made. Verjus was a common condiment on salads in the winter season, when lemons were scarce. Today it is used as an alternative to lemon juice to flavor water, salads, and fish. Verjus is available at wineries and in gourmet markets.

Walnuts

Walnuts are found in almost every course on the Arab table, from Tahini Walnut Sauce drizzled over sea bass to many pastries on the dessert table. English or Persian walnuts are used in these recipes. Shelled walnuts should be large, plump, and crisp when you bite into them. If they are at all soft, they are old. Store walnuts in resealable plastic bags in the refrigerator for up to 3 months. They can be frozen for up to 1 year. To enhance the nuts' flavor, toast them in a preheated 350°F oven for 7 minutes.

Wine (nabeeth)

Wine is not used in Arab cooking, but it is very much enjoyed with food. You can enjoy your regular selections or try Lebanese or Jordanian wine. The Lebanese wineries Kefraya, Ksara, and Château Musar produce some excellent Cabernet Sauvignon and Chardonnay. Some Middle Eastern stores carry the wine, but your best bet is to ask your wine merchant, who can easily get it for you if he or she does not already carry it.

Yogurt (laban)

Yogurt is essential to Arab cooking. For eating and for making *labneh,* yogurt cheese, I recommend the Greek brand Total, which is readily available in large supermarkets and of course in Greek and Middle Eastern shops. Woodstock water-buffalo-milk yogurt, made in Vermont, is nice and thick—almost like Greek yogurt. I also like Stonyfield Farms organic yogurt. To make authentic Yogurt Cheese Balls, use goat's-milk yogurt—it is available in gourmet and health food stores, packaged in plastic bottles.

I use full-fat yogurt for cooking. But for health reasons, I use fat-free to make labneh. (Total is the only store-bought yogurt that does not need to be drained before cooking.)

Zaatar

This pungent mix of thyme, oregano, sumac, and sesame seeds is as essential to the Arabic kitchen as salt. Named for its primary ingredient, *zaatar,* a wild thyme that grows throughout the Middle East, the mix is used as a flavoring for both cooked and raw foods and also as a dry dip for bread drizzled with olive oil. The true essence of zaatar's flavor is in the freshness and aroma of its various herbs. Although zaatar is now widely available in many shops, the mix still tastes best when made at home with your own freshly dried oregano and thyme. While the herbs can be ground in a food processor, I favor the old-fashioned method of crushing the dried herbs by rubbing them in my hands and then passing them through a sieve. This gives the zaatar an authentic consistency—slightly coarse and somewhat powdery at the same time.

Zucchini (kousa)

Zucchini, also called Lebanese squash, is about the length of your hand and has a delicate green skin. It is available year-round but is highly perishable and will keep in the refrigerator for just 2 or 3 days. Some recipes will explain how you can prepare them and freeze them for later use. If your market has only large, dark green zucchini, choose the smallest, narrowest ones you can find—they will be sweeter and have fewer seeds.

Basics

SPICE MIXES AND SAUCES ARE PART of every dish on the Arab table. Tahini Onion Sauce and Parsley Sauce are enjoyed with seafood dishes, from simple fried fish to elaborate Fish Kibeh. Spicy, delicious Tomato Sauce is spooned over aromatic rice dishes, and Stewed Tomato Sauce is drizzled over Pasta and Lentils.

In most Arab kitchens, you will find jars of Zaatar and Toasted Wheat and Spice Mix. These are staples for sprinkling over bread and stirring into olive oil. I mix my own spices in small quantities to keep them fresh. The spice mixes I've included in this chapter are the ones you can use in all of your cooking to enhance the flavor of almost any dish you prepare.

I've also provided tips and techniques for drying and storing fresh herbs, chopping parsley for the perfect Tabouleh, frying onions, and toasting nuts to the perfect golden color.

Tahini

TAHINI

3 small cloves garlic, mashed

1 cup sesame paste (tahini)

¾ cup fresh lemon juice

Red pepper flakes, to taste

Salt, to taste

Chopped fresh parsley, for
garnish

*T*ahini, a mixture of sesame paste, garlic, and lemon juice, is used in
every course of a Middle Eastern meal. It appears as a dipping sauce
for Fried Cauliflower on the mezza table, as a dressing for Jerusalem Salad,
and as a sauce for main-dish Kafta Burgers. It even shows up in dessert, as
a glaze for Yellow Diamonds. In the same way that ketchup is essential to a
hamburger, Tahini is always served with Shawarma and Falafel.

The mark of good Tahini is its color. The best is pale—almost
white—indicating that the proper amount of lemon juice has been
added to the paste. I often add a tablespoon of freshly squeezed orange or
clementine juice and ½ teaspoon of the zest to give the sauce an extra
kick. But if you prefer a nutty flavor, go easy on the lemon juice. The best
Tahini is one you taste as you go and adjust to your liking.

The consistency of commercial sesame pastes varies by brand, which is
why I add water gradually until the sauce is thinned to my liking. The
sauce will keep, tightly covered, in the refrigerator for up to 1 week. It
will thicken if it sits for any period of time; just add a little water to liq-
uefy it before you use it.   *Makes 2 to 2½ cups*

Whisk the garlic and sesame paste together in a small bowl. Add the
lemon juice, whisking until the mixture turns into a firm white
paste. Gradually add up to ⅔ cup cold water, whisking constantly,
until the sauce has the desired consistency. Season with the red
pepper flakes and salt. Serve in a bowl, garnished with parsley.

GARLIC: PEELING AND CRUSHING

Garlic, an essential ingredient in the Arab pantry, is used liberally in many dishes in this book—
some recipes call for fifteen or more cloves. There's an easy way to do this, if you plan ahead. Soak
as many cloves as you need—or several heads for later use—in a bowl of warm water for 30 to 60
minutes. The peels should then come off effortlessly. If you are not using them immediately, place
the peeled cloves in a plastic or glass container with a tight-fitting lid, cover them with a dry paper
towel, and close the container tight. The garlic cloves will keep, refrigerated, for up to 10 days.

Most of the recipes that call for garlic specify "mashed" garlic. Rather than using a press,
I prefer to pound garlic cloves to a paste with a mortar and pestle. To do this, add a pinch of
salt for every 3 cloves and pound until the garlic is smooth and creamy.

Tahini Onion Sauce

TAGEN

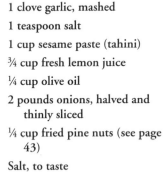

1 clove garlic, mashed

1 teaspoon salt

1 cup sesame paste (tahini)

¾ cup fresh lemon juice

¼ cup olive oil

2 pounds onions, halved and thinly sliced

¼ cup fried pine nuts (see page 43)

Salt, to taste

*T*he secret to making delicious Tagen is to very slowly cook, or caramelize, the onions until they are golden brown and almost melting. I prefer Spanish onions because they caramelize so well. Serve Tahini Onion Sauce with Fish Kibeh, Warm Lentils with Rice, or any grilled fish. ***Makes 3 cups***

Combine the garlic, salt, and sesame paste in a medium bowl. Add the lemon juice and whisk until the mixture becomes a firm white paste. Gradually add up to 1 cup cold water, whisking constantly, until the mixture has the consistency of heavy cream. Set it aside.

Heat the olive oil in a medium skillet over medium heat. Add the onions and stir to coat. Then reduce the heat to low and cook, stirring occasionally, until most of the liquid has evaporated, about 10 minutes. Slide a heat diffuser under the skillet and continue to cook, stirring frequently, until the onions are soft and translucent and all the liquid has evaporated, 10 minutes. Using a slotted spoon, transfer the onions to paper towels to drain.

Add the drained onions to the tahini mixture and stir well. Add the pine nuts, reserving a few for garnish. Season with salt.

Spoon the sauce into a serving bowl, and scatter the reserved pine nuts on top.

Stewed Tomato Sauce

DAMAA'

Damaa' is the Arabic word for "teardrop" as well as the name given to this spicy Egyptian sauce—which you can make as hot as you like, even so hot that it makes you cry. Serve it with Baked Sea Bass, Onion Rice, or Pasta with Lentils.   **Makes about 2 cups**

3 tablespoons olive oil

1½ pounds onions, finely diced

7 cloves garlic, mashed

One 15-ounce can crushed tomatoes

1 teaspoon white vinegar

1 teaspoon salt

1 teaspoon black pepper

Cayenne pepper, to taste

Heat the olive oil in a large skillet over medium heat. Add the onions and sauté until soft and translucent, about 5 minutes. Add the garlic and tomato sauce, and stir until the onions are coated. Then cover the skillet and bring to a boil. Reduce the heat to medium and simmer for 20 minutes.

Add the vinegar, salt, black pepper, and cayenne, and simmer for 3 minutes. Add more vinegar, salt, or pepper to taste. Serve hot, in a sauceboat.

Spicy Tomato Sauce

DAKOUS

¼ cup extra virgin olive oil

5 cloves garlic, mashed

2 jalapeño peppers, seeded and finely chopped

5 pounds tomatoes, peeled and seeded, or four 14½-ounce cans "petite" diced or crushed tomatoes

2 tablespoons tomato paste

1 teaspoon salt

1 teaspoon black pepper

¼ teaspoon ground cinnamon

*T*his sauce is a specialty of the Gulf region and is typically served with Lamb Beryani and Kabsa. It makes a zesty dipping sauce for grilled vegetables, too. If you're using canned tomatoes, omit the salt and season the sauce to taste just before serving. Dakous can be made ahead and refrigerated, tightly covered, for up to 2 days. **Makes 6 cups**

Heat the olive oil in a large saucepan over high heat. Add the garlic and jalapeños and sauté until soft and fragrant, about 2 minutes. Reduce the heat to medium-low and add the tomatoes, tomato paste, salt, pepper, and cinnamon. Cook, partially covered, for 30 minutes, breaking up the tomatoes with the back of a spoon. The finished sauce will resemble spaghetti sauce.

Transfer the sauce to a sauceboat and serve it alongside a main course, or use as directed in a recipe.

PEELING TOMATOES

Bring a saucepan of water to a boil. Fill a bowl with ice water. Using a sharp knife, cut a small X in the bottom of each tomato. Drop the tomatoes into the boiling water and leave them for just 25 seconds. Then use a slotted spoon to transfer them to the bowl of ice water, and let them cool. The skin will peel away easily.

Parsley Sauce

BAKUDONSEEYA

1 cup sesame paste (tahini)

½ cup fresh lemon juice, plus more to taste

½ teaspoon salt, plus more to taste

3 cloves garlic, mashed

1 packed cup chopped fresh parsley

1 small tomato, peeled, seeded, and chopped

I find this lemony sauce addictive. The sharp bite of the parsley cuts the richness of the tahini, making it bright enough in flavor to serve alongside any fish dish or as a dip with plain toasted or fried Arab bread. It also makes an excellent dressing for chopped romaine lettuce. I serve it, with a little red pepper added, with Kafta. To make a delicious salad dressing, thin the sauce with a bit of water or lemon juice, adding the liquid gradually until you achieve the consistency you like.

Makes 2 cups

Combine the tahini, lemon juice, and salt in a medium bowl. Stir until the mixture becomes firm and pale. Gradually add up to ½ cup cold water, stirring constantly, until the mixture has the consistency of thick cream. Stir in the garlic, parsley, and tomatoes. Season to taste with more salt and lemon juice.

Garlic Paste

TOUM BI ZEIT

20 cloves garlic, peeled (see page 32)

½ teaspoon salt, plus more to taste

2 teaspoons Arab Yogurt Cheese (page 110)

⅓ cup extra virgin olive oil

1 tablespoon fresh lemon juice, plus more to taste

I make this pungent garlic sauce the way my mother did, by mashing the garlic and salt together in a large mortar and pestle, then slowly adding the olive oil until the mixture becomes smooth and creamy. The lemon juice is added at the end to finish the sauce. Here, however, I suggest using a small food processor (a large one won't do a very good job of whipping the ingredients to a creamy consistency)—but by all means use a large mortar and pestle if you have one. If the sauce is too strong for your taste, add some mayonnaise, boiled potatoes, or more Labneh. Toum Bi Zeit can be made a day ahead and refrigerated; add any leftover sauce to salad dressings or use it whenever crushed garlic is called for in a recipe. Serve the sauce with Kibeh Balls.   *Makes ½ cup*

Combine the garlic and salt in a mini processor or a blender and pulse three or four times, until the garlic is minced. Add the Arab Yogurt Cheese and pulse until incorporated. With the processor running, add the olive oil in a steady stream, processing until it is thoroughly incorporated and the mixture forms a paste. Add the lemon juice and pulse a few more times. Taste, and add more salt and lemon juice as desired.

Zaatar

ZAATAR

¼ cup sesame seeds

10 ounces oregano leaves, washed, dried, and crushed (see page 45; 1 cup crushed)

5 ounces thyme leaves, washed, dried, and crushed (see page 45; ½ cup crushed)

3 tablespoons ground sumac

2½ tablespoons coarse salt

½ teaspoon ground allspice

¼ teaspoon caraway seeds (optional)

Zaatar, a spice blend, is ubiquitous in Arab cooking, but it varies slightly by region and personal preference. In Palestine, for example, caraway seeds are added to the blend. My version features twice as much oregano as thyme, for which the blend is named, which is the way most Lebanese cooks make it. Zaatar is used in hot and cold dishes, from Grilled Halloumi Cheese Triangles to Oregano Salad. ***Makes 2 cups***

Put the sesame seeds in a nonstick skillet and place it over high heat. Cook, stirring constantly, until the seeds begin to pop and crackle like popcorn. *Watch carefully.* As soon as some seeds start to turn light brown, remove the skillet from the heat. *Keep stirring:* the seeds will continue to cook. When they are a uniform light brown, immediately transfer them to a plate to cool.

While the sesame seeds are cooling, set a fine-mesh sieve over a bowl, and pass the crushed oregano and thyme through the sieve. Mix the sumac, salt, allspice, and caraway seeds, if using, into the sieved herbs. Stir in the cooled sesame seeds. Taste, and add more sumac if you like it tart, or more allspice if you like it more aromatic.

Store the Zaatar in an airtight jar for up to 1 year.

Toasted Chickpea Flour and Spice Mix

DUKKA

¼ pound chickpea flour

1 tablespoon coriander seeds

1 tablespoon caraway seeds, toasted

1 tablespoon dill seeds, toasted

1 tablespoon ground sumac

1 tablespoon sesame seeds, toasted and pounded to a powder in a mortar

½ tablespoon coarse salt, or to taste

¾ teaspoon cayenne pepper, or to taste

*T*his blend of chickpea flour, sesame, dill, caraway, coriander, and sumac is as ubiquitous on the Arab table as Zaatar, the thyme seasoning blend (page 38). And like Zaatar, the combination and quantities of spices vary from one home to the next. Dukka can be served dry on a small plate, as a dip for an olive oil–soaked piece of bread, or it can be sprinkled right on the bread and then served. Sometimes I cut Arab bread in triangles, brush them with olive oil, then dust them with Dukka, and toast them to make chips. You can buy Dukka at Middle Eastern stores or make it the way I do, as described here. **Makes 1 cup**

Combine the chickpea flour, coriander seeds, caraway seeds, and dill seeds in a spice grinder and grind to a fine powder, working in batches if necessary. Combine the spice powder with the sumac, sesame powder, coarse salt, and cayenne in a bowl and mix together with a spoon (make sure the spoon is perfectly dry). Adjust any one of the seasonings to taste.

Store in a glass jar with a tight-fitting lid in the pantry, or in a resealable plastic bag in the freezer, for up to 1 year.

Saudi Spice Mix

BAHARAT SAUDIYA

¼ cup sweet paprika

2 tablespoons black pepper

2 tablespoons chat masala (see page 16)

1 tablespoon ground coriander

1 tablespoon ground cinnamon

1 tablespoon ground cloves

2 tablespoons ground cumin

1 teaspoon ground cardamom

1 tablespoon grated nutmeg

1 tablespoon ground lime (*loumi*)

You will rarely find two identical recipes for this mixture, since each Saudi cook varies it a bit to suit his or her taste. When I first began to cook, I never bothered to make my own spice mixes, but when we moved to London, I was forced to put my own seasonings together since they weren't available commercially. Buy spices from a busy purveyor to guarantee their freshness. The chat masala, a spice mix itself, is fragrant of dried mango, mint, and pomegranate. Both the masala and the loumi can be purchased at Middle Eastern markets. If you can't find loumi, make the spice mix anyway, and add a little lime zest to the pot when you add the dried spices. ***Makes 1 cup***

Mix all the spices together in a small bowl. The mixture will keep in a glass jar with a tight-fitting lid for 1 year.

Kuwaiti Spice Mix

BAHARAT KUWAITI

½ cup black pepper

¼ cup cayenne pepper

1½ teaspoons ground coriander

1½ teaspoons ground cumin

1½ teaspoons ground ginger

1½ teaspoons ground cinnamon

1½ teaspoons ground cloves

1½ teaspoons grated nutmeg

*G*round ginger and cayenne pepper distinguish this spice mix from those used in the cooking of the Eastern Mediterranean. But the mixtures vary not only from country to country, but from household to household. That's why I encourage you to tinker with the combination of spices listed here until you come up with a mix that suits your palate.

Makes about 1 cup

Combine all the spices in a small bowl and mix well. Store in a jar with a tight-fitting lid for up to 1 year.

Yemeni Spice Mix

BAHARAT YEMENI

¼ cup black peppercorns

2 tablespoons caraway seeds

2 teaspoons saffron threads

2 teaspoons cardamom seeds

1 tablespoon plus 1 teaspoon ground turmeric

*T*his gold-flecked spice mix can be used in place of the Saudi Spice Mix in Kabsa (page 40), the festive rice and lamb dish so popular in that country, to make it the Yemeni way.   ***Makes about ½ cup***

Combine the peppercorns, caraway seeds, saffron, and cardamom seeds in a spice grinder and grind to a fine powder. Transfer the powder to a glass jar, add the turmeric, and stir to mix it in thoroughly. Seal tightly and store in the pantry for up to 1 year.

Arab Chips

KHOUBEZ MOHAMAS

Three 7-inch loaves Arab
flatbread

¼ cup extra virgin olive oil

2 tablespoons Dukka or Zaatar
(pages 39, 38)

*S*nacks and mezza often feature a variety of dips, flavored oils, or sauces that are scooped up with small pieces of Arab bread. When I first came to America, I learned that chips of all kinds—including "pita chips"—were popular snacks used in much the same way. Here's how to make them at home. Of course the recipe can easily be doubled or tripled.

When making Arab bread chips, I alternate between my family's two favorite spice mixtures, sprinkling on bit of Zaatar or Dukka, but you can use just about any flavoring or herb. Try crushed garlic, basil, oregano, thyme, cayenne pepper, black pepper, parsley, sumac, chipotle pepper powder, or any infused oil—the possibilities are virtually endless.

Makes 36 chips

Preheat the oven to 425°F.

Split open the Arab bread, using the tip of a knife to pry apart the top and bottom layers. Brush the insides of the bread halves with olive oil, and then sprinkle with Dukka or Zaatar. Replace the bread halves on top of each other.

Using a knife or scissors, cut the breads in half, and then cut each half into 3 triangles. Separate the triangles and arrange them in a single layer, flavored side up, on a baking sheet. Bake until lightly browned, crisp, and firm to the touch, about 10 minutes.

Arab bread chips can be stored in a plastic bag for up to 1 week.

Fried Nuts

QOLOBAT MAKLIYEH

¼ cup olive oil

½ cup pecans, cashews, or pine
nuts

The trick to getting uniformly golden nuts is to stir them constantly as they fry—and to remove them from the heat just before they turn the color you want them to be; they continue to cook in the oil even when they're off the heat, and they can burn very easily. Fried nuts can be stored in a sealed container in the refrigerator or freezer for up to 3 months. ***Makes ½ cup***

Pour the olive oil into a skillet that is large enough to accommodate the nuts in a single layer. Heat the oil over medium-high heat. Add the nuts, reduce the heat to low, and stir actively until they begin to darken slightly, about 1 minute. Remove the pan from the heat, and use a slotted spoon to transfer the nuts to a paper towel–lined plate to drain. (Alternatively, dump the nuts into a medium-mesh sieve set over a container to catch the cooking oil.) Let them cool completely.

Fried Onions

BASAL MAKLI

Canola oil for frying

A quantity of onions, thinly sliced into rings or halved and thinly sliced

*F*ried onions flavor some of my favorite Arab dishes, including Sautéed Greens with Crispy Onions and Warm Lentils with Rice. I like to make a big batch and freeze them.

Pour enough canola oil into a deep skillet or a Dutch oven to cover the onions by ½ inch. Heat the oil over high heat. Add the onions and fry, stirring occasionally, until they begin to turn yellow, about 3 minutes. Then reduce the heat to medium-low and continue cooking, stirring frequently, until they are golden brown, 20 to 30 minutes. (The onions will rise to the surface.) Using a slotted spoon, transfer the onions to a paper towel–lined plate or a colander to drain.

To freeze the onions, spread them in a single layer on a baking sheet and freeze overnight. Then transfer them to a rigid container with a tight-fitting lid, and freeze for up to 6 months.

Clarified Butter

SAMNA

Makes 1½ cups

1 pound unsalted butter

Cut the butter into small pieces and place them in a saucepan. Heat over low heat, being careful not to let the butter brown. Remove the pan from the heat and set it aside for 3 minutes. Then skim off the froth that has formed on the surface and discard it. The golden liquid underneath is butter that has been separated from its milk solids, or clarified. Carefully pour it into a clean container with a tight-fitting lid and set it aside to cool completely.

Alternatively, melt the butter in a microwave-safe container in a microwave on high power. This will take about 2½ minutes. The butter will separate into three layers: Skim off and discard the foamy layer on top. The clear, golden yellow layer in the middle is the clarified butter; pour it into a clean container as described above. The bottom layer consists of milk solids and should be discarded.

Samna will last for a year in a cool, dry place, providing you always use a clean spoon to scoop out what you need.

DRIED HERBS

Dried herbs, particularly oregano, thyme, and mint, are widely used in Arab cooking. Although you can find dried herbs in every grocery store and ethnic market, I prefer to dry my own. This way, I know how old (or new) they are and can be sure that they will impart the desired flavor to my food. What's more, I prefer organically grown herbs, since the plants are so greatly affected by the soil and water they grow in.

To dry herbs at home, first pick the leaves off the stems. Place the leaves in a bowl of cold water and swirl them around to wash off any dirt and debris. Using your hands, lift the herbs out of the bowl (pouring them out will just put the dirt right back on them) and place them in another bowl filled with fresh cold water. Repeat until there is no longer any sediment or dirt in the bottom of the bowl.

Spread the washed herbs on a tray lined with a triple layer of paper towels. Place the tray in a dry spot out of the sun, and leave it until the leaves are thoroughly dried, about 24 hours. Store them in a glass container with a tight-fitting lid for up to 1 year.

If you must use packaged herbs, opt for those stored in glass jars; herbs stored in plastic tend to lose their flavor faster.

CILANTRO AND PARSLEY

Cilantro (fresh coriander) and parsley are two of the most important herbs in the Arab kitchen. Both are easy to find in American markets these days.

Cilantro and parsley are usually quite gritty and must be thoroughly rinsed and dried before you use them. Fill a large bowl (or a clean sink) with cold water. Remove the rubber band or twist tie holding the bunch of herbs together. Gather as many stems as you want to wash, forming an even bunch, and retie it firmly. Cut off the stems so only 3 inches remain. Then submerge the bunch in the cold water, and swish it around so the dirt is released and sinks to the bottom. Lift the herbs out, pour off the water and grit, and repeat two or three times, until the water is clean. Then set the whole bunch in a colander, leaves up but not pressed together, and let it air-dry for a couple of hours. (Put the colander in the sink or on a plate to catch dripping water.)

CHOPPING FRESH HERBS

To chop any fresh herbs, they must be completely dry. You must have a sharp knife and an even surface; if the knife is not sharp, you will end up bruising and mashing the leaves instead of cutting them. Lay a wet paper towel under the cutting board to prevent it from sliding while you chop.

To chop a large quantity of an herb such as cilantro or parsley, lay a bunch on a chopping board and grab the entire pile of leaves near the tie, as close to the leaves as possible, squeezing them together as you close your first around the leaves. Using a chef's knife, cut all the extra stems and throw them away. Then slice through the leaves that are poking out of your fist, chopping them as called for in the recipe. After a few chops, stop, regroup the bunch, and then continue to chop. To make a fine chop, use the back of the knife to scrape the chopped herbs back into a pile and go over them one more time, making a small back-and-forth motion with the knife. Now you can measure the herbs for your recipe.

If you are planning to chop fresh mint, cool it in the fridge first. This will prevent it from bruising when it is chopped, and it will retain its fragrance.

CLEANING LEAFY VEGETABLES

Fill a large bowl (or clean sink) with cold water, and submerge the leaves in it. Swirl the leaves around to wash off any dirt. Then, using your hands, lift the leaves out of the water. Discard the water, refill the bowl, and repeat one or two more times, until the water is clear. Set the rinsed leaves in a colander and let them air-dry for a couple of hours. (Put the colander in the sink or on a plate to catch dripping water.)

Mezza

THE TRADITION OF MEZZA, OR appetizers, best exemplifies the lavish hospitality for which Arabs are famous. Guests—invited or unexpected—are never asked if they would like something to eat or drink when they arrive at an Arab home; food is offered as a matter of course.

Small portions of different mezza are served on small plates, and depending on the country, can range from the simple offerings on the Egyptian table, such as cheese, Arab flatbread, sardines, and lentil dip, to the elaborate spreads of warm and cold salads, savory pastries, dips, and meat preparations typical in Lebanon. No matter what the country, mezza dishes are always bountiful and presented with pride. Each one is garnished with, at the very least, parsley or mint sprigs, a slice of tomato or lemon, or a sprinkling of zaatar. An edible centerpiece of romaine lettuce leaves, cucumber strips, sliced sweet peppers and carrots, whole radishes, chile peppers, and scallions, garnished with bunches of parsley and mint, is placed on the table. In the summer I add farmstand tomatoes and make them easy to eat by coring them, packing their centers with coarse salt, and placing them in a bowl of crushed ice. Pickled cucumbers, eggplants, turnips, and cauliflower are staples on my mezza table. These can be purchased at Middle Eastern markets, packed in jars or cans.

The recipes here are mostly Lebanese in origin, since the tradition of mezza is so highly prized there. Although I favor the Lebanese way of serving a variety of cooked and cool appetizers with a broad range of flavors, the beauty of mezza is in its versatility. Any of these recipes can be a side dish to a main course, or you can group several together for a meal, as is the custom in Syria, Jordan, and Palestine. Once you have stocked up on the basic Arab pantry ingredients—tahini, yogurt, walnuts, garlic, lemons, pomegranate syrup, and olive oil—putting together an impromptu mezza is easy.

Cold Mezza

Hot Green Olives

ZEITOUN

1 pound brine-cured Arab green
    olives in their brine

2 serrano chiles, halved, seeded,
    and thinly sliced

1 teaspoon red pepper flakes

¼ cup fresh lemon juice

Extra virgin olive oil

My favorite way to eat zeitoun *is as the simple snack eaten by day laborers, schoolchildren, and businessmen alike all over the Middle East: pitted olives, along with a slice of ripe tomato and a slice of white onion, wrapped in a piece of Arab flatbread. If you can't find Arab olives (Lebanese Soury, Jordanian Suri, Syrian Sorani, Palestinian Sorri, Tunisian Gerboui, Egyptian Tofahi, Morrocan Meslala), substitute the firm, green Greek Nafplion olives or Italian Cerignola.*

Don't throw away the marinade once you've used all the olives; simply add more of the spiced olive mixture to it, top it off with more olive oil, and repeat the process. **Makes 3 to 4 cups**

In a large bowl, mix the olives and half of their brine with the chiles, red pepper flakes, and lemon juice. Transfer the mixture to a 1½-quart lidded glass container, and add olive oil to cover. Seal the jar and let the olives marinate at room temperature for at least 4 hours or, preferably, overnight.

IS IT EXTRA VIRGIN?

I always use extra virgin olive oil to dress salads, to swirl into dips, and whenever oil is called for in an uncooked dish, such as tabouleh. Here's one way to determine if the olive oil you are using is truly extra virgin: Pour a small amount into a clear glass and place it in the refrigerator for 3 to 4 days. If the oil crystallizes and becomes hard, it is extra virgin.

STORING OLIVE OIL

Direct sunlight affects both the color and the flavor of olive oil and can turn the oil rancid. If your favorite olive oil comes in a clear glass bottle, do yourself a favor and decant it into a dark glass vessel or a metal container. This will prevent the oil from breaking down. If you can't decant it, simply wrap the clear bottle in aluminum foil. Store your olive oil in a cool, dark place.

OLIVES, THE FAMILY FRUIT

When Thomas Jefferson said that the olive tree was surely the richest gift of heaven, he was expressing a centuries-old sentiment. Certainly in the Arab world, the fruit of the olive tree, its branches, and its leaves have all held deep social and religious significance. The ancient Egyptians considered olives to be the ultimate embodiment of the riches of the Mediterranean. In ancient Greece, the Olympic flame was burned using olive oil. Judeo-Christian and Islamic traditions say that a dove brought an olive branch to Noah on the Ark to herald the end of the great Flood.

To the ancients, olive oil provided food, beauty, and utility. Olive oil was the preferred source of fuel for cooking fires and ceremonial flames. It was also thought to be an effective moisturizer that helped healed wounds—principles still followed in the Arab world, where the hands are treated with a mixture of lukewarm olive oil and lemon juice.

Although olive trees were first found in Asia, they have been cultivated in Palestine, Syria, Lebanon, Jordan, Algeria, Tunisia, Morocco, and Egypt for thousands of years. Olive groves are as integral to life in this region today as they were thousands of years ago. In Palestine, olives probably are the most widely planted tree.

Thirty-nine varieties of olives grow in Arab countries—only a fraction of the different kinds grown in Italy and Spain, yet they play a major role nevertheless.

In my extended family, olives are a way of life. To this day my uncle sends us green olives and olive oil from trees that grow on our family farm in Jordan. The harvest, which takes place in the beginning of the rainy season in November and continues through early December, is a special family event. Men, women, and children set out for the groves with blankets to spread under the trees, a ladder to climb them, and a well-ventilated plastic bucket to transport the just-picked olives. The younger boys nimbly climb the ladders to get at the higher branches while the women and girls pick the lower branches clean. Sometimes sticks are used to shake the higher branches so the olives will fall to the blanket below.

The bright green olives are spread out on huge cloths on the village rooftops to dry in the sun for a few days. The olives are then picked over, cracked, and stored in glass jars, in a brine made of purified water and salt. (The proper ratio of salt to water is achieved when a raw egg bobs to the surface.) To make black olives, the fresh olives are left to ripen on the rooftops until they turn black. They are then stored in the same brine as the green olives. Fully ripe olives—the color turns from green to violet black—are collected and pressed, with the pit, to make olive oil.

As important as the olives themselves, olive oil is considered so valuable that it is given as a gift—just as it was in ancient times. Back home in Jordan, we always shared the fresh crop of olives and olive oil with our closest friends—but not before my father gave the oil his stamp of approval. Whenever I open a bottle here in the U.S., I am reminded of the tasting my father conducted after the first press of olives: My mother would pour some of the golden-green liquid into a drinking glass. Like a person scrutinizing a fine wine, my father would raise the glass of oil to the light to inspect its color. He was pleased when it was a deep, dark green. Next he would smell its bouquet, always looking for a slightly nutty, almond-like fragrance. After an initial sip, he would dip a piece of bread into the glass, to make sure that the flavor of the oil held up with food. Once my father gave the olive oil his approval, it was decanted from storage cans into dark bottles to preserve its color and flavor.

Tomato Spread

BANDORA BI ZEIT ZEITOUN

6 cloves garlic, mashed

1 teaspoon salt

2 pounds ripe tomatoes, peeled
and finely diced

¼ cup extra virgin olive oil

1 jalapeño pepper, seeded and
minced

Coarsely chopped fresh cilantro
leaves, for garnish

There is usually a batch of this tasty cooked tomato salsa in my refrigerator all summer long. It tastes best when made with juicy farm-stand tomatoes—an heirloom variety called Ugli tomatoes is especially good. We scoop the mixture with triangles of fluffy Arab bread, spoon it over grilled whitefish, and spread it on warm bread for a quick appetizer. If you like your salsa very hot, add some of the pepper's seeds to the mix. Bandora bi Zeit Zeitoun will keep, covered, in the refrigerator for up to a week. ***Makes 3 cups***

Combine the garlic, salt, tomatoes, olive oil, and jalapeño in a medium saucepan and bring to a boil over high heat, stirring occasionally. Reduce the heat to medium, cover the pan, and cook until the tomatoes have broken down, about 40 minutes. Turn the heat to very low, or slide a heat diffuser under the pan, for the last 10 minutes.

Uncover the pan and cook, stirring two or three times, for 5 minutes.

Pour the tomatoes into a rimmed serving dish and garnish with the cilantro. Serve warm or at room temperature.

Chickpea Dip

HUMMUS

2 cups dried chickpeas, *or* three 15-ounce cans

¼ teaspoon baking soda (for dried chickpeas)

2 cloves garlic, mashed

½ teaspoon salt, plus more to taste

½ cup sesame paste (tahini)

½ cup fresh lemon juice, plus more to taste

Extra virgin olive oil, for drizzling

Paprika-dusted cucumber slices, *or* pine nuts, *or* whole cooked chickpeas, for garnish

Cayenne pepper, for garnish

*P*erhaps the most popular dish to make the trip from the Middle East to the U.S., this Arab staple is almost always part of a mezza, as a dip served with toasted Arab bread. I often swab some into the pocket of a flatbread for a protein-rich vegetarian sandwich. A good hummus will be slightly tart, with a strong flavor of garlic and olive oil. It should be silky smooth, too, which is easy to achieve if you peel the chickpeas as described here. I prefer dried chickpeas to canned because it results in a more robust dip that stands up even when frozen. If you plan to freeze hummus, omit the garlic and add it when the dip is defrosted.

Serve hummus with torn pieces of Arab bread, either soft or toasted, and sprigs of parsley (for cleansing the breath after eating the garlicky dip). ***Makes 2 cups***

If using dried chickpeas, place them in a bowl and add water to cover by 1 inch. Add the baking soda and let soak overnight. Then drain the chickpeas and rinse them under cold running water. Combine the chickpeas with 6 cups water in a saucepan, and bring to a boil over high heat. Cook, skimming the foam from the surface until no more appears, about 15 minutes. Then reduce the heat, cover the pan, and simmer until the beans are tender and break easily when pressed with the back of the spoon, 1½ hours. Drain, reserving the liquid, and pour the chickpeas into a large bowl of cold water. Gather a handful of chickpeas and rub them between your palms to remove their skins. Once the surface of the water is covered with transparent skins, pour off the water, refill the bowl, and continue to rub the chickpeas between your palms until most of the skins are removed. Drain the chickpeas thoroughly and set aside.

If using canned chickpeas, drain and rinse them three times. Place the chickpeas in a saucepan and add water to cover by 1 inch. Bring to a boil, reduce the heat, and simmer for 1 to 2 minutes. Drain, reserving some of the liquid, and set aside.

Place the garlic and salt in a food processor and pulse three times. Add the chickpeas, sesame paste, and lemon juice, and pulse until the mixture is thick and creamy. Using a rubber spatula, scrape down the sides of the bowl. Then process the paste until it has the consistency of sour cream, about 5 minutes. Add a little of the chickpea cooking liquid—about 2 tablespoons—if the mixture is too dry. Season to taste with additional salt and lemon juice if desired.

Spoon the hummus onto a rimmed plate or a shallow bowl and smooth it out evenly, using the back of the spoon to push the mixture out toward the edge of the plate to create a raised border. Then use the back of the spoon to form indentations all over the hummus in which the olive oil can pool. Drizzle with olive oil.

Dampen your thumb, place it in the paprika, and then press it around the edges of the cucumber slices. Garnish the plate with the cucumbers. (Alternatively, mound pine nuts or whole chickpeas in the center of the dish.) Sprinkle the cayenne on top, and serve.

CHICKPEAS

In some recipes I suggest using canned chickpeas because they are easier to work with, even though I feel that dried chickpeas provide better taste and texture. When using canned chickpeas, it's important to drain off the liquid, then rinse the peas under cold water for a minute or so. For the best flavor, boil the canned chickpeas in water to cover for 1 to 2 minutes; then drain.

Because I prefer using dried chickpeas, I prepare a large quantity in advance, divide them into 2-cup containers, and freeze them. They will keep in the freezer for up to 6 months.

To prepare dried chickpeas, place them in a bowl and add water to cover by 1 inch. Add baking soda (¼ teaspoon for 2 cups chickpeas) and let soak overnight. Then drain the chickpeas and rinse them under cold running water. Place the chickpeas in a saucepan, cover generously with water, and bring to a boil over high heat. Cook, skimming the foam from the surface until no more appears, about 15 minutes. Then reduce the heat and simmer until the beans are tender and break easily when pressed with the back of the spoon, 1½ hours. Let them cool completely in the cooking liquid. Then freeze the chickpeas, in their cooking liquid, to use at a later time.

A Variation for Meat Lovers

Heat ¼ cup extra virgin olive oil in a small skillet over high heat. Add ¼ pound ground sirloin, ¼ teaspoon ground allspice, ⅛ teaspoon ground cinnamon, and ¼ teaspoon salt. Cook, breaking up the meat into coarse crumbs, until the beef is evenly browned, about 5 minutes. Spread the prepared hummus on a plate, creating a raised border as described, and spoon the cooked beef mixture onto the center of the hummus. Garnish with fried pine nuts (see page 43).

Spicy Lebanese Cheese Dip

SHANKLEESH MUTABAL

*S*hankleesh *is a fermented goat cheese that is coated with a rind of thyme, salt, and cayenne pepper. The dense cheese, which is the size and shape of a golf ball, was traditionally made at home during the summer, when goat's milk is abundant. Before it was stored for eating in the winter, this staple of Lebanese mezza was air-dried on a cloth for 5 days so that its rind could harden a bit. Today shankleesh is rarely, if ever, made at home since it is readily available in Middle Eastern groceries, either packed in olive oil or dried and vacuum-packed. Some varieties feature an herb-coated rind, while in others the herbs are mixed in with the cheese. If you can't find shankleesh, feta is a fine substitute.*

As with any Arab cheese, shankleesh can be served on its own with Arab bread. Its sharp taste makes it an excellent companion to fresh vegetables. I often serve it tossed with tomatoes in a tangy vinaigrette, with toasted bread on the side for dipping. Vacuum-packed shankleesh keeps in the refrigerator for up to 6 months or in the freezer for up to a year. To defrost it, simply set it out on the kitchen counter for a couple of hours.

Serves 6

Two 5-ounce balls *shankleesh*

1 cup plus 1 tablespoon finely chopped firm plum tomatoes

20 scallions, white and light green parts only, finely chopped (about ¾ cup)

2 jalapeño peppers, seeded and minced

2 tablespoons fresh lemon juice

3 tablespoons extra virgin olive oil, plus more for drizzling

1 teaspoon salt

Chopped fresh flat-leaf parsley, for garnish

Arab flatbread, torn into bite-size pieces and toasted

Peel the thin rind from the *shankleesh* with a paring knife and discard it. (It's not imperative to remove every last bit of rind.) Cut small, uneven pieces of cheese from the ball, dropping them directly into a medium serving bowl. Add the tomatoes, scallions, jalapeños, lemon juice, olive oil, and salt. Toss together gently with a wooden spoon. Taste, and adjust the seasonings if needed. Drizzle with olive oil, garnish with parsley, and serve with the toasted Arab flatbread.

Roasted Eggplant Spread

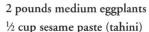

BETINJAN MUTABAL

*T*he distinctive flavor of this dish comes from getting a good char on the eggplants. The intensely smoky flavor of Betinjan Mutabal makes it an excellent accompaniment to grilled meats and chicken. It is thick and creamy enough, too, to spread on Arab bread or to scoop up with crudités. My mother's version, which I give here, is particularly smooth thanks to the addition of yogurt as a "secret" ingredient.

The spread can be prepared 2 days in advance and refrigerated. Alternatively, you can prepare the eggplants only: Roast, peel, and seed them. Submerge them in a bowl of lemon juice, then drain, and freeze in resealable freezer bags. Defrost at room temperature until soft. **Serves 6**

2 pounds medium eggplants

½ cup sesame paste (tahini)

⅔ cup fresh lemon juice, plus more to taste

¾ teaspoon coarse salt, plus more to taste

1 teaspoon mashed garlic

2 tablespoons full-fat plain yogurt

1 teaspoon red pepper flakes

Sliced radishes, for garnish

Chopped scallions, for garnish

Julienned red or green chiles, for garnish

Extra virgin olive oil, for drizzling

Preheat the oven to 400°F.

Pierce the eggplants in a few places with a sharp paring knife, and place them on an aluminum foil–lined baking sheet 4 inches from the heat source. Roast, turning the eggplants a quarter turn every 5 minutes, until the skin blisters and cracks all over.

To determine doneness, press the top of an eggplant between your index finger and thumb. If it is soft, they are cooked. Let the eggplants cool until they are comfortable to handle. Then, holding the still-warm eggplants, at the stem end, peel them from the top down. Cut them in half and gently scrape out the seeds with a spoon, leaving as much flesh behind as possible.

Place the eggplant flesh in a bowl, and mash it with a potato masher or a pestle until smooth. Mix the sesame paste with the lemon juice,

GETTING THAT SMOKY FLAVOR, INDOORS OR OUT

I roast eggplants the same way my grandmother did, by grilling them on top of a heavy wire mesh square fitted directly over the stovetop flame. A heat diffuser is ideal for this purpose. Of course, setting them directly over the coals on a barbecue grill results in the smokiest flavor of all. If you do your roasting in an oven, preheat it to 400°F, place the eggplants on a baking sheet, and set it on a rack about 4 inches from the heat source. Turn them as the skin blisters.

salt, garlic, yogurt, and red pepper flakes in a small bowl. Add this to the eggplant and stir until the mixture is thoroughly combined. Season to taste with additional lemon juice and salt if needed.

Spoon the eggplant spread onto a serving plate and garnish with the radishes, scallions, and chiles. Drizzle with olive oil, and serve.

EGGPLANT LORE

Gracing the tables of rich and poor alike, eggplant is often called "the noble fruit" in the Arab world. In Syria, where eggplant is probably the most appreciated, a woman is likened to an eggplant if she is particularly helpful and good. In Palestine, a woman's ability to manage the household is judged by how many ways she can prepare eggplant.

Cucumber and Yogurt

KHIYAR BI LABAN

3 cups full-fat plain yogurt

1 Lebanese cucumber or 2 Kirby cucumbers, peeled, seeded, and finely chopped

1 clove garlic, mashed

¼ teaspoon salt

1 teaspoon dried mint, preferably spearmint

*T*hroughout this book, you will notice that I suggest serving quite a few dishes with this cool, creamy, and chameleon-like dish. Khiyar bi Laban can be a salad eaten on its own, a dip for scooping up with Arab bread or vegetables, a cold summertime soup, or an accompaniment to rice, meat, and kibeh dishes. It all depends on the consistency of the yogurt and the different herbs you use. My favorite herb combination is mint, dill, and chives, but feel free to use whatever herbs you have on hand.

Whenever I can find them, I use the skinny, straight Middle Eastern cucumbers—sometimes called "Lebanese" or "Armenian" cucumbers—for this dish because they generally have fewer and smaller seeds. Kirbys (pickling cucumbers) and seedless English cukes are good choices, too. If you can only find slicing cucumbers, peel them first, then use a teaspoon to scoop out all the seeds and watery pulp before chopping them.

Khiyar bi Laban can be made ahead and kept in the refrigerator for a week. Omit the garlic if you plan to make it in advance, and add it just before serving. This version is thick, to be used as a dip. *Serves 6*

CUCUMBER, YOGURT, AND . . .

Cucumber and Yogurt with dried mint is often served with Kibeh Balls and with Spiced Beef with Rice. Cucumber and Yogurt with dried dill goes well with Karfta Burgers and Kafta Fingers. Combine Cucumber and Yogurt with chives and harissa for a dip to serve with vegetables or chips.

LABNEH BAG

Used for draining yogurt, labneh bags are a fixture in an Arab kitchen. My mother and her mother made labneh bags from new white cotton pillowcases. Here I have found that the easiest way to make one is with a new white cotton t-shirt. Cut across the shirt just under the arms, creating a large wide tube. Using a tight stitch, machine-sew one of the open sides closed to create a sack that will hold the yogurt while it drains.

After each use, wash the labneh bag by hand, using dish detergent or a mild color- and odor-free soap, and hang it up to dry. The bag should not come into contact with non-food-safe items, so don't wash it in the washing machine or with other material.

Remove excess water from the yogurt: Put the yogurt in a bowl, place a couple of layers of paper towels on the surface, and set it aside for a few minutes. The paper will become soaked very quickly. Remove the towels, stir, and repeat with fresh paper towels if necessary. (This step isn't necessary if using Total® Greek yogurt.)

In a large glass or ceramic bowl, combine the yogurt, cucumbers, garlic, and salt. Taste, and add more garlic and salt if desired.

Garnish with the mint, and serve.

GRANDMOTHER NAZLEH'S YOGURT FROM SCRATCH

Like olive oil and bread, yogurt is an essential element of the Arab kitchen used in everything from appetizers to salads to drinks. It is strained to make *labneh,* the Arab yogurt cheese; cooked together with stuffed zucchini, kibeh, and all kinds of beef and lamb; served straight from the container as a side dish at almost every meal; and diluted, seasoned with salt, and garnished with fresh mint to make a refreshing drink called *ayran* (page 291). It is also highly regarded as a salve for sunburned skin—we often slathered it all over our faces after a day in the sun—and as an antidote to the side effects of antibiotics. As a result Arabs are quite serious about their yogurt, and more often than not, they make it at home rather than buying it at the grocery store, despite the availability of good-quality packaged brands.

My grandmother was the chief yogurt-maker in our family. One night each week, she would make a big pot of it—enough to last seven days. But it wasn't until I was newly married and moved to Kuwait that I began to make my own yogurt from scratch. Luckily, my parents were living there at the time too, and my mother set aside a day to come to my kitchen and teach me the delicate, though not difficult, art of making yogurt the way her mother made it. Traditionally, fresh milk is used to make yogurt, but at the time, powdered milk was more available in Kuwait, where there were limited milk-bearing herds.

These days I buy yogurt—Stonyfield Farms and Greek Total are two of my favorite brands—for convenience' sake, but occasionally I return to the recipe that goes back several generations.

Combine 4 cups powdered milk with 12 cups cold water in a mixing bowl, and beat with a hand-held electric mixer on medium speed until smooth. Pour the mixture through a strainer into a large pot, and place it over high heat. Heat the mixture just to the boiling point, then immediately remove it from the heat. (Alternatively, use 1 gallon full-fat milk.) Allow the mixture to cool until it is warm to the touch (or as we used to say, "baby warm"), and then remove the skin that has formed on the surface. (My grandmother used to scoop up some of this thickened liquid, sprinkle it with sugar, and offer it to us as a treat.)

Next, combine ½ cup of the scalded milk with ½ cup store-bought full-fat yogurt (or, as my grandmother did, with ½ cup of last week's yogurt) and add it to the pot. Stir well. Cover the pot and wrap it in a fleece blanket (Grandmother had a special woolen blanket—a *herram labneh*—expressly for the purpose of "proofing" the yogurt), and leave the pot undisturbed overnight. The mixture will become thick and creamy, the consistency of delicious yogurt.

Whether you make your own yogurt or purchase it, always drain off the liquid, or whey, before using it.

Dressed Chickpeas

BALILA

*T*his simple salad, fragrant of cumin, is traditionally eaten only as a mezza, but I often add feta and chopped tomatoes to turn it into a satisfying lunch. To make the salad taste more intensely of cumin, toast the whole seeds in a dry skillet until fragrant, about 1 minute, then grind them in a spice grinder or with a mortar and pestle. You can also toast cumin that is preground. Balila will keep in the refrigerator, covered, for up to 3 days. Serve it with Arab flatbread. *Serves 8*

1 cup dried chickpeas, *or* two 15-ounce cans

⅛ tcaspoon baking soda (for dried chickpeas)

½ pound white onions, finely chopped

1 jalapeño pepper, seeded and minced

2 cloves garlic, mashed

1¼ teaspoons salt

1½ teaspoons ground cumin

¼ cup fresh lemon juice

⅓ cup extra virgin olive oil

1 medium tomato, chopped, for garnish

2 tablespoons coarsely chopped fresh parsley, for garnish

¼ teaspoon cayenne pepper, for garnish

If using dried chickpeas, combine the chickpeas, 3 cups water, and the baking soda in a large bowl and soak overnight. Then drain the chickpeas and rinse them under cold running water. Place them in a saucepan and add water to cover by 1 inch. Bring to a boil over high heat. Cook, skimming the foam from the surface until no more appears, about 15 minutes. Then reduce the heat, cover the pan, and simmer until the beans are tender and break easily with the back of a spoon, 1½ hours. Drain, reserving the liquid, and set aside.

If using canned chickpeas, drain them and rinse them three times under cold running water. Place them in a saucepan and add water to cover by 1 inch. Bring to a boil and cook for 1 to 2 minutes. Drain, reserving some of the liquid, and set aside.

CHICKPEA TREATS

I love chickpeas all ways, but the most delicious memory I have of them is from my childhood summers, when, in the early weeks of the season, fresh chickpeas, or *hamleh malyaneh*, were sold by the bunch on the side of the road all over Lebanon, Syria, Jordan, and Palestine. My father always bought several bunches, and as a special treat for my sisters and me, he salted them and roasted them to make a fragrant savory snack. This was his version of the cumin-spiced fried chickpeas that are popular on the streets of many Arab cities, especially in Egypt.

Pour the drained chickpeas into a large bowl of cold water. Gather a handful of chickpeas in your hand and rub them between your palms to remove their skins. Once the surface of the water is covered with transparent skins, pour off the water, refill the bowl, and continue to rub the chickpeas between your palms until most of the skins are removed.

Place the drained chickpeas in a large bowl and add the onions and jalapeño.

Whisk the garlic, salt, cumin, lemon juice, and olive oil together in a small bowl until well blended. Taste, and adjust the seasonings. Pour the dressing over the chickpea mixture and stir gently to coat the salad.

Spoon the salad onto a serving plate, and garnish with the tomatoes, parsley, and cayenne.

FREEZING CHICKPEAS

Like most Arab cooks, I keep a generous supply of precooked chickpeas on hand in my freezer (I prefer their flavor to the canned variety). If you want to do this, simply make more than the Balila or the Hummus recipe calls for and freeze the extra—in its cooking liquid—in a freezer bag or rigid container. When you want to use the chickpeas, defrost them overnight in the refrigerator or on the kitchen counter until they are soft. Drain them in a colander.

Beets with Tahini

SHAMANDAR MUTABAL

½ cup plain full-fat yogurt

1 pound small beets, leaves trimmed, beets rinsed and scrubbed

1 teaspoon salt

¼ teaspoon white vinegar

4 cloves garlic, mashed

⅔ cup fresh lemon juice

⅓ cup sesame paste (tahini)

White and red radish slices, for garnish (optional)

In my grandmother's kitchen, nothing went to waste—not even cooking liquid. Growing up, my sisters and I loved it when she cooked beets. Not because she made a delicious and exuberantly tinted Mutabal (which she did), or because the greens are loaded with vitamins that she insisted staved off anemia (they are rich in folate, potassium, and vitamin C), but because of the ruby red cooking water that was left in the pot once the beets were cooked. Traditionally, this water is used for pickling turnips and for dyeing Easter eggs, but when we were in our teens, we used it to make one-of-a-kind tie-dyed t-shirts. Rather than tying the shirts in knots, we clipped clothespins all over them, dunked the bright white tees right into the pot full of colorful liquid, and left them on the balcony to dry.

To make the best Shamandar Mutabal, buy small beets, since they are more tender and flavorful than the baseball-size variety. Whatever kind you buy, choose ones that are of roughly equal size so they will cook evenly. I always add vinegar to the cooking liquid to retain the beets' vibrant color.

This savory dish might be found on a mezza table with several kinds of kibeh, including Kibeh Balls and Potato Kibeh, Cucumber and Yogurt, and Roasted Eggplant Spread. The beet dip will keep, covered, in the refrigerator for up to 5 days.　　*Serves 6 to 8*

Place the yogurt in a small bowl. Fold a sheet of paper towel in quarters and place it directly on top of the yogurt to soak up the excess liquid. (This step isn't necessary if using Total® Greek yogurt.) Set it aside.

Place the beets in a saucepan and add enough water to cover them completely. Add the salt and vinegar, and cook over high heat until you can easily insert a fork into them, about 1½ hours. Drain, and set aside until they are cool enough to handle.

Peel the beets by hand (the skin should come off easily); in places where the skin doesn't fall away easily, use a paring knife. Place the beets in a food processor and pulse 3 times to make smooth paste. (Alternatively, use a potato masher or the back of a fork.) The beet pieces and the juices should come together to form a very smooth paste.

Add the yogurt, garlic, lemon juice, and sesame paste, and stir to incorporate evenly. Taste, and add more salt and lemon juice if desired. Garnish with the radish slices, and serve cold or at room temperature.

Variation: Use zucchini (unpeeled) in place of the beets; cook it until tender, about 15 minutes.

Zucchini with Bread and Mint

TREEDEH KOOSSA

1½ pounds zucchini, cubed,
   or the pulp left over from
   3 pounds hollowed-out
   zucchini

½ pound white onions, finely
   chopped

3 tablespoons extra virgin olive
   oil, plus extra for drizzling

1 small clove garlic, mashed

2 tablespoons fresh lemon juice

Half of a 7-inch loaf of stale
   thick flatbread, torn into
   bite-size pieces

½ teaspoon salt

¼ teaspoon black pepper

1 teaspoon dried mint,
   preferably spearmint

Fresh mint leaves, for garnish

My grandmother wouldn't dream of discarding bits and pieces of trimmed vegetables. If she had leftover pulp from the tiny zucchinis she hollowed out for stuffing, she would make Treedeh Koossa, my favorite cold mezza. Treedeh is the name given to any dish that features bread for soaking up the juices and flavors of its companion ingredients. Make this dish in the summertime, when fresh zucchini are abundant. Treedeh Koossa will keep, tightly covered, in the refrigerator for up to 4 days.   *Serves 4 to 6*

Combine the squash and 1 cup water in a saucepan and bring to a boil over medium-high heat. Cover the pan, reduce the heat to medium, and cook for 20 minutes.

Drain the zucchini in a colander, transfer it to a large bowl, and mash with the back of a fork. Drain the zucchini again and return it to the bowl. Add the onions, olive oil, garlic, lemon juice, and bread. Stir gently to combine. Season with the salt, pepper, and dried mint. Stir again gently so that the seasonings are well distributed.

Serve warm or at room temperature, drizzled with olive oil and garnished with fresh mint leaves.

Eggplant with Toasted Bread and Pomegranate Syrup

TREEDEH BETINJAN

2½ pounds eggplant

2 teaspoons salt

¾ pound tomatoes, seeded, diced, and drained

¾ pound white onions, diced

10 cloves garlic, mashed

1 jalapeño pepper, or more to taste, seeded and finely chopped

¼ cup pomegranate syrup

1 tablespoon fresh lemon juice

One 7-inch loaf Arab flatbread, cut into 1-inch squares and toasted

¼ cup extra virgin olive oil

Fresh pomegranate seeds, for garnish (optional)

Dried mint, preferably spearmint, for garnish

My grandmother always said that there are over a hundred ways to cook eggplant. Treedah Betinjan, a chunky dip of diced eggplant and tomatoes bathed in pomegranate syrup, was among her favorites. It can be served on its own as a salad or with several different small dishes on the mezza table. Jalapeño is always added to give Treedah a bit of a kick, and I like to make mine very hot with two chile peppers. Adjust the amount to suit your taste.

Treedeh Betinjan can be made 2 days in advance as long as you wait to toast the bread and mix it in just before adding the garnishes and serving. **Serves 6 to 8**

Preheat the oven to 400°F.

Using a vegetable peeler, peel the skin from the eggplants lengthwise, leaving a few thin strips here and there. Cut the eggplants into 2-inch-thick rounds; then cut each round into 2-inch cubes. Combine the eggplant, 5 cups water, and 1 teaspoon of the salt in a medium saucepan. Cook, covered, over high heat until the eggplants are fork-tender, about 25 minutes. Drain in a colander and set aside to cool completely.

Combine the eggplant, tomatoes, onions, garlic, jalapeño, pomegranate syrup, lemon juice, and remaining 1 teaspoon salt in a medium bowl. Mix well. Taste, and adjust the seasonings if needed. Add the toasted Arab flatbread and mix gently. Transfer the salad to a serving bowl and drizzle the olive oil over it. Garnish with the pomegranate seeds, if using, and mint.

A FAMILY PASSION FOR POMEGRANATES

Some of my fondest memories of my childhood in Kuwait are not of the special banquets or the holiday feasts we celebrated, but of the afternoons during pomegranate season. Every day after school, my mother insisted that we gather around the dining room table to talk about our studies while she peeled at least a dozen ruby red pomegranates to produce enough pulp for us to snack on. (We consumed more than the average family, so my father bought them by the box, not the kilo.) She scored and sectioned each pomegranate like a magician, making swift cuts into the leathery skin and using her nimble fingers to release the sparkling fruit from the yellow membranes. No matter how fast our mother worked, we always grew impatient, so she would appease us by giving us a section to work on ourselves. I loved this part—making a mess and letting the juice run all over my hands. And it meant we put off our homework for a good hour or so.

To this day, when I visit my mother in London, we have pomegranates and tea at five o'clock in the afternoon. And despite the fact that I have continued this ritual with my three boys—and have become a speedy sectioner myself—my mother still insists on taking over the job when I am with her.

There are six varieties of pomegranates in the Middle East, but just one, the sweet eating pomegranate known as "Wonderful," is available in the United States. This is the type of pomegranate that Arabs cut open to extract the pulp—to eat out of hand or to garnish a dish—or to make a refreshing pitcher full of juice. You are likely to see these sweet pomegranates piled high in the produce section of large supermarkets and gourmet food shops as early as September and as late as December. Look for those that are about the size of a navel orange, with tight, shiny, ruby-colored skin.

Cooking with pomegranates, on the other hand, is generally done with the concentrated juice of the sour or sweet-sour variety of the fruit, which is not available fresh in the U.S. This concentrated liquid—*debs al ruman* in Arabic, or "syrup and molasses"—can range in thickness from the consistency of maple syrup to that of slow-pouring molasses. It is typically paired with eggplant and lends a piquant, somewhat smoky flavor to Eggplant Salad, Eggplant Pomegranate Salad, Eggplant with Toasted Bread and Pomegranate Syrup, and Tibsi Red Snapper. The amount you add to a dish will vary according to its thickness; the denser the syrup, the less you need. My favorite brand is Cortas; the label reads "concentrated pomegranate juice." It can be found at Middle Eastern shops and is available by mail order (see Sources).

AN EASY WAY TO PEEL POMEGRANATES

It may take more time than peeling an orange, but with a bit of practice, peeling a pomegranate will become just as easy. To do it the way my mother taught me, first cut off the end of the pomegranate opposite the stem end with a sharp knife, being careful not to puncture any of the seeds. Next, score the skin vertically in wedges, beginning at the cut end and dragging the knife to the stem end. Insert the tip of the knife into the center of the pomegranate through the cut end. Wiggle the knife to loosen the pulp in the center, and pull it out. Break apart the scored sections with your thumbs; each one will reveal a multitude of ruby red seeds. Separate the pulp from the membranes that surround them, using your fingers, and place it in a bowl. Eat the pulp by the spoonful, sprinkle it on salads, or use it as a sparkling garnish on Roasted Eggplant Spread or Eggplant Salad.

Pomegranates also make delicious and healthful juice. (It is higher in vitamin C than orange juice, and offers substantial amounts of potassium and fiber.) To make 1 cup, peel 3 pomegranates and pass the pulp and seeds through a food mill. While freshly pressed juice is always preferable to bottled, several brands are widely available in supermarkets. I prefer the Cortas brand.

Pomegranate pulp will keep, tightly covered, in the refrigerator for up to 3 weeks. To freeze it, spread the pulp in a single layer on a baking sheet and freeze until firm; then pack into resealable plastic bags or rigid containers. It will keep for up to 4 months.

Stuffed Grape Leaves

WARAK ENAB BI ZEIT

One 16-ounce jar grape leaves
(look for Orlando or
Al-Afaia brand), drained
and rinsed

1½ cups short-grain rice, rinsed
(see page 165), soaked, and
drained

1 pound onions, finely chopped

1½ pounds tomatoes, seeded,
chopped, and drained

5 cups chopped fresh flat-leaf
parsley

½ cup chopped fresh mint, or
3 tablespoons dried

2 cups fresh lemon juice, plus
more to taste

1 cup extra virgin olive oil

1 jalapeño pepper, seeded and
minced

1¼ tablespoons salt, plus more
to taste

1 tablespoon black pepper

To line the pan:
1 pound tomatoes, cut into
½-inch-thick rounds

½ pound onions, cut into
½-inch-thick rounds

½ pound potatoes, cut into
½-inch-thick rounds

For serving:
Lemon wedges

A specialty of the Eastern Mediterranean, grape leaves are perhaps the best known and most popular wrap for savory fillings in the Arab world.

When I first encountered stuffed grape leaves in the States—in big-city delis and at some Middle Eastern restaurants—I was shocked at how chubby they were. Authentic stuffed grape leaves are slender: about the width of a woman's pinky finger and no more than 1½ inches long. Though making them can be time-consuming, the yield is quite large, and they can be frozen.

Cook stuffed grape leaves the day before you plan to serve them, so the flavors can develop. **Makes 10 dozen stuffed grape leaves**

Separate a few grape leaves, spread them out flat, and hang them over the edge of a colander to drain well. As you fill the leaves, arrange the remaining leaves around the rim of the colander.

Combine the rice with the onions, chopped tomatoes, parsley, mint, 1 cup of the lemon juice, the olive oil, jalapeño, salt, and pepper in a medium bowl. Mix the ingredients together and taste (avoiding biting into the uncooked rice); add more salt and lemon juice if necessary.

Working with 1 leaf at a time, snip the stem off with kitchen shears or a sharp knife. Spread the leaf out on a plate or clean work surface, shiny side down and stem end facing you. If the leaf has deep indentations between the segments, close the gap by bringing the two segments together, overlapping them slightly, or by patching the gap with a torn piece of another leaf. If any of the leaves are more than 4 inches across, cut them in half. Reserve any torn or broken leaves for lining the cooking pot. Trim and stack all the whole leaves.

Prepare the cooking pot before you begin rolling the leaves, so you can place them directly into it as you make them: Scatter the reserved pieces of grape leaves over the bottom of a wide 4-quart pot or Dutch oven. Top with a layer of the sliced tomatoes, followed by the onions and ending with the potatoes. Place the pot nearby.

Now stuff the leaves: Place 1 heaping teaspoon of the rice mixture in the center of a leaf, close to where the stem begins. If the filling is wet, squeeze the excess liquid back into the bowl; you will use it as the cooking liquid. Bring the bottom of the leaf up over the filling, then fold the sides of the leaf onto the filling (in the same way a butcher wraps meat). Roll the leaf away from you, wrapping it tightly around the filling as you go. Repeat with the remaining leaves and rice mixture. As you fill them, place the stuffed grape leaves, scam side down, in the cooking pot, arranging them in concentric rings, beginning with the outside ring and working your way to the middle. The rolls should fit snugly side by side. When the bottom of the pot is covered, layer the remaining rolls on top until they are all in place.

Pour just enough of the liquid from the rice mixture into the pot to reach the bottom of the top layer of rolls. If there is not enough liquid, add salted water—½ teaspoon salt per 1 cup water—to reach that level.

Invert a heatproof plate over the rolls; the plate should be large enough to reach within ¼ inch of the edge of the pot. Place a weight, such as a large can of tomatoes or foil-wrapped brick, on top of the plate. Cover the pot. (If you use a can that sits higher than the rim of the pot, use foil to cover the pot.) Bring the liquid to a boil over high heat, and cook for 30 minutes. Then reduce the heat to medium and add the remaining 1 cup lemon juice. Cover the pot and cook for 1½ hours more. After the rolls have been cooking for 1½ hours, taste, and add salt and lemon juice if needed.

Reduce the heat to low, remove the weight from the plate, and re-cover the pot. Place a heat diffuser under the pot. Cook until the grape leaves and the filling are tender, about 1 hour.

The liquid should be reduced to a glaze consistency. Remove the pan from the heat and set aside to cool completely. Refrigerate the stuffed grape leaves, still in the cooking pot, for at least 4 hours or, preferably, overnight. (The rolls will hold together better if refrigerated overnight.)

While holding the rolls in place with the plate, tilt the pot to pour the cooking liquid into a bowl. Remove the plate, and invert a tray or platter over the pot. Flip the pot and tray together but do not remove the pot. Leave it there for at least 15 minutes or up to 1 hour. This gives the rolls time to settle into a cake shape.

Gently lift off the cooking pot. Remove the layers of torn leaves, potatoes, onions, and tomatoes. Return any stray rolls to their places. Use a paper towel to soak up any excess liquid around the platter. Garnish with lemon wedges, and serve.

Variation: Add 2 tablespoons pomegranate syrup to the cooking liquid, the way the Syrians do.

FREEZING STUFFED GRAPE LEAVES

Fill a rigid container with uncooked stuffed grape leaves, and seal it with a tight-fitting lid; they will keep for up to 1 month. Freeze the liquid from the rice mixture in another container. The day before you plan to cook them, defrost the grape leaves overnight in the refrigerator, just to the point where they are still slightly frozen; then arrange them in the cooking pot as described (it is easier to do this when they are still slightly firm).

Steak Tartare, Lebanese Style

KIBEH NAYEH

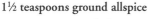

1½ teaspoons ground allspice

2 teaspoons ground cinnamon

1 tablespoon salt, plus more to taste

½ teaspoon finely ground high-quality black pepper, such as Tellicherry

½ teaspoon finely ground white pepper

1 cup fine bulgur, picked over

1 yellow onion, quartered

1½ pounds lean beef filet, cut into 1-inch cubes

2 tablespoons extra virgin olive oil

Mint leaves, for garnish and serving

Chile oil or hot sauce

Arab flatbread, for serving

2 white onions, cut into wedges

*T*his recipe is a variation on the beloved national dish of Lebanon and Syria, where eating Kibeh Nayeh is a revered ritual. Authentic Kibeh Nayeh is made with ground lamb, bulgur, onions, and seasonings, all pounded to a paste in a *jurn*, or large mortar. In the Arab world, most home cooks and chefs still make it this way, but more and more city dwellers are using food processors to work the meat. Not only do I use a processor, but I prefer tender beef filet for my Kibeh Nayeh. Whether you use beef or lamb, it must be of tartare grade and purchased very fresh—never frozen—from a reputable butcher. The lamb should come from young early summer stock. Ask your butcher to trim all the fat and gristle away for you. Fresh goat meat, almost impossible to find in this country, is commonly used in the mountain villages of Lebanon, including Douma, where my Auntie Nina is famous for her buttery hand-pounded Kibeh Nayeh.*

The traditional way to eat Kibeh Nayeh is to spoon some of it onto your plate and flatten it with the back of your fork. Drizzle olive oil over it, followed by chile oil or hot sauce. Tear a piece of soft Arab bread from a loaf and roll it into a cone shape. Use the cone to scoop up the Kibeh Nayeh, take a bite, and follow it with a wedge of white onion or bite of scallion and a mint leaf. In Lebanon, we always serve Kibeh Nayeh with a glass of arak, *but here we pour a full-bodied white wine.*　　*Serves 6*

Combine the allspice, cinnamon, salt, and black and white pepper in a small bowl. Stir well and set aside.

Wash the bulgur in a bowl of cold water, wading through it with your fingers. Repeat three times, using fresh water each time. Then use your hands to lift the bulgur out of the water, squeeze to release the liquid, and transfer it to a bowl.

Fill a large bowl with ice water and set it on a damp kitchen towel.

Place the quartered yellow onion in a food processor and pulse to form a paste. Add the bulgur and ½ teaspoon of the spice mixture, and process until the mixture returns to a paste. Transfer the paste to a medium bowl and set it in the ice-water bath.

Place the meat in the food processor and pulse several times, scraping down the sides of the bowl, until it forms a very smooth paste, about 1 minute. The meat should maintain its pinkish tone; don't overprocess, or the heat of the machine will "cook" the meat and turn it pale gray. Work in batches if your processor is too small.

Add the meat paste to the bulgur mixture and knead them together in the bowl. Add the remaining spice mixture, 1 tablespoon at a time, dipping your hands into the ice water as you work, and knead until the mixture is silky smooth, 7 to 10 minutes. Add more ice to the bath if necessary to keep it cold. Add more salt to taste.

To serve the kibeh, spread it on a serving plate and smooth it with the back of a spoon. Create a decorative pattern by making impressions in the kibeh with the back of the spoon. Drizzle the olive oil over the kibeh, letting it pool in the indentations. Garnish with a few mint leaves. Serve with the chile oil, Arab flatbread, white onion wedges, and more mint leaves alongside.

THE MUSIC IN THE MORTAR

Most Arab Americans don't bother with the traditional method for making Kibeh Nayeh, opting instead for grinding the meat from a well-trimmed leg of a lamb in a food processor and then combining it with the chopped onion and spices. But the ritual of preparing kibeh the traditional way is one of my most treasured memories of growing up in Lebanon. Every Sunday morning, my sisters and I awoke to the sound of the pounding of the kibeh. I can still see Samira, our kitchen helper, sitting on a small stool in front of the huge mortar—it was about a foot and a half high and a foot wide—transfixed by the movement of her own hands as she pounded, as if she were directing the world's greatest symphony. The *jurn,* or stone mortar, sat on the floor, a towel slipped underneath to absorb the sound of the pounding and to protect the floor. Samira wrapped her legs around it and used her big hands to grip the heavy wooden *madak,* or pestle, in order to comfortably pound the meat for up to 2 hours. The Lebanese believe that it takes special talent to pound kibeh, and Samira surely had it. Her hands had the special rhythm that made the pestle hitting the mortar sound like music.

A FAMILY RECIPE FOR SEVEN-SPICE MIX

From city to city, village to village, and house to house, the amount and combination of spices that are mixed into Kibeh Nayeh vary. In Beirut, for example, you will often find it seasoned with dried basil or a prepackaged seven-spice mix called *baharat*. My recipe was passed down by my grandmother, who always had a fragrant jar of these ground spices in her kitchen. If you want to try her recipe in your kibeh, omit the spices called for in the recipe on page 226. My Auntie Nina omits the cloves, nutmeg, and coriander, while our good friend Rafat Mattar, whose family lives in southern Lebanon, adds *kamounih,* a mixture of spices and dried rose petals.

Grandmother Nazleh's Seven-Spice Mix

Grandmother would use no cinnamon other than Ceylon cinnamon in this spice mix because, like most Arabs, she believed it to be superior to all others. In fact, unlike the cinnamon available in tins in the supermarket, buff-colored Ceylon cinnamon is the true spice, with a sweeter, less astringent flavor than its cheaper, teak-colored imposters. You can find it at gourmet food shops and specialty stores.   *Makes a scant ½ cup*

- 2 tablespoons ground allspice
- 2 tablespoons black pepper
- 1 tablespoon white pepper
- 1½ teaspoons ground Ceylon cinnamon
- 1½ teaspoons ground cloves
- 1½ teaspoons grated nutmeg
- 1½ teaspoons ground coriander

Mix the spices together and store in an airtight container in a cool, dry place. This will keep for up to 1 year.

Warm Mezza

Fried Halloumi Cheese

HALLOUMI MAKLI

Extra virgin olive oil

½ pound halloumi cheese, cut
    into 1-inch-thick slices

Arab flatbread

1 pound tomatoes, thinly sliced

*A*lways popular at my dinner table, this delicious pan-fried cheese should be made at the last minute and served straight from the hot pan.

Although my version calls for Cypriot halloumi cheese, it is traditionally made with nablusy, a salty, brine-cured sheep cheese made only in Nablus, Palestine. When I no longer had access to nablusy, I substituted halloumi, which is very similar in flavor and texture but far less salty. I prefer the Greek Pittas brand of halloumi, which I buy in large quantities and freeze for several months; it takes only a few hours to defrost at room temperature. (If I'm short on time, I put the frozen halloumi in the microwave oven for 1½ minutes, rotate it, and heat it for another 1½ minutes.)

Pleasantly salty, with a bite similar to aged mozzarella, Halloumi Makli is best served simply—with just a few slices of ripe tomato. A well-loved snack in my family, it is also popular for dinner, the lightest meal in an Arab's day.

Serves 6

Pour enough olive oil into a large skillet to coat the bottom, and heat it over high heat. Add the cheese slices, working in batches if necessary, and sauté until they are golden on one side, 1 minute. Flip them over and sauté until golden on the other side, another minute.

Serve immediately, with the Arab flatbread and sliced tomatoes.

Grilled Halloumi Cheese Triangles

HALLOUMI KULAGE

Four 8-inch loaves Arab
flatbread, each cut into
6 wedges

½ cup extra virgin olive oil

2 pounds halloumi cheese, cut
into ½-inch-thick slices

3 pounds tomatoes, cut into
½-inch-thick slices

¼ cup Zaatar (page 38)

Fresh mint leaves, for garnish

*These little cheese sandwiches, seasoned with Zaatar, make perfect
cocktail party food; they are easy to hold in one hand and are small
enough to be eaten in two bites. Halloumi Kulage taste particularly delicious with arak, beer, or a glass of chilled white wine.*

*Although I usually use a sandwich press to make these, placing the tri-
angles under the broiler, or using a skillet in the same way that you
would to make a grilled cheese sandwich, works well too.*

Makes 24 triangles

Preheat the broiler.

Open each bread triangle without separating the layers. Brush some
olive oil inside the bread, and tuck a piece of cheese and a slice of
tomato into the pocket. Sprinkle some Zaatar over the tomatoes.
Arrange the triangles on a baking sheet, and broil until the bread is
lightly browned and crisped and the cheese is beginning to melt,
about 4 minutes. (Alternatively, press the triangles in a sandwich
press.)

Arrange the triangles on a plate and garnish it with the mint leaves,
inviting your guests to tuck them into their sandwiches. Serve
warm.

DESALTING HALLOUMI

**Middle Eastern groceries carry several varieties of halloumi, each with subtle flavor
differences. Taste the different brands and decide which one you like. If you find that
halloumi is too salty for your taste, slice it and place it in a bowl with cold water to cover.
Change the water about every 5 minutes, for a total of 15 minutes.**

Fried Eggplant with Hot Chiles

BETINJAN MAKLI

2 small eggplants (about
   3 pounds total)

2 teaspoons salt

1 clove garlic, mashed

1 tablespoon fresh lemon juice

1 tablespoon white vinegar

1 cup vegetable oil

4 to 6 jalapeño peppers

Ground sumac, for garnish

2 loaves Arab flatbread,
   quartered

You can eat these golden rounds without any adornment other than a simple garlic lemon sauce, as we do here, or you can prepare them the way our Egyptian nanny used to, by wrapping a piece of Arab pocket bread around a slice of fried eggplant and a whole fried jalapeño. To my mind, this is the best way to eat eggplant. Occasionally I sprinkle a little sumac over the eggplant before serving it, the way the Lebanese do. Use young vegetables for this dish—they're sweeter and more tender than the mature ones. For an informal mezza menu, serve these with Arab Salsa, Cucumber and Yogurt, and Spinach Triangles.   **Serves 4 to 6**

Peel the eggplants with a vegetable peeler, leaving a few thin strips of skin on (this will hold the eggplant together when it is fried). Cut the flesh into ½-inch-thick rounds and place them in a colander set over a bowl. Sprinkle the salt over the eggplant slices and set aside until the juices have drained, at least 1 hour.

Meanwhile, mix together the garlic, lemon juice, and vinegar, and set aside.

Pat the eggplant slices dry with paper towels. Heat the vegetable oil in a large skillet over high heat. Carefully slide the eggplant slices, one at a time, into the hot oil, using a slotted spoon or your hands. Fry until the edges darken, the center is golden brown, and the flesh is fork-tender, about 4 minutes per side. Using a slotted spoon, transfer the slices to a paper towel–lined plate to drain.

While the eggplant is draining, make one or two slits in each jalapeño with a sharp knife, and slide them into the hot oil. When the peppers blister and turn white all over, use a slotted spoon to transfer them to paper towels.

Arrange the eggplant slices on a platter, spoon the lemon dressing over them, and arrange the fried jalapeños on top. Sprinkle with some sumac, if desired. Serve the Arab flatbread on the side.

Fried Cauliflower

ARNABEET MAKLI

About 2 cups canola oil (enough to cover the cauliflower)

1 head cauliflower, washed and cut into bite-size florets

1 cup chopped fresh flat-leaf parsley, for serving

1 cup Tahini (page 32)

*C*auliflower is considered a poor man's vegetable in the Arab world, where it grows in great abundance. But it is anything but lowly when fried and dressed with tart Tahini. This is the perfect dish for a casual gathering (I never serve it for formal dinner parties) as a passed appetizer. Do not let the cauliflower sit in the oil too long, or it will lose its shape and crunch. *Serves 4 to 6*

Heat the canola oil in a heavy-bottomed pot over high heat. When the oil is hot enough—it will spit when you add a piece of cauliflower—slide the cauliflower florets into the pot. Fry, turning them occasionally, until they are golden brown all over, 5 to 8 minutes. (You may have to do this in batches.) Using a slotted spoon, transfer the cauliflower to a paper towel–lined plate to drain.

To serve, arrange a bed of chopped parsley on a platter and place the cauliflower on top. Set a bowl of the Tahini on the platter for dipping.

Fried Kafta Triangles

KAFTA ARAYES

5 loaves (one 16-ounce package)
white Arab flatbread,
quartered

3 tablespoons unsalted butter,
at room temperature, plus
more for spreading

½ recipe Kafta (page 234)

Vegetable oil, for frying

Lemon slices, for garnish

Sliced pickled cucumbers
(store-bought), for garnish

Fresh mint leaves, for garnish

Undeniably indulgent, these little filled and fried sandwiches are among the heartiest mezzas, making them a good choice if you are serving only a selection of small dishes rather than a traditional menu of appetizer, main course, and salad. My mother used to fry arayes *in lard, which gives the bread an incomparable crispness, but since moving to the U.S., I prepare them with vegetable oil with delicious results. Baking the triangles is a nice no-fuss and lower-fat alternative. Fried Kafta should always be served immediately.* **Makes 20 pieces**

Open each wedge of bread without separating the layers, and spread some butter on one side. Place about 1 tablespoon of the Kafta on the buttered side, and spread it all over with your fingers. Close the triangle and flatten it between the palms of your hands. Repeat, filling all the triangles.

To fry: Pour enough vegetable oil into a heavy skillet to cover the bottom, and place it over high heat. Working in batches, carefully slide the filled bread triangles into the skillet. Reduce the heat to medium and cook, pressing down a few times on the bread with the back of a spatula, until one side is golden brown, about 3 minutes. Flip the bread over and cook the other side the same way. Serve immediately.

To bake: Preheat the oven to 400°F.

Generously grease a baking sheet with vegetable oil, and place the triangles on it. Bake for 15 minutes. Then flip the bread over with a spatula and bake for 10 minutes more.

To serve, place the fried triangles on a platter, and surround them with the lemon slices, cucumbers, and mint leaves.

Sautéed Lamb's Liver

KIBDEH MAKLI

1 pound fresh lamb's liver

¼ cup olive oil

1 pound onions, finely chopped

4 cloves garlic, mashed

½ teaspoon salt

½ teaspoon black pepper

1 tablespoon pomegranate
   syrup

1 tablespoon fresh lemon juice

Lemon slices, for garnish

Sliced seeded jalapeño peppers,
   for garnish

Fresh flat-leaf parsley leaves, for
   garnish

Arab flatbread

I learned how to make this simple mezza the best way—at my father's side. At our house, Kibdeh Makli was his specialty. No matter where we lived, whether it was Kuwait, Lebanon, Jordan, or London, he made sure to know which butchers carried the best lamb. Whenever my father arrived home from a shopping trip with his prized package of livers, he headed straight for the kitchen. If I was home, I chopped the onions and garlic while my mother put away the rest of the groceries.

I always serve Kibdeh Makli cooked rare, but in Lebanon—where it is known as kasba suda, *which means "black log,"—it is eaten raw, accompanied by a glass of arak.*   *Serves 4*

Trim the gristle from the liver and discard it. Slice the liver into 1-inch-wide strips. Set it aside.

Heat the olive oil in a medium skillet over medium-high heat. Add the onions and garlic, and sauté until the onions are soft, 5 to 7 minutes. Add the liver, and season with the salt and pepper. Sauté, turning frequently, until the liver loses its color, 2 to 3 minutes.

Remove the skillet from the heat, add the pomegranate concentrate juice and lemon juice, and stir. Transfer the liver and the juices to a rimmed platter, and garnish with the lemon slices, jalapeños, and parsley. Serve immediately, with the Arab flatbread.

Sautéed Chicken Gizzards

QUANIS DAJAJ

½ pound chicken gizzards

1 cup white vinegar

4 tablespoons fresh lemon juice

4 tablespoons (½ stick) unsalted butter

1 pound onions, finely chopped

2 cloves garlic, mashed

½ teaspoon salt

½ teaspoon black pepper

1 tablespoon pomegranate syrup

Fresh parsley leaves, for garnish

Quanis Dajaj is very common throughout the Arab world. It can be made ahead, then covered and refrigerated overnight. Just before serving, reheat the gizzards in a very hot pan and finish with the lemon juice, pomegranate and parsley.   *Serves 6*

Place the gizzards in a bowl, and add the vinegar and 2 tablespoons of the lemon juice. Set it aside for 20 minutes.

Drain the gizzards, rinse them under cold water, and pat them dry with paper towels.

Heat the butter in a medium skillet over high heat. Add the gizzards and sauté, turning frequently, until golden, about 15 minutes. Then add the onions, garlic, salt, and pepper and sauté until the onions are very soft and tender, 10 minutes. Add the remaining 2 tablespoons lemon juice and the pomegranate syrup, and cook over high heat to deglaze the skillet, about 3 minutes.

Serve hot, garnished with parsley.

Meat Pies

SAFIHA

These open-face tartlets are often served with other savory pastries, including Spinach Triangles and Oregano Cakes, and a green salad. The filling can be made the day before you bake them; just cover it tightly and put it in the refrigerator. To get the right texture, be sure to use powdered whole milk in the dough. I prefer the Nido brand. One last hint: Don't be tempted to open the oven door as these bake; the oven temperature must remain constant in order for them to brown evenly.

Safiha can be frozen in a tightly covered rigid container for up to 3 months. If you plan to freeze them, bake the meat pies for only 20 minutes, or until they are puffed and firm to the touch; then cool and freeze. Thaw them at room temperature, and bake in a preheated 400°F oven, with the rack in the upper third of the oven, for 10 to 15 minutes.

Makes 50 pies

For the dough:

2 teaspoons (1 packet) active dry yeast

1 cup warm water (110°F)

½ teaspoon sugar

5 cups all-purpose flour, sifted

2 tablespoons powdered whole milk or powdered buttermilk

1 teaspoon baking powder

2 teaspoons salt

2 large eggs

1 cup canola oil

2 tablespoons plain yogurt

Olive oil

For the filling:

2 tablespoons canola oil

½ pound onions, finely chopped

1 pound lean ground lamb or beef

1 teaspoon ground allspice

½ teaspoon ground cardamom seeds (see page 15)

½ teaspoon ground coriander

½ teaspoon crushed black pepper

1½ teaspoons salt

3 large cloves garlic, mashed

¼ cup fresh lemon juice

¼ cup sesame paste (tahini)

2 tablespoons plus 1 teaspoon white vinegar

¼ cup plain yogurt

2 drops Tabasco or other hot pepper sauce, or to taste (optional)

½ cup pine nuts

Prepare the dough: Combine the yeast, warm water, and sugar in a small bowl and stir to dissolve. Set the bowl aside until the mixture is foamy and has doubled in size, about 10 minutes.

Using an electric mixer: Sift the flour, powdered milk, baking powder, and salt together into the bowl of a standing mixer fitted with the dough hook. Stir in the eggs and canola oil. Add the yeast mixture, yogurt, and ½ cup water. Give the mixture a good stir with a wooden spoon. Then mix the dough on medium speed until it pulls away from the sides of the bowl, 3 minutes. (If the dough doesn't come away from the sides, add 1 tablespoon flour.) Raise the speed to high and mix until the dough is smooth and elastic, about 2 minutes.

By hand: Sift the flour, salt, and baking powder together, and dump it in a mound on your work surface. Make a well in the top of the mound, using two fingers. Mix the canola oil and ½ cup water into the yeast mixture. Pour a small amount of this mixture into the well, then use a fork to gather up some flour from the perimeter of the mound and add it to the well. Stir the flour into the liquid until it is absorbed. Continue adding liquid and mixing the flour into it until all of the liquid is absorbed. Then knead the dough by pressing down on it with the heel of your hand, then stretching the dough forward, pushing it away from your body. Fold it in half and press down on it to seal the fold. Rotate it a quarter-turn, then knead again. Continue kneading, folding, sealing, and rotating the dough until it is smooth and elastic, about 7 minutes.

Shape the dough into a ball. Coat your hands and a large glass or ceramic bowl with olive oil, and place the dough in it. Turn the dough so that it is coated all over with oil. Cover loosely with plastic wrap and set aside in a warm, draft-free place until the dough has doubled in size, about 1 hour. (During the colder months, it may take longer to rise.)

Prepare the filling: Heat the canola oil in a large saucepan or a Dutch oven over medium heat. Add the onions and sauté until soft, about 3 minutes. Add the meat and cook, breaking it up with a wooden spoon, until it loses any pink color, about 5 minutes.

Stir in the allspice, cardamom, coriander, black pepper, and 1 teaspoon of the salt. Reduce the heat to low and cook, breaking up the meat with the back of the spoon until it resembles coarse crumbs, the mixture is a rich dark brown, and the onions and spices are well incorporated, about 30 minutes. Set it aside to cool completely. Then add the garlic, lemon juice, sesame paste, vinegar, yogurt, remaining ½ teaspoon salt, and Tabasco. Stir to mix well. Taste, and adjust the seasonings as desired. The meat mixture should taste strongly of vinegar, lemon juice, tahini, and pepper; these assertive flavors will mellow as the pies bake. (Reserve the pine nuts.)

Preheat the oven to 400°F, with one rack in the lower third of the oven and the other in the upper third. Grease two baking sheets generously with olive oil.

Punch down the dough. Pinch off a piece about the size of a baseball, and squeeze it between your thumb and index finger until a ball about the size of a walnut comes through. Separate the ball from the dough in your palm by pinching your thumb and index finger together tightly. Set the ball on a prepared sheet pan and repeat, placing the pieces of dough 1 inch apart, until all of the dough is used. Let the balls rest for 10 minutes.

Press 1 teaspoon of the filling into each ball, allowing a rim of dough to form around the meat. Place 3 pine nuts on top of the meat filling in each pie.

When you finish filling one sheet of meat pies, place it on the lower rack in the oven and bake until they are puffy and golden brown, about 15 minutes. At this point, the second sheet should be ready to go into the oven. Transfer the first batch to the top rack and slide the second sheet onto the lower rack. Bake until the meat pies on the top rack are golden brown, 10 to 15 minutes. Remove them from the oven and transfer the second batch to the top rack. Bake until they are golden brown, about 15 minutes. (Each batch should bake for a total of 30 minutes.)

Immediately transfer the meat pies from the baking sheets to a platter. Serve hot or at room temperature.

Lebanese Meat Pies

In Lebanon, tomatoes and pomegranate syrup are mixed into the seasoned beef filling, which is spooned raw into the dough and baked.

½ pound onions, finely chopped

2 tablespoons ground coriander

1 teaspoon ground allspice

½ teaspoon black pepper

1 teaspoon salt

¼ cup (½ stick) unsalted butter, at room temperature

1 pound lean ground lamb or beef

1 pound tomatoes, peeled and finely chopped

1 teaspoon cayenne pepper, or to taste

½ cup pine nuts

1 tablespoon pomegranate syrup

Combine the onions, coriander, allspice, black pepper, and salt in a large bowl and mix together with your hands until the onions have absorbed the spices. Add the butter, lamb, tomatoes, cayenne, pine nuts, and pomegranate syrup, and mix well. Scoop 1 tablespoon into each tartlet and bake as above.

Oregano and Cheese Crescents

ZAATAR WA JIBNEH

For the dough:
1 tablespoon active dry yeast
½ teaspoon sugar
1½ cups warm water (110°F)
5 cups all-purpose flour
⅓ cup powdered whole milk
1 teaspoon salt
1 egg
⅓ cup vegetable oil

Olive oil

For the filling:
½ pound fresh oregano leaves
   (about 5 cups), picked over,
   washed, and patted dry
1 pound halloumi cheese, rinsed
   (see page 75), shredded on
   the large holes of a box
   grater
½ pound mozzarella cheese,
   shredded on the large holes
   of a box grater
⅓ cup extra virgin olive oil
1 teaspoon salt

1 egg white
2 tablespoons whole milk

These half-moon-shaped pastries have always been a favorite of my middle son, Basil. When he was younger, he asked for them in his lunchbox, and he loved them as an after-school snack too. Though I often serve them as an appetizer with cocktails, I still take great delight in making them for Basil, even though he lives thirty minutes away. Nothing makes me happier than to deliver a warm plate of these cheese pastries to his doorstep, and to watch him take the first bite.

If you plan to freeze the pastries for later use, bake them for only 15 minutes. Let them cool, and then arrange them in layers, separated by wax paper, in a rigid container. When you are ready to serve them, defrost them on the countertop for 3 hours and then bake as directed.

Makes about 50 pastries

Prepare the dough: Combine the yeast, sugar, and warm water in a small bowl and stir to dissolve. Set it aside until the mixture is foamy and has doubled in size, about 10 minutes.

Using an electric mixer: Sift the flour, powdered milk, and salt together into the bowl of a standing mixer fitted with the dough hook. Stir in the egg, vegetable oil, and ¾ cup water. Add the yeast mixture and give the mixture a good stir with a wooden spoon. Then mix the dough on medium speed until it pulls away from the sides of the bowl, 3 minutes. (If the dough doesn't come away from the sides add 1 tablespoon flour.) Raise the speed to high and mix until the dough is smooth and elastic, about 2 minutes.

By hand: Sift the flour, powdered milk, and salt together, and dump it in a mound on your work surface. Make a well in the top of the mound, using two fingers. Mix the vegetable oil and ¾ cup water into the yeast mixture. Pour a small amount of this mixture into the well. Using a fork, gather up some flour from the perimeter of the mound and add it to the well; stir it into the liquid until it is absorbed. Continue adding liquid and mixing the flour into it until all of the liquid is absorbed. Then knead the dough by pressing down on it with the heel of your hand, then stretching the dough forward, pushing it away from your body. Fold the dough in half

WILD ZAATAR

Zaatar is the name given to both wild thyme and the spice mixture that contains thyme, sumac, and sesame seeds (see page 38). It is not to be confused with another wild plant, *zaatar akhdar* or green zaatar, which is actually oregano, the fresh leaves of which are used in pastries and salads. In Palestine, Syria, Jordan, and other countries in the Eastern Mediterranean, the appearance of *zaatar akhdar*'s light pink flowers poking up on the mountainsides is the surest sign that spring has arrived.

Today both wild thyme and oregano are cultivated in Palestine, Lebanon, Jordan, and Syria. You can find zaatar spice mixture and *zaatar akhdar* at Middle Eastern shops or order them by mail (see Sources).

and press down on it again with the palm of your hand to seal the fold. Rotate the dough a quarter-turn and knead again. Repeat kneading, folding, sealing, and rotating until the dough is smooth and elastic, about 7 minutes.

Coat a deep bowl with olive oil. Shape the dough into a ball and place in the bowl. Turn the dough to coat it all over with the oil. Cover the bowl with plastic wrap and a kitchen towel, and set it aside in a warm, draft-free place until it has doubled in size, 2 to 3 hours.

Meanwhile, make the filling: Mix the oregano leaves, halloumi, mozzarella, olive oil, and salt together in a bowl, and set it aside.

Shape and bake the pastries: Preheat the oven to 370°F, with two racks in the center. Brush a baking sheet with olive oil.

Whisk the egg white and milk together in a small bowl, and set it aside.

Remove half the dough from the bowl and place it on a work surface that has been generously dusted with flour. Roll it out to form a ¼-inch-thick round. Using a 2½-inch cookie cutter, cut out rounds of dough. Holding a round of dough in the palm of your hand, place 2 teaspoons of the filling in the middle. Then fold the round in half over the filling to make a half-moon shape. Pinch the edges together, sealing them tightly so the filling doesn't spill out during baking. Place the pastries on the prepared baking sheet, spacing them about ½ inch apart. Repeat with the remaining dough and filling.

Brush the crescents with the egg wash. Bake in the lower rack in the oven until the bottoms are light golden, about 15 minutes. Then transfer the baking sheet to the upper rack and bake for 5 minutes more. Serve the pastries right out of the oven or at room temperature.

Oregano Cakes

AKRASS ZAATAR

For the dough:

1 teaspoon active dry yeast

⅛ teaspoon sugar

1¼ cups warm water (110°F)

2 cups all-purpose flour

1 cup coarse semolina

½ teaspoon baking powder

1 teaspoon salt

½ cup olive oil, plus extra for
  your hands, the bowl, and
  the work surface

For the filling:

½ pound fresh oregano leaves
  (about 5 cups), washed and
  patted dry

1 teaspoon salt

*F*luffier and softer than crackers, yet not as light and airy as yeast bread, these little semolina cakes are a delicious snack with feta cheese, a simple salad of chopped tomatoes and olives, or a cup of hot tea. This recipe is a contemporary, lighter version of the traditional cakes made in early spring in rural areas all over the Arab world, when oregano first appears in the fields. Though not as heavy, the flavor and aroma are the same; your kitchen will be fragrant with yeast and oregano.

Baked Zaatar Akrass can be stored in a tightly sealed container in the refrigerator for up to 1 week, or frozen for up to 3 months. Alternatively, you can partially bake the cakes and finish the baking when you want to serve them: Simply take them out of the oven after 15 minutes, let them cool, and then refrigerate or freeze. Defrost them on the countertop for 2 hours; then reheat them in a 350°F oven until warmed through, about 10 minutes. **Makes about 23 cakes**

Prepare the dough: Combine the yeast, sugar, and ½ cup of the warm water in a small bowl and stir to dissolve. Set it aside until the mixture is foamy and has doubled in size, about 10 minutes.

Using an electric mixer: Sift the flour, semolina, baking powder, and salt together into the bowl of a standing mixer fitted with the dough hook. Stir in the yeast mixture, olive oil, and remaining ¾ cup warm water. Mix the dough on medium speed until it pulls away from the sides of the bowl, 3 minutes. (If the dough doesn't come away from the sides, add 1 tablespoon flour.) Raise the speed to high and mix until the dough is smooth and elastic, about 2 minutes.

By hand: Sift the flour, semolina, baking powder, and salt together and dump it into a mound on a work surface. Make a well in the top of the mound, using two fingers. Mix the yeast mixture with the oil and remaining ¾ cup warm water. Pour a small amount of this mixture into the well. Using a fork, gather up some flour from the perimeter of the mound and add it to the well. Stir it into the liquid until it is absorbed. Continue adding liquid and mixing the flour into it until all of the liquid is absorbed. Then knead the dough by pressing down on it with the heel of your hand, then stretching the dough forward, pushing it away from your body. Fold it in half and press down on it with the palm of your hand to seal the fold. Rotate the dough a quarter-turn, and knead it again. Repeat the kneading, folding, sealing, and rotating until the dough is very smooth and shiny, about 5 minutes.

Adding the filling: Toss the oregano with the salt, and pour it over the dough. Coat your hands with olive oil and knead the dough until the oregano is just mixed in. Coat a glass or ceramic bowl with olive oil, place the dough in the bowl, and turn it to coat it well with the oil. Cover the bowl with plastic wrap and set it aside in a warm place until the dough has doubled in size, about 1 hour.

Form and bake the cakes: Preheat the oven to 400°F, with one rack on the second position from the bottom and the other on the top position. Lightly oil two baking sheets.

Punch down the dough, and knead it until it is soft and smooth. Cut the dough into 5 equal pieces and place them on a lightly oiled surface. Roll out each piece of dough until it is ¼ to ½ inch thick. Cut out rounds using a 3-inch cookie cutter, and place them on the prepared baking sheets. Tuck in any oregano leaves that poke out from the dough. Place the baking sheets on the oven racks and bake for 10 minutes. Then reverse their positions and bake until golden brown, another 10 minutes. Serve warm.

Spinach Triangles

FATAYER BI SABANEKH

Arabs always use fresh spinach for these savory filled pastries, but I've used frozen spinach with fine results. Whichever you use, make sure the spinach is not too wet, or the filling will saturate the dough and steam open the triangles. Be sure to taste the filling before you begin shaping the triangles—it should be assertively lemony from the sumac, if not downright sour. As the triangles bake, the flavor will mellow. The North African version of this filling includes currants or raisins and often features a variety of greens, including purslane, dandelion greens, and wild chicory.

I often make a double batch of these and put some in the freezer, where they will keep for up to 3 months. If you are planning to freeze Fatayer bi Sabanekh, bake them for 20 minutes, then let them cool on a wire rack. Pack them in an airtight container with wax paper separating the layers. To serve, thaw them at room temperature for 2 to 3 hours, then bake them in a preheated 400°F oven for about 10 minutes, or until heated through. **Makes 15 triangles**

For the dough:

3 cups all-purpose flour

⅓ cup extra virgin olive oil, plus extra for the bowl, the baking sheet, and brushing the pastry

¼ teaspoon salt

For the filling:

2 pounds fresh baby spinach, stemmed, washed, and patted dry, or 20 ounces frozen chopped spinach, thawed, drained, and squeezed dry

2 teaspoons salt

1½ pounds onions, minced

⅔ cup plus 1 teaspoon ground sumac

½ teaspoon black pepper

¼ cup extra virgin olive oil

½ cup fresh lemon juice

1 tablespoon pine nuts

1 tablespoon pomegranate syrup (optional)

To prepare the dough with a electric mixer: Combine the flour, olive oil, and salt in the bowl of a standing mixer fitted with the dough hook, or in a food processor fitted with the plastic blade. Mix on medium speed, gradually adding up to 1⅛ cups water, until the dough pulls away from the sides of the bowl and forms a smooth ball, 3 to 5 minutes.

To make the dough by hand: Combine the flour and salt in a bowl, and pour it onto a work surface, forming a mound. Use two fingers to make a well in the center. Combine the oil and 1⅛ cups water in a small bowl. Gradually pour the liquid into the well, whisking it into the flour with a fork, beginning at the bottom center of the well and working outward. Continue until all of the liquid is absorbed. Then knead the dough by pressing down on it with the heel of your hand, then stretching the dough forward, pushing it away from your body. Fold it in half and press down on it with the palm of your hand to seal the fold. Rotate the dough a quarter-turn and knead it again. Repeat the kneading, folding, sealing, and rotating until the dough is very smooth and shiny, about 7 minutes.

Coat a glass or ceramic bowl with olive oil, place the dough in the bowl, and roll it around to coat it with the oil. Cover, and set aside in a warm place to rest for 1 hour.

Meanwhile, make the filling: Make sure the spinach is as dry as possible. Coarsely chop the spinach and place it in a large bowl. Sprinkle 1 teaspoon of the salt over the spinach, and then rub the spinach between the palms of your hands until it wilts.

Place the onions in another bowl, and add the sumac, pepper, and remaining 1 teaspoon salt. Rub the onions between the palms of your hands until they soften. Add the mixture to the spinach. Add the olive oil, lemon juice, and pine nuts, and stir until thoroughly incorporated. Taste; the flavor should be very tart. If it's not, add about 1 tablespoon pomegranate syrup (rather than more lemon juice, which will make the filling too wet).

Preheat the oven to 400°F with one rack on the second position from the bottom and the other on the top position. Generously grease two baking sheets with olive oil.

Divide the dough into 3 balls. Roll out 1 ball of dough on a floured surface to a thickness of about ¼ inch. Using a 3-inch biscuit cutter or the rim of a glass, cut out rounds of dough. Place a round of dough in the palm of one hand, and with the other hand, stretch it to fit the size of your palm. Place a heaping teaspoon of filling in the center of the dough. Pinch the dough together at the bottom third of the round to create two sides of a triangle. Bring the remaining arc of the circle up to meet them to create the third side. If the dough does not seal well, dip your fingers in flour before pressing it together. Place the triangles 1 inch apart on the prepared baking sheets. Repeat with the remaining dough and filling.

Brush the triangles with olive oil, and place the baking sheets on the oven racks. Bake for 10 minutes. Then reverse their positions and bake until golden on the bottom, another 10 minutes.

Serve hot.

EID AL ADHA
THE FEAST FOR THE END OF THE PILGRIMAGE

Eid al Adha is the most important holiday on the Muslim calendar, a three-day celebration filled with family gatherings, drop-in visits, and almost non-stop eating! Yet like other religious holidays, this Eid, which means "festival" or "feast" in Arabic, is rooted in a sacred aspect of Islam: the annual pilgrimage, or hajj, to Mecca. As a culmination of the hajj, those who have journeyed to Mecca must sacrifice a sheep or a lamb. At the same time, Muslims around the world begin the Eid with a family feast that offers lamb or other meat, symbolizing that all Muslims are participating in the feast of the sacrifice—which is what *Eid al Adha* means.

Of all the big meals I prepare during the year, the first-day feast for Eid al Adha is the one most anticipated by my family. The menu here is one I often make for the Eid at our home. I serve it Arab-style, arranging beautiful platters of every appetizer and main course on buffet tables before anyone enters the dining room. It is a joy to see my guests marvel at the grand display and return to the buffet again and again to fill their plates.

- Simple Salad
- Spinach Triangles
- Sautéed Greens with Crispy Onions
- Kibeh Balls
- Stuffed Leg of Lamb
- Baked Sea Bass with Tahini Walnut Sauce

- Cucumber and Yogurt
- Arab Flatbread

- Shredded Pastry with Cheese
- Semolina Cake

- Baklava
- Fruit platter: strawberries, grapes, melon, and other fruits in season

- Lemonade
- Jalap (date and grape molasses drink) (store-bought)
- Mulberry juice (store-bought)
- Fresh-squeezed orange juice
- Arab Coffee

The Big Eid and the Little Eid: Two Busy Holidays

Eid al Adha comes seventy days after Eid al-Fiter, the holiday that concludes Ramadan. With these two major Islamic festivals coming so close together, we sometimes distinguish between them by referring to Eid al Adha as the "big Eid" (Eid al Kibeer) and Eid al-Fiter as the "little Eid" (Eid al Sageer). In terms of its religious significance, Eid al Adha is somewhat more important, and so we call it "big." But in the Arab world today, both are big deals: they start with great feasts and then pass in a whirl of visits and food and friends, with no work or school for three days!

We love the Eids, but all that socializing can be a challenge. It's a time-honored custom in the Arab world that you must visit every relative on both sides of the family sometime during both Eids to exchange holiday wishes and partake of the wonderful sweets they always offer. In large Arab families, this takes some planning.

When we lived in Beirut and Kuwait City, Aref and I would start paying courtesy visits on the first day, as soon as we could move after the feast. We planned our itinerary carefully, visiting everyone in a certain part of town—elder relatives first, out of respect—before driving on to the next. At each stop, we had to eat a bit of the proffered delicious pastries, cookies, Jordan almonds, dates, and chocolate, plus coffee and tea to drink.

Completing our rounds often took us into the second day of the Eid—and then it was our turn to receive visits from all the relatives (and friends) at our house, and to offer them pastries and cookies. With a constant stream of guests from morning to night, the Eids were no vacation! Yet we felt our ties to family and friends grow stronger all the time, and I value these holiday customs to this day.

Having two major Eids also helps to solve a common domestic dilemma. The first-day feast is traditionally held at the house of the head of the family, usually grandparents who welcome their grown children and grandchildren. When we got married, Aref and I had to decide: whose family would we go to for the Eid? The diplomatic and convenient solution was to go to my parents' for the little Eid and then to Aref's parents' for the big Eid, two months later—and vice versa the next year. Since we moved to the United States, I have observed that many of our friends follow this same strategy at Thanksgiving and Christmas.

Greetings for the Eid

During Eid al Adha and Eid al-Fiter, the first thing we do on meeting family and friends is to exchange special holiday greetings:

- *Eid muburak!*—"Blessed Eid!"
- *Eid saeed!*—"Happy Eid!"
- *Assakoum-min-awadeh*—"May the blessings come back to you"
- *Kul am wa antum bi khair*—"May every year be a joyous one"

The Pilgrimage and the Sacrifice— A Pillar of Islam

The hajj, to which Eid al Adha is linked, is the annual pilgrimage of Muslims from all over the world to Mecca, in Saudi Arabia, the birthplace of the prophet Muhammad. Like the yearly fast of Ramadan and *zakat* (alms-giving to the needy), the hajj is one of the Five Pillars of Islam. Every Muslim individual (man or woman) must make the journey to Mecca once in his lifetime if possible, as an act of penitence and to show devotion to God.

In recent years, the hajj has brought literally millions of Muslim men and women to Mecca, where they followed prescribed set of rituals at the holy sites over a period of several days. The sacrifice of an animal—a lamb or a sheep—is one of the final rituals, commemorating Abraham's willingness to sacrifice his son Isaac at God's command.

The enormous number of people who journey to Mecca has changed the nature of the sacrifice. Due to the physical impossibility of providing a sacrificial animal for every one of the millions of pilgrims, a symbolic sacrifice can be made by paying an official agent for the cost of a lamb. This money is used to buy lambs for poorer people who can't afford their own. In recent years, Saudi authorities have created a system that processes these thousands of sacrificial lambs, freezes the meat, and distributes it all over the Muslim world.

In places far from Mecca, Muslims follow the same custom of helping others who cannot afford to purchase their own lamb. Everyone who has the means buys lamb for their family feast and also makes a donation that is used to buy lamb for those with less means. When we lived in Kuwait, Aref was in the food service business and he was able to provide such assistance in a direct way. His big kitchens would roast several whole lambs that were then delivered to a mosque or charitable agency, fully cooked and ready for someone's table, on the first day of the Eid.

Bread

AT BREAKFAST, LUNCH, AND dinner, with every cup of tea or coffee in between, and whenever friends and family gather around an Arab table, there is always plenty of fresh bread to pass around. The breads can be fluffy or flat, round or free-form, plain or flavored with herbs and spices. Bread is also appreciated for its versatility: a piece may be folded into a small cone to scoop up dips, or sandwiched between the fingers to pick up an olive on the mezza table. It may be sliced in half and filled with halloumi cheese and tomatoes, Falafel, or strips of chicken and beef; cut into tiny squares and toasted to top salads; or used stale, scattered on the bottom of layered dishes to soak up flavorful sauces.

Essentially made from water, wheat, and salt and sometimes yeast, bread is so revered in the Arab culture that if a piece is found on the ground, it must be picked up immediately and then a prayer recited.

Breads in the Arab world vary from country to country and from city to small village within

each. In my family, we eat more of the Lebanese-style bread—referred to throughout this book as Arab flatbread—than any other. Also known as pita bread, it comes in various diameters and thicknesses, depending on the brand and whether it is made from white or whole-wheat flours or a combination of both.

These flatbreads are found only in the towns and cities in Lebanon. In the mountains *markouk,* huge unleavened sheets of bread made with a combination of whole-wheat and white flour, or entirely of whole-wheat flour, are baked in homes every day. Despite being exclusive to mountain villages, markouk is considered the national bread of Lebanon and Syria. Both Arab flatbread and markouk can be purchased at Middle Eastern grocery stores.

In most Arab countries, bread is baked against the hot walls of a round clay oven called a *tannur.* The baker skillfully throws the dough onto the sides of the hot oven and when it is properly baked, the bread falls to the oven floor, where it is removed with a long wooden paddle. In Palestine, bread is traditionally baked in a *taboun,* a cylindrical piece of metal that is set in the ground over hot pebbles.

While many women still make fresh bread for every meal, most people buy their bread from bakeries. I occasionally bake my own bread, but I find that there are many excellent brands available. One superior version is Farahat Pita Bread, made in Jacksonville, Florida (see Sources).

Arab Flatbread

KHOUBEZ

2¼ teaspoons active dry yeast

2 cups warm water (110°F),
   plus ¾ cup if using
   whole-wheat flour

1¼ teaspoons sugar

5½ cups all-purpose or
   whole-wheat flour, plus extra
   for kneading

2 teaspoons sea salt

4 tablespoons extra virgin
   olive oil

*W*hen my boys were very young, I made Khoubez every Sunday. Its yeasty aroma told them that there was a big breakfast awaiting. These days most cooks in my homeland, as well as my Arab-American friends here in the States, use frozen dough to make this bread. There are excellent packaged brands available in Middle Eastern groceries (see Sources).

Whether you make the dough yourself or use packaged dough, the loaves can be rolled out in advance, flattened, stacked directly on one another, sealed in a plastic bag, and refrigerated for 2 to 3 days or frozen for up to a month. When you are ready to serve it, bring the bread to room temperature and then bake it in a preheated 500°F oven for 10 minutes. ***Makes seven 6- to 7-inch loaves***

Combine the yeast, 1 cup of the warm water, and the sugar in a small bowl and stir to dissolve. Set it aside until the mixture is foamy and has doubled in size, about 10 minutes.

Sift the flour and salt together into the bowl of a standing mixer fitted with the dough hook. Make a well in the center and add the remaining 1 cup warm water (or 1¾ cups if using whole-wheat flour), the yeast mixture, and 2 tablespoons of the olive oil. Mix the ingredients on low speed until they are incorporated. Turn the speed to high and mix until the dough pulls away from the sides of the bowl and forms a ball around the dough hook, 2 minutes.

Transfer the dough to a floured work surface. Sprinkling as little flour on the dough and your hands as possible, knead the dough: Push down on it with the heel of your hand. Using one hand, stretch the dough away from you while holding it in place with the other. Then fold the dough in half and press down on it with the palm of your hand to seal the fold. Rotate the dough a quarter-turn and repeat, continuing to knead, fold, seal, and turn until the dough is smooth and elastic and doesn't stick to your fingers, 5 minutes.

Coat a large bowl with the remaining 2 tablespoons olive oil and place the dough in it, turning it to coat it all over the oil. Cover the bowl with plastic wrap and a kitchen towel, and set in aside in a warm draft-free place until the dough has doubled in size, about 2 hours.

Meanwhile, lightly dust a baking sheet with flour. Dust a large kitchen cloth or a folded cotton sheet with flour.

Punch the dough down and transfer it to a floured work surface. Knead it for 2 minutes. Then divide the dough into 7 equal pieces, roll each one into a ball, and place them on the prepared baking sheet. Working with 1 ball of dough at a time, flatten them gently on a lightly floured surface, using a dry rolling pin lightly dusted with flour. Roll the dough out until it is about ¼ inch thick and 5 to 6 inches in diameter. Lay the loaves on the floured towel, sprinkle some flour over them, cover with a second towel, and let them rest for 30 minutes.

Preheat the oven to 500°F, with a rack in the lowest position. Preheat a baking sheet on the rack for 10 minutes.

Arrange 2 loaves on the preheated baking sheet, spacing them 1 inch apart, and bake until they puff up, 5 to 7 minutes. Transfer the loaves to a wire rack to cool, and repeat with the remaining loaves.

To freeze baked flatbread, package it in resealable freezer bags, squeezing the air out of the bread as you zip it closed. It will keep in the freezer for 6 months. Defrost the bread in the refrigerator. If you want to warm the defrosted bread, heat it in a 300°F oven for 10 minutes. Then quickly cover it with a towel or napkin, as it will dry out easily. Alternatively, wrap a stack of frozen bread in a paper towel and defrost it in the microwave for 30 minutes. For a casual mezza table, I cut Arab flatbread into triangles and serve it in plastic bags, which prevents it from drying out. It isn't beautiful, but it's practical!

DON'T TOSS THAT BREAD!

An Arab cook never wastes food—not even stale bread. Break up hardened loaves of Arab Flatbread and use it in Chicken and Rice with Creamy Yogurt Sauce or wherever a recipe calls for toasted or fried bread.

Holy Bread

URBAN

2 tablespoons active dry yeast

2 cups plus ½ teaspoon sugar

2¼ cups warm water (110° F)

1 cup whole milk, warmed

1½ teaspoons ground mahlab
   (see page 22)

3 tablespoons rose water

8 cups bread flour

2 teaspoons baking powder

Olive oil, for the bowl

Rose water, for brushing
   (optional)

*T*his sweet leavened bread is subtly flavored with mahlab, *the spice ground from the pits of black cherries. It is a traditional Easter bread for Arab Christians, and it is also baked as an offering to God in thanks for answering a prayer. For example, when my friend's son was very sick, she pledged to make ten loaves of bread and offer them up to God if her son recuperated. When he recovered, she left ten freshly baked loaves of Holy Bread at the entrance to her church. Whenever there is an offering of Holy Bread, the congregation is invited to taste it as they leave the church. Urban is also traditionally wrapped in festive paper and ribbons and given to guests at a child's christening.*

I make round loaves, but you can also roll each ball of dough into long strands (about 11 inches long and 2 inches wide), place them close together on the baking sheet, and braid them; then brush with the egg wash and bake as directed. Whatever shape they are, the loaves taste best warm. **Makes eight 5-inch loaves**

Combine the yeast, ½ teaspoon of the sugar, and ½ cup of the warm water in a small bowl, and stir to dissolve. Set it aside until the mixture is foamy and has doubled in size, about 10 minutes.

Combine the remaining 2 cups sugar, remaining 1¾ cups lukewarm water, the warm milk, and the mahlab in a large bowl. Add the rose water and the yeast mixture, and set aside.

In another large bowl, combine the flour and baking powder. Whisk the milk mixture into the flour mixture until it comes together. Transfer the dough to a lightly floured surface and knead it: Push down on the dough with the heel of your hand. Using one hand, stretch the dough away from you while holding it in place with the other. Then fold the dough in half and press down on it with the palm of your hand to seal the fold. Rotate the dough a quarter-turn and repeat, continuing to knead, fold, seal, and turn until the dough is smooth, 8 minutes.

Coat a bowl with olive oil, place the dough in the bowl, and turn to coat it all over with the oil. Cover with plastic wrap and a kitchen towel, and set it aside in a warm, draft-free place until it has doubled in size, about 2 hours.

Divide the dough into 8 equal pieces, shape them into balls, and place them on a lightly floured baking sheet or tray. Dust each piece with a little flour, cover them with a kitchen towel, and let them rest for 20 minutes.

Preheat the oven to 375°F, with a rack in the center.

Working in batches, flatten the balls to form 1-inch-thick rounds, and place them on a heavy-bottomed baking sheet. Prick the surface of the dough all over with the tines of a fork to make a decorative pattern. Bake until golden, 15 to 20 minutes.

Remove the bread from the oven and brush the tops with a little rose water if desired. Transfer the loaves to a wire rack to cool a bit. Serve warm. The bread will keep, tightly wrapped, at room temperature for 2 days.

Mountain Bread

MANAKEESH

1 package (2¼ teaspoons) active dry yeast

¼ teaspoon sugar

1 cup warm water (110°F)

6 cups bread flour, sifted

1½ cups water

1 tablespoon salt

3 tablespoons extra virgin olive oil, plus extra for the bowl

Zaatar Spread, Tomato Zaatar Spread, and/or Halloumi Topping (recipes follow)

These aromatic herbed flatbreads are especially heavenly when eaten warm from the oven. They make a perfect casual breakfast when served with Labneh, green olives, sliced tomato and cucumber, and a pot of hot tea.

If you do not have time to prepare fresh dough, you can use pizza dough or frozen bread dough, as many young Arab and Arab-American cooks do. When my boys were in college, they used to make "instant" Manakeesh on ready-made pizza bread simply by adding olive oil and sprinkling Zaatar on top and warming it in a 350°F oven for few minutes.

You can make Manakeesh any size you like—the traditional loaves are about 5 inches in diameter. Sometimes I make mini Manakeesh for appetizers by rolling out a large portion of dough and cutting out small rounds with a biscuit cutter.

The dough can be made ahead and frozen for up to 3 months: Wrap each of the 15 pieces in wax paper and place them in a resealable plastic bag. You can also freeze fully prepared manakeesh—with toppings—by baking the bread for 5 minutes, then cooling and freezing it as described above. Defrost the bread at room temperature and finish baking it in a preheated 500°F oven until heated through, about 5 minutes. To freeze fully baked Manakeesh, fold each one in half (to prevent the spread from falling off) before sliding wax paper between them.

Makes fifteen 5-inch loaves

Combine the yeast, sugar, and warm water in a small bowl and stir to dissolve. Set it aside until the mixture doubles in size, about 5 minutes.

Using an electric mixer: Combine the flour, water, salt, olive oil, and yeast mixture in the bowl of an electric mixer fitted with the dough hook. Mix on medium speed until the dough leaves the sides of the bowl and is very smooth, 3 to 4 minutes.

By hand: Sift the flour and salt together onto a clean work surface, forming a mound. Mix the yeast mixture, olive oil, and water together in a bowl. Using two fingers, make a well in the middle of the mound of flour. Pour a small amount of the liquid into the well. Using a fork, gather up some flour from the perimeter of the mound and add it to the well. Stir it into the liquid until it is absorbed. Gradually add the remaining liquid, mixing the flour into it in the same way, until it is all absorbed. Then knead the dough by pressing down on it with the heel of your hand, then stretching the dough forward, pushing it away from your body. Fold it in half and press down on it with the palm of your hand to seal the fold. Rotate the dough a quarter-turn, and knead it again. Repeat the kneading, folding, sealing, and rotating until the dough is very smooth and shiny, 7 minutes.

Coat a bowl with olive oil, place the dough in the bowl, and turn it to coat the entire surface with the oil. Cover with plastic wrap and a kitchen towel, and set it in a warm, draft-free place (85° to 95°F) until it has doubled in size, about 1 hour.

Preheat the oven to 500°F, with a rack in the lower third of the oven. Place a pizza stone or a heavy baking sheet on the rack to preheat.

Punch the dough down. Place it on a lightly floured board and cut it into 15 equal pieces. Roll out each piece of dough to form a ¼-inch-thick round. Crimp the edges to make a border like a pizza crust, and make impressions with your fingertips inside the border.

Spoon 1½ tablespoons of the desired topping onto each round of dough, and spread it out evenly with the back of the spoon. Slide the loaves, in batches, onto the hot pizza stone or baking sheet, and bake until the bottoms are golden brown, 10 to 15 minutes. Serve immediately.

Zaatar Spread

Makes enough for 15 loaves

2 cups Zaatar (page 38)
1½ cups extra virgin olive oil

Whisk the Zaatar and olive oil together in a medium bowl. Transfer the spread to a container with a tight-fitting lid, and store in the refrigerator for up to 3 days. Bring it to room temperature before using.

Tomato Zaatar Spread

Makes enough for 15 loaves

1½ cups Zaatar (page 38)
1½ cups extra virgin olive oil
1 pound tomatoes, seeded and finely diced
½ pound white onions, finely diced
Red pepper flakes, to taste (optional)

Combine the Zaatar, olive oil, tomatoes, onions, and red pepper flakes, if using, in a medium bowl and stir together. Transfer the spread to a container with a tight-fitting lid, and refrigerate for up to 1 day. Bring it to room temperature before using.

Halloumi Topping

Makes enough for 15 loaves

3 pounds halloumi cheese, soaked (see page 75), cut into 1-inch cubes
½ cup extra virgin olive oil
2 tablespoons nigella or sesame seeds

Combine the halloumi, olive oil, and nigella seeds in a medium bowl and stir until the cheese is coated. Transfer to a container with a tight-fitting lid, and refrigerate for up to 5 days. Bring it to room temperature before using.

MAKING MANAKEESH IN THE MOUNTAINS

In my early teens, we often spent part of the summer in Bihamdoun, a village in the mountains of Lebanon. In most Lebanese villages back then, *manakeesh* was made through a happy collaboration between the local baker and the villagers. The baker supplied the dough and the ovens, or *forun*, and his customers brought their own savory toppings to the bakery, where they rolled out the dough and spread the toppings themselves. Each Sunday morning, my sister Haifa and I would wake at sunrise in order to get to the bakery in time to secure our place at the long table, where we would clear a space for our large baking tray and the big bowl of Zaatar and olive oil our mother had prepared the night before. The baking table was always full of young girls and boys, as well as adults, gossiping and chatting. One by one, the baker would take each customer's order. When it came time to give ours, Haifa always ordered at least twelve loaves—and often more when friends were visiting.

The baker would bring the plump pieces of dough, set on a long wooden plank, to our table. As the adults gossiped around us, we children set to work on the dough. We took it very seriously, carefully crimping the edges, then quickly tapping the centers of the flattened pieces with our fingertips so they didn't rise too much before they went into the oven. Five minutes after returning our *manakeesh* to the baker, he pulled it from the huge wall oven, piping hot and fragrant with thyme and melted cheese. Haifa and I slid the hot *manakeesh* onto our tray, and because we always forgot our pot holders, swaddled the hot tray in layers of newspapers. Then we rushed home so the aromatic bread would make it onto the breakfast table piping hot.

Pull-Away Cheese Rolls

TABAT JIBNEH

For the dough:

1½ teaspoons active dry yeast

¼ teaspoon sugar

1 cup warm water (110°F)

3 cups all-purpose flour, sifted

¼ teaspoon salt

½ cup powdered whole milk

1 egg

½ cup vegetable oil

Olive oil, for coating the bowl and the pan

For the filling:

One 5-ounce package halloumi or akawi cheese

¼ cup finely chopped fresh flat-leaf parsley

5 ounces mozzarella cheese, shredded on the small holes of a box grater (about ½ cup)

1 tablespoon finely chopped fresh oregano or thyme leaves

¼ cup sesame seeds

2 teaspoons nigella seeds

¼ cup olive oil, plus extra for drizzling

*I*n Kuwait it's common for women to gather at least twice a week for a couple of hours before lunch. When I lived there, most of the women at these gatherings were not employed outside the home, making these subheys, which means "mornings," a cherished part of our social life. We enjoyed visiting one another and sampling the delicious refreshments that were always an important feature of the get-togethers. Savory pastries, sweets, and coffee were usually served, and there was always an unspoken challenge to come up with uniquely delicious recipes in order to impress one another. Since I love cheese, and especially the combination of cheese and bread, I invented these fragrant cheese-filled rolls to serve at one of our subheys.

Tabat Jibneh can be frozen uncooked, right in the pan, for up to 6 weeks. Double-wrap the pan with one layer of plastic wrap and another of heavy-duty aluminum foil. When you are ready to bake them, defrost the rolls in the refrigerator, then bake them in a preheated 425°F oven until they are pale gold, 30 minutes. You can also freeze fully baked Tabat Jibneh, tightly wrapped, for up to 2 weeks.

Makes 30 to 36 rolls

Prepare the dough: Combine the yeast, sugar, and warm water in a small bowl, and stir to dissolve. Set it aside until the mixture is foamy, about 5 minutes.

Combine the flour, salt, and powdered milk in the bowl of an electric mixer fitted with the dough hook. Add the egg and vegetable oil, and give the mixture a good stir. Add the yeast mixture and mix on medium speed until the ingredients are incorporated. Then raise the speed to high and continue to mix until the dough pulls away from the sides of the bowl, 3 minutes.

Coat a glass or ceramic bowl with olive oil, put the dough in the bowl, and roll it around to coat it with the oil. Cover with a kitchen towel or plastic wrap, and set it aside in a warm, draft-free place until the dough has doubled in size, about 1 hour.

Prepare the filling: Rinse the halloumi under cold running water; or, if you are using akawi packed in brine, submerge it in water, changing the bath three times to rid it of overly salty brine. Drain the cheese and shred it on the large holes of a box grater. Combine the halloumi, parsley, mozzarella, and oregano in a bowl, and stir to mix.

Form and bake the rolls: Preheat the oven to 425°F. Combine the sesame and nigella seeds on a plate. Coat a 12-inch cake pan with olive oil. Fill a small bowl with the ¼ cup olive oil. Liberally coat your hands with olive oil.

Punch the dough down. Pull off a piece about the size of a baseball and squeeze it between your thumb and index finger until a ball about the size of a walnut comes through. Separate the ball from the dough in your palm by pinching your index finger over your thumb. Flatten the ball in the palm of your hand, stretching it to fit your palm. Place 1 tablespoon of the filling in the center and gather the edges around it, pinching to seal it, forming a purse shape. Dip the smooth side into the olive oil, then into the seed mixture, and place it, sealed side down, in the cake pan. Repeat with the remaining dough and filling, arranging the rolls tightly in concentric circles, beginning with the outer ring and working your way to the center.

Drizzle a little olive oil over the rolls and bake until they are pale gold, about 25 minutes. Transfer the pan to a wire rack and let the rolls cool for a bit.

Run a knife around the rim of the pan to loosen the rolls. Invert a plate over the pan, flip the plate and pan together, and remove the pan. Invert a second plate over the rolls and flip again, so the rolls are seed side up. Place the plate on the table and let your guests pull one roll at a time from the loaf.

Breakfast

Breakfast in the Arab world is relatively simple compared to the noon and evening meals, but it is still a more elaborate production than the usual American breakfast of a bowl of cereal and a cup of coffee.

A typical weekday breakfast includes a bowl of Labneh (yogurt cheese) to spread on flatbread, accompanied by small bowls of Zaatar and Dukka, the spice mixes, for seasoning the cheese and a third bowl with olive oil for drizzling over the whole thing—or just for dipping into with a piece of bread. Tea flavored with mint or sage is the traditional beverage. Coffee is never served at breakfast.

On most weekends and always on holidays, the morning meal is served at a later hour and is considerably more elaborate. In addition to the staple weekday offerings, salty black and green cured olives, sliced tomatoes, crisp cucumber slices, and pickles are served on individual small plates. Other dishes include Fava Beans seasoned with fresh lemon, Chickpea Dip with hard-boiled eggs, and Falafel. Fragrant loaves of freshly baked Mountain Bread are offered alongside Arab flatbread. At least one egg dish is on the table, from a simple omelet to a more elegant offering such as Baked Eggs with Eggplant.

Homemade jams and preserves—date, rose petal, and apricot are among my favorites—are always offered for spreading on warm bread; good-quality brands are available at Middle Eastern grocery stores. Look there, too, for *dibis,* a molasses made from carob seeds that is often mixed with tahini to make a spread for bread. Halvah, the honey-sweetened confection found in every Arab cook's pantry, is also typically served on the brunch table.

Fava Beans

FUL MUDAMAS

Two 15-ounce cans fava beans, with their liquid

6 cloves garlic

1 jalapeño pepper, seeded and minced

1 teaspoon chopped fresh dill

1 teaspoon salt, plus more to taste

1½ tablespoons sesame paste (tahini)

3 tablespoons fresh lemon juice, plus more to taste

1 medium tomato, seeded and diced

¼ cup extra virgin olive oil

Arab flatbread, for serving

It is the national breakfast of Egypt, yet Ful Madamas is eaten the Arab world over, and at all times of the day. Sometimes Ful Madamas is combined with hamine, *a traditional Egyptian breakfast dish in which whole eggs are cooked in a pot of water, flavored with onion skins and sometimes a bit of ground coffee, over very low heat for as long as 4 hours; the melt-in-your mouth eggs are peeled and served over the* ful. *Other times, the eggs are cooked in the pot with the beans.*

For lunch, ful *is commonly eaten with two other essential mezza dishes, Hummus and Betinjan Mutabal. It is often a part of dinner— traditionally a light meal—with fried Zucchini-Egg Cakes and some sliced tomatoes and pickles.* Ful *is not only served at home, however. In Cairo and other cosmopolitan cities in the Arab world, office workers and students line up to buy lunch from street vendors who cook the beans in big brass urns and serve them up in small, round earthenware bowls. Sometimes they spoon the beans right into a split loaf of fluffy pocket bread. Garlic, lemon juice, olive oil, and eggs are optional.*

Here in the U.S., I often serve Ful Madamas with grilled meats because its sturdy consistency and smoky flavor are strong enough to stand up to the assertive flavor of anything grilled.

Taste the fava beans before you serve them—they should be distinctly lemony but not overly tart. Serve them hot, with whole scallions for biting into after a few spoonfuls of the beans, and offer pickles, radishes, and fresh spearmint leaves on the side. **Serves 6**

Pour the fava beans and their liquid into a saucepan and bring to a boil over high heat, stirring once or twice. Reduce the heat to medium-low, cover, and cook until the beans are easily smashed with the back of a spoon, about 15 minutes.

Meanwhile, using a mortar and pestle, crush the garlic, jalapeño, dill, and salt together to make a paste.

Drain the beans and transfer them to a bowl. Mash them slightly with a pestle or a potato masher, pressing down just enough to split them; the beans should remain largely intact. Stir in the paste,

Fava Beans *(continued)*

sesame paste, and lemon juice, and mix until fully incorporated. Taste, and add more lemon and salt if needed.

Spoon the Ful Madamas into a serving bowl, garnish with the tomatoes, and drizzle with the olive oil. Serve warm, with the Arab flatbread alongside for scooping.

Deep-Fried Fava Bean Patties

FALAFEL

1 pound dried split fava beans, picked over

½ pound dried chickpeas, picked over

15 large cloves garlic

1 medium onion, coarsely chopped

1 leek, white part only, chopped

1 packed cup coarsely chopped fresh cilantro

½ cup coarsely chopped fresh flat-leaf parsley

2 teaspoons ground coriander

1 teaspoon ground allspice

1 teaspoon ground cumin

½ teaspoon cayenne pepper

½ teaspoon ground cinnamon

2 tablespoons salt

½ teaspoon black pepper

2 teaspoons baking soda

1 tablespoon baking powder

¼ cup sesame seeds

4 cups canola oil

Accompaniments:
Arab flatbread
Tahini (page 32)
Sliced tomatoes
Thinly sliced onions
Pickled wild cucumbers (store-bought; Ziyad is my favorite brand)
Pickled turnips (store-bought)

*I*f there's one Arab dish that's familiar to many Americans, it's the spicy seasoned patties known as falafel. Although it likely originated in Egypt, where it is called ta'amia, *Falafel is now a pan-Arab street food, just as popular in Syria, Lebanon, Palestine, Israel, and Jordan as it is in its homeland. Though it varies from region to region (mainly in the ratio of fava beans to chickpeas), the occasions for eating Falafel are the same: At breakfast it is used to scoop up Chickpeas with Yogurt; for lunch the savory cakes and chopped cucumbers are wrapped in Arab pocket flatbread and drizzled with Tahini or arranged atop salad greens; and for an appetizer or snack it is eaten plain or with a bit of Tahini.*

Making Falafel takes some planning since the dried beans—I never used canned because they make the mixture mushy—must be soaked ahead of time and the "dough" must rest for a couple of hours. A meat grinder makes the fluffiest, lightest dough, but the grinder attachment on a standing mixer is a good substitute. Don't use a food processor; it makes the mixture too runny to shape into patties. You can shape the Falafel by hand or use an aleb *(see page 109), a simple tool that makes uniformly shaped patties.*

At home I serve Falafel on a bed of chopped parsley, with sliced tomatoes and onions arranged around it. There's always sliced pickled cucumber and pickled turnips on the side, and a bowl of Tahini for guests to dress their own Falafel. If I'm serving Falafel as part of a casual gathering, such as a Super Bowl party, I cut 6-inch pocket breads in half, then place four patties in each pocket and set them on a serving platter, surrounded by the condiments so guests can tuck whatever they wish into their own sandwiches.

The Falafel mixture can be frozen, tightly covered, for 3 months; defrost it overnight in the refrigerator, and then remove it from the refrigerator 2 hours before frying.

Makes forty-five to fifty 1½-inch patties

Place the fava beans and the chickpeas in a strainer and rinse them under cold running water. Drain, place them in a bowl, and add water to cover by 1 inch. Soak for 12 hours or overnight.

Drain the beans and set them aside until they are completely dry (if the beans are wet, the mixture will be runny).

Combine the beans, garlic, onions, leeks, cilantro, and parsley in a large bowl if you are using a meat grinder (fit it with the fine grinding plate), or in the bowl of a standing mixer fitted with the grinder attachment. Spoon the bean mixture into the grinder funnel in batches, pressing down as needed with the plunger tool. Continue until all of the bean mixture has been ground.

Pass the mixture through the grinder a second time, finishing with a small piece of Arab flatbread to push the last of the mixture through the machine.

Add the coriander, allspice, cumin, cayenne, cinnamon, salt, and black pepper to the bean mixture, and knead by hand until all the ingredients are well incorporated, about 2 minutes. The "dough" should be coarse yet cohesive, similar to cooked polenta. Cover, and let rest for 2 hours at room temperature.

About 30 minutes before you plan to shape the falafel, add the baking soda and baking powder, and knead the mixture by hand for 1 to 2 minutes.

Meanwhile, line two trays—one for the uncooked Falafel, the other for the fried Falafel—with two layers of paper towels. Spread the sesame seeds on a dinner plate.

Heat the canola oil in a large deep pot (I find a wok actually works best) to 365° to 375°F.

While the oil is heating, begin to shape the Falafel: Wet your hands with cold water. Scoop a walnut-size portion of the mixture into your hands and roll it into a ball. Gently flatten it between your palms. Make an indentation in the center of the Falafel, using your index finger, and then lightly press the indented side into the sesame seeds. Set the patty on the prepared tray and continue, forming about half of the "dough."

Once the oil is hot, begin frying the Falafel. (If you don't have a deep-frying thermometer, drop a tiny amount of the Falafel mixture into the oil. If it bubbles vigorously and floats to the top, the oil is ready.) Gently slide each piece into the oil, using your hands or a slotted spoon. Do not crowd the pot. When the pieces bob to the surface, use a slotted spoon to flip them over, and continue to cook until they are a rich brown, 5 minutes in all. Finish shaping the remaining Falafel dough while the earlier batches are frying.

Using the slotted spoon, transfer the Falafel to the other prepared tray. To keep the Falafel warm, slide them onto a sheet pan in a low oven.

Serve hot, with the Arab flatbread, Tahini, tomatoes, onions, pickled cucumbers, and pickled turnips alongside.

Using an aleb*:* An aleb will form 24 larger balls. They will take slightly longer to cook in the hot oil.

ALEB FALAFEL

Those who make falafel frequently use a special shaping tool called an *aleb falafel.* Found in Middle Eastern grocery stores, it costs less than $2 and resembles a cylinder with a disk attached to the top. Within the disk there is a smaller plate where the falafel mix is molded and formed. The disk is then depressed by the lever on the handle (cylinder) of the aleb. To use an aleb falafel, hold it in your non-dominant hand, and using your thumb, depress the lever on the side of the tool. This will lower the disk upon which the falafel sits. Using the small spatula that comes with the aleb, smooth the falafel paste onto the disk as if you were pressing ice cream onto a cone. Carefully release the lever and gently slide the formed falafel directly into the hot oil as directed in the recipe.

Arab Yogurt Cheese

LABNEH

32 ounces plain yogurt

1 teaspoon salt

¼ cup extra virgin olive oil, for drizzling

Zaatar (page 38) *or* dried mint, preferably spearmint, *or* fresh oregano *or* mint leaves

*L*abneh is simply plain yogurt drained of its whey. It is luxuriously creamy, no matter what kind of yogurt you use—even fat-free yogurt tastes rich, almost decadent. Depending on how long you allow the yogurt to drain, you can make a looser cheese that is the perfect consistency for dipping or spreading, or a much stiffer version that can be shaped or molded. Arabs use Labneh to make everything from cheese balls and sandwich spreads, to fillings for Kibeh in the tray, to dips for fruits and vegetables. It is often flavored with dried spice mixes, such as Zaatar or Dukka, or just a single spice, such as dried mint. Jam, too, is sometimes swirled into the cheese to make a breakfast spread. Like Hummus, Labneh is a staple on the mezza table.*

Although you can find Labneh in any Middle Eastern market, it's so easy to make at home that it's worth the small effort. I use dried spearmint whenever I can find it because its flavor is closest to the mint of my homeland. If you are serving this cheese with fruits and vegetables for dipping, omit the olive oil. If you are serving it as a thicker cheese on the mezza table, place a small pitcher of olive oil nearby and invite guests to drizzle it onto their portion. ***Makes 1 cup***

Line a fine-mesh strainer with three layers of 100% cotton cheesecloth or with an appropriately sized coffee filter. (Alternatively, use a labneh bag; see page 57.)

Spoon the yogurt into the cheesecloth, add the salt, and stir. (If using a labneh bag, roll the edges down as you would a pastry bag and fill it with the yogurt.) Twist the cheesecloth tightly around the yogurt and place it, in the strainer, over a large bowl. Be sure there is plenty of space between the bottom of the strainer and the bottom of the bowl—you don't want the gradually thickening yogurt to come into contact with the drained whey. Cover with plastic wrap and refrigerate for 6 to 8 hours to achieve sour cream consistency, 24 hours if you want the yogurt to thicken to a cream cheese–like texture.

Remove the Labneh from the cheesecloth and place it in a rigid storage container. Discard the whey. Cover the Labneh tightly, and refrigerate until ready to use. (It will keep for up to 2 weeks.)

To serve, spoon the Labneh into a serving dish. Use the back of the spoon to push the cheese out toward the edge of the dish, creating a well in the center, and to make indentations in the cheese. Drizzle the olive oil into the indentations. Sprinkle the Zaatar or dried mint all over the cheese, or garnish with the fresh oregano or mint.

Variation: The thicker version of Labneh (drained for at least 24 hours) can be molded in almost any shape. Simply line the mold with plastic wrap, and chill for 6 hours. Unmold onto a serving plate, remove the plastic wrap, and garnish with strawberries, cherry tomatoes, and cucumber wedges.

Yogurt Cheese Balls

TABAT LABNEH

16 ounces firm Labneh (drained for 48 hours; see page 110)
Extra virgin olive oil

*T*abat Labneh is just one example of how the Arab cook makes the most out of a single ingredient. Walnut-size balls of yogurt cheese, with the consistency of chèvre and the appearance of little mozzarella balls, Tabat Labneh was traditionally made in the summer, when fresh yogurt was most abundant and there was always plenty of Labneh to spare. The extra Labneh was formed into balls, set out to dry over the course of a few days, then packed in olive oil for use throughout the winter. The yogurt must drain for at least 2 days for the Labneh to achieve the proper consistency for these cheese balls. The result, firm Tabat Labneh, can be rolled in Zaatar or Dukka and served with Arab flatbread for breakfast, or threaded onto skewers with tomato and mint, or served plain on the mezza table. **Makes about 40 cheese balls**

Line a nonmetallic tray with three layers of paper towels, and set it aside.

Scoop out 1 tablespoonful of Labneh and place it in the palm of your hand. Roll the Labneh between your palms to form a ball. Place the ball on the paper towels, and repeat until all the Labneh has been formed into balls.

Gently place three layers of paper towels on top of the completed balls, and refrigerate the tray. Check the balls once or twice a day, and when the paper towels are very damp, replace both top and bottom layers with fresh paper towels. Repeat this process as needed until the Labneh balls are firm and dry. This will take 3 to 4 days.

Place the balls in a clean glass jar and cover with olive oil. They will keep, refrigerated, for up to 6 months as long as a clean, dry fork or tongs are used to remove them from the jar.

Variations:

Place fresh thyme sprigs between layers of the cheese balls in the jar before adding the olive oil.

Before storing the Tabat Labneh in the olive oil, roll the dry cheese balls in Zaatar or crushed red pepper flakes and chill them in the refrigerator for 5 hours. Then place the spiced Tabat Labneh in the jar and add olive oil to cover.

Yogurt Cheese Wraps

AROOSE LABNEH

Six 12-inch loaves Arab
flatbread, or 6 loaves
markouk

⅔ cup Labneh (page 110),
spreading consistency

½ cup extra virgin olive oil

4 teaspoons Zaatar (page 38;
optional)

Optional fillings:

Chopped tomatoes

Chopped cucumbers

Pitted green olives

Fresh mint leaves

Fresh basil leaves

Whenever my family traveled between Lebanon and Syria, we stopped in the Lebanese village of Shtura, which is famous for both its dairy products and its delicious aroose labneh, *a rolled breakfast sandwich made with* markouk, *the unleavened Lebanese mountain bread, spread with a thick layer of creamy Labneh and seasoned with Zaatar. It has always been popular in our house, though each of my sons prefers a different combination with the Labneh. Wasfi likes it with tomatoes and Zaatar, olives are Basil's choice, and Naji prefers it with cucumber.*

While Aroose Labneh is traditionally eaten as a single rolled sandwich for breakfast, I often cut the rolls into inch-thick pieces and serve them as appetizers.   *Serves 6*

Pull apart the two sides of each loaf of Arab bread and spread evenly with the Labneh. (Alternatively, unfold the *markouk* and spread a thin layer of Labneh over it.) Drizzle the olive oil evenly over the Labneh, and sprinkle the Zaatar, if using, on top. Arrange any or all of the fillings in a line down the center of one half of the bread (or in the center of the *markouk*).

Tightly roll the bread forward from one end until it is rolled into a log. Serve as a roll.

To serve it as an appetizer: Roll the Aroose Labneh in plastic wrap and place it in the freezer for 30 minutes to firm up. Then remove it from the freezer, place it seam side down on a cutting board, and slice it into ½-inch-thick rounds. If the Aroose Labneh begins to unravel, pierce it with a cocktail pick to hold it together.

Phyllo Cheese Pie

JIBNEH MALFOFEH

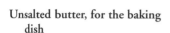

Unsalted butter, for the baking
   dish

1¼ pounds white cheddar
   cheese, grated on the large
   holes of a box grater

¼ pound mozzarella cheese,
   grated on the large holes of a
   box grater

8 sheets frozen phyllo dough,
   thawed (see page 25)

3 cups whole milk

6 eggs

1 tablespoon ground cinnamon

1 teaspoon salt

½ teaspoon black pepper

*I*ndividual spirals of rolled phyllo filled with cheese are tucked tightly
into a baking dish and drenched in cinnamon-scented custard in this
aromatic brunch dish. The beauty of Jibneh Malfofeh is that you can
vary the seasonings and cheeses to your liking. I often substitute ground
caraway for the cinnamon and use halloumi or Gruyère in place of the
mozzarella or cheddar for a more distinctive flavor. Jibneh Malfofeh
must be served straight from the oven; the crisp top becomes soggy if it sits
too long. For an informal brunch, serve it with a Simple Salad. Or for a
more elaborate gathering or for supper, serve it with Fried Eggplant with
Hot Chiles, Tomato Spread, Dressed Chickpeas, and Sautéed Lamb's
Liver.   *Serves 6 to 8*

Coat a shallow 4-quart ovenproof dish with butter.

Set aside 3 tablespoons of the cheddar. Combine the remaining
cheddar and the mozzarella in a medium bowl, and toss with your
hands. Set aside.

Stack the sheets of phyllo on a clean work surface and cover them
with a kitchen towel. Working with 1 sheet at a time, place the
phyllo on a clean surface with the long side facing you. Spoon ⅓
cup of the cheese mixture along the long near edge of the sheet.
Roll the dough away from you, around the cheese, to create a long
tube. Coil the tube around itself, making a spiral. Place the spiral in
the baking dish. Repeat with the remaining dough and cheese,
arranging the spirals tightly in a single layer. Set aside.

Whisk the milk, eggs, cinnamon, salt, and pepper together in a
large bowl, and pour the mixture over the phyllo spirals. Cover the
dish with plastic wrap and refrigerate until the dough has absorbed
about three quarters of the liquid, 2 to 3 hours. The spirals will
resemble pasta in a creamy white sauce.

Remove the dish from the refrigerator and bring it to room
temperature. Preheat the oven to 350°F.

Sprinkle the reserved 3 tablespoons cheddar on top of the spirals
and bake until the top is golden, 40 to 50 minutes. Serve warm.

Arab Omelet

AIJEH ARABIA

½ pound red onions, finely chopped

2 teaspoons salt

1 teaspoon white pepper

8 eggs, beaten

1 cup finely chopped fresh flat-leaf parsley

3 tablespoons extra virgin olive oil

Fresh flat-leaf parsley leaves, for garnish

Compared to a traditional French omelet, Aijeh is a bit flatter and denser—more like a frittata. It is prepared as a single dish—all of the egg mixture is poured into a large skillet at once. In Kuwait I always cooked this omelet in clarified butter, but I use olive oil to slick the pan in my American kitchen. You can add crumbled dried mint or any other favorite herb to the mixture. Serve Aijeh hot for breakfast, with sliced tomatoes and Arab flatbread, or cold, tucked inside Arab flatbread, for lunch. *Serves 6*

Combine the onions, salt, and pepper in a large bowl. Using your hands, work the salt and pepper into the onions. Add the eggs and whisk until frothy. Add the chopped parsley and whisk until it is incorporated.

Heat the olive oil in a large nonstick skillet over high heat. Add the egg mixture and cook, moving the edges with a spoon to ensure it does not stick. When the edges are almost dry, place a plate or platter over the pan and flip the omelet onto the plate. Slide the omelet back into the skillet and cook the other side for 2 to 3 minutes.

Garnish with the parsley and serve.

Sumac Fried Eggs

BAYD MAKLI BI SUMAC

2 tablespoons extra virgin
   olive oil

8 eggs

Salt, to taste

White pepper, to taste

1 tablespoon ground sumac

My oldest sister, Ikram, used to make these simple fried eggs for us on the occasional night when she was left in charge of cooking dinner. The sumac transforms these eggs; it adds a wonderful tart flavor and looks beautiful, too. Serve Bayd Makli bi Sumac with Arab Flatbread, sliced tomatoes, green olives, and a cup of tea.

Serves 6

Heat the olive oil in a large skillet over medium-high heat. Break the eggs, one by one, into the skillet. Season with the salt and pepper. Sprinkle the sumac all over the eggs. Reduce the heat to low and cook, covered, until the yolks are firm, 7 minutes. Serve immediately.

Eggs with Ground Beef and Sumac

BAYD BI LAHEMEH

2 tablespoons extra virgin
    olive oil
½ pound yellow onions, diced
1½ pounds lean ground beef
½ teaspoon ground allspice
1½ teaspoons salt
½ teaspoon black pepper
⅛ teaspoon ground cinnamon
8 eggs
1½ teaspoons ground sumac

Eggs cooked sunny-side-up and dusted with cherry-red sumac are nestled on top of cinnamon and allspice–seasoned ground beef in this skillet breakfast. Serve it with Cucumber and Yogurt and Labneh.

Serves 4

Heat the olive oil in a large skillet (one that has a tight-fitting lid) over medium heat. Add the onions and sauté until translucent, about 5 minutes. Add the ground beef, breaking it up with the back of a spoon, and sauté until it loses its pink color, about 5 minutes. Add the allspice, salt, pepper, and cinnamon, and stir to incorporate into the meat. Reduce the heat to medium-low and continue sautéing the beef, breaking it up until it resembles coarse dark crumbs, about 5 minutes.

Raise the heat to high. Break the eggs over the beef and sprinkle the sumac on top. Reduce the heat to medium-low, cover the skillet, and cook for 15 minutes. Serve immediately.

Breakfast Potatoes with Eggs

MUFARAKAT BATATA BI BAYID

¼ cup extra virgin olive oil

¼ pound onions, chopped

1½ pounds small red potatoes, peeled and diced

Salt and black pepper, to taste

12 eggs

Fresh flat-leaf parsley leaves, for garnish

I *have fond memories of making this very old and beloved dish with my sisters on Saturday nights, when our parents went out to dinner. It is so simple to prepare, and was especially so for four young girls who set up the preparation in assembly-line fashion. My oldest sister, Ikram, was always the conductor, making sure the preparation was going smoothly while dicing the potatoes that I had peeled. Haifa, the second oldest, would set the table—a job that fell to her for all meals, with just family or when company came. My youngest sister, Maha, was the chief taster. Occasionally she would mix up a green salad. When all of the preparations were finished and the bread was warm in the oven, the olives were on the table, and the water glasses were filled, Ikram would begin adding the eggs to the skillet.*

If you have fresh herbs on hand, chop them up and add them to the skillet just before you add the eggs. For brunch or a light supper, serve Mufarakat Batata bi Bayid straight from the skillet with Arab flatbread, sliced tomatoes, and a Simple Salad or Baby Arugula Salad.

Serves 6

Divide the olive oil between two large skillets and heat over medium heat. Dividing the ingredients between the two skillets, add the onions and cook until soft, about 5 minutes. Add the potatoes, cover the skillets, and cook until they are fork-tender, 10 to 15 minutes.

Season the potato/onion mixture with salt and pepper. Break the eggs over the mixture and stir gently with a wooden spoon until the eggs are cooked to your liking—about 3 minutes for a soft, loose consistency and 5 minutes for a firmer one. Garnish with the parsley leaves, and serve.

Variation: To make a heartier version of this dish, add ½ pound ground beef to the pan after you sauté the onions. Sauté the beef, breaking it up with the back of a spoon, until it loses its pink color. Then proceed with the recipe.

Baked Eggs with Eggplant

MUFARAKAT BETINJAN

1 pound eggplant, peeled and
    cut into ½-inch cubes

2 tablespoons salt

½ cup olive oil

½ pound onions, finely chopped

5 cloves garlic, mashed

8 eggs

Salt and black pepper, to taste

This simple egg dish is my grandmother's idea of the perfect brunch for children. She used to make these sunny-side-up eggs for us when we visited, a ritual I continued with my own boys. Occasionally I substitute zucchini for the eggplant. The eggplant mixture can be made a day in advance and refrigerated; add the eggs and finish the dish in the oven just before serving time. Serve Mufarakat Betinjan with Arab flatbread and olives.
         Serves 6

Place the eggplant in a strainer and sprinkle the salt over it. Toss gently to coat the pieces with salt. Set the strainer in the sink or over a bowl and let it drain for 30 minutes. Then pat the eggplant dry with paper towels.

Preheat the oven to 350°F.

Heat the olive oil in a large ovenproof skillet over high heat. Add the onions and garlic and sauté, stirring, until soft and translucent, about 2 minutes. Reduce the heat to medium-high, add the eggplant, and cook, stirring frequently, until it is yellow-gold, about 10 minutes.

One egg at a time, break the eggs into a bowl and then slide them onto the eggplant. Season with salt and pepper. Cover the skillet, place it in the oven, and bake until the yolks are firm (they should not run when you pierce them with a fork), 4 minutes.

If the olive oil pools around the rim of the skillet, pat it with paper towels to absorb any excess. Serve hot, straight from the skillet.

Zucchini-Egg Cakes

AJET BAYD BI KOOSSA

1 pound zucchini, cut into 1-inch-thick rounds

¼ pound onions, coarsely chopped

3 cloves garlic

½ cup fresh flat-leaf parsley leaves

8 large eggs

Salt, to taste

1 teaspoon white pepper, or to taste

Canola oil, for frying

Chopped fresh parsley or mint, for garnish

These savory pancakes can be made as much as 2 days in advance and rewarmed or served cold. They can be part of a mezza spread, or served with a green salad for breakfast or brunch. Do not overcook the zucchini, or the batter will be too runny. Serve the pancakes with Arab flatbread. ***Makes 14 to 16 cakes***

Place the zucchini in a saucepan, add water to cover, and bring to a boil over high heat. Reduce the heat to low and simmer until just fork-tender, 10 minutes. Drain, and transfer the zucchini to the bowl of a food processor. Add the onions, garlic, and parsley, and pulse until the mixture is finely chopped. Then add the eggs, salt, and pepper, and pulse just until the eggs are incorporated.

Line a baking sheet with paper towels and set it nearby.

Fill a large, heavy-bottomed, nonstick skillet with canola oil to a depth of ½ inch, and heat over high heat. Working in batches of 2 or 3 cakes, pour the batter into the oil, ⅓ cup per cake, and fry until both sides are golden brown, 3 to 4 minutes per side. Using a slotted spoon, transfer the cakes to the paper towel–lined baking sheet. As you cook the remaining batches, skim off the brown foam that forms around the edges of the skillet, to keep the oil clean.

Serve warm or at room temperature, garnished with the parsley.

LENT AND FASTING

In the Arab Christian tradition, the main periods of fasting usually occur before important dates in the church calendar. In addition to the forty days of Lent before Easter Sunday, devout Christians fast for twenty-five days before Christmas Day and for the first two weeks in August, to mark the Feast of the Assumption, which is celebrated by the majority of Christian traditions on August 15.

Some Arab Christians choose to fast on a weekly basis year-round. The traditions of the Eastern and Western churches vary, as do their calendars. However, it is generally perceived that those following the Orthodox (Greek/Russian) traditions fast every Wednesday and Friday and exclude all animal products from their meals, whereas those who follow the Western (Roman) traditions fast on Fridays only and exclude meat and poultry but not fish, which is usually the main meal of the day.

During the forty days of Lent, fasting means strict abstinence from meat, animal fats, eggs, and treats like chocolate as well. In Lebanon and neighboring regions of the Eastern Mediterranean, where I lived and learned to cook, the abundance of fresh produce and the rich cuisine of vegetable and bean dishes mean that the meals of Lent, though meatless, are quite varied and delicious.

Lenten dishes include

- Roasted Eggplant Spread
- Stuffed Grape Leaves
- Fried Cauliflower
- Fava Bean Salad
- Eggplant Pomegranate Salad
- Orange Lentil Soup
- Brown Lentil Soup with Chard Leaves
- Warm Lentils with Rice
- Pureed Split Lentils
- Chickpeas with Yogurt
- Braised Fava Beans
- Bulgur and Fava Beans
- Spiced Bulgur with Tomatoes
- Pasta with Lentils
- Yellow Diamonds
- Fruit Salad with Rose Water

EASTER
THE CELEBRATION OF CHRIST'S RISING

For millions of Arab Christians, as for Christians all over the world, the observance of Easter is the most sacred time of the year. And though the specific rites differ among the various Christian denominations in the Arab world, the celebration of Christ's resurrection is commonly known by the Arabic name *Eid al Fes-eh*.

In Middle Eastern villages, a lamb is slaughtered in celebration of Easter and food is distributed to poorer families. Church bells ring, children color eggs and wear their best clothes to church on Sunday morning, and the whole family gathers for lunch at the patriarchal family home.

In preparation for Easter Sunday, an entire week of rituals takes place in the household. The women in the family, as well as female friends and neighbors, get together several times during the week to prepare the lunch menu, which will consist mainly of meat, poultry, and fish—all that is forbidden during Lent.

One or two days of this week are dedicated to making *ka'ak* and *ma'amoul,* cookies baked especially for Easter. Consisting of a mixture of semolina and butter, they are formed in three different shapes and stuffed with three types of filling. Each shape is symbolic of Christ's suffering: a ridged donut-shaped cookie (stuffed with dates) represents the crown of thorns Jesus wore; round cookies (stuffed with walnuts) symbolize the stones that were thrown at Him while He carried the cross; and an oblong cookie (stuffed with pistachio nuts) represents the tomb where Jesus' body was buried after His crucifixion.

The task of making the *ma'amoul* is meticulous and time-consuming, and is a lot more fun when shared with friends. Mothers and daughters, cousins and aunts, all gather in one kitchen to share the work: one will mind the oven, one will chop the nuts, and one will measure out portions of semolina . . . They sing hymns and catch up on news and gossip while their fingers are at work shaping and decorating the *ma'amoul,* often with beautiful, intricate designs.

The week before Easter is a solemn time and is treated by some Arab Christians as a period of mourning. Some women wear black clothes in remembrance of Christ. Churches hold mass more often than usual and leave their doors open for the entire week. On the Thursday preceding Easter, known as *Khamees al-Ghusol* (Cleansing, or Maundy, Thursday), the priest washes the feet of twelve children, or the Archbishop washes the feet of twelve priests, in remembrance of Jesus' washing the feet of the twelve apostles as a demonstration of His humility before them, before being betrayed that evening. The following day, Good Friday, or *Jima'a al-Hazineh,* the last day of fasting, is also a sad and solemn occasion, as it represents the day Christ was nailed to the cross.

On Saturday the veil of sadness is lifted as children get together to paint and decorate eggs. When we were young, celebrating the holiday with our Christian friends, we colored the eggs using natural coloring from beets or from red or yellow onion peel. Nowadays artificial coloring is widely available and makes the task easier. These carefully prepared and decorated eggs will be the cause of much laughter the following day, when children and adults compete to crack each other's eggs: The eggs are offered around when family members and friends gather for lunch on Easter day. Each person chooses an egg and challenges a brother, parent, or neighbor to crack their eggs together. The participant with the last remaining unbroken egg is declared the winner.

Some people choose to break the fast at midday

on Saturday—the time when Jesus' tomb was discovered empty. Others wait to break the fast on Easter Sunday, the day Christ is declared risen.

No matter which tradition is followed, Easter Sunday is the main day of celebration, the end of Lenten fasting and the culmination of weeks of preparation. On Easter day people attend a celebratory mass and later visit each other to offer their good wishes. Families get together for lunch, and children compete to see who holds the strongest egg.

Easter Sunday Lunch

- Chickpea Dip
- Zucchini with Bread and Mint
- Meat Pies
- Eggplant Salad
- Chicken Freka with Ground Beef
- Lamb with Rice and Yogurt
- Baked Whole Red Snapper
- Warm Lentils with Rice
- Holy Bread
- Arab Flatbread
- Olives
- Pastries with Walnuts, Pistachios, and Dates
- Bread Pudding with Syrup
- Semolina Pistachio Layer Cake
- Arab Coffee
- White Coffee

Soups and Stews

ALTHOUGH MY MOTHER made soups and stews only when someone was sick, for new mothers, and for those breaking the fast during Ramadan, she had a rather impressive repertoire of recipes. We never tired of her soups because the variety was so great: grain and bean soups, chunky beef and lamb stews, pureed and rustic vegetable soups, soups made with freka, a smoky-flavored roasted wheat, and soups prepared with lentils and chickpeas.

It was not until I began attending boarding school that I came to love eating a piping hot bowl of soup for lunch or dinner. During the winter months, I enjoyed a bowl of thick, creamy vegetable lentil soup almost every day. The secret to the distinctive flavor of this and most meat- and poultry-based soups is the stock. Arab soups begin with stocks infused with allspice and cardamom, to which the freshest vegetables, lamb or beef, chicken, or fish is added.

Rice, bulgur, couscous, noodles, beans, lentils, and chickpeas are flavorful thickeners, while spices, including cumin, coriander, paprika, and cinnamon, are typical seasonings. Often a squeeze of lemon, pomegranate syrup, sumac, or, in the case of Fish Soup, a drizzle of apple cider vinegar, is added to brighten the flavor just before serving. As with all Arab dishes, garnishes are essential, from a sprig of parsley and a pinch of chopped cilantro to some fried pine nuts or chopped scallions.

Spiced Chicken Stock

MARAQ DAJAJ

One 3-pound chicken *or* 2 skin-on, bone-in breasts, rinsed and patted dry

2 pounds onions, quartered

3 cardamom pods, *or* ¼ teaspoon ground cardamom

Two 3-inch cinnamon sticks

1 tablespoon ground allspice

5 black peppercorns

2 bay leaves

1 teaspoon salt

This basic chicken stock is assertively flavored with fragrant cardamom, cinnamon, and allspice—the trinity of spices in Arab cuisine. You may want to tailor the quantities of the spices to suit your own taste, but an Arab cook would never omit any of them. Reserve the succulent chicken meat for sandwiches and salads. If you aren't using the stock right away, cool it in an ice water bath in order to prevent bacteria growth. The stock will keep, tightly covered, in the freezer for 6 months. Thaw frozen stock in the refrigerator or the microwave—not at room temperature—before using. **Makes 3 quarts**

Combine all the ingredients in a large stockpot and add water to cover by 2 inches. Cover, and bring to a boil. Then reduce the heat to medium-low and simmer for 2 hours, adding water as necessary to keep the chicken covered by 2 inches. Skim the foam off the surface of the stock as it simmers until no more foam is collecting there. Partially uncover the pot for the second hour of cooking.

Remove the chicken from the stock. Strain the liquid through a fine-mesh sieve into a bowl. Allow it to cool, and then refrigerate. When the stock is thoroughly chilled, remove the layer of fat that has congealed on the surface.

Use within 2 days, or freeze.

Chicken Soup with Vermicelli

SHORABAT DAJAJ BI SHAIRIYEH

One 4-pound chicken (or parts), rinsed and patted dry

1 pound onions, quartered

Two 3-inch cinnamon sticks

6 cardamom pods

1½ teaspoons salt, plus more if needed

½ teaspoon white pepper, plus more if needed

1 tablespoon allspice berries

2 bay leaves

1 cup vermicelli pieces (thin spaghetti broken into 1-inch lengths)

Fresh flat-leaf parsley leaves, for garnish

Every mother in the Arab world knows how to make this healing soup, fragrant with allspice, cardamom, and cinnamon. And as soon as her daughters or daughters-in-law become mothers, she teaches them how to make it too, to "build the bones back," as the older women say and to nourish their own children when they are sick.

When we celebrate Christmas with our Christian friends, we serve a special version of this soup for the festive holiday meal: Baked Kibeh Balls and some crushed mastic (tied in cheesecloth) are added to the simmering soup about 30 minutes before it is taken off the heat. All of the Kibeh Balls have been hollowed and sealed closed without a filling— except one, which is filled with pitted olives and is good luck for the person who finds it in his soup bowl. Serves 6 to 8

Combine the chicken, onions, cinnamon sticks, cardamom pods, salt, pepper, allspice berries, bay leaves, and 9 cups water in a large pot and bring to a boil over high heat. Skim off the foam as it forms on the surface of the liquid. Reduce the heat to medium, cover the pot, and cook until the chicken is tender, about 45 minutes. Remove from the heat. Remove the chicken from the pot and set it aside until it is cool enough to handle.

FAVORITE CHICKEN SOUPS

For every country in the Arab world, there is a different version of chicken soup. In any of them, you might find the vermicelli replaced with short-grain rice, bulgur, or couscous.

In Tunisia, tomato paste and turmeric are added to the strained stock, and a beaten egg is added during the last 5 minutes of cooking.

In Yemen, equal amounts of fenugreek, cumin, turmeric, and Yemeni Spice Mix (page 41) flavor the strained stock.

In Libya, chopped tomatoes, tomato paste, chickpeas, and cayenne are added to the strained stock, and the soup is garnished with dried mint.

In Iraq, crushed garlic, cilantro, chopped tomatoes, and chickpeas are traditional additions to the strained stock.

In Morocco, tomato paste, chopped tomatoes, chopped celery, cinnamon, saffron, and a boiled egg are added to the strained stock.

Gently tear the chicken meat off the bones and shred it into bite-size pieces. Place the shredded chicken in a saucepan and set a strainer over it. Pour the stock through the strainer into the pan; you should have about 8 cups of liquid. Bring the stock to a boil over high heat. Stir in the vermicelli, reduce the heat to medium, and cook for 15 minutes. Season with more salt and pepper, if desired. Ladle into soup bowls, garnish with the parsley, and serve.

Moroccan Chicken Soup

SHORABAT DAJAJ WA HUMMUS

*C*hickpeas are used in many Moroccan soups, not only to add texture
but also to make them hearty enough to serve as a main course.
You can use canned chickpeas with this recipe, but be sure to rinse
them well before adding them to the soup.   *Serves 6 to 8*

1 cup dried chickpeas, soaked
    for 6 hours or as long as
    overnight (see page 52),
    drained and rinsed *or* one
    15-ounce can chickpeas,
    drained and rinsed

2 tablespoons olive oil

1 medium onion, diced

6 cloves garlic, mashed

2½ pounds chicken, whole or
    parts, rinsed and patted dry

2 bay leaves

½ teaspoon ground cumin

1 teaspoon hot paprika

½ teaspoon black pepper

2 tablespoons tomato paste

2 teaspoons harissa (see page
    21)

10 cups boiling water

¼ teaspoon ground cinnamon

¼ teaspoon ground cardamom

2 teaspoons salt

1 cup couscous

2 teaspoons dried mint,
    preferably spearmint

Cook the chickpeas: If using dried chickpeas, put them in a pot,
add water to cover, and bring to a boil over high heat. Cook,
skimming the foam from the surface until no more appears, about
15 minutes. Then reduce the heat, cover the pot, and simmer until
the beans are tender and are easily crushed with the back of a
spoon, 1½ hours. Drain and set aside. If using canned chickpeas,
rinse them 3 times under cold water, place them in a pot with water
to cover, bring to a boil, and then drain immediately; set them
aside.

While the chickpeas are cooking, heat the olive oil in a large pot
over high heat. Add the onions and garlic, and sauté until soft and
golden, about 2 minutes. Add the chicken, bay leaves, cumin,
paprika, pepper, tomato paste, and harissa. Stir, and cook until the
chicken loses its pink color, about 5 minutes. Add the boiling water,
cover the pot, and bring to a boil. Skim the foam from the surface
of the liquid. Reduce the heat to medium, cover the pot, and cook
for 1 hour.

Remove the chicken and bay leaves from the pot, and set the
chicken aside until it is cool enough to handle. Then pull the
chicken meat off the bone and cut it into 1-inch pieces. Return the
cut-up chicken to the pot and add the chickpeas, cinnamon,
cardamom, and salt. Simmer over medium heat for 10 minutes.
Add the couscous and simmer for 10 minutes more. Ladle the soup
into bowls, and garnish with the dried mint.

Orange Lentil Soup

SHORABAT ADAS

*C*umin lends a unique flavor and aroma to this popular Ramadan soup. Sometimes, for a heartier version, I add Kafta balls just after I puree the lentils and let them cook together. Lemon juice is thought to aid the body in absorbing the iron in the lentils, so I always squeeze some into each serving—it brightens the flavor, too.

Shorabat Adas is delicious the next day; just add a little water to the cold lentils, which will be very thick, before reheating it. You can freeze it, too, in a tightly covered rigid container for up to 6 months.

Serves 6 to 8

2 tablespoons extra virgin olive oil, plus more for the croutons

1 medium onion, coarsely chopped

2 cups orange lentils, picked clean and rinsed

6 cups Spiced Chicken Stock (page 125), Beef Stock (page 131), *or* low-sodium canned chicken or beef broth

3 slices whole-wheat or white bread, crusts removed

2 teaspoons ground cumin

1 teaspoon salt

½ teaspoon white pepper

Lemon wedges, for serving

Red radishes, for serving

Olives, for serving

Heat the olive oil in a large pot over medium heat. Add the onions and sauté until soft, about 5 minutes. Add the lentils and stir to coat them in the oil. Add the stock and bring it to a boil. Then reduce the heat to medium, cover the pot, and cook, removing any foam that rises to the surface, until the lentils are soft, about 45 minutes. Remove the pot from the heat and set it aside to cool for 15 minutes.

Meanwhile, preheat the oven to 400°F.

Brush olive oil over both sides of the bread slices, and cut them into small cubes. Place the cubes in a single layer in a baking dish, and toast in the oven until golden and crisp, about 7 minutes. Set the croutons aside.

Transfer the lentils, with their liquid, to a blender, in batches if necessary, and puree. Return the soup to the pot. (Alternatively, puree the lentils right in the pot with an immersion blender.) Add the cumin, salt, and pepper and give the soup a good stir. Bring it to a boil over medium-high heat, stirring frequently. Reduce the heat to low and simmer, uncovered, for 15 minutes.

Ladle the soup into bowls, and sprinkle a few croutons on top of each serving. Serve with the lemon wedges, radishes, and olives alongside.

Variation: Mix 1 cup low-fat yogurt, ¼ cup fresh lemon juice, and the grated zest of 1 lemon together in a small bowl. Spoon a bit into each bowl before serving.

Lentil Soup with Chard Leaves

SHORABAT ADAS BI HAMOD

I usually make this soup for a light lunch with a refreshing Mixed Vegetable Salad as an accompaniment. Syrian and Lebanese cooks combine lentils with chard, but in North Africa, kale or spinach is common. Present-day Arabs often use baby spinach in place of the chard because it requires just a quick rinse and no chopping.   **Serves 6 to 8**

2 cups brown lentils, picked over

1 large onion, chopped

11 cups Spiced Chicken Stock (page 125) *or* low-sodium canned broth

2 teaspoons salt, plus more if needed

2 large potatoes, cut into ½-inch cubes

1 pound chard or spinach leaves, rinsed, stemmed, and coarsely chopped

½ teaspoon black pepper

¼ cup extra virgin olive oil

5 cloves garlic, mashed

1 teaspoon ground coriander

1 teaspoon ground cumin

¾ cup chopped fresh cilantro

1 tablespoon all-purpose flour

¼ cup fresh lemon juice, plus more if needed

Lemon slices, for garnish

Olives, for serving

Rinse the lentils in cold water and drain in a colander. Combine them with the onions and stock in a large pot, cover, and bring to a boil over high heat. Reduce the heat to medium, uncover the pot, and cook for 30 minutes, skimming the foam from the surface. Add the salt and potatoes, reduce the heat to low, cover the pot, and cook, stirring occasionally, for 15 minutes. Add the chard in batches, submerging it with the back of a spoon. Add more salt, if needed, and the pepper. Cook, stirring occasionally, until all of the potatoes sink to the bottom of the pot, about 15 minutes.

Meanwhile, heat the olive oil in a skillet over medium heat. Add the garlic, coriander, cumin, and cilantro, and sauté until the cilantro wilts, about 5 minutes. Add the flour and stir until it is dissolved. Set the skillet aside.

Add the cilantro mixture to the soup and simmer for 10 minutes. Stir in the lemon juice. Taste, and add more salt and lemon juice if needed. Ladle the soup into deep bowls, garnish with the lemon slices, and serve with olives alongside.

Note: This soup will keep, tightly covered, in the freezer for up to 3 months. To reheat it, stir 1 cup of water into the pot just before putting it on the stove.

The stems of the chard leaves can be made into an appetizer or side dish: Cut the stems into bite-size strips and wash them well. Place them in a saucepan, and add a small amount of salt and water to cover. Bring to a boil, then reduce the heat and cook until tender. Drain, and allow to cool thoroughly. Make a small amount of the Tahini sauce and add it to the cooked stems. Serve it alone or with soft Arab flatbread.

Beef Stock

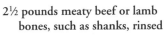

MARAKIT LAHMEH

2½ pounds meaty beef or lamb
    bones, such as shanks, rinsed

2 carrots, quartered lengthwise

1 large onion, peeled down to
    one layer of skin, quartered

1 celery stalk, quartered
    lengthwise

2 tablespoons canola oil

1 tablespoon black peppercorns

3 cardamom pods, crushed

1 teaspoon ground allspice

2 bay leaves

Salt, to taste

Cardamom and allspice, two of the most used spices in the Arab pantry, give this fragrant stock its distinctive Middle Eastern flavor. I often double this recipe and freeze a batch so that I will always have some on hand. If you aren't using the stock right away, cool it quickly in an ice water bath in order to prevent bacteria growth. Similarly, thaw frozen stock in the refrigerator or in the microwave, not on the counter. Trim the cooked meat from the bones and reserve it for use in soups, sandwiches, and salads. ***Makes about 2½ quarts***

Preheat the oven to 450°F.

Place the beef bones in a large shallow roasting pan and surround them with the carrots, onions, and celery. Drizzle the canola oil over the vegetables and toss to coat them with the oil. Roast for 30 to 45 minutes.

Transfer the bones and vegetables, with any pan juices, to a large pot, and add water to cover by 2 inches. Add the peppercorns, cardamom pods, allspice, and bay leaves, and bring to a boil over high heat. Reduce the heat to medium and simmer, uncovered, for 1½ to 2 hours, skimming the foam from the surface until the stock is clear. Strain, and season to taste with the salt.

If you are not using it right away, let the stock cool (see headnote) and then refrigerate it for up to 2 days or freeze it for up to 6 months.

Tomato Soup with Vermicelli

SHORABAT BANDORA

My cousin Leila, who lives in Jordan, always makes this soup during Ramadan because it is light after a day of fasting. Have your butcher trim the lamb shank for you, and ask him to give you a few of the bones for flavoring the soup.

Serves 6

1 tablespoon canola oil

¾ pound onions, coarsely chopped

1 pound lamb shank meat, cut into 1-inch cubes, bones reserved

2 pounds tomatoes, peeled, seeded, and chopped

2 cups Beef Stock (page 131) *or* one 15-ounce can low-sodium broth

2 tablespoons tomato paste

½ cup vermicelli pieces (thin spaghetti broken into 1-inch lengths)

Salt and black pepper, to taste

Chopped fresh parsley *or* dried mint, preferably spearmint, for garnish

Heat the canola oil in a large stockpot over medium heat. Add the onions and meat, and sauté until the onions are soft and the meat loses its pink color, about 15 minutes. Add the tomatoes, shank bones, stock, and tomato paste. Cover and bring to a boil. Then reduce the heat to medium and simmer until the meat is tender, about 1¼ hours.

Using a slotted spoon, remove the bones from the soup. Add the vermicelli and cook, uncovered, until it is tender, 5 to 7 minutes. Season with salt and pepper, and garnish with the parsley. Serve hot.

Rice and Meatball Soup

SHORABAT RUZ BI LAHIM

This soup is traditionally served to break the Lenten fast during the Easter season. It is also a typical winter lunch for children and is often recommended for new mothers. I don't like to use canned broth here because the soup relies on the quality of the stock for its flavor.

Serve 6 to 8

Vegetable oil, for the baking sheet

1 pound ground beef

2 teaspoons salt, plus more if needed

1 teaspoon white pepper, plus more if needed

½ teaspoon ground cardamom seeds (see page 15)

¼ cup pine nuts

7 cups Beef Stock (page 131)

½ cup short-grain rice

Chopped fresh parsley, for garnish

Preheat the oven to 400°F. Coat a rimmed baking sheet with vegetable oil.

Combine the beef, 1 teaspoon of the salt, ½ teaspoon of the pepper, and the cardamom in a food processor and pulse until the mixture is smooth. Transfer the mixture to a bowl, add the pine nuts, and mix them in with your hands. Working with about 1 tablespoon of the beef mixture at a time, form the mixture into walnut-size meatballs and set them on the prepared baking sheet.

Bake the meatballs, turning them once, until they are a soft brown and the juices have been absorbed, about 15 minutes. Remove the baking sheet from the oven and cover it with foil to keep the meatballs warm.

In a medium saucepan, combine the stock, remaining 1 teaspoon salt, and remaining ½ teaspoon pepper. Bring to a boil over high heat. Add the rice and the meatballs, and give the soup a good stir. Then reduce the heat to medium, cover the pan, and simmer until the rice is tender, about 45 minutes. Taste, and add salt and pepper if needed. Transfer the soup to a serving bowl, garnish with the parsley, and serve.

Beef and Freka Soup

SHORABAT FREKA

2 cups freka (see page 20),
    picked over

¼ cup vegetable oil

1 medium onion, finely
    chopped

2½ pounds beef shanks, rinsed
    and patted dry

1 teaspoon ground cardamom

5 cardamom pods

2 bay leaves

One 3-inch cinnamon stick

1 teaspoon ground allspice

1 teaspoon black pepper

10 cups boiling water

1 tablespoon salt, plus more if
    needed

Lemon wedges

¼ cup chopped fresh flat-leaf
    parsley

The distinctive flavor of this soup comes from freka, *the green wheat kernels commonly used in Palestine and Jordan. Open-fire roasting of newly harvested wheat kernels is what gives freka its subtle smoky flavor. During the roasting process, some of the kernels break; these are gathered and used for soup, while the intact kernels are kept to cook in the same manner as rice. I call for whole freka grains in this recipe, however, since you are unlikely to come across a quantity of soup-grade freka. Beef and lamb shanks are traditional soup starters in the Middle East, but I occasionally substitute chicken. If you want to flavor this soup with a bit of tomato, as Jordanian cooks do, add 1½ pounds coarsely chopped peeled tomatoes when you add the salt.*　　*Serves 6 to 8*

Wash the freka: Fill two medium bowls with water. Put the freka in one bowl, swirl it around with your hand, then lift the grains out and transfer them to the second bowl. Repeat, refilling the first bowl with fresh water until there is no debris on the bottom of the bowl. Drain the freka and set it aside.

Heat the vegetable oil in a large pot over medium heat. Add the onions and sauté until they are soft and translucent, about 5 minutes. Add the beef shanks, ground cardamom, cardamom pods, bay leaves, cinnamon stick, allspice, and pepper. Stir to coat the meat, about 3 minutes. Then add the boiling water, cover the pot, and bring to a boil.

Skim the foam from the surface of the soup. Reduce the heat to medium, cover, and cook for 45 to 60 minutes.

Reduce the heat to low, add the freka and salt, cover, and simmer until the meat is fork-tender, 30 to 45 minutes. Taste, and add more salt if needed. The freka should be slightly crunchy.

Uncover the pot and remove the shank bones, pulling the meat away from them. Cook for 2 to 3 minutes. Ladle into soup bowls, squeeze a little lemon juice into each, garnish with the parsley, and serve.

Fish Soup

SHORABAT AL SAMAK

Cardamom perfumes this chunky fish soup, which is popular in the northern Lebanon port city of Tripoli and all along the Gulf coast, where fish is available year-round. It originated the way most fish soups do—as a way to use leftover pieces of fish. Serve it with lemon wedges and toasted pieces of Arab flatbread. **Serves 6**

½ cup olive oil

1 small yellow onion, finely chopped

3 ribs celery, finely chopped

1 carrot, finely chopped

2 cloves garlic, mashed

1 pound tomatoes, peeled, seeded, and finely chopped

¼ cup cider vinegar

Grated zest of 1 orange

½ cup chopped fresh cilantro

½ teaspoon saffron threads

½ teaspoon ground cardamom

½ teaspoon cayenne pepper (optional)

1 tablespoon plus 2 teaspoons salt

½ teaspoon black pepper

8 cups boiling water

¼ cup sesame paste (tahini)

½ cup fresh lemon juice

2 pounds sea bass, grouper, snapper, or cod, cut into 1-inch pieces and rinsed

16 large shrimp (16 to 20 per pound), peeled and deveined

3 tablespoons chopped fresh parsley

Heat the olive oil in a large pot over high heat. Add the onions, celery, carrots, and garlic, and sauté until the vegetables are soft, about 10 minutes. Add the tomatoes, vinegar, orange zest, cilantro, saffron, cardamom, cayenne, if using, salt, and black pepper, and sauté until fragrant, about 5 minutes. Then add the boiling water and bring to a boil. Reduce the heat to medium-high, cover the pot, and cook for 15 minutes.

Remove the pot from the heat, and stir in the sesame paste and lemon juice. Puree the mixture, in batches, in a blender, and return the puree to the pot. (Alternatively, use an immersion blender to puree it right in the pot.) Set the pot over medium-high heat, and add the fish and shrimp. Cook until the fish begins to flake with the prick of a fork and the shrimp is pink, about 7 minutes. Garnish with the parsley, and serve hot.

Meatball Stew

YAKHNI LAHMEH BI DEBIS RUMAN

½ teaspoon ground cinnamon

½ teaspoon ground allspice

½ teaspoon ground cardamom

1 teaspoon salt

¼ teaspoon black pepper

1½ pounds lean ground beef

¾ pound onions, finely chopped

1 tablespoon butter

¼ cup pine nuts

1 pound pearl onions, ends trimmed and peeled, *or* one 15-ounce package frozen pearl onions, thawed and drained

3 tablespoons all-purpose flour

5 cups boiling water

1 tablespoon pomegranate syrup

*P*omegranate syrup flavors this filling stew, which makes an excellent meal when accompanied by a green salad. If you can't find pomegranate syrup, substitute 2 tablespoons lemon juice or verjus. I make this for weekday dinners with my family; for company, I add desert truffles, the best of which grow in Syria, where the Bedouins pray for lightning during truffle season because they believe the bolts force the truffles to pop up out of the sand. You can find canned desert truffles in Middle Eastern groceries. To serve Yakhni Lahmeh, ladle it over rice with vermicelli, or mashed potatoes.   *Serves 6*

Preheat the oven to 400°F.

Combine the cinnamon, allspice, cardamom, salt, and pepper in a small bowl and stir together. Combine the beef, chopped onions, and 2 teaspoons of the spice mixture in a large bowl and mix well, using your hands. Working with about 1 tablespoon of the mixture at a time, roll the meat between your palms to form it into balls. Place the meatballs in a single layer in a broiler pan without letting them touch each other. Roast, turning once, for 15 minutes.

Meanwhile, melt the butter in a large skillet over medium heat. Add the pine nuts and sauté, stirring constantly, until they are pale gold, about 45 seconds. Using a slotted spoon, transfer the pine nuts to a plate. Add the pearl onions to the same skillet and sauté until they are soft and translucent, about 5 minutes. Transfer them to a plate, using a slotted spoon. Add the flour to the skillet and whisk to dissolve it in the butter. Add the boiling water and stir to blend. Add the remaining 2¼ teaspoons spice mixture and the reserved pearl onions to the skillet. Cover and simmer until the liquid coats the back of a spoon, about 15 minutes.

Add the meatballs and simmer for 10 minutes. Stir in the pomegranate syrup and remove the skillet from the heat. Transfer the stew to a serving bowl or soup terrine, garnish with the pine nuts, and serve.

Eggplant and Pomegranate Stew

TABBAKH ROHO

Tabbakh roho means "it cooks by itself," and this stew really does. Not only is it easy to make, it is economical and doesn't require any special ingredients. This Syrian stew came into being the way many of the best dishes do, by tossing a little bit of this and a little bit of that—essentially whatever vegetables and meat were on hand, combined with eggplant and pomegranate syrup, which are found in every Arab kitchen—into a pot and letting it cook without much intervention. Add Kibeh Balls to the stew for an even heartier version. Serve the stew over white rice. Serves 6

3 pounds eggplant, halved and cut into 1-inch chunks

1 tablespoon plus 2 teaspoons salt

4 tablespoons vegetable oil

2 pounds stew beef or lamb (trimmed from the leg)

½ teaspoon black pepper

½ teaspoon white pepper

½ teaspoon ground allspice

Boiling water

2 medium onions, halved and thinly sliced

1 pound carrots, cut into 1-inch-thick rounds

1 green bell pepper, seeded and cut into 1-inch pieces

2 tablespoons tomato paste

3 cloves garlic, mashed

2 teaspoons pomegranate syrup

1 teaspoon dried mint

Place the eggplant in a colander and sprinkle 1 tablespoon of the salt over it. Set the colander over a bowl or in the sink to drain.

Heat 1 tablespoon of the vegetable oil in a large pot over high heat. Add the beef and cook, turning, until it is browned on all sides, about 10 minutes. Add ¼ teaspoon each of the black pepper, white pepper, and allspice, and turn the meat to coat it in the spices. Add boiling water to cover by 1 inch. Bring the water to a boil, skimming the foam from the surface. Cover, reduce the heat to medium, and cook for 30 minutes.

Meanwhile, heat the remaining 3 tablespoons vegetable oil in a large pot over medium heat. Add the onions and sauté until they release their juices and are soft, about 5 minutes. Pat the eggplant dry. Add the eggplant, carrots, and green peppers and cook, stirring occasionally, until they are soft, about 10 minutes. Add the tomato paste and the meat with its liquid, and give the mixture a good stir. Add the remaining ¼ teaspoon each of black pepper, white pepper, and allspice. Bring the stew to a boil. Then reduce the heat to medium, cover the pot, and cook until the meat is tender, about 1 hour.

Stir in the garlic, pomegranate syrup, mint, and remaining 2 teaspoons salt. Taste, and adjust the seasonings as needed.

Eggplant with Ground Beef

MONAZALLET BI ASWAD

1 pound eggplant, sliced into
    1-inch-thick rounds

Salt

2 tablespoons canola oil

½ pound minced lean beef

½ pound onions, finely chopped

¼ teaspoon black pepper

1 pound tomatoes, sliced into
    1-inch-thick rounds

2 green bell peppers, seeded and
    sliced into 1-inch-thick rings

1 teaspoon pomegranate syrup

1 cup Beef Stock (page 131) *or*
    low-sodium canned broth

This classic Middle Eastern combination is prepared slightly differently from one country to the next. I make the Syrian version, which is flavored with tangy pomegranate syrup and served over white rice. To make the Iraqi version, add a cup of cooked chickpeas and serve it in deep soup bowls lined with pieces of fluffy flatbread.

Serves 6 to 8

Place the eggplant slices in a colander set over a bowl. Sprinkle salt over the eggplant and set it aside for at least 1 hour.

Meanwhile, preheat the oven to 450°F.

Pat the eggplant slices dry with paper towels, and arrange them in a single layer in an ovenproof dish. Fill any large gaps with cut pieces of eggplant. Drizzle 1 tablespoon of the canola oil over the eggplant and roast, turning the slices once, until they are golden and puffy, 3 to 4 minutes per side.

Reduce the oven temperature to 350°F.

Heat the remaining 1 tablespoon canola oil in a medium skillet over high heat. Add the beef and onions, and sauté until the meat loses its pink color and the onions are soft, about 5 minutes. Season with ½ teaspoon salt and the pepper.

Spoon the meat mixture evenly over the eggplant. Arrange the tomatoes on top, followed by the green peppers. Stir the pomegranate syrup thoroughly into the stock, and pour it over the vegetables. Cover the dish with aluminum foil and bake for 40 minutes. Then uncover, and bake until the broth has thickened to a light sauce, 20 to 25 minutes. Serve hot.

Tomato Stew

BANDORA YAKHNI

¼ cup olive oil

¼ cup pine nuts

2 pounds onions, finely
chopped

1 pound ground beef

½ teaspoon ground allspice

½ teaspoon ground cinnamon

1 tablespoon salt, plus more if
needed

½ teaspoon black pepper, plus
more if needed

4 pounds ripe tomatoes, peeled,
seeded, and chopped

There are as many variations of this stew as there are cooks who make it. My version is thick with ground beef and tomatoes and tastes faintly of cinnamon and allspice, while my mother prefers lamb and seasons hers heavily with cinnamon. Serve the stew over white rice or rice with vermicelli.   *Serves 6*

Heat the olive oil in a large skillet over high heat. Add the pine nuts and sauté, stirring constantly, until golden and fragrant, about 45 seconds. Using a slotted spoon, transfer the pine nuts to a paper towel–lined plate.

Add the onions to the skillet and sauté over medium heat until soft and translucent, about 5 minutes. Add the beef and sauté, breaking it up with a wooden spoon, until it loses its pink color, 7 minutes. Stir in the allspice, cinnamon, salt, and pepper. Sauté, continuing to break the meat up with the back of a spoon, until it is a deep mahogany color and resembles coarse crumbs, 10 minutes. Stir in the tomatoes. Cover, and cook until the beef and tomatoes come together, about 15 minutes. Reduce the heat to medium-low and simmer with the lid ajar until the sauce thickens slightly, about 10 minutes. Taste, and add more salt and pepper if needed. Transfer the stew to a deep serving dish or soup terrine, garnish with the pine nuts, and serve.

Lamb and Pea Stew

YAKHNI BAZILLA

¼ cup plus 2 tablespoons olive oil

1 pound lamb shank or shoulder meat, trimmed

1 pound onions, coarsely chopped

10 cups boiling water

1 teaspoon ground allspice

½ teaspoon black pepper

1 pound carrots, sliced into ½-inch-thick rounds

2 pounds fresh or frozen peas

Two 15-ounce cans tomato sauce

Salt, to taste

5 cloves garlic, mashed

1 packed cup chopped fresh cilantro

This chunky stew varies from country to country, primarily in the seasonings that are added in the final minutes of cooking. In Iraq you won't find sautéed cilantro swirled in at the end as it is here, while in the Gulf States the warm flavors of curry and saffron infuse the stew. However you choose to season this stew, the slower you cook it, the better it will be. Though it can be made in as little as 90 minutes, Yakhni Bazilla benefits from a long session over low heat, so let it simmer for as long as you can before serving it over white rice. If you have the extra time, cook the meat on low heat for 60 minutes instead of 20 minutes.

Serves 6

Heat 2 tablespoons of the olive oil in a large pot over high heat. Add the lamb and onions and sauté, stirring occasionally, until the meat is browned all over, about 10 minutes. Add the boiling water and bring it back to a boil, skimming the foam from the surface as it appears. Reduce the heat to medium, add the allspice and pepper, and cook, covered, for 20 minutes. Then reduce the heat to low and simmer for another 25 minutes. Add the carrots, peas, tomato sauce, and salt, and cook for 30 minutes.

Heat the remaining ¼ cup olive oil in a skillet over high heat. Add the garlic and cilantro and sauté, stirring, until the mixture is fragrant and the cilantro has brightened, about 2 minutes. Add the cilantro mixture to the stew and stir to incorporate it. Simmer, partially covered, for 10 minutes. Serve hot.

Spinach and Ground Lamb Stew

SABANEKH YAKHNI

2 tablespoons vegetable oil

1 pound onions, coarsely chopped

1 pound ground lamb or beef

1 tablespoon ground allspice

1 teaspoon black pepper, plus more if needed

2 teaspoons salt, plus more if needed

2 pounds fresh spinach, rinsed, drained, and chopped *or two* 10-ounce packages frozen chopped spinach, thawed and well drained

4 cloves garlic, mashed

¼ cup whole milk

½ cup fresh lemon juice

½ cup fried pine nuts (see page 43)

This stew—a typical lunch offering—is served with rice and plain yogurt, common accompaniments with most Middle Eastern stews. My grandmother used to pour a cup of milk into the pot during the last half hour of cooking; she said it not only made the stew taste better, but it promoted better absorption of the minerals in the spinach. Indeed, a cup of milk does add richness to the broth, so if you are inclined, stir some in. Serve Sabanekh Yakhni with a Simple Salad for a healthy lunch.   *Serves 6*

Heat the vegetable oil in a stockpot over medium heat. Add the onions and sauté until soft and translucent, about 5 minutes. Add the lamb and sauté, breaking it up with a wooden spoon, until it loses its pink color, about 7 minutes. Stir in the allspice, pepper, and salt. Cook, continuing to break up the meat with the back of a spoon, until it is a deep mahogany color and resembles coarse crumbs, 10 minutes.

Add the spinach and 1 cup water. Cook, covered, over high heat until the meat has lost all of its pink color and the spinach has wilted, about 20 minutes. Add the garlic, give the mixture a good stir, and cook for 15 minutes more. Then reduce the heat to medium, add the milk, and cook, stirring once or twice, for 5 minutes. Taste, and add more salt and pepper if needed. Remove the pot from the heat and stir in the lemon juice. Ladle the stew into rimmed soup bowls, garnish with the pine nuts, and serve hot.

Okra Stew

YAKHNI BAMYEH

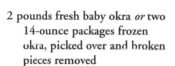

2 pounds fresh baby okra *or* two 14-ounce packages frozen okra, picked over and broken pieces removed

⅔ cup plus 2 tablespoons canola oil

2 medium onions (about 1 pound), finely chopped

2 pounds boneless lamb shanks, cut into thirds

1 pound beef neck bones

4 cups boiling water

½ teaspoon ground allspice

½ teaspoon ground coriander

¼ teaspoon ground cardamom

½ teaspoon salt, plus more if needed

½ teaspoon black pepper, plus more if needed

Two 15-ounce cans tomato sauce

7 cloves garlic, mashed

1 jalapeño pepper, seeded and chopped

1 packed cup chopped fresh cilantro leaves

2 tablespoons fresh lemon juice

Basmati Rice (page 164)

Yakhni Bamyeh is popular in Iraq, where okra is abundant. I never ate this stew as a child because my mother and grandmother were not particularly fond of it, but after I was married I learned how to make it because it is one of Aref's favorite. "He who lives with someone for forty days either becomes one of them or leaves them," the saying goes, and now my boys and I love Bamyeh. If you want to make it the Algerian and Egyptian way, substitute basil for the cilantro. **Serves 6 to 8**

Trim the stem ends of the okra with a paring knife. Trim around the cap only; do not chop it off or the okra will release a slimy liquid. Wash the okra under cold running water and transfer to a paper towel to dry.

Heat 2 tablespoons of the canola oil in a large pot over medium heat. Add the onions and sauté, stirring occasionally, until they become translucent, 5 minutes.

Meanwhile, rinse the meat under cold running water and pat it dry.

Add the meat to the pot and sauté until it loses its pink color, about 10 minutes. Add the beef bones, boiling water, allspice, coriander,

IT'S NOT OKRA STEW WITHOUT CHILE PEPPERS

Most people sit down to a bowl of stew and begin eating it by dipping their spoon into the piping hot liquid. Not Aref. Before he takes a single taste of my Yakhni Bamyeh, my Gaza-born husband engages in a bit of ceremony. He chops a green chile pepper into tiny pieces (we have them at every meal, since Gazans eat them like candy!), slices a lemon into wedges, and assembles them on a plate along with some olives. On another small plate, he squeezes some juice from the lemons, bathes the chile pieces in it, and eats a few. Next, he scoops up the stew with some warm, fluffy Arab flatbread and follows it with an olive. He repeats the ritual for every spoonful of stew he eats!

ISTIKBAL

My grandmother used to tell me stories about the *istikbals* that she used to host. During her time, as in ours today, women developed their networks of friends and neighbors to help in happy times and in crisis. Friendship and neighborly relations were maintained by women supporting each other.

Once a month my grandmother received her friends, to socialize and share food, but often there was an underlying desire to talk about something important: perhaps to solve a problem, or to help one of the women plan her daughter's wedding.

A typical Arab woman today opens her house to friends and relatives, who come and socialize. Information and opinions are exchanged, and sometimes individual situations are discussed and advice is offered. However, in many instances these gatherings are just to gossip and have light-hearted conversations.

On most occasions coffee or tea is served with a simple sweet or savory dish. However, sometimes a woman will pull out all the stops and set an elaborate table with her finest linens and silver, serving a great spread of desserts and savory dishes, along with drinks such as fresh-squeezed orange juice, coffee, and tea.

cardamom, salt, and pepper. Reduce the heat to medium, cover the pot, and simmer for 45 minutes.

Meanwhile, heat the remaining ⅔ cup canola oil in a medium pot over high heat. Add the okra and sauté until the ridges on the okra turn dark and the pared tips are golden, 3 to 4 minutes. Fresh okra will turn completely white. Using a slotted spoon, transfer the okra to a paper towel–lined plate to drain.

Using a slotted spoon, remove the bones from the stew and discard them. Add the tomato sauce and the drained okra, and continue to simmer until the meat and okra are fork-tender, about 30 minutes. Then reduce the heat to very low (if necessary, slide a heat diffuser under the pot).

Combine the garlic, jalapeño, and cilantro in a small bowl and mix together. Add the mixture to the stew and stir gently with a wooden spoon (avoid crushing the okra). Taste, and add salt and pepper if needed. If the sauce is too thick, add water. Simmer for 10 minutes. Remove from the heat and stir in the lemon juice. Serve hot, over the Basmati Rice.

Salads

UNTIL RECENTLY, VEGETABLE VENDORS in many Arab countries walked, with their carts, the residential streets of towns and cities every morning, calling loudly to get the attention of potential buyers. Housewives waited with anticipation, and when they heard the vendor, they lowered a basket from their balconies or windows. The merchant filled the basket with the vegetables requested. Once emptied, the basket was lowered again with the money. Today, vegetables are purchased from open-air markets, corner stores, or supermarkets.

Fresh as well as cooked vegetable salads are served in abundance on the Arab table. Some are served as light side dishes as accompaniments to substantial vegetable, meat, and rice preparations.

Other salads are part of an extensive mezza spread on all tables.

Although salads often seem simple to prepare, care in choosing ingredients and preparation makes all the difference. For best results, vegetables must be thoroughly washed and dried, for easier chopping and so as not to dilute the dressing.

When preparing salads, experiment with the ingredients. Think about adding some green you have not used before, or sprinkle the salad with fresh or dried mint, fresh parsley, or oregano.

A simple mixture of extra virgin olive oil, freshly squeezed lemon juice, salt, and pepper makes the perfect dressing.

PARSLEY STAINS

To prevent my hands from getting stained, I always wear rubber gloves when chopping parsley. If you prefer to grip the knife with bare hands and they do get stained, simply wash your hands with fresh lemon juice. To remove parsley stains from countertops and chopping boards, use a solution of bleach and water.

Simple Salad

SALATAT ARABI

1 pound hearts of romaine lettuce, rinsed, dried, and cut into bite-size pieces

1 pound small cucumbers, thinly sliced

5 scallions, white and light green parts, coarsely chopped

¾ pound tomatoes, cut into wedges

½ cup extra virgin olive oil

⅓ cup fresh lemon juice

1 teaspoon coarse salt

½ teaspoon black pepper

This mix of romaine, tomato wedges, cucumber slices, and scallions is served the same way all over the Arab world, from North Africa to the Arabian Gulf. Arabs prefer baby heads of romaine for this salad. Rather than buying just the hearts, I buy several whole heads and peel away the outer leaves, which I save to use in Mixed Vegetable Salad. You can substitute verjus for the lemon juice, to make the dressing the way those living in the Lebanese mountains do during the winter months. I often add fresh parsley and dried mint to this salad, and occasionally I substitute sliced red onions for the scallions. *Serves 6*

Toss the lettuce, cucumbers, scallions, and tomatoes in a bowl.

Combine the olive oil, lemon juice, salt, and pepper in a jar with a tight-fitting lid, and shake well.

Pour the dressing over the salad, and toss to coat all of the greens and vegetables. Serve immediately.

Jerusalem Salad

SALATAT KUDSIYEH

1½ pounds firm tomatoes, seeded and finely chopped

3 small pickling cucumbers, such as Kirby cucumbers, *or* 1 English cucumber, finely chopped

5 scallions, white and light green parts only, finely chopped

1 green bell pepper, seeded and finely chopped

2 packed cups finely chopped hearts of romaine lettuce

¼ cup fresh lemon juice

¼ cup extra virgin olive oil

⅓ cup sesame paste (tahini), plus more if needed

2 tablespoons white vinegar

Salt and black pepper, to taste

My cousin Mona, who grew up in Jordan and eventually came to the United States to study, made this salad whenever she was homesick—it was a vivid reminder of her father, who loved the piquant tahini dressing. Mona always served Jerusalem Salad with Warm Lentils with Rice, just as her father did. Although she passed away several years ago, it's as if Mona is in my kitchen every time I make this. It is delicious with grilled meats, or spooned onto Falafel in place of the tomato and onion slices. Serves 4 to 6

Combine the tomatoes, cucumbers, scallions, green peppers, and lettuce in a large bowl.

In another bowl, whisk the lemon juice, olive oil, sesame paste, vinegar, salt, and pepper together until the dressing is creamy and pale. If the dressing is too thick, gradually add a little water, whisking, until it reaches the desired consistency. If it is too thin, gradually add more sesame paste.

Just before serving, pour the dressing over the vegetables and toss thoroughly to coat. Serve immediately, to prevent the salad from becoming soggy.

Mixed Vegetable Salad

FATTOUSH

One 7-inch loaf Arab flatbread,
   cut into ½-inch squares

2 heads romaine lettuce, cut
   into ¼-inch pieces

2 pounds tomatoes, diced

3 small pickling cucumbers,
   such as Kirby cucumbers, *or*
   1 English cucumber, peeled
   and diced

4 radishes, trimmed and finely
   chopped

8 scallions, white and light
   green parts only, finely
   chopped

¾ cup finely chopped fresh
   mint leaves, preferably
   spearmint, or 1 tablespoon
   dried

5½ cups finely chopped fresh
   parsley

1 cup mâche, purslane, or other
   soft green, rinsed, patted dry,
   and finely chopped

¼ cup fresh lemon juice

½ cup extra virgin olive oil

3 tablespoons ground sumac

Salt and black pepper, to taste

*T*raditionally served for the fast-breaking Iftar meal during Ramadan, this salad of finely diced vegetables is distinguished by the tart, slightly woodsy flavor that comes from finely ground sumac, the deep burgundy seasoning that is essential to making a proper Fattoush. Be sure to rinse and thoroughly dry all of the vegetables before chopping them, to prevent the salad from becoming soggy.   *Serves 6*

Preheat the oven to 400°F.

Place the bread squares on a baking sheet and toast in the oven until lightly browned, 8 to 10 minutes. Set aside to cool.

Meanwhile, combine the lettuce, tomatoes, cucumbers, radishes, scallions, mint, parsley, and mâche in a large serving bowl. Toss, and set aside.

Combine the lemon juice, olive oil, sumac, salt, and pepper in a jar with a tight-fitting lid, and shake until blended.

Just before serving, pour the dressing over the vegetables and toss to coat them well. Scatter the bread squares over the salad, and serve.

Parsley Salad

TABOULEH

½ pound yellow onions, finely chopped, *or* 6 scallions, white and light green parts, finely chopped

1 teaspoon black pepper

½ cup fine bulgur (or more if desired), picked over and rinsed (see page 225)

1 pound tomatoes, finely chopped

6 packed cups chopped fresh parsley

¼ cup finely chopped fresh mint leaves, preferably spearmint

½ teaspoon finely chopped jalapeño pepper

¾ cup fresh lemon juice, or more to taste

1 cup extra virgin olive oil

1 tablespoon salt, or more to taste

Romaine lettuce leaves, cabbage leaves, or endive spears

When I was young, it was traditional for girls to learn various home arts, including sewing, embroidery, cooking, needlepoint, etiquette, and ballroom dancing. To gain these skills, my sisters and I attended finishing school at a convent in Lebanon's Brumana mountains each summer. On Sundays, the students prepared a picnic that always included tabouleh, which is not only a traditional Middle Eastern lunch dish but is often served for afternoon tea and with late-morning coffee. I had the job of chopping the parsley, which, as one of the nuns taught me, should be done with a gentle touch in order to make the lightest, fluffiest tabouleh. Avoid chopping it too much; the parsley will bruise and then wilt once the dressing is added. Use the best possible quality olive oil for this dish; it will come through in every bite.

In the Arab world, the proportions of the ingredients in tabouleh vary from country to country, and within countries too. The most common version is made with only a little bulgur—unlike most American versions I've tasted, which often have more bulgur than parsley in the mix. In the Lebanese mountains, we made it with equal amounts of bulgur and tomatoes. Whatever proportions you choose, the mark of a good tabouleh is its combination of tartness (from the lemon juice) and richness (from the olive oil).

To make Tabouleh in advance, prepare the parsley and refrigerate it. Combine the onions, peppers, bulgur, and tomatoes; cover, and refrigerate for up to 6 hours. When you are ready to serve the salad, add the remaining ingredients, toss, and serve as described in the recipe.

Serves 6

Combine the onions and black pepper in a bowl, and mix together with your fingers until well incorporated. Add the bulgur, tomatoes, parsley, mint, and jalapeño, and toss. Then add the lemon juice, olive oil, and salt. Mix well, until all the ingredients are coated with the dressing. Taste, and add more lemon juice or salt as desired.

To serve family-style, line a serving bowl with the romaine leaves and spoon the salad into them. For a formal dinner, spoon individual servings into cabbage leaves. For a cocktail party, arrange endive leaves on a platter and fill each one with about 2 tablespoons of the Tabouleh.

CLOCKWISE FROM BOTTOM LEFT:

Sumac, lentils, chickpeas, cinnamon sticks, dates, yogurt cheese, cumin

OPPOSITE, CLOCKWISE FROM TOP LEFT: *Mountain Bread with Zaatar (page 98),*
mint tea, Arab Yogurt Cheese (page 110), Zaatar (page 38), dukka (page 19), olive oil (page 24)

THIS PAGE, CLOCKWISE FROM TOP LEFT: *Yogurt Cheese Balls (page 112),*
Fried Halloumi Cheese (page 74), mountain flatbread (purchased), Dressed Chickpeas (page 60),
Cucumber and Yogurt (page 57), Arab Flatbread (page 94), Hot Green Olives (page 48)

Beets with Tahini (page 62)

OPPOSITE, CLOCKWISE FROM TOP: *Oregano Cakes (page 86), vegetable plate (mint, lettuce, tomatoes, hot peppers), Fried Cauliflower (page 77), Stuffed Grape Leaves (page 68), Hummus (page 51), Zucchini with Bread and Mint (page 64), Hot Green Olives (page 48)*

Fried Halloumi Cheese in Arab flatbread (page 74)

≺ *Stuffed Grape Leaves (page 68)*

Falafel (page 107)

Arab cheese tray ➤

Fattoush (page 148)

≺ *Phyllo Cheese Pie (page 114)*

Oregano Salad (page 151)

Moroccan Chicken Soup (page 128) ➢

Fish Soup (page 135)

≺ *Orange Lentil Soup (page 129)*

Stuffed Artichoke Hearts (page 195)

Chicken Freka with Ground Beef (page 184) ➤

Lamb with Rice and Yogurt (page 211)

◄ *Rice and Ground Beef in Phyllo Pockets (page 200)*

Beef with White Beans (page 221)

Lamb Kebabs (page 215) ➤

Kafta Balls with Spicy Tomato Sauce (pages 35 and 234)

≺ *Kibeh Balls (page 230)*

Tibsi Red Snapper in Pomegranate Syrup (page 252) ➤

Sautéed Greens with Crispy Onions (page 269)

≺ *Shrimp with Garlic and Cilantro (page 255)*

Eggplant in Pomegranate Syrup (page 273)

Pastries with Walnuts, Pistachios, and Dates (page 303) ➤

CLOCKWISE FROM BOTTOM LEFT:
Mughli (page 326), Semolina Cake (page 320), nougat (purchased), halvah (purchased), Milk Pudding (page 322), Ladies' Arms (page 305), Cheese and Walnut Crescents (page 337)

◄ *Semolina Pistachio Layer Cake (page 316)*

Apricot Juice (page 288)

Oregano Salad

SALATAT ZAATAR

6 cups (about eight ¾-ounce packages) fresh oregano, stemmed, rinsed, and patted dry

1 medium white onion, finely chopped

15 scallions, white and light green parts only, chopped (about ½ cup)

½ pound tomatoes, seeded and diced

1 clove garlic, mashed

⅓ cup extra virgin olive oil

¼ cup fresh lemon juice, or more to taste

1 teaspoon salt, or more to taste

2 tablespoons ground sumac

White onions, halved and thinly sliced, for garnish

Arab flatbread, for serving

In the Arab world, oregano is believed to strengthen the memory, which makes it a popular herb among students, who often make eating Zaatar, the oregano and thyme seasoning, part of a pre-exam ritual. Regardless of its mind-sharpening powers, tender leaves of oregano tossed with tomatoes and onions makes for a tongue-tingling, palate-cleansing salad.

Because oregano grows wild all over the Middle East, we think nothing of using large amounts of it in a dish. If you find it difficult or prohibitively expensive to use the quantity of oregano I call for in this salad, substitute another soft herb, such as marjoram, thyme, or sage. Serve the salad with pitted olives and Labneh for brunch, or with grilled meat or chicken for dinner.

As with all recipes that call for fresh herbs, I prefer to use the organic variety because they are generally smaller and more tender than commercially grown herbs. Avoid using overly large, tough leaves in this fresh salad. Salatat Zaatar does not hold up for very long after it has been dressed, so toss it in the lemon juice mixture just before you bring it to the table.　　　　　　　　　　　　　　　　　　　　　　*Serves 6*

Combine the oregano leaves, onions, scallions, and tomatoes in a medium bowl.

Whisk the garlic, olive oil, and lemon juice together in a small bowl, and pour the dressing over the salad. Toss, so that all the oregano leaves are coated with the dressing. Season with the salt. Taste, and add more salt or a bit more lemon juice if desired. Sprinkle the sumac over the salad, reserving a bit for garnish, and toss again.

Transfer the salad to a serving platter or bowl, garnish with the onions, and sprinkle the remaining sumac over the onions. Serve immediately, with wedges of Arab flatbread.

Baby Arugula Salad

SALATAT JARJEER

1 pound baby arugula

1 medium red onion, thinly
 sliced

¼ cup fresh lemon juice

⅓ cup olive oil

2 cloves garlic, mashed

1½ teaspoons salt

½ teaspoon black pepper

Arugula is called jarjeer *in Palestine and Jordan and* rocca *in Lebanon—a word that the French translated into* roquette, *or "rocket," during their extended occupation of the area in 1920. I use baby arugula leaves since the more mature leaves can have a strong, somewhat bitter taste. If you buy arugula with the roots attached, chop them off and wash it very thoroughly to remove all of the sand and grit. I serve this salad for lunch, with Meat Pies and a side dish of plain yogurt.* ***Serves 6 to 8***

Wash the arugula leaves by immersing them in a big bowl of cold water and swirling them to remove any dirt. Lift them out of the water with your hands. Repeat as necessary, in clean water, until the leaves are clean; then transfer them to a salad spinner and spin dry. Chop the arugula into 1-inch pieces and place them in a large bowl. Add the onions and toss.

Combine the lemon juice, olive oil, garlic, salt, and pepper in a jar with a tight-fitting lid, and shake vigorously.

Just before serving the salad, drizzle the dressing over it and toss it well. Serve immediately.

Shredded Cabbage Salad

SALATAT EL MALFOOF

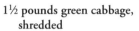

1½ pounds green cabbage, shredded

¾ pound tomatoes, seeded and diced

½ pound white onions, halved and thinly sliced

⅓ cup fresh lemon juice

½ cup extra virgin olive oil

4 cloves garlic, mashed

2 teaspoons salt

½ teaspoon black pepper

*W*hen I was in boarding school, Salatat el Malfoof was served with Kibeh in the Tray every Thursday. I still love this crunchy salad, despite having eaten it so regularly as a young girl. It is an excellent choice for entertaining because it can be made in advance and doesn't wilt readily; the flavor actually improves the longer it sits. Serve it with Warm Lentils with Rice.   ***Serves 6 to 8***

Combine the cabbage, tomatoes, and onions in a large bowl.

Combine the lemon juice, olive oil, garlic, salt, and pepper in a jar with a tight-fitting lid, and shake it vigorously. Pour the dressing over the vegetables and toss to thoroughly coat. Cover the bowl with plastic wrap and refrigerate for at least 1 hour, or up to 4 hours, to let the flavors blend. Serve cold.

Potato Salad

SALATAT BATATA

3 pounds white potatoes, cut
    into ½-inch cubes

¼ cup extra virgin olive oil

¼ cup fresh lemon juice

Salt, to taste

½ teaspoon black pepper

4 cloves garlic, mashed

½ cup finely chopped fresh
    cilantro leaves

A staple on Middle Eastern steakhouse, or mashawi, *menus, this cilantro and garlic–seasoned potato salad is a typical accompaniment to Lamb Kebabs, Chicken Kebabs, and other grilled foods. In this recipe, the potatoes are cooked in their skins, but you can peel them before cooking if you prefer. I call for white potatoes because these are the only kind that were available when I was growing up, but you could use red or Yukon Gold if you prefer.*   *Serves 6*

Place the potatoes in a large pot and add water to cover by 2 inches. Bring to a boil. Then reduce the heat to medium and cook, covered, until fork-tender, about 20 minutes. Drain immediately and rinse under cold running water. Transfer the potatoes to a large bowl.

Combine the olive oil, lemon juice, salt, pepper, and garlic in a jar with a tight-fitting lid, and shake vigorously to blend. Pour the dressing over the potatoes and toss with two wooden spoons to coat. Garnish with the cilantro, cover with plastic wrap, and refrigerate for at least 1 hour and up to 4 hours. Bring to room temperature before serving. (If you prepare the salad a day ahead, do not add the garlic until just before serving.)

Beet Salad

SALATAT SHAMANDAR

2 pounds cooked beets, peeled,
  ends trimmed, cut into
  eighths

½ pound onions, thinly sliced

½ cup white vinegar

⅔ cup extra virgin olive oil

4 cloves garlic, mashed

½ teaspoon salt

1 cup chopped fresh flat-leaf
  parsley

Make this salad a few hours ahead to allow the flavors of the beets, vinegar, and parsley to come together. Serve it at room temperature with grilled meats, such as Kafta. If you're in a hurry and don't have any cooked beets on hand, used canned beets—the whole variety—rinsed and cut into wedges.   *Serves 6 to 8*

Combine the beets and onions in a large bowl.

Combine the vinegar, olive oil, garlic, and salt in a jar with a tight-fitting lid, and shake vigorously. Taste, and adjust the seasoning to your liking.

Pour the dressing over the beets and toss gently to thoroughly coat them. Transfer the salad to a serving dish, and garnish with the parsley. Cover and refrigerate up to 6 hours. Serve at room temperature.

Fava Bean Salad

SALATAT FUL AKHDAR

28 ounces frozen fava beans

1 teaspoon baking soda

14 ounces frozen artichoke
bottoms

½ cup plus 1 tablespoon fresh
lemon juice (reserve the
lemon shells)

4 cloves garlic, mashed

⅓ cup extra virgin olive oil

2 teaspoons salt

1 tablespoon chopped fresh
cilantro or parsley

Because my father traveled so much for business, my mother often spent her evenings preparing ingredients for the next day's meals—peeling beans, coring zucchini, stemming herbs for drying. I have crystal-clear memories of her sitting in front of the television, peeling the beans for this salad while nudging us to help her by turning the whole operation into a competition among us sisters. It always worked.

I rely on the frozen Egyptian beans that are available in every Middle Eastern grocery for this simple salad—creamy fava beans tossed in a garlic-lemon dressing. But whenever they're available, I use fresh Italian fava beans. You can peel them while talking on the phone, watching the evening news, or helping the kids with their homework. If you prepare the fresh beans in advance, store them in a tightly covered container in the refrigerator until ready to use. I use frozen artichoke bottoms rather than working with fresh artichokes; either will taste delicious here. If you want to make this salad in advance, refrigerate it, tightly covered, and bring it to room temperature before serving. **Serves 6**

Rinse the beans in cold water, place them in a saucepan or a bowl, and add water to cover. Stir in the baking soda and set them aside for about 30 minutes.

Drain the beans, place them in a large pot, and add water to cover by 1 inch. Bring to a boil over high heat, and cook for 2 minutes. Drain the beans in a colander and rinse them under cold water. The skins should be loose enough to peel away easily. To do this, gently press a bean between your thumb and index finger and squeeze to nudge the bean from its skin. Discard the skins and set aside the peeled beans.

Trim any tough skin off the artichoke bottoms. Rinse them, place them in a large pot, and add water to cover. Add the squeezed lemon halves and 1 tablespoon of the lemon juice, and bring to a boil. Cook until the artichoke hearts are easily pierced with a fork, about 10 minutes. Drain them in a colander and set them aside until they have cooled. Discard the lemon halves.

Meanwhile, make the dressing: Combine the garlic, olive oil, remaining ½ cup lemon juice, and salt in a jar with a tight-fitting lid and shake well. Use a fork to break up the mashed garlic if it doesn't incorporate easily.

Trim the artichoke bottoms, paring a thin piece from the bottom, so they will sit flat on a platter. Combine them with the beans and the dressing in a large bowl. Toss to coat all of the ingredients with the dressing.

To serve, pick the artichoke bottoms out of the mix, arrange them around the rim of a platter, and fill each one with beans. (Alternatively, slice the artichokes into ½-inch-thick slices and set them around the rim of the platter.) Spoon the remaining beans in the middle of the plate, and if there is dressing left in the bowl, drizzle it over all. Garnish with the cilantro, and serve.

Eggplant Salad

FATTOUSH BETINJAN

The classic Syrian pairing of eggplant and pomegranate is featured in this salad. To make it the customary way, toss the croutons right into the salad. If I am serving it as part of a buffet, however, I prefer to pile them in the center so that they stay crisp.　　*Serves 6 to 8*

4 pounds eggplant, peeled, cut into ¾-inch-thick slices, and then cubed

Salt

Vegetable oil, for deep-frying

Two 7-inch loaves Arab flatbread, cut into ½-inch squares

2 packed cups chopped fresh parsley

5 scallions, white and light green parts only, finely chopped

1½ pounds tomatoes, seeded and finely chopped

1 tablespoon pomegranate syrup

½ cup fresh lemon juice, plus more if needed

½ cup extra virgin olive oil

6 cloves garlic, mashed

¼ teaspoon black pepper

Place the eggplant in a strainer and sprinkle it with 1 teaspoon salt. Set the strainer in the sink or over a bowl, and let the eggplant drain for 30 minutes.

Meanwhile, pour vegetable oil into a large, deep skillet to a depth of 2 inches, and place it over high heat. Using a slotted spoon, slide the Arab flatbread, in small batches, into the hot oil and fry until golden brown, 5 minutes per batch. Transfer the croutons to a paper towel–lined plate to drain.

Pat the eggplant dry with paper towels. Place the same skillet over high heat and fry the eggplant, in small batches, in the oil until golden brown, about 12 minutes. Transfer the eggplant to a paper towel–lined baking sheet to drain and cool completely.

Combine the eggplant, parsley, scallions, and tomatoes in a medium bowl and toss.

Combine the pomegranate syrup, lemon juice, olive oil, garlic, 1 teaspoon salt, and the pepper in a jar with a tight-fitting lid, and shake vigorously. Just before serving, drizzle the dressing over the salad, and toss to coat it thoroughly. Taste, and add salt and more lemon juice if needed. Transfer the salad to a serving bowl, and either toss the croutons in it or spoon them into the center in a small mound. Serve immediately.

Eggplant Pomegranate Salad

SALATAT AL RAHIB

2 pounds eggplant

2 pounds firm tomatoes, seeded and diced

4 scallions, white and light green parts only, chopped

1 green, red, yellow, or orange bell pepper, seeded and finely diced

1 jalapeño pepper, minced

1 tablespoon pomegranate syrup

4 cloves garlic, mashed

½ cup extra virgin olive oil

¼ cup fresh lemon juice

½ teaspoon salt

⅛ teaspoon black pepper

2 tablespoons chopped fresh flat-leaf parsley

Fresh mint leaves, for garnish

Pomegranate seeds, for garnish (optional)

No one knows the origin of this dish's name, which means "priest's salad." The tang of the pomegranate makes Salatat al Rahib a good side dish with grilled meats. It is one of the few salads that are typically served as an accompaniment to a main course, rather than eaten on their own for lunch. I always chop the vegetables quite fine for this salad because in my homeland, that is considered a symbol of elegance.

Serves 6

Preheat the oven to 400°F, with a rack about 4 inches from the heat source. Line a baking sheet with aluminum foil.

Using a fork, pierce the eggplants in a few places. Place them on the prepared baking sheet and bake, turning them a quarter-turn every 5 minutes, until the skin blisters and cracks, 20 minutes in all. (Alternatively, slide a heat diffuser over a gas flame and set the eggplants directly on it, turning them as the skin blisters and cracks.) Set the roasted eggplants aside until they are cool enough to handle.

Holding the eggplant at the stem end, peel away the skin, using your hands or a knife. Set them aside to cool completely.

PREPARING EGGPLANT

Recipes often call for placing peeled eggplant in a colander, sprinkling it generously with salt, and allowing it to sit for at least 30 minutes and up to 1 hour. This leaches out the bitter juices. If the eggplant is then going to be fried, pat it dry with a paper towel to keep it from becoming soggy.

If you are baking a whole eggplant, pierce it in several places so it won't burst. You can also microwave a whole eggplant, which is speedier but will not impart the delicious smoky flavor that results from baking it in the oven: Microwave the eggplant on high power for 3 to 5 minutes, turning it over halfway through cooking. Once you remove the eggplant from the oven or microwave, peel it as soon as you can comfortably handle it—it's much easier to take the skin off while the eggplant is still hot. Seed the eggplant before chopping it by slicing it lengthwise and running a soupspoon down the middle to loosen and remove the seeds.

If the eggplant is mashed or pureed and you are preparing it in advance of assembling the recipe, add a bit of lemon juice to prevent discoloration.

Meanwhile, combine the tomatoes, scallions, bell peppers, jalapeño, pomegranate syrup, garlic, olive oil, lemon juice, salt, and black pepper in a medium bowl.

Chop the eggplants into 1-inch chunks and add them to the vegetables. Stir the salad gently with a wooden spoon (to avoid breaking the eggplant). Garnish with the parsley, mint, and pomegranate seeds, if using, and serve.

Variation: I often use Japanese eggplants for this dish. Rather than cutting them into 1-inch chunks, I halve them, scoop out the flesh, and add the flesh to the mixture; then I serve the salad in the hollowed-out shells. Because there isn't much flesh in this variety of eggplant, I always roast a small Italian eggplant, peel it, and cut it into chunks to add to the salad.

Tomato Salad

SALATAT BANDORA

1½ pounds firm tomatoes, seeded and diced

1 cup green olives, pitted and chopped

½ pound white onions, coarsely chopped

¼ cup fresh lemon juice

¼ cup extra virgin olive oil

2 teaspoons salt

1 teaspoon black pepper

In the Arab world, a person's nationality can often be determined by the way they pronounce bandora, *the word for "tomato." Those who say "bana-doora" are probably Lebanese, while people who pronounce it "ban-doora" are likely to come from Palestine or Jordan. Salatat Bandora is particularly nice when served on Arab flatbread with Warm Lentils with Rice or Pureed Split Lentils as part of a mezza spread.*

Serves 6

Combine all the ingredients in a large serving bowl and toss until the tomatoes, olives, and onions are well coated with the dressing. Serve immediately.

Tomato and Dill Seed Salad

DAKKA

2 cloves garlic, mashed

2 jalapeño peppers, seeded and finely chopped, plus more if needed

2 tablespoons dill seed

1 teaspoon salt, plus more if needed

1½ pounds ripe tomatoes, seeded and diced

1 shallot, minced

2 tablespoons fresh lemon juice, plus more if needed

3 tablespoons olive oil

*T*he men in Middle Eastern families most often make Dakka, for reasons that are unknown. They prepare it in the traditional way, using a mortar and pestle to pound the garlic, jalapeño, and dill seed into a creamy paste. In the southern regions of Palestine, where this salad originated, a special black earthenware mortar with a wooden pestle is used. In my American kitchen, I prepare the salad and Aref adds the final touches—usually a good dose of jalapeño since he likes this salad very hot. Adjust the heat to suit your own taste. Dakka is excellent spooned over grilled fish or on its own, as a dip. Prepare it an hour before serving to allow the flavors to develop.

Serves 6

Combine the garlic, jalapeños, dill seed, and salt in a mortar and pound to a creamy paste (or use a mini processor).

Combine the tomatoes, shallots, and lemon juice in a medium bowl, and stir in the jalapeño mixture. Taste, and adjust the lemon juice, jalapeño, and salt to taste. Transfer the salad to a serving dish, drizzle with the olive oil, and serve.

Rice

Until recent times, in most of the Arab countries, rice was considered a luxury food to be served on the tables of the rich and for special occasions. Grains such as wheat, barley, and corn were less expensive and more readily available to most people. During the 1940s, new agricultural methods made it possible for rice to be grown in Egypt, Syria, and southern Iraq.

There are several varieties of rice grown in the Arab world. Anbar, which is highly esteemed and grown in Iraq, is a long-grain, aromatic rice, but it is expensive and hard to find. Rashidi, grown in Egypt and parts of Syria, is a short-grain rice that is harvested while still slightly green. Long-grained and aromatic basmati rice from India is my favorite rice and the one recommended for most recipes in this book. Short-grained rice is used in stuffings. Long-grain American rice can also be used in these recipes with excellent results.

Each cook has her own way of preparing rice. In most of my cooking, I sauté the rice before adding the water; this method is referred to as *timam*. Although this method produces delicious rice and looks easy, it does require your attention. To prevent moisture from escaping, don't uncover the pot unless absolutely necessary. And always wrap your rice in an old blanket for one to three hours; this step makes a big difference in the end. By wrapping the rice, you give it time to "open up" slowly to produce a better flavor.

Another technique is to add the rice to boiling water. Once the water is absorbed, a bit of oil is added to finish it off.

In the Arab Gulf, the rice is first parboiled in spiced water, then drained and finished with oil and more spices, or by adding sugar or molasses to make a sweet rice.

Basmati Rice

RUZ MUFALFAL

3 tablespoons vegetable oil or
    ghee
3 cups basmati rice, rinsed (see
    page 165), soaked, and
    drained
3 cups boiling water
1 tablespoon salt
Ground cinnamon, for garnish

*W*ho cooked the rice?" was the first thing my father, the food connoisseur in our family, always asked as he sat down to dinner.
Whenever my mother replied that it was Aunt Maha's rice, a broad smile
would come over his face. "Ahhh. Rice the *timam way.*" Timam, *which
means "to slowly separate," is the Iraqi method for preparing basmati,
and it is the method I use. The steps vary from cook to cook: Some do not
sauté the rice before adding the water, but rather add the fat to the pot at
the end. Others, mainly in the Gulf States, boil the rice like pasta, drain
it, and then incorporate the fat and some spices just before serving.*

The timam *method, one commonly used in the Arab world, is simple, but it requires close attention. Do not be tempted to lift the lid from
the pot unless it is necessary to add spices or other ingredients; the steam
inside is essential for proper cooking. And don't skip the resting step at
the end: Wrapping the pot in a blanket or thick piece of wool for a minimum of 1 hour—preferably 3—allows the grains to open up.*

Serves 6 to 8

Heat the vegetable oil in a medium saucepan over high heat. Add
the rice and stir to coat each grain with oil, about 1 minute. Then
add the boiling water and the salt, cover the pan, and cook for 3
minutes. Reduce the heat to medium-low, slide a heat diffuser
under the pot, and cook for 10 minutes. Reduce the heat to low and
continue to simmer until the rice is tender when you bite into it, 10
minutes.

Remove the pan from the stove and wrap it tightly in a fleece
blanket. Set it aside for at least 1 hour (it will stay hot wrapped this
way for 3 hours).

Fluff the rice with a fork and serve, garnished with a dusting of
cinnamon.

ARAB-STYLE RICE: THE BASICS

Here are some tips that will help you make perfect rice every time:

- Buy basmati rice: This fragrant rice is the standard rice of Arab cooking. I prefer imported Indian basmati. For short-grain rice, use Egyptian rice.

- Rinse rice before cooking: I rinse my rice three times, enough to remove any debris but not so much that all the starch is rinsed away: Put the rice in a mixing bowl and fill it with cold water to cover by a few inches. Stir the rice with your fingers, releasing any debris. Let the rice settle in the bowl, and pour off the water. Repeat twice.

- Soak rice for 10 minutes after rinsing.

- Add an equal amount of boiling water: Arab-style rice is made with the same amount of water as rice, not twice the amount as is common here. Have the water boiling (this cooks the grains faster) and pour it into a heatproof measuring cup.

- Use a "flame tamer": A heat-diffusing flame tamer is an essential kitchen tool for cooking rice slowly, without burning. After the water has been absorbed by the rice (3 to 5 minutes), put the saucepan on the flame tamer for the rest of the cooking time.

- For the best rice, let it rest and keep it warm: After cooking it, always leave rice in its covered pot for at least 1 hour to "open up" and moisten. Wrap the pot in a piece of wool or fleece cloth to retain the heat; it will stay hot for 3 hours.

WHITE RICE

Arabs eat white rice (*ruz mufalfal* in Palestine, Jordan, Syria, and Lebanon; *timan* in Iraq; *aish* in the Gulf States), but it is rarely served plain. Here are a few ways we enhance it:

- Steep a pinch of saffron threads in 2 tablespoons rose water or orange-blossom water, and add this to the pot 15 minutes into the cooking time. Do not stir it in, but rather gently drizzle it on top of the cooking rice. Garnish the finished rice with pine nuts and raisins.

- Give white rice a glorious golden color by combining ½ teaspoon ground turmeric with the salt before adding it to the pot.

- Add ½ teaspoon ground cinnamon, ground cardamom, or grated nutmeg to the cooking oil just before adding the rice.

- Spray a mold with unflavored cooking spray and spoon the cooked rice into it; press down with the back of a spoon, then invert onto a serving plate. Or make some plain white rice and some yellow rice (add saffron and rosewater as above) and spoon them into the mold in alternating layers; invert onto a serving platter and garnish with fried nuts.

Sweet Rice

MUHAMAR

¼ teaspoon saffron threads, plus
  2 more threads

1¼ teaspoons ground
  cardamom

¼ cup rose water

2 cups basmati rice, rinsed (see
  page 165), soaked, and
  drained

2 tablespoons vegetable oil

2 cups sugar

Cardamom pods, for garnish

This method of cooking rice is common in the Gulf States, where it is served on festive occasions such as weddings and the birth of a child. In Kuwait it is served on the second day of Eid al Adha (see page 90) with roasted leg of lamb, or Tibsi Red Snapper in Pomegranate Syrup, or Shrimp with Garlic and Cilantro.   *Serves 6*

Combine ¼ teaspoon of the saffron threads, 1 teaspoon of the ground cardamom, and the rose water in a small bowl and set it aside.

Bring 6 cups water to a boil in a large pot. Add the rice and bring to a boil over high heat, stirring occasionally.

Reduce the heat to medium and cook for 7 minutes, until the rice is still a bit chewy. Strain it and set it aside in a bowl to cool completely.

In the same pot, heat the vegetable oil over medium heat. Add the remaining ¼ teaspoon cardamom and 2 threads of saffron, and cook until fragrant, about 1 minute. Meanwhile, add the sugar to the rice and stir to thoroughly combine.

EATEN TO SWEETEN THE CATCH

Before the discovery of oil in the Gulf States, the economies of the region relied heavily on the fruits of the sea—most people made their living from it. And whether it was fish or pearls they sought, divers would eat a healthy portion of rice sweetened with date syrup—it was thought to give them energy and to warm their blood—before they entered the water. With a wooden clothespin pinching their noses and weights on their feet, they would tie a rope around their waist and lower themselves to the bottom of the sea, looking for oysters that might contain pearls. A partner on land would pull them up by the rope, and together they would examine the catch.

Add the rice to the seasoned oil and stir to coat it. Raise the heat to high, cover the pot, and cook until the rice has dried out and is tender, about 10 minutes. Reduce the heat to low, pour the rose water mixture over the surface of the rice (do not stir it in), and return the cover to the pot. Slide a heat diffuser under the pot and cook until the rice is tender and fluffy, 30 minutes.

Serve immediately or, preferably, wrap the pot in a fleece blanket to keep the rice warm until ready to serve. To serve, stir the rice with a fork to separate the grains, then transfer it to a serving dish and garnish with the cardamom pods.

Onion Rice

RUZ BI BASAL

½ cup canola oil

2 pounds onions, finely chopped

1½ teaspoons ground cumin

1 teaspoon ground coriander

½ teaspoon ground allspice

1 teaspoon salt

¼ teaspoon black pepper

¼ teaspoon ground cinnamon

⅛ teaspoon grated nutmeg

⅛ teaspoon ground cloves

2⅔ cups boiling water

2⅔ cups basmati rice, rinsed (see page 165), soaked, and drained

My grandmother Nazleh made this rice better than anyone in my family. I don't know if it was the plain aluminum cup she used to "measure" out the rice, or the quality of the rice itself, which hung in a huge brown mesh sack—food was never to touch the ground—in her pantry. Or perhaps it was because I had expertly picked over the rice (one of my first jobs in her kitchen, along with peeling garlic and squeezing lemons). Whatever it was, my grandmother had just the right touch. The real secret, I believe, is in the sautéing of the onions. They should be cooked over medium-low heat and stirred constantly to avoid burning. As my husband likes to say, "You cannot multitask when cooking rice." Another key to making this rice perfectly is to wrap the pot in a fleece blanket and let it rest for at least 30 minutes before serving.

Ruz bi Basal is traditionally served with fish and seafood, such as Fried Fish and Shrimp with Garlic and Cilantro, in North Africa and along the Eastern Mediterranean. **Serves 6**

Heat the canola oil in a heavy pot over high heat. Add the onions and lower the heat to medium. Sauté until they're soft and the edges have darkened, about 10 minutes.

Reduce the heat to low and stir in the cumin, coriander, allspice, salt, pepper, cinnamon, nutmeg, and cloves. Add the rice to the pot. Stir to coat the kernels with the spices, about 2 minutes.

Add the boiling water to the pot, give it a good stir, cover, and bring to a boil over high heat. Reduce the heat to medium and cook until all of the liquid has been absorbed, about 10 minutes. Then reduce the heat to low, slide a heat diffuser under the pot, and cook until the rice is tender, 35 minutes.

Remove the pot from the heat, and let the rice rest, wrapped in a fleece blanket, for 30 minutes before serving.

Egyptian Rice

RUZ MASRI MUFALFAL

2 cups Egyptian rice

2 tablespoons ghee or vegetable oil

1 teaspoon salt

3 cups boiling water

¼ teaspoon ground cinnamon or paprika, for garnish

Egyptian rice kernels are shorter and starchier than basmati rice; they resemble sushi rice. In Egypt and North Africa this is the preferred rice, while in other Arab countries it is used primarily for stuffing vegetables (Stuffed Zucchini, Stuffed Grape Leaves), in soups (Rice and Meatball Soup), and in lentil dishes (Lentils with Caramelized Onions) because its high starch content allows it to combine easily with other ingredients.

When I make this rice, I prepare it the way the Egyptians do, with ghee. Vegetable oil is an acceptable substitute, but it will not have the slightly nutty flavor that ghee imparts to dishes. (Ghee is readily available in Middle Eastern stores; it may be labeled samna.*) You can also use broth in place of the water, or a mix of broth and water. Sometimes I add crushed cardamom pods to the ghee to vary the flavor of this delicious rice.*

Serves 6

Wash the rice three times over, as for basmati (see page 165), and then soak it in fresh cold water for about 15 minutes.

Heat the ghee in a saucepan over high heat until it has melted, about 1 minute. Drain the rice thoroughly and add it to the pan. Add the salt and stir until the rice is well coated with the ghee. Add the boiling water, stir, and cover the pan. Bring the mixture to a boil. Reduce the heat to medium and cook until the water has been absorbed, 15 minutes. Reduce the heat to low, slide a heat diffuser under the pan, and simmer until the rice is soft, about 15 minutes more.

Remove the pan from the stove, wrap it in a fleece blanket, and set it aside for 1 hour.

Fluff the rice with a fork and transfer it to a serving dish. Smooth the surface with the back of a spoon, and garnish with a dusting of cinnamon.

Lentils with Fried Onions

MUJADARA

2 cups brown lentils, picked over and rinsed

1 pound onions, chopped

1 cup extra virgin olive oil

⅓ cup Egyptian, sushi, or other short-grain rice, rinsed (see page 165), soaked, and drained

1 teaspoon ground cumin

1 tablespoon salt, plus more if needed

½ teaspoon black pepper

For the fried onions:

¼ teaspoon salt

2 pounds onions, halved and thinly sliced

Vegetable oil, for deep-frying

By Arab standards, Mujadara is not fancy enough to serve to guests—it's reserved for family or perhaps a casual get-together—but I often include it among a selection of more elaborate choices, partly because I love it myself! I learned to make this, the Lebanese version, from my Auntie Nina, though anyone from Lebanon would be surprised to find cumin in it, which is perhaps a habit rooted in my Palestinian origins; we add cumin to every pulse we cook. Mujadara consists of lentils and rice cooked to the consistency of a pudding and garnished with fried onions. A summertime dish, it is served at room temperature.

After you pour the Mujadara onto a plate and it cools off, it should have a smooth surface. If the surface cracks, you can cover it with the onions or put it back in the pot, add ¼ to ½ cup water, let it cook for a few minutes, and pour again. (This method also works well when you prepare it a day or two before serving it. Just give it a quick boil and pour it onto your serving plate. It will look as though you just made it.)

Serve Mujadara with Shredded Cabbage Salad or Arab flatbread, with pickles and radishes in small bowls on the side. **Serves 6**

Combine the lentils, chopped onions, ½ cup of the olive oil, and 5 cups water in a large pot. Cover and bring to a boil over high heat. Then reduce the heat to low and simmer until the lentils can easily be mashed with the back of a spoon, about 30 minutes. Skim the foam from the surface as the lentils simmer.

Remove the pot from the heat and allow to cool. Working in batches, transfer the lentil mixture to a blender and puree until smooth and the texture of a creamy soup. If the mixture is thicker than that, gradually add up to 1 cup water until it reaches the desired consistency. Return the pureed lentils to the pot and set it aside.

Combine the rice with 2 cups water in a medium saucepan. Bring to a boil over high heat and continue to cook, uncovered, until tender, about 20 minutes.

Meanwhile, sprinkle the salt over the onion slices and toss. Fill a deep 3-quart pot with vegetable oil to a depth of 2 inches, and heat over high heat. Add the onions and sauté, stirring occasionally, until they are golden, about 5 minutes. Reduce the heat to medium and continue to cook, stirring, until the onions are mahogany brown, 15 to 20 minutes. Transfer the onions to a paper towel–lined plate.

Drain the rice in a colander; then stir it into the lentils. Stir in the cumin, salt, and pepper. Place the pot over medium heat, add the remaining ½ cup olive oil, and cook, uncovered, until the lentils begin to boil. Reduce the heat to low and cook, stirring occasionally, for 5 to 8 minutes. The lentils may bubble up and spit out of the pot, so wear an oven mitt when you stir. Taste, and add more salt if needed.

To serve, spoon the lentil-rice mixture into a shallow rimmed plate or bowl, and garnish with the fried onions. Serve at room temperature.

LENTIL BASICS

Unlike other legumes, lentils do not need to be presoaked. But they do need to be picked over and rid of any debris. To do this, spread them on a plate in a single layer and remove any unwanted material; then rinse them under cold running water. When cooking lentils, always skim off the foam that forms on the surface of the cooking water. Add salt to the pot only after the lentils are cooked.

Warm Lentils with Rice

MUDARDARA

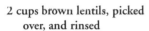

2 cups brown lentils, picked over, and rinsed

2 tablespoons plus ½ cup extra virgin olive oil

1 small onion, finely chopped

1½ cups basmati or other long-grain rice, rinsed (see page 165), soaked, and drained

1 tablespoon salt, plus more as needed

½ teaspoon black pepper

1¼ teaspoons ground cumin

4 medium onions, quartered and thinly sliced (4 cups)

This version of rice and lentils is never served any way but warm, and is different than Mujadara in that the lentils are left whole and are mixed with basmati rather than short-grain rice. In the south of Lebanon, you often see this dish made with coarse bulgur instead of rice. If you choose to make it that way, add another ½ cup water to the pot. Serve this hearty dish with Cucumber and Yogurt.   *Serves 6*

Combine the lentils with 5 cups water in a large pot. Cover and bring to a boil over high heat. Then lower the heat to medium, give the lentils a good stir, and cover the pot. Simmer until the lentils are tender, 20 minutes.

Remove the lentils from the heat and strain, reserving the cooking liquid.

Heat 2 tablespoons of the olive oil in the same pot over medium heat. Add the chopped onions and sauté until translucent, 10 minutes. Then stir in the lentils, rice, salt, pepper, and cumin. Measure out 1½ cups of the reserved lentil cooking liquid and add it to the pot. Stir, cover, and bring to a boil. Reduce the heat to medium and cook until the liquid has been absorbed and the rice is tender, about 10 minutes. Taste, and add salt if needed. Reduce the heat to low, slide a heat diffuser under the pot, and cook until the rice is done, 15 to 20 minutes.

Remove the pot from the heat and let it rest for 10 minutes, or wrap it in a fleece blanket and keep warm for up to 4 hours.

Meanwhile, sprinkle the sliced onions with a dash of salt. Heat the remaining ½ cup olive oil in a medium skillet over high heat. Add the onions and fry, stirring constantly, until they are golden, 8 to 10 minutes. Transfer the onions to a paper towel–lined plate to drain.

To serve, spoon the lentil-rice mixture into a shallow serving dish and garnish with the fried onions.

Spiced Beef with Rice

HASHWEH

1 teaspoon ground allspice

1 teaspoon ground cardamom

1 teaspoon Seven Spice Mix
(page 73)

½ teaspoon ground cinnamon

¼ teaspoon grated nutmeg

¼ teaspoon ground cloves

1 teaspoon salt

½ teaspoon black pepper

2 tablespoons canola oil

1 pound ground beef
(preferably 90% lean)

3 cups white basmati rice,
rinsed (see page 165),
soaked, and drained

3 cups boiling water *or* half
boiling water and half Spiced
Chicken Stock (page 125) *or*
low-sodium canned broth

*H*ashweh *means "stuffing," which is just one of the ways this fragrant dish is used. Of the many magnificent rice dishes in the Arab repertoire, this beautifully spiced one is my favorite. You can simply serve it on its own with a dish of Cucumber and Yogurt alongside, or you can make it part of a larger, more elaborate presentation—for example, mounded on a platter, topped with large pieces of poached chicken, and garnished with fried pine nuts. (It is not unusual to find main courses on the Arab table that feature a combination of chicken and beef or lamb.) Hashweh is also stuffed into whole chickens and enveloped in butterflied leg of lamb. Seven Spice Mix, a staple in the Lebanese kitchen, is used almost as frequently as salt.*

Serves 8 (makes about 10 cups)

Mix the allspice, cardamom, Seven Spice Mix, cinnamon, nutmeg, cloves, salt, and pepper together in a small bowl.

Heat the canola oil in a large, heavy pot (one with a tight-fitting lid) over high heat. Add the ground beef and break it apart with a big spoon as it sizzles and starts to brown. After 2 minutes, stir in the spice mixture. Cook another minute or so over high heat, stirring frequently, until the meat is evenly browned. Then lower the heat and cook, stirring occasionally, for 3 minutes more.

Add the rice to the pot and raise the heat to high. Stirring and scraping vigorously, cook the rice and meat together for 3 minutes or so, adjusting the heat if necessary to prevent burning.

Pour in the boiling water and stir only once. Cover the pot, bring to a boil, and immediately reduce the heat to low. Cook until all the water has been absorbed, about 10 minutes.

Slide a heat diffuser under the pot and cook, covered, for another 10 minutes. Stir the mixture, re-cover, and cook for 5 minutes more.

If the rice is to be served the next day or used for stuffing, uncover the pot, let the rice cool, and then refrigerate it overnight. If the rice is to be served the same day, wrap the pot in a fleece or wool blanket and let it sit for at least 1 hour.

To reheat the rice: Place it in a bowl, top with a vented cover, and reheat in a microwave. Or return it to a heavy pot, stir in a couple of tablespoons of water or stock, cover, and set the pot on a heat diffuser over very low heat for about 30 minutes.

Main Courses

*A*RAB COOKS TAKE GREAT pride in their main-course meat, chicken, and fish dishes. Most are prepared in quantities suitable for twice as many people as are expected at the table—the first step in a dance between host and guests that is choreographed to convey how much they respect each other. While presenting a bountiful spread of the best dishes a host can afford is an unwritten rule of Arab etiquette, the amount of food that guests eat is directly connected to how much they esteem the host. In other words, turning down "seconds" is impolite.

Each Arab country claims a national dish that is prepared for special celebrations such as weddings, births, or the return home of a loved one. Lamb is the ultimate symbol of Arab hospitality and is always prominently featured on a special-occasion table. Jordanians have their Mansaf, a layered extravaganza of rice and stewed lamb presented on a huge tray. Saudis love their Kabsa—fragrant, slow-cooked lamb and rice topped with pine nuts and raisins. In Palestine, Kidra, a baked dish of lamb, chickpeas, and whole heads of garlic, is offered at feasts. In Kuwait, Sabour Mashwi, a whole

grilled fish stuffed with dates, is a source of great culinary pride.

Family suppers throughout the Arab world feature one copious main course, set in the center of the table, accompanied by several side dishes.

Ground meat dishes, seasoned with various combinations of warm spices such as cinnamon and allspice, are staples of Arab cookery. The meat is often mixed with rice and stuffed into vegetables, wrapped in phyllo, or rolled up inside grape leaves. Every Arab cooks knows how to make several variations of Kafta, a mixture of ground lamb, parsley, onion, and spices that is grilled or baked. And most Arabs can't live without Kibeh, ground lamb moistened with bulgur that is fried, grilled, or baked.

In dishes that contain meat, Muslim Arabs must use *halal,* or lawful, meat, which means that the animal must be butchered by a Muslim. When I first moved to America, it was nearly impossible to find good-quality lamb, not to mention halal lamb. Much has changed since then. Excellent fresh lamb, though not halal, is now available from places such as Jamison Farms (see Sources) and in many quality markets. With the increasing population of Muslims—about 7 million in the U.S.—it is now much easier to buy halal meat, especially in large cities.

I use only fresh lamb, steering clear of the frozen varieties from Australia and New Zealand, which are pallid by comparison. When I can't buy fresh lamb, I substitute beef, usually from the shanks.

As in many other countries, in the Arab world chicken is abundant and relatively inexpensive. It is cooked in a great number of ways. In Lebanon it is usually grilled and served with hummus and garlic. It is also served with couscous, as it is in Morocco. In other Mediterranean countries chicken is also grilled, sometimes served with rose water and saffron-flavored rice.

Fish dishes are served in abundance along the coast of North Africa and the Eastern Mediterranean, where gray and red mullet, as well as mackerel, rule supreme. Those countries also enjoy a great variety of shellfish. In the Arab countries bordering the Red Sea and the Arabian Gulf, shrimps, grouper and *zubaidi* are served with rice, both sweet and savory.

Moroccan Couscous

COUSCOUS BI KHODRA WA DAJAJ

For the Moroccan spice mix:

1 tablespoon allspice berries

1 tablespoon cumin seeds

1 tablespoon black peppercorns

1 tablespoon cardamom pods, crushed

1 tablespoon coriander seeds

1 tablespoon ground ginger

One 3-inch cinnamon stick

2 teaspoons whole cloves

2 teaspoons cayenne pepper

1½ teaspoons saffron threads

1 tablespoon ground cinnamon

1 tablespoon salt

For the masala (onion topping):

¼ cup vegetable oil

1 teaspoon saffron threads

2 pounds onions, halved and thinly sliced

2 cups Spiced Chicken Stock (page 125) *or* low-sodium canned broth

½ cup golden raisins

1 cup canned chickpeas, drained and rinsed

Salt, to taste

For the Cornish hens:

½ cup vegetable oil

½ pound onions, finely chopped

4 Cornish hens, rinsed and split in half lengthwise

6 to 8 cups boiling water

1 teaspoon salt

*A*lthough I have traveled in that beautiful country, I learned how to cook Moroccan food primarily from my friend Zubaida, who was living in London at the time Aref and I and our three boys lived there. Zubaida used to help me prepare food for dinner parties and celebrations. That was twenty years ago, when we made couscous from scratch in a couscousière (a double-boiler-like setup in which the top pot has a perforated bottom that allows the couscous granules to steam) and preparing this dish was truly an all-day affair. Now that instant couscous is available (Moroccans use the fine yellow grains that resemble sand) it is a bit more streamlined, but there's no denying that this one-platter party dish asks more of your time than many other Arab specialties (even though many parts of it can be made ahead). To make it a proper Arab one-dish meal, stew some beef and arrange it on the platter with the chicken, and serve it with a Simple Salad. *Serve 10 to 12*

Prepare the Moroccan spice mix: Combine all the ingredients in a bowl. Set aside one third of the spice mix, including the cinnamon stick, and grind the remainder in a spice grinder. Set the ground mixture aside as well.

Prepare the masala: Heat the vegetable oil in a small saucepan over medium heat. Add the saffron and 3 tablespoons of the ground Moroccan spice mix, and sauté until fragrant, about 3 minutes. Add the onions and sauté until they are soft and translucent, about 5 minutes. Deglaze the pan by adding the broth and using a wooden spoon to scrape up any browned bits from the pan. Add the raisins, cover, and cook until the onions have almost melted, about 15 minutes. Add the chickpeas and cook, uncovered, until they are heated through and soft enough to mash with the back of a spoon, about 5 minutes. Season with salt to taste, and set aside.

Cook the Cornish hens: Heat the vegetable oil in a medium pot over medium heat. Add the onions and sauté until soft and translucent, about 5 minutes. Add the reserved unground Moroccan spices and sauté until fragrant, 3 to 4 minutes. Arrange

For the vegetables:

½ cup vegetable oil

1½ pounds red onions, chopped

½ pound carrots, cut into
½-inch cubes

¾ pound sweet potatoes, cut
into ½-inch cubes

1½ pounds turnips, cut into
½-inch cubes

1 pound butternut squash, cut
into ½-inch cubes

1 tablespoon salt

1 teaspoon black pepper

One 14-ounce can tomato sauce

2 cups Spiced Chicken Stock
(page 125) *or* low-sodium
canned broth

½ pound zucchini, cut into
½-inch cubes

For the couscous:

Spiced Chicken Stock (page
125) *or* low-sodium canned
broth, if needed

4 cups instant couscous

2 tablespoons clarified butter
(see page 45)

Salt and black pepper, to taste

For the garnish:

Chopped fresh flat-leaf parsley

Ground cinnamon

the Cornish hens, skin side down, in the pot and cook until the skin is golden brown, about 10 minutes. Add enough of the boiling water to cover the hens by 1 inch. Add the salt, cover the pot, and cook until the meat is tender and cooked through, about 30 minutes. Transfer the hens to a plate and cover them with foil. Strain the broth and set it aside. Discard the whole spices.

Cook the vegetables: While the Cornish hens are cooking, heat the vegetable oil in a medium pot over medium-high heat. Add 3 tablespoons of the ground Moroccan spices and sauté until fragrant, about 3 minutes. Add the onions, carrots, sweet potatoes, turnips, squash, salt, and pepper, and cook until the onions are translucent, about 15 minutes. Reduce the heat to medium, add the tomato sauce and chicken stock, and cover the pot. Cook until the sweet potatoes are fork-tender, about 20 minutes. Add the zucchini, cover, and cook for 5 minutes more. Remove the pot from the heat and wrap it in a fleece blanket to keep it warm until the dish is ready to be assembled.

Cook the couscous: Pour the reserved broth from the Cornish hens into a large pot, adding enough chicken stock to make 4 cups. Bring it to a boil over high heat.

Pour the couscous into a large heatproof bowl, and pour the hot broth over it. Cover the bowl with a plate or plastic wrap, and set it aside for 5 minutes.

Uncover the couscous and add the clarified butter. Fluff the couscous with a fork, mixing the butter in evenly. Season to taste with salt and pepper. Cover with foil and set aside until ready to serve.

Assemble the dish: Spoon the couscous onto a large serving platter, forming a dome shape. Arrange some of the vegetables around it, along the rim of the platter. Arrange the Cornish hen pieces over the couscous, and spoon the masala mixture over the meat and the vegetables. Garnish the dish with the chopped parsley and ground cinnamon. Serve the remaining vegetables and their broth in a bowl on the side.

Lebanese Couscous

MUGRABIEH

Two 3- to 4-pound chickens, rinsed

1 pound boneless lamb shanks, cut into 2-inch cubes, rinsed and patted dry

½ pound onions, chopped

1 tablespoon ground cinnamon

Two 3-inch cinnamon sticks

1 bay leaf

¼ teaspoon black pepper, plus more if needed

2 teaspoons salt, plus more if needed

3 tablespoons plus 2 teaspoons extra virgin olive oil

16 pearl onions, peeled

½ cup fresh chickpeas, soaked overnight and cooked (see page 51), or one 15-ounce can chickpeas, rinsed three times, and drained

2 teaspoons ground caraway seeds

¼ teaspoon white pepper

2 tablespoons plus 1 teaspoon butter, softened

3 cups Lebanese couscous

1 teaspoon all-purpose flour dissolved in ½ cup water

*N*amed for the North African region of Maghreb, where couscous is king, Mugrabieh is mentioned in cookbooks dating to the thirteenth century. Both the dish and the ingredient are known as couscous. The grains themselves vary from Morocco and Palestine to Lebanon, Syria, and Jordan. Pellet-size Lebanese couscous is considerably larger than the tiny North African grains, though both are made from semolina. In Palestine, couscous isn't semolina at all, but rather toasted grains of a mixture of bulgur and flour called maftool, *which is larger than Moroccan couscous and smaller than Lebanese couscous.*

Lebanese couscous has a reputation for taking hours and hours to make, but that's because the traditional method involves long hours of steaming the grains until they are tender. Store-bought couscous needs only about 35 minutes to cook. This couscous should taste distinctly of caraway and cinnamon, so if you find that these fragrant spices do not come through, add some more. To make Mugrabieh ahead, you can prepare everything up to the point at which you add the stock to the couscous for its final cooking. About 15 minutes before the couscous is cooked, place the lamb mixture on the stove to reheat and rewarm the chicken in the oven.

Mugrabieh is an excellent menu choice for a crowd; we always serve it for the Iftar during the month of Ramadan.   *Serves 6 to 8*

Combine the chicken and the lamb in a large pot and add water to cover (about 7 cups). Add the onions, ½ teaspoon of the ground cinnamon, and the cinnamon sticks, bay leaf, and black pepper. Cover the pot and bring to a boil over high heat. Boil for 20 minutes, skimming off any foam that forms on the surface. Then reduce the heat to medium, add 1 teaspoon of the salt, and simmer until the chicken falls away from the bone when you poke it with a fork, 45 minutes. Using a slotted spoon, transfer the chicken to a plate. Transfer the lamb to a 3-quart pot. Strain the stock, and add 3 cups of it to the lamb. Reserve the remaining stock.

Meanwhile, heat 2 tablespoons of the olive oil in a large skillet over high heat. Add the pearl onions and sauté until they are golden, about 10 minutes.

Using a slotted spoon, transfer the pearl onions to the pot containing the lamb and broth. Add the chickpeas, ½ teaspoon of the caraway, and the remaining 1 teaspoon salt. Bring to a boil, and boil for 10 minutes. Then remove the pot from the heat and set it aside. Taste, and adjust the seasoning if needed.

Meanwhile, preheat the oven to 350°F.

Debone the chicken and cut it into 8 pieces. Season the pieces with the white pepper, ¼ teaspoon of the cinnamon, and 1 teaspoon of the butter (smear the butter over the chicken). Place the chicken on a baking sheet and bake until it is golden and crisp, about 20 minutes.

Prepare the couscous: Bring 4 cups salted water to a boil in a saucepan. Add the 2 teaspoons olive oil and the couscous, give it a good stir, and bring to a boil over high heat. Continue boiling the couscous until the grains are tender when you bite into them, about 3 minutes. Pour the couscous into a strainer and rinse under cold running water. Set it aside.

Bring 3½ cups of the remaining stock to a boil in a saucepan over high heat.

Meanwhile, heat the remaining 2 tablespoons butter and 1 tablespoon olive oil in a large pot over high heat. Add the couscous, 1¼ teaspoons of the cinnamon, and the remaining 1½ teaspoons caraway and sauté, stirring, until the mixture is fragrant and all the grains are coated, about 5 minutes. Reduce the heat to low, add the hot stock, cover, and simmer until all the stock has been absorbed and the grains are soft, about 30 minutes. Taste, and adjust the seasonings if needed.

Meanwhile, bring the lamb and chickpea mixture to a boil over high heat. Add the flour/water mixture to the pot and stir until it is incorporated. Reduce the heat to medium and simmer for 15 minutes. Taste, and adjust the seasonings if needed.

To serve: Spoon the couscous onto a large serving dish, spreading it out to cover the entire surface. Arrange the chicken pieces on top. Spoon half of the lamb mixture over the chicken, and season with the remaining 1 teaspoon cinnamon. Place the remaining lamb mixture, with its broth, in a deep bowl and serve it on the side.

THE TRADITIONAL WAY TO CLEAN CHICKEN

Whenever my mother (or grandmother or aunts) was going to cook chicken, she first cleaned the raw flesh with a combination of lemon juice and vinegar—and often with a flour rub as well. This not only removed sliminess and odors but also made the food taste better. I continue to use these traditional techniques today, even with perfectly fresh products. And while these steps are optional, if you follow them, I think you'll agree that they make the dishes even more delicious.

To clean chicken pieces, combine ⅔ cup bottled lemon juice (don't bother with fresh-squeezed) and 1 cup white vinegar in a large glass bowl or pan. Rinse the chicken pieces under cold running water; then place them in the bowl with the acidic liquids. If necessary, add more lemon juice and vinegar so the pieces are covered. Let them soak for 15 to 20 minutes; then rinse with water before continuing with the recipe.

To clean a whole chicken, rinse it well under cold water, pulling any veins, fat, and fleshy bits from the cavity. Drizzle some of the lemon juice and vinegar into the cavity, and rub the whole surface with about 2 tablespoons all-purpose flour. Rinse it well. Then soak the outside of the chicken in the bowl of lemon juice and vinegar for 15 minutes, turning to make sure it has all been cleansed. Rinse, and proceed with the recipe.

Chicken Stuffed with Spiced Beef and Rice

DAJAJ MAHSHE

Two 4-pound chickens, excess
   fat removed, rinsed and
   patted dry

2 teaspoons ground allspice

½ teaspoon ground cloves

½ teaspoon grated nutmeg

1 teaspoon ground cardamom

1½ teaspoons ground cinnamon

1 teaspoon black pepper

2 teaspoons salt

Spiced Beef with Rice (page
   173), cooled

4 medium onions, quartered

6 to 8 shallots

2 bay leaves

Three 3-inch cinnamon sticks

¼ cup fresh lemon juice

½ cup fried pine nuts (see page
   43)

½ cup peeled almonds, fried
   (see pages 12, 43)

*O*ne of the highlights on my Auntie Nina's Christmas table is her *Dajaj Mahshe*, a huge platter laid with a bed of seasoned rice and beef and topped with two succulent roasted chickens, both marinated overnight in a dry spice rub and then filled with the same rice and beef mixture. The best part? There are always leftovers.

You don't have to wait for a holiday to serve this delicious chicken dish. Dajaj Mahshe is wonderful for company, served with just a Simple Salad and Cucumber and Yogurt.   *Serves 6 to 8*

Sew the necks of the chickens closed with a trussing needle and thread.

Combine the allspice, cloves, nutmeg, cardamom, cinnamon, pepper, and salt in a small bowl, and stir well. Rub this all over the chickens, inside and out, and then refrigerate them, covered with plastic wrap, for at least 4 hours or as long as overnight.

Preheat the oven to 450°F. Line a large roasting pan with two sheets of aluminum foil, one spanning the length of the pan, the other spanning the width, with at least 6 inches overhanging on all sides.

Spoon the Spiced Beef with Rice into the chickens, reserving any extra to serve on the side. Seal the chicken cavities closed with a trussing needle and thread. Place the chickens in the middle of the prepared roasting pan and arrange the onions, shallots, bay leaves, and cinnamon sticks around them. Pour ½ cup water around the chickens, and then wrap the foil around them tightly. Fill the pan with at least 1 inch of water and the lemon juice. Roast for 2 hours, refilling the pan with water as it evaporates.

Reduce the heat to 350°F and roast for 2 hours more.

Meanwhile, put the remaining Spiced Beef with Rice in an ovenproof dish, sprinkle with 2 tablespoons water, and cover tightly with foil. Warm the rice in the oven with the chicken for the last 30 to 45 minutes of cooking. (Alternatively, heat the rice in a microwave oven.)

Remove the pan from the oven, and pour off any remaining water. Open the foil wrappings carefully (the steam could burn your hand). Using two dessert plates as implements, lift the chickens onto your serving plate. Snip and pull off the trussing thread. Surround the chickens with Spiced Beef with Rice, and scatter the pine nuts and almonds over the chickens and the rice. Discard the quartered onions, bay leaves, and cinnamon sticks. Put the shallots and the juices from the chicken in a sauceboat to serve along with the chicken. Present the whole chickens at the table before slicing.

When ready to serve, carve the chickens. Give each guest a slice with some of the rice stuffing, additional rice from the platter, and some juice.

For the leftovers: The day after the holiday festivities, Auntie Nina made this delicious savory "cake" with the leftovers: Shred the leftover chicken and arrange it in the bottom of a cake pan. Smooth the rice over it. Sprinkle 2 tablespoons water over the rice, and bake in a preheated 350°F oven for about 30 minutes. Let it cool slightly, then invert the cake pan onto a serving plate and unmold the "cake." Garnish it with fried pine nuts, and serve hot.

Chicken Freka with Ground Beef

DAJAJ BI FREKA

3 tablespoons butter

3 tablespoons canola oil

1 pound onions, grated on the large holes of a box grater

1 pound ground beef

2 cups freka, picked over, rinsed, and drained

1 teaspoon ground allspice

¼ teaspoon grated nutmeg

¼ teaspoon ground cardamom

⅛ teaspoon ground cloves

1½ teaspoons ground cinnamon

2½ teaspoons salt

1 teaspoon black pepper

2½ cups stock from cooking the chicken (see below), Spiced Chicken Stock, Beef Stock (pages 125, 131), *or* canned low-sodium broth

4 pounds chicken parts, boiled in water to cover by 2 inches, skinned, and deboned

¼ cup fried pine nuts (see page 43)

½ cup fried peeled almonds, (see pages 12, 43)

Freka are greenish brown underripe wheat grains that have been roasted and either left whole or cracked. They impart a smoky, nutty flavor to dishes, making an excellent accompaniment to hearty winter foods. Though it is grown only in Egypt, Syria, and Jordan and was once considered peasant food, freka *has become very fashionable among cosmopolitan Arabs and is now found on restaurant menus in such cities as Amman, Damascus, and Beirut. Freka is available in most Middle Eastern markets. There are different types, and the cooking times may vary; the green grains take a little longer to cook than the brown variety. Properly cooked freka should have the texture of risotto, without the creaminess. Here it is cooked together with spiced ground beef and served with succulent pieces of chicken.* Serves 6

Heat the butter and canola oil in a large pot over medium heat. Add the onions and sauté until translucent, about 15 minutes. Add the beef and sauté, breaking it up with the back of a spoon, until it loses its pink color, about 10 minutes. Add the freka and stir until the grains are coated with the oil, about 4 minutes. Stir in the allspice, nutmeg, cardamom, cloves, ½ teaspoon of the cinnamon, 2 teaspoons of the salt, and ½ teaspoon of the pepper. Add 1½ cups of the chicken stock, give the mixture a good stir, cover the pot, and bring to a boil. Continue boiling for 15 minutes. Then reduce the heat to low, slide a heat diffuser under the pot, and cook, stirring often, for 1 hour. The freka should be tender to the bite—not at all crunchy—but still hold its shape. Remove the pot from the stove, wrap it in a fleece blanket, and set it aside for at least 30 minutes or up to 3 hours.

Meanwhile, preheat the oven to 300°F.

Arrange the chicken pieces in an ovenproof dish and season with the remaining ½ teaspoon salt and ½ teaspoon pepper. Pour the remaining 1 cup stock into the dish (enough to just cover the bottom), and cover the dish with foil. Reheat in the oven.

To serve, spoon the freka onto a serving dish and arrange the chicken pieces on top. Garnish with the pine nuts and almonds, and dust sparingly with the remaining 1 teaspoon cinnamon.

Chicken and Rice with Creamy Yogurt Sauce

FATET DAJAJ

32 ounces plain full-fat yogurt

10 cloves garlic, mashed

Salt, to taste (optional)

¾ cup fresh lemon juice

3 tablespoons vegetable oil

1 loaf Arab flatbread, cut into
    ½-inch squares

One 6- to 8-pound chicken,
    rinsed

¼ cup Spiced Chicken Stock
    (page 125) *or* low-sodium
    canned broth

½ teaspoon salt

½ teaspoon black pepper

1 tablespoon butter, cut into
    small pieces

Basmati Rice (page 164), kept
    warm

½ cup fried pine nuts (see page
    43)

Chopped fresh parsley, for
    garnish

Paprika or red pepper flakes, for
    garnish

This layered "casserole" is one of the oldest dishes in Arab cuisine. Some like to serve it without the yogurt, but I think it is a wonderfully cooling and creamy counterpoint to the tangy garlic and lemon–soaked croutons. Make sure you sink the serving spoon all the way to the bottom of the dish to get a sampling of each layer. Serve Fatet Dajaj the same day you make it; it doesn't hold up well overnight.

Serves 6 to 8

Spoon the yogurt into a bowl and set two paper towels directly on top of it to absorb the excess liquid. (This step isn't necessary if you are using Greek Total brand yogurt.) Replace the paper towels when they become saturated. After about 10 minutes, remove and discard the paper towels.

Add half of the garlic to the yogurt and mix thoroughly. Taste the mixture—it should have only a subtle garlic flavor—and add a little salt if desired. Whisk the remaining garlic and the lemon juice together in a small bowl. Set both mixtures aside.

Heat the vegetable oil in a large skillet over high heat. Add the bread pieces, in batches, and fry, stirring constantly, until crisp, about 1 minute. Using a slotted spoon, transfer the croutons to paper towels to drain.

Preheat the oven to 350°F.

Cut the chicken into small pieces (at least 8 pieces), and skin and debone them. Place the meat in a baking pan and add the stock. Season with the salt and pepper, and scatter the butter over the chicken. Bake, covered, for 20 minutes.

Spread the croutons in a deep 8 by 13-inch baking dish, completely covering the bottom. Drizzle the lemon-garlic mixture over the croutons and toss so that every piece is soaked. Spread the Basmati Rice on top, smoothing it with the back of a spoon. Cover the rice with the yogurt mixture, spreading it evenly over the grains, and top with the chicken pieces. Scatter the pine nuts over all, and garnish with the parsley and paprika. Serve immediately.

Rose Water–Scented Chicken with Saffron Rice

MASHBOUSE AL DAJAJ

During the years we lived in Kuwait, one of Aref's friends married my friend Jumana, and in the same span of time, they also had three boys. Of course our friendship went far beyond the sharing of recipes, but my boys will always remember Jumana for this succulent chicken. When she visited us in the U.S. for the first time, Jumana shared this recipe with me and it has now become a part of our Thanksgiving celebration. Mashbouse Al Dajaj takes some time—about 3 hours—but you can prepare it in stages: Make the onion mixture a day or two ahead and reheat it before adding; cook the chicken a day ahead, up to the point of sautéing; then finish it the day you plan to serve the dish. And you can also cook the rice several hours ahead.   *Serves 6*

For the chicken:

1 teaspoon ground allspice

1 teaspoon ground cardamom

½ teaspoon ground cinnamon

2 teaspoons salt

½ teaspoon black pepper

5 pounds chicken parts *or* 3 Cornish hens, rinsed

2 medium onions, thinly sliced

6 cloves garlic

6 allspice berries

6 black peppercorns

Three 3-inch cinnamon sticks

6 cardamom pods

1 dried lime (*loumi*)

For the onions:

½ cup vegetable oil

3 pounds medium onions, finely chopped

1 teaspoon ground allspice

½ teaspoon white pepper

⅛ teaspoon ground cinnamon

⅛ teaspoon ground cloves

⅛ teaspoon grated nutmeg

½ teaspoon ground cardamom

1 teaspoon salt

1 cup raisins, soaked in 1½ cups warm water for 30 minutes

For the tomato sauce:

¼ cup extra virgin olive oil

10 cloves garlic, mashed

2 jalapeño or serrano peppers, seeded and finely chopped

Cook the chicken: Combine the allspice, cardamom, cinnamon, 1 teaspoon of the salt, and pepper in a small bowl, and mix well. Rub this spice mix all over the chicken pieces. Place the chicken in a large pot and add cold water to cover. Add the onions, garlic, allspice berries, peppercorns, cinnamon sticks, cardamom pods, and dried lemon. Cover the pot and bring to a boil over high heat. Skim off the froth that forms on the surface. Reduce the heat and simmer until the chicken meat falls away from the bone when you prick it with a fork, about 45 minutes. Strain the chicken, reserving the broth. Remove the bones from the chicken pieces, and season the chicken meat with the remaining 1 teaspoon salt. Place the chicken on a dish and set it aside. Set the broth aside as well. Discard the whole spices and the dried lemon.

Cook the onions: Heat the vegetable oil in a large skillet over high heat. Add the onions, allspice, white pepper, cinnamon, cloves, nutmeg, cardamom, and salt, and sauté until the onions are soft and translucent, 15 to 20 minutes. Drain the raisins, add them to the pot, and stir to incorporate. Remove the onion mixture from the heat and cover to keep it warm.

Make the tomato sauce: Heat the olive oil in a small pot over high heat. Add the garlic and jalapeño and sauté, stirring constantly, until fragrant, about 2 minutes. Reduce the heat to medium-high

2½ pounds tomatoes, peeled
    and chopped

3 tablespoons tomato paste

1½ teaspoons salt

1 teaspoon black pepper

½ teaspoon ground cinnamon

For the rice:

2 tablespoons butter

3 cups basmati rice, rinsed (see
    page 165), soaked, and
    drained

1 teaspoon salt

3 strands saffron, steeped in ¼
    cup rose water for 2 hours

For sautéing the chicken:

10 threads saffron, steeped in 2
    cups rose water for 2 hours

½ cup fresh lemon juice

1 tablespoon ground cardamom

1 cup vegetable oil

and add the tomatoes, tomato paste, salt, pepper, and cinnamon. Cook, partially covered, until the mixture forms a thickened sauce, about 25 minutes. Set it aside and keep warm.

Cook the rice: Heat the butter in a large pot over high heat. Add the rice and salt. Stir to coat the rice. Add 2¾ cups of the reserved chicken broth; stir. Cover the pot and cook until almost all the broth has been absorbed, about 5 minutes. Then reduce the heat to low and gently pour the rose water mixture on top of the rice; do not stir. Cover the pot, slide a heat diffuser under it, and cook until the rice is tender, 15 to 20 minutes. Remove the pot from the heat and wrap it in a fleece blanket to keep it warm.

Sauté the chicken: Preheat the oven to 300°F.

Combine the rose water–saffron mixture, lemon juice, and cardamom in a wide, shallow bowl and set it aside. This will be a "wash" for the chicken.

Heat the vegetable oil in a large skillet over high heat. Drag a few pieces of chicken through the wash and slide them into the skillet. Sauté until the pieces are golden yellow, 3 to 4 minutes on each side. Transfer the chicken to an ovenproof dish. Repeat with the remaining chicken. Cover the dish with aluminum foil and keep it warm in the oven.

To serve: Spoon the rice onto a large rimmed platter. Scatter the onion mixture over the rice, covering the entire surface. Arrange the chicken pieces on top of the onions in a spiral pattern, beginning in the center and working your way out to the rim of the platter. Place the tomato sauce in a bowl, and serve it alongside the rice and chicken.

Poached Chicken with Garlic-Chile Relish

FATET DEJAJ GAZAWEH

This special-occasion dish dates back to the Middle Ages, when the Egyptians living across the river Nile in the Sinai made bread without yeast, which meant that the round, flat loaves turned dry and stale fast. They combined the hardened bread with stock, rice, and meat or chicken to make this threed, *or "food of the Arab." I learned to make* fatet *from my friend Jumana Al Shawa. Her husband, like mine, is from Gaza, where the cuisine is influenced by the cooking of neighboring Egypt.* **Serves 6 to 8**

1 recipe Spiced Chicken Stock made with 4 to 5 pounds chicken parts (page 125), strained, chicken parts reserved, kept hot

Salt and black pepper, to taste

20 cloves garlic, mashed (see page 32)

1½ cups fresh lemon juice

3 jalapeño peppers, seeded and finely chopped

3 to 4 loaves *markouk* (see page 22) or other paper-thin soft flatbread

2½ cups Basmati Rice (page 164), kept hot

½ cup fried pine nuts (see page 43)

½ cup fried slivered almonds (see page 43)

Preheat the broiler.

Season the chicken pieces with salt and pepper and place them on a baking sheet. Broil until the chicken is golden, about 2 minutes. Cover with aluminum foil and set aside.

Combine the garlic, lemon juice, and jalapeños in a small bowl, and set aside.

To assemble the *fatet* for serving, place one piece of *markouk* in the middle of a large platter, tucking its edges under to form a rim. Tear the remaining *markouk* into 4-inch pieces and arrange them around the edge of the platter. Drizzle ½ cup of the lemon juice mixture and ½ cup of the chicken stock over the bread. Spoon the rice over the center bread, mounding it high and leaving the rim of the bread uncovered. Arrange the chicken pieces over the rice. Garnish with the pine nuts and almonds.

Use a large spoon to serve each portion, and be sure to include a little bit of each layer—bread, rice, and chicken—on each guest's plate. Serve the remaining lemon juice mixture on the side.

Chicken Kebabs

SHISH TAWOOK

10 cloves garlic, mashed

½ cup fresh lemon juice

⅓ cup olive oil

2 tablespoons plain yogurt

½ teaspoon ground cardamom

1 teaspoon salt

1 teaspoon white pepper

2 pounds boneless, skinless chicken breasts, rinsed and cut into 1-inch pieces

Garlic Paste (page 37)

1 loaf *markouk* (see page 22) *or* other paper-thin soft flatbread

I use white breast meat for these kebabs, but you can use a mix of light and dark, as long as you do not combine the two on a single skewer; light meat cooks faster than dark. Unlike Shish Kebab, Shish Tawook is not traditionally grilled with vegetables, but I occasionally thread chunks of green bell peppers and onions onto the skewers. Sometimes I stray a bit from tradition and add dried oregano to the marinade, too. To save yourself from running back and forth between the kitchen and the grill, bring a large piece of foil with you on your first trip out—be sure it doesn't touch the raw meat—and once you've put all the skewers on the coals, cover the platter with the foil; then place the fully cooked skewers on it. I always prefer a grilled kebab to one broiled in the oven, but you can certainly use the broiler for these. Serve Shish Tawook with Hummus, Roasted Eggplant Spread, or Broad Bean Salad.

Serves 6 (makes 8 skewers)

Combine the garlic, lemon juice, olive oil, yogurt, cardamom, salt, and pepper in a shallow glass or ceramic dish. Stir well. Add the chicken and turn to coat it all over. Cover with plastic wrap and refrigerate for at least 2 hours or as long as overnight.

Prepare a charcoal grill or preheat the broiler.

Thread the chicken onto metal skewers, dividing the pieces evenly among them. Grill, turning the skewers at least twice, until the chicken is cooked through, about 6 minutes in all. Just before taking the skewers off the grill, brush each one with the Garlic Paste.

To serve, unfold a loaf of markouk onto a large platter and arrange the kebabs on one half of the loaf. Fold the other half over to cover them.

Chicken Shawarma

SHAWARMA DAJAJ

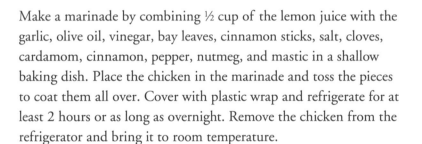

1 cup fresh lemon juice

10 cloves garlic, mashed

6 tablespoons olive oil

2 tablespoons white vinegar

4 bay leaves

Two 3-inch cinnamon sticks, broken

2 teaspoons salt

¼ teaspoon ground cloves

2 teaspoons ground cardamom

½ teaspoon ground cinnamon

½ teaspoon white pepper

¼ teaspoon grated nutmeg

4 pebble-size pieces mastic, crushed (see page 22)

4 pounds boneless, skinless chicken thighs, rinsed and cut into 2 by ½-inch pieces

1 tablespoon Garlic Paste (page 37)

1 loaf *markouk* (see page 22) *or* other paper-thin soft flatbread

I never eat this addictive chicken before I have a social commitment! There are ten cloves of garlic in the marinade alone—and then a tangy garlic sauce is drizzled over the chicken just before it is served. *Shawarma Dajaj* will always remind me of my years at boarding school in Lebanon, where my friend Wafa and I ate the succulent pieces of chicken wrapped in Arab flatbread whenever we studied late into the night. In the Arab world, they are as popular with students as pizza is here in the States. To serve the Shawarma sandwich-style, wrap it in Arab pocket bread with Tahini or Hummus, sliced tomatoes, and thinly sliced onions rubbed with sumac. **Serves 10**

Make a marinade by combining ½ cup of the lemon juice with the garlic, olive oil, vinegar, bay leaves, cinnamon sticks, salt, cloves, cardamom, cinnamon, pepper, nutmeg, and mastic in a shallow baking dish. Place the chicken in the marinade and toss the pieces to coat them all over. Cover with plastic wrap and refrigerate for at least 2 hours or as long as overnight. Remove the chicken from the refrigerator and bring it to room temperature.

Preheat the oven to 400°F, with a rack in the lower third of the oven.

Using your hands, squeeze the chicken pieces dry of the marinade—it is important to rid them of as much liquid as possible, or the chicken will steam—and place them in a single layer in an ovenproof dish. Bake the chicken, using a spatula to turn it occasionally, until it is golden and browned on the edges, 30 to 45 minutes.

Meanwhile, prepare the sauce: Mix the remaining ½ cup lemon juice and the Garlic Paste together, and set it aside.

Transfer the chicken to a serving platter, drizzle with the sauce, cover with the *markouk,* and serve immediately.

Chicken Kibeh

KIBEH DAJAJ

For the filling:

⅓ cup extra virgin olive oil

¼ cup pine nuts

3 pounds onions, finely diced

½ teaspoon ground allspice

⅛ teaspoon grated nutmeg

⅛ teaspoon ground cinnamon

1 tablespoon ground sumac

1 teaspoon salt

¼ teaspoon white pepper

¼ cup walnut pieces

For the Kibeh:

1 pound skinless, boneless
    chicken breasts

3 cups fine bulgur, picked over
    and rinsed (see page 281)

½ pound onions, quartered

1 teaspoon salt

½ teaspoon white pepper

1¼ teaspoons ground allspice

½ teaspoon ground cinnamom

¼ teaspoon grated nutmeg

½ teaspoon ground cardamon

1 tablespoon extra virgin olive
    oil, plus more for the baking
    dish

3 tablespoons butter

Fresh parsley leaves, for garnish

*W*hen we moved to Kentucky, there was no fresh lamb available in the markets, so Aref located a farmer who was willing to butcher one for me. Much to my surprise, Aref purchased the whole lamb, which I didn't find out until he walked into the kitchen and unloaded it on the kitchen counter! I spent hours trimming the meat to make traditional *kibeh*, which turned out to be much more time-consuming than it was worth. And that's how Chicken Kibeh came to be. Though this is not authentically Middle Eastern, it is a perfect example of how I have melded my old and new lives together in the kitchen. I use organic chicken to make this layered dish of ground chicken and spiced onions, which has been adopted by my family and friends. Serve it hot with Roasted Eggplant Spread or Hummus. Kibeh can be prepared and frozen, tightly covered, either before baking or after. Defrost it in the refrigerator and bake as directed.   *Serves 6*

Prepare the filling: Heat the olive oil in a skillet over high heat and fry the pine nuts, stirring them constantly to prevent them from burning, about 45 seconds. Using a slotted spoon, transfer them to a paper towel–lined plate.

Add the onions to the skillet and sauté over medium heat until they are soft and tender, about 10 minutes. Stir in the allspice, nutmeg, cinnamon, sumac, salt, and white pepper. Reduce the heat to medium and continue to cook, stirring occasionally, until the onions are soft and slightly golden, about 25 minutes. Transfer the onion mixture to a plate lined with paper towels, add the pine nuts and walnuts, and set aside.

Make the Kibeh: Rinse the chicken breasts and pat them dry with paper towels. Trim away any excess fat and cut the breasts into 3-inch pieces. Cover and refrigerate.

Combine the bulgur and the onion quarters in a food processor and pulse several times, scraping the bowl down as necessary, until the mixture forms a smooth, somewhat runny paste. Transfer the bulgur mixture to a bowl and set it aside.

Fill a large bowl with ice and set a slightly smaller mixing bowl in it. Working in batches if necessary, pulse the chicken pieces in the food processor until they form a paste. Transfer the chicken paste to the smaller mixing bowl. Add the bulgur mixture and stir to evenly incorporate it. Add the salt, pepper, allspice, cinnamon, nutmeg, and cardamom. Wet your hands with ice water and knead the mixture in the bowl for about 10 minutes. Keep your hands wet with ice water as you work with the "dough." Return the kibeh to the food processor, and working with small batches, pulse each batch three times, adding 2 pieces of ice to each batch to keep it cold.

Preheat the oven to 350°F, with two racks in the top third of the oven. Coat a 9 by 13-inch baking dish, or a 13-inch round baking dish, with olive oil. Place two thirds of the kibeh dough between two sheets of wax paper and roll it out to about 1-inch thickness—it should be a few inches larger than the baking dish. Remove the top piece of wax paper and invert the dough into the dish, pressing it up the sides of the dish. Remove the second piece of wax paper. Spoon the filling evenly over the kibeh dough, and smooth it with the back of a spoon.

Roll out the remaining kibeh dough, as before, and transfer it to the dish as you did the bottom layer, placing it over the filling. Seal the bottom and top layers by folding the edges of the bottom layer of dough over the top layer. Dip your hands in ice water and smooth the top layer. Score the surface of the kibeh with a sharp knife, making a pattern of triangles or squares.

Heat the butter with the olive oil in a small pan over medium-high heat. Pour the mixture evenly over the kibeh. Bake on the lower of the oven racks for 40 to 45 minutes. Then raise the oven temperature to 400°F, transfer the dish to the top rack, and bake until the top is golden brown, about 10 minutes.

Cover the kibeh with a plate, and holding it in place, tilt the baking dish to pour off the fat that has accumulated on the surface.

To serve, cut the kibeh along the score marks, transfer the pieces to a serving platter, and garnish with the parsley.

Stuffed Zucchini in Yogurt Sauce

KOOSSA BI LABAN

2 pounds (about 15) baby
  zucchini, rinsed, stem end
  trimmed

1½ teaspoons salt

1 cup short-grain rice, rinsed
  (see page 165), soaked, and
  drained

1 pound lean ground beef

2 tablespoons canola oil

3 cloves garlic, mashed

1 tablespoon ground allspice

½ teaspoon black pepper

For the yogurt sauce:

64 ounces plain full-fat yogurt

1 egg

1 tablespoon all-purpose flour

½ teaspoon salt

6 cloves garlic, mashed

2 tablespoons dried mint

*S*tuffed vegetables, or mahashi, *are Arab comfort food. You could say that Arabs are born with the urge to stuff or roll any vegetable available to them. A mixture of seasoned ground meat and rice is the most common filling, and it is spooned into everything from cucumbers, tomatoes, and onions to cabbage and chard leaves.*

  To store leftover Koossa, transfer the zucchini to a container with a tight-fitting lid and pour the yogurt into a second container. It will keep in the refrigerator for up to 3 days. To reheat, whisk a little water into the yogurt sauce, combine it with the zucchini in a pot, and warm over low heat.   *Serves 6*

Using a zucchini corer, gently hollow out the zucchini from the stem end, making sure the root end remains intact. Place the zucchini in a deep bowl and season with 1 teaspoon of the salt. Add water to cover and set aside.

Meanwhile, place the rice in a large bowl. Add the beef, canola oil, garlic, allspice, remaining ½ teaspoon salt, and the pepper. Using your hands, mix until the stuffing is thoroughly combined.

Transfer the zucchini to a colander and shake well to drain any excess liquid. Using your hands, fill each zucchini three fourths full with stuffing, gently pounding the root end in the palm of your hand to coax the filling all the way to the bottom. Do not pack the zucchini too tightly. Place the filled zucchini in a large pot, arranging them in layers as you fill them. Add water to cover by 2 inches, cover the pot, and cook over high heat for 15 minutes. Then reduce the heat to medium-low and simmer until the zucchini can be easily pierced with the tip of a knife, about 30 minutes. Using a slotted spoon, transfer the zucchini to a platter.

Make the yogurt sauce: Place the yogurt in a large pot. Set a stack of five paper towels directly on the surface of the yogurt to absorb any liquid. Repeat three times or until there is no liquid visible. (This step is not necessary if you are using Total brand yogurt.) Add the egg and beat it into the yogurt until it is incorporated. Combine the flour with ½ cup water in a small bowl, and stir to dissolve. Whisk the flour mixture into the yogurt. Add the salt. Bring the yogurt mixture to a boil over high heat, stirring constantly. Reduce the heat to low and gently add the zucchini, one at a time. In a small bowl, combine the garlic with the mint, rubbing the mint between your palms to crush it. Add the garlic-mint mixture to the yogurt and pick up the pot with both hands to swirl the mixture around. (To avoid breaking the zucchini, do not stir with a spoon.) Cook, uncovered, for 15 minutes to allow the flavors to come together.

To serve: Using a slotted spoon, transfer the zucchini to a platter. Pour the yogurt sauce into a bowl to serve on the side.

Variations:

Tomato Sauce: Cover the layers of zucchini in the pot with three 15-ounce cans tomato sauce and 5 mashed garlic cloves. Cook over high heat for 15 minutes. Then reduce the heat to low, cover, and cook for 30 minutes more. Place the zucchini on a platter and serve the tomato sauce on the side.

Sautéed Zucchini: Whenever she made Koossa, my mother always reserved a few for sautéing in equal parts ghee and olive oil. My father loved this simple version.

Kibeh Balls in Yogurt Sauce: Drop raw Kibeh Balls (page 230) into the yogurt sauce and cook for 15 minutes over medium heat. Substitute 1 cup finely chopped fresh cilantro for the dried mint, and serve over rice with vermicelli.

Beef and White Bean Stew with Yogurt Sauce: Add Beef with White Beans (page 221) to the yogurt sauce for the last 20 minutes of cooking time. Substitute 1 cup minced onions sautéed in 2 tablespoons butter for the garlic and mint. Serve over rice, or with Bulgur and Fava Beans (page 281). Garnish with fresh dill.

Stuffed Artichoke Hearts

ARDICHOKEH MAHSHI

12 fresh or frozen artichoke hearts

Zest of 1 lemon, removed with a vegetable peeler (for preparing fresh artichokes)

¼ cup fresh lemon juice (for preparing fresh artichokes)

2 tablespoons vegetable oil

2 medium onions, minced

1 pound lean ground beef or lamb

2 teaspoons ground allspice

¼ teaspoon ground cinnamon

1 teaspoon salt

1 teaspoon black pepper

¼ cup pine nuts

For the sauce:

3 tablespoons all-purpose flour

2 tablespoons butter

3 cups Beef Stock (page 131) *or* low-sodium canned broth, heated

2 tablespoons fresh lemon juice, plus more if needed

1 teaspoon salt

1 teaspoon black pepper

For the garnish:

Chopped fresh parsley

Lemon slices

When we lived in Kuwait, one of my favorite seasons was early spring, when the boxes of fresh artichokes would arrive. Every surface in my kitchen was covered with kharshouf, *the artichokes cultivated in North Africa, Syria, and Egypt. Because their season was so short, I used to stock up and then spend days peeling, cleaning, and preparing them for the freezer for use in the wintertime.*

Since moving to the U.S., I have stopped preparing fresh artichokes to freeze because the frozen artichokes from Egypt, available in Middle Eastern groceries, are quite good—and require a lot less work! Do try, however, making this dish at least once with fresh artichokes when they are at their peak. Serve this with plain white rice or rice cooked with vermicelli.

To serve Ardichokeh Mahshi as a side dish, add 1 cup frozen peas to the meat mixture before stuffing it in the artichokes.   Serves 6

If using frozen artichoke hearts, while they are still frozen, trim off any tough areas with a paring knife. Slice a thin piece off the bottom so the artichoke hearts sit upright. Reserve the trimmings. Set the artichoke hearts out on the kitchen counter to thaw. Pat them dry before cooking.

To prepare fresh artichoke hearts, have ready a bowl of salted ice water mixed with fresh lemon juice. Toss the lemon zest into the water as well. Remove the tough outer leaves of each artichoke; you should be able to peel them away easily with your fingers. When you reach the soft, yellow interior leaves, peel them away too. Using kitchen shears, trim the tip of the artichoke, leaving ¼ inch attached to the heart. Next, cut off the stem with a knife. Use a small spoon to scoop out the hairy choke, which is revealed when you cut away the tip. The heart is all that remains. Slice a thin piece off from the bottom of the artichoke, reserving the trimming, and drop the heart into the bowl of acidulated water. Repeat with the remaining artichokes.

Heat the vegetable oil in a large skillet over high heat. Add the artichoke hearts and sauté until golden, about 4 minutes on the bottom and 2 minutes on the top. Remove them with a slotted spoon and transfer to a paper towel–lined plate.

Reduce the heat to medium and add the onions to the skillet. Sauté until they are soft and have released some of their juices, about 5 minutes. Add the ground beef and cook, breaking it up with the back of a spoon, until it loses its pink color, about 10 minutes. Add the allspice, cinnamon, salt, and pepper, and stir until they are incorporated into the meat. Cook until the meat is a rich mahogany brown, about 15 minutes. Then stir in the pine nuts. Taste, and adjust the seasoning if necessary. Set the meat mixture aside to cool.

To fill the hearts, hold one in the palm of your hand and spoon about 1 tablespoon of the filling into its center. Press the filling firmly into the cup with your thumb, and cover it with some of the trimmings. Repeat with the remaining hearts, filling, and trimmings. Arrange the stuffed artichokes in a 10 by 12-inch baking dish and set it aside.

Preheat the oven to 350°F, with a rack in the middle.

Prepare the sauce: Combine the flour and butter in a saucepan over medium-high heat and cook, whisking constantly, until the flour is golden brown, 5 to 8 minutes. Remove the pan from the heat and slowly add the hot stock, whisking constantly to prevent lumps. Return the pan to the heat and cook until it thickens to a creamy consistency, about 5 minutes. Add the lemon juice, salt, and pepper. Taste, and add more lemon juice and salt if desired.

Pour the sauce over the artichoke hearts; the artichokes should be half submerged in the sauce. Cover with aluminum foil and bake until the artichokes are fork-tender, about 20 minutes.

Serve straight from the cooking dish, or transfer the artichoke hearts to a serving platter. Spoon some of the sauce over them, and garnish with the parsley and some lemon slices.

Grape Leaves Stuffed with Lamb and Rice

WARAK ENAB BI LAHMEH

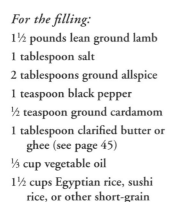

For the filling:

1½ pounds lean ground lamb

1 tablespoon salt

2 tablespoons ground allspice

1 teaspoon black pepper

½ teaspoon ground cardamom

1 tablespoon clarified butter or ghee (see page 45)

⅓ cup vegetable oil

1½ cups Egyptian rice, sushi rice, or other short-grain rice, rinsed (see page 165), soaked, and drained

One 16-ounce jar grape leaves, drained and rinsed

1 pound tomatoes, cut into ½-inch-thick slices

1 teaspoon salt

½ teaspoon black pepper

1 pound yellow onions, cut into ½-inch-thick slices

2 pounds lamb cutlets, trimmed from the neck, sliced into 1-inch-thick pieces

3 pounds zucchini, cut into ½-inch-thick slices

1 cup fresh lemon juice

Lemon slices, for garnish

Chopped fresh parsley, for garnish

Every time I make Warak Enab bi Lahmeh, I am reminded of my early days in the U.S., when everything familiar to me was so far away—my mother was back in Jordan and my close friends were in London, the Middle East, or several states away, and it was difficult to find the ingredients I was accustomed to using. When I first made these, I couldn't find the tiny zucchini—about the length of an index finger—that my mother insisted were essential, nor could I get the right cut of lamb at the supermarket. But I found that wrapping grape leaves around a filling was a comforting occupation, so I made do. Of course as time went on, I found better sources, but I never did replace the beautiful stone I used in Kuwait to weight the rolls in the pot—I was unable to take it when we settled in the United States in the early 1990s. Aref, who was eager for me to be happy in our new circumstances, found the solution in an old brick. I covered it with several layers of foil and it worked just fine.

Serve these with Cucumber and Yogurt, Simple Salad, and Arab flatbread for dipping into the broth. To make a meal, serve the stuffed grape leaves with Chicken Kibeh, Meat Pies, Hummus, and Roasted Eggplant Spread.   *Serves 6*

Make the filling: Combine the lamb, salt, allspice, pepper, cardamom, clarified butter, vegetable oil, and rice in a large bowl and mix together with your hands until the ingredients are blended. Set the filling aside.

Separate a few grape leaves, spread them out flat, and hang them over the edge of a colander to drain well. As you fill the leaves, arrange the remaining leaves around the rim of the colander.

Working with 1 leaf at a time, snip the stem off with kitchen shears or a sharp knife. Spread the leaf out on a plate or a clean work surface, shiny side down and the stem end facing you. If the leaf has deep indentations between the segments, close the gap by bringing the two segments together, overlapping them slightly, or by patching the gap with a torn piece of another leaf. If any of the leaves are more than 4 inches across, cut them in half. Reserve any torn or broken leaves for lining the cooking pot. Trim and stack all the whole leaves.

Prepare the cooking pot before you begin rolling the leaves, so you can place them directly into it as you make them: Scatter the reserved pieces of grape leaves over the bottom of a 4-quart pot or Dutch oven. Top with a single layer of the sliced tomatoes, and season with some of the salt and pepper. Follow with a layer of the onions. Season the lamb on both sides with the remaining salt and pepper, and then arrange it in a layer in the pot. Place the pot nearby.

Now stuff the leaves: Place 1 tablespoon of the rice mixture in the center of a leaf, close to where the stem begins. Bring the bottom of the leaf up over the filling, then fold the sides of the leaf onto the filling (in the same way a butcher wraps meat). Roll the leaf away from you, wrapping it tightly around the filling as you go. Repeat with the remaining leaves and filling.

As you fill them, arrange the stuffed grape leaves on top of the lamb, placing them seam side down in concentric rings, beginning with the outside ring and working your way to the middle. The rolls should fit snugly side by side, and the lamb should be covered entirely.

Arrange a layer of zucchini on top of the first layer of grape leaves. Layer the remaining rolls and zucchini until they are all in place. Pour 2 cups water into the pot.

Invert a heatproof plate over the rolls; the plate should be large enough to reach within ¼ inch of the edge of the pot. Place a weight, such as a foil-wrapped brick or a large can of tomatoes, on top of the plate. Cover the pot. (If you use a can that sits higher than the rim of the pot, use foil to cover the pot.) Bring the liquid to a boil over high heat, and cook for 20 minutes. Then reduce the heat to medium and cook for 45 minutes to 1 hour.

Reduce the heat to low, remove the weight from the plate, and add the lemon juice. Cover, and cook for 2 to 3 hours. After the rolls have been cooking for 1½ hours, taste, and adjust the salt and lemon if needed. Slide a heat diffuser under the pot for the last hour of cooking. If the liquid begins to evaporate, add ½ cup water mixed with ¼ teaspoon salt and ½ cup fresh lemon juice. The rolls are done when the grape leaves are easy to bite into and taste intensely of lemon.

Remove the pot from the heat, wrap it in a fleece blanket, and set it aside for 15 to 20 minutes.

While holding the rolls in place with the plate, tilt the pot to pour the cooking liquid into a bowl. Remove the plate and invert a platter over the pot. Holding the two together, flip the pot over, but do not remove it; leave it there for at least 5 minutes (this gives the rolls time to settle into a cake shape). Then gently remove the pot. Lift off the layers of leaves, tomatoes, onions, and lamb, and return any stray rolls to their places. Arrange the lamb around the rolls. Use a paper towel to soak up any excess liquid around the platter. Garnish with the lemon slices and parsley. Pour the juices from the pot into a sauceboat, and serve alongside.

Rice and Ground Beef in Phyllo Pockets

BOUQUAJ

One 3 inch cinnamon stick, broken

2 bay leaves

½ teaspoon black peppercorns

½ teaspoon allspice berries

4 cardamom pods

1½ cups Beef Stock (page 131) or low-sodium canned broth

2 tablespoons vegetable oil

1 pound ground beef or lamb

½ teaspoon ground allspice

Dash of grated nutmeg

Dash of ground cinnamon

2 teaspoons salt

½ teaspoon plus a dash of white pepper

1 package (10 ounces) frozen peas

3 cups basmati rice, rinsed (see page 165), soaked, and drained

2 tablespoons butter

Clarified butter (see page 45), melted

12 sheets frozen phyllo dough, thawed

1 egg

¼ cup milk

¼ cup almonds, peeled (see page 12) and split

In Syria and Lebanon, this fragrant, spicy ground meat encased in flaky phyllo is known as ouzi. *In Iraq it is called* barda belaw, *and boiled eggs and raisins are added to the mix. Rather than making individual servings, as we always did in Jordan, the Syrians, Iraqis, and Iranians line a bowl with sheets of phyllo, spoon the filling into the bowl, brush the overhanging pieces of phyllo with butter, and seal them together on top. The baked pastry is inverted onto a serving platter to reveal a show-stopping golden dome of filled phyllo. You can make Bouquaj this way, too.*

My mother would never have dreamed of baking these pockets ahead—they must be eaten piping hot—but in fact, I have made them a day in advance and reheated them just before serving without compromising the tender phyllo or the moist filling. If you want to substitute chicken for the beef, simply cut the chicken into small cubes and cook the rice with chicken broth. **Makes 12 pockets**

Tie the cinnamon stick, bay leaves, peppercorns, allspice berries, and cardamom pods in a cheesecloth bundle and set it aside.

Combine the beef stock with 1½ cups water in a saucepan, and bring to a boil.

Meanwhile, heat the vegetable oil in a large pot over high heat. Add the beef and sauté, breaking up the pieces with a spoon, until it loses its pink color, about 5 minutes. Stir in the allspice, nutmeg, cinnamon, salt, and ½ teaspoon of the pepper. Add the cheesecloth bundle. Cook for 5 minutes more. Stir in the peas and the rice. Drop the butter into the pot and stir until the rice is coated and the butter is completely melted. Add the boiling stock, give it a good stir, cover, and bring to a boil. Reduce the heat to low and cook until the broth has been absorbed and the rice is moist, about 15 minutes.

Slide a heat diffuser under the pot and cook for 20 minutes more. If you can crush a kernel of rice between your fingers, it is done. Taste, and add more salt if desired. Remove the pot from the heat, wrap it in a fleece blanket, and set it aside for at least 30 minutes. Then spoon the mixture onto a platter, spreading it in a thin layer to allow it to cool quickly.

Preheat the oven to 350°F, with a rack in the middle. Coat a baking sheet with a bit of clarified butter.

Cut the phyllo into 10 by 16-inch rectangles. Keeping the remainder covered with a damp cloth, work with 1 sheet of phyllo at a time. Position a short side in front of you, and brush the bottom half of the sheet with clarified butter. Fold the top half over it. Place the phyllo in a bowl with a 6-inch opening (I use a cereal bowl), letting the excess hang over the rim. Spoon 1 cup of the rice mixture into the phyllo. Fold the dangling edges over the filling, dabbing each fold with a bit of clarified butter to help the next fold stick to it. Once all of the dough is covering the filling and it is sealed, flip the bowl over onto the palm of your hand to catch the pocket. Place it, smooth side up, on the prepared baking sheet. Repeat with the remaining dough and filling.

Using a fork, stir the egg, milk, and dash of pepper together in a bowl. Brush the entire surface of the pockets with this egg wash. Dip the almonds in clarified butter and arrange 3 pieces on the center of each pocket. Bake until the phyllo is golden and crisp, 20 minutes. Serve hot.

If you are not serving the Bouquaj immediately, bake them only until the phyllo begins to color, about 10 minutes. Remove them from the oven, cover with foil, and set aside for up to 2 hours. To reheat, return them to a 350°F oven and bake for 30 minutes.

Sautéed Ground Beef with Zucchini

MUFARAKAT KOSSA

This quintessential family dish—rarely, if ever, offered on a formal table—is fragrant with allspice and cinnamon. Arab children grow up on Mufarakat Kossa, with a bit of plain yogurt swirled into the mixture and the whole thing spooned over white rice. Not only is it simple and quick to prepare, but it can be frozen for up to 6 months. Serve Mufarakat Kossa with white rice with vermicelli, with Cucumber and Yogurt alongside.   *Serves 6*

2 teaspoons canola oil

1 pound onions, finely chopped

1 pound ground beef

½ teaspoon Seven Spice Mix (page 73)

1 teaspoon ground allspice

Pinch of black pepper

½ teaspoon salt

2 pounds zucchini, cut into ¼ by 2-inch strips or 1-inch cubes

Heat the canola oil in a large, deep skillet over medium heat. Add the onions and sauté until tender, about 5 minutes. Stir in the ground beef, spice mix, allspice, pepper, and salt. Cook, stirring to break the beef into coarse crumbs, until it is dark—almost black—and fragrant, about 5 minutes. Add the zucchini, and cover the skillet. Cook, stirring occasionally, until the zucchini is fork-tender, about 35 minutes. Serve hot.

Baked Lamb with Rice and Chickpeas

KIDRA

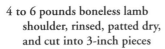

4 to 6 pounds boneless lamb shoulder, rinsed, patted dry, and cut into 3-inch pieces

2 medium onions, quartered

2 teaspoons allspice berries

2 teaspoons whole cloves

2 teaspoons ground cardamom

2 bay leaves

1 tablespoon plus 2 teaspoons salt

2½ teaspoons black pepper

6 heads garlic

4 cups basmati rice, rinsed (see page 164), soaked, and drained

¼ cup osfour (optional; see page 24)

1 tablespoon ground allspice

2 large onions, cut into ½-inch-thick rings

One 15-ounce can chickpeas, drained and rinsed three times

2 cups boiling water, plus more if needed

3 tablespoons butter

This recipe for Kidra (pronounced "idra") comes from Aref's family in Gaza, where, before the turn of the twentieth century, lamb was cooked the traditional way—in clay pots set into an outdoor oven known as a tanour, *which is just a large hole in the ground lined with coal. The big black pot had a slender neck—about the size of a fist—that was sealed shut with dough made from flour and water. The Kidra was left to cook for hours, sometimes overnight. Eventually, when homes were built closer to each other and bakeries began to appear in small villages, home cooks began sending their pots of Kidra to the local bakery to cook in the large wood-burning ovens. The desert population, however, continued to cook their Kidra in the ground into the 1940s, and in some areas of Iraq and Jordan well into the 1950s. I've modified Aref's family recipe to suit a standard home oven and the results, according to Aref, are as close as it gets to the dish he enjoyed as a child.*

I always show my guests how to handle the baked garlic: serve a whole or half head to each guest, and have them press on the base of the head with a fork to release the sweet pulp. Mix the pulp into the rice and enjoy.

Osfour, the stigma of the safflower, is added just to give the dish some color. You can omit it without any change in flavor. **Serves 6 to 8**

Place the lamb in a large pot and add cold water to cover by 3 to 4 inches. Add the quartered onions, allspice berries, cloves, cardamom, bay leaves, and 1 teaspoon each of the salt and pepper. Cover and bring to a boil over high heat, occasionally skimming off the foam that forms on the surface. Reduce the heat to medium and cook until the meat is fork-tender, about 1 hour, adding boiling water as necessary to keep the meat covered.

Meanwhile, peel away the thicker outer layers of the garlic heads, leaving the transparent skin that holds the head together. Trim off the root end of each head. (If it is too tough to trim, soak the head in a bowl of water for about 30 minutes to soften the root.) Rinse the garlic heads under cold water and set them aside.

Place the rice in a bowl, and stir in the 1 tablespoon salt and the osfour. Set it aside.

Using a slotted spoon, transfer the lamb to a bowl. Season it with the remaining 1 teaspoon salt, 2 teaspoons of the ground allspice, and 1 teaspoon of the pepper. Set it aside. Strain the broth and set it aside.

Preheat the oven to 300°F.

When you are ready to assemble the Kidra for baking, arrange the onion slices in a heavy-bottomed 3½-quart pot or Dutch oven. Spread half of the rice mixture over the onions. Then arrange the meat, garlic heads, and chickpeas on top of the rice. Season with the remaining 1 teaspoon ground allspice and ½ teaspoon black pepper. Then spread the remaining rice over everything. Pour 2 cups of the reserved lamb broth and the 2 cups boiling water into the pot. Cut the butter into 3 pieces and tuck them into the center of the rice. Cover the pot and bring it to a boil over high heat. Then reduce the heat to medium-low and simmer for 10 minutes, or until all of the water is absorbed. If the rice appears dried out, add ½ cup boiling water to the pot.

Gently turn the top layer of rice with a wooden spoon. Cover the pot and transfer it to the oven. Bake for 1 hour, stirring the Kidra gently after 30 minutes. If the rice appears dry, sprinkle a bit of hot water over it with your hands, or wet two paper towels and lay them on top of the rice to keep it moist. If you don't plan to serve the Kidra right away, reduce the oven temperature to 250°F and leave the pot in the oven for up to 1 hour.

To serve, use a small saucer to transfer the contents of the pot to a serving platter. (A spoon would break apart the meat and crush the chickpeas.) Arrange the lamb and garlic on a bed of rice and chickpeas, and serve hot.

Lamb in Creamy Sheep's-Milk Yogurt

MANSAF

¼ cup vegetable oil

2 pounds onions, chopped

11 pounds lamb, trimmed from the leg and shoulder, cut into 4-inch pieces, rinsed and patted dry

1 tablespoon allspice berries

5 black peppercorns

One 3-inch cinnamon stick

10 cardamom pods

1 teaspoon ground cardamom

1 teaspoon ground allspice

1 teaspoon salt, plus more if needed

1 teaspoon white pepper

About 6 quarts boiling water

32 ounces liquid *jameed* (available in Middle Eastern groceries; see page 206)

4 loaves *tanour* or *markouk* (see pages 29, 22)

4 cups Basmati Rice (page 164), cooked with ghee and in beef stock, kept warm or reheated

½ cup fried pine nuts (see page 43)

½ cup fried almonds (see page 43)

Mansaf, or "large tray," is the traditional festive dish of Jordan, where the slow-cooked lamb stew is prepared for big celebrations such as weddings. A huge platter is lined with flatbread and piled high with rice, then crowned with large chunks of tender lamb. However, Mansaf isn't restricted to special occasions—it is also served for family gatherings and weekend lunches. Serve Mansaf with wedges of white onion, olives, pickles, and thinly sliced serrano chiles.

Serves 10

~ ~ ~

Cook the lamb: Heat the vegetable oil in a large pot over medium heat. Add the onions and cook until soft and translucent, about 5 minutes. Add the lamb, allspice berries, peppercorns, cinnamon stick, cardamom pods, ground cardamom, ground allspice, salt, and white pepper. Stir to coat the meat with the spices. Add enough of the boiling water to cover the lamb by 3 inches. Bring to a boil, skimming off the foam that appears on the surface. Reduce the heat to medium, cover the pot, and cook until the meat is fork-tender, about 2 hours.

Using a slotted spoon, transfer the lamb to a second large pot. Pour the stock through a fine-mesh strainer into a bowl.

Add the *jameed* to the lamb. Pour 6 cups of the reserved stock into the pot, stir, and bring it to a boil over high heat, stirring slowly with a wooden spoon to avoid breaking the lamb apart. Reduce the heat to low and simmer for 30 minutes. Taste, and add salt if needed.

Compose the dish: Fold 1 piece of *tanour* or *markouk* underneath itself to create a mound, and place it in the center of a large platter. Arrange torn pieces of a second piece of *tanour* around the rim of the platter. Drizzle some of the jameed broth over the bread. Spread the rice over the mound of bread in the middle. Lift the lamb from the pot with a slotted spoon, and arrange it over the rice. Sprinkle the pine nuts and almonds on top. Place the platter in the middle of the table, making it the centerpiece of your meal. Pour some of the jameed broth into a sauceboat and place it next to the platter. Serve the remaining *tanour* alongside.

To serve: Use shallow rimmed soup bowls. Scoop some rice from the platter, using the bread pieces as your spoon, and place it in the bowl. Place a piece of lamb, with some nuts, on top of the rice and ladle a bit of broth over the whole thing.

JAMEED

It used to be that *jameed* was available only in the dried form—chalk-white globes of tart dried sheep's-milk yogurt the size of tennis balls—that had to be softened and diluted to make a proper Mansaf. To dilute it for cooking, we broke the balls into small pieces with a hammer, rinsed them under cold water several times, and then soaked them in water overnight. The next day, we massaged them into a cream inside the rough surface of an earthenware *juron,* which is similar to a mortar. Today I use a blender for this step and find that breaking the *jameed* into even tinier pebble-size pieces makes it easier to achieve a creamy consistency. The liquid is then passed through a very-fine-mesh sieve, and the massaging (or blending) and straining is repeated two or three times to achieve the proper creamy consistency.

Today liquid jameed is available in Middle Eastern grocery stores, making for much less work.

Lamb with Sumac and Chickpeas

SUMAKIYAH

¼ cup dried chickpeas, soaked overnight (see page 52), rinsed, and drained *or* 1 cup canned chickpeas, drained and rinsed three times

2 tablespoons vegetable oil

1¼ pounds onions, finely chopped

2 pounds boneless lamb stew meat, cut into 2-inch cubes

1 teaspoon salt, plus more to taste

1 teaspoon black pepper, plus more to taste

1 tablespoon ground allspice

½ teaspoon ground cardamom

2 bay leaves

2 pounds Swiss chard leaves, coarsely chopped

12 cloves garlic, mashed

1 small jalapeño pepper, seeded and finely chopped

½ teaspoon dill seed

2 cups ground sumac

¼ cup all-purpose flour

1 cup sesame paste (tahini)

Fresh lemon juice, to taste

Arab flatbread, for serving

*T*his is an ancient specialty dish from Gaza in the south of Palestine, where it is cooked only by the older generation of women. It is typically made for feasts and celebrations and always features an abundance of lamb on the platter to demonstrate to guests how important they are. Unlike many other Arab meat dishes in which the meat is served with vegetables and rice, Sumakiyah is served on its own, in a sauce thickened with chickpeas and chard. I first tasted this soon after I was married, when a distant cousin of Aref's showed up at our door holding a deep covered dish of Sumakiyah. It was her way of telling me that she accepted me into the family, even though I did not grow up in Gaza, where it is customary to marry within the community. Serve this with Arab flatbread, olives, and a plate of hot peppers, whole radishes, and quartered white onions. *Serves 6 to 8*

Place the dried chickpeas, if using, in a saucepan, add water to cover, and bring to a boil over high heat. Boil for 10 minutes. Then drain and set aside.

Heat the vegetable oil in a large stockpot over medium heat. Add the onions and sauté until soft and translucent, about 5 minutes. Add the lamb and cook, stirring, until it loses its pink color, about 20 minutes.

Add the 1 teaspoon salt, 1 teaspoon pepper, allspice, cardamom, bay leaves, and 8 cups water to the pot. Cover, and cook until the meat is fork-tender, about 1½ hours. Add the chard and the chickpeas and cook 40 minutes more.

Meanwhile, combine the garlic, jalapeño, and dill seed in a mortar, and crush to a paste with the pestle.

Add the garlic paste to the pot, stir, and leave the pot on very low heat, stirring it occasionally.

Combine the sumac and 3 cups water in a saucepan, cover, and bring to a boil over high heat. Boil for 10 minutes. Then pour the mixture into a blender and process to blend. Pour the mixture through a fine-mesh strainer into a bowl. Gradually whisk the flour into the strained liquid, stirring constantly to combine.

Pour the sumac mixture slowly into the pot, stirring constantly, and bring to a boil. Reduce the heat to low and simmer until the broth thickens, about 20 minutes. Then add the sesame paste and cook, stirring, until the sauce thickens slightly, 5 minutes. Season with salt, pepper, and lemon juice, and cook 5 minutes more.

The lamb can be eaten hot or at room temperature.

To serve, ladle the lamb and sauce into shallow rimmed soup bowls. Provide torn pieces of Arab flatbread alongside, for scooping up the meat.

Stuffed Leg of Lamb

FAKHDEH MEHSHI KHODRA

4 packed cups chopped fresh
flat-leaf parsley

1 packed cup chopped fresh
mint leaves

25 cloves garlic, mashed (see
page 32)

2½ pounds carrots, sliced into
¼-inch-thick rounds

½ teaspoon finely chopped
jalapeño pepper

2 tablespoons ground allspice

1 teaspoon ground cardamom

½ teaspoon grated nutmeg

½ teaspoon ground cloves

2 teaspoons salt

1 teaspoon black pepper

4½ pounds boneless leg of
lamb, butterflied, trimmed
of excess fat, rinsed, and
patted dry

1 pound onions, halved

One 3-inch cinnamon stick

2 bay leaves

¼ cup red wine vinegar

1 cup red wine, Spiced Chicken
Stock (page 125),
low-sodium canned chicken
broth, *or* verjus

1 to 2 tablespoons all-purpose
flour

*W*hen there is a whole lamb on the Arab table, the occasion is a
special one. It is prepared to celebrate the birth of a child, a
marriage, the return from a pilgrimage, or the recuperation from illness.
For the host, it is an opportunity to honor the guests, showing them how
important they are. When I was growing up, my mother always prepared
it for the Eid al Adha, the celebration for the end of the pilgrimage to
Mecca.

It used to be that only families of little means, who could not afford to
buy a whole lamb, stuffed the shoulder, neck, or leg. These days, anyone
who is preparing dinner for a small gathering will stuff just the leg, as I
do here, with a mix of herbs, garlic, and carrots. You can also stuff it
with Spiced Beef with Rice. I prefer farm-raised fresh lamb for this dish,
for its tender, delicate meat. Ask your butcher to butterfly the leg of lamb
and to leave the thin membrane on the leg; it retains the meat's juices as
it cooks.   *Serves 6 to 8*

Preheat the oven to 400°F. Line a roasting pan with four layers of
aluminum foil, each three times the length of the pan, with two
layers extending crosswise across the pan.

Combine the parsley, mint, garlic, carrots, and jalapeño in a
medium bowl and stir together. Set aside.

Lay the lamb flat on a clean work surface. In a small bowl, mix
together the allspice, cardamom, nutmeg, cloves, salt, and pepper.
Rub this spice mix all over both sides the lamb. Spoon the reserved
herb mixture down the middle of the lamb (there may be too
much—pack in as much as possible). Roll the lamb up over the
stuffing and secure it with lengths of kitchen string tied around it
every few inches.

Arrange the onions, cinnamon stick, and bay leaves in the foil-lined
pan. Sprinkle the vinegar over all. Place the meat on top, and wrap
it tightly in the foil. Pour enough water into the pan to fill it to
about 1 inch. Bake for 3 hours, adding water to the pan every hour

if necessary to maintain the level. The lamb should be very tender and browned.

Remove the pan from the oven and pour off the water. Carefully open the foil, standing far away from it to avoid the steam. Ladle as much liquid as you can out of the foil and into a small saucepan. Reseal the foil to keep the meat warm. Add the red wine to the broth in the saucepan and bring to a boil over high heat. Whisk in the flour and cook until the sauce is smooth and has thickened a bit, 8 minutes. Remove from the heat.

Transfer the lamb to a serving platter by sliding two lunch plates underneath it, on either side, to lift it out of the foil. Cut away the string. Arrange the onions around the lamb. Slice the lamb into ½-inch-thick pieces, and serve with the red wine sauce on the side.

MY MOTHER'S CELEBRATION LAMB

The aroma of lamb sizzling in fragrant ghee marked the beginning of the preparations for the Eid al Adha in my childhood home. My mother used to prepare a whole stuffed lamb on the stovetop, first rubbing it inside and out with her special spice mixture, then filling the cavity with Hashweh and sealing it with a basting needle and thread. She slicked ghee all over the huge pan, which spanned two burners on the stove. When the ghee was hot, Mother set the whole lamb into the pan (with some help!) to the warm sound of searing. When a delicate crust had formed on one side of the lamb, she enlisted a helper to assist her in turning it onto its other side, using two large plates as her "potholders" to grasp the lamb tightly and rotate it. Once properly browned, the lamb was placed in a huge pot filled with water, onions, and whole spices and was left to simmer for at least 5 hours—which seemed like an eternity to me, as I anticipated my mother setting this grand dish at the center of the table and the festivities beginning.

Lamb with Rice and Yogurt

FATET LAMICE

For the lamb shanks and stock:

7 pounds lamb shanks or leg of lamb, boned, trimmed of fat, and cut into 3-inch pieces

¼ cup vegetable oil

2 large onions, quartered

Three 3-inch cinnamon sticks

1 teaspoon allspice berries

1 teaspoon black peppercorns

1 teaspoon ground cardamom

1¼ teaspoons ground allspice

½ teaspoon black pepper

4 bay leaves

10 to 12 cups boiling water

1 tablespoon salt

¼ teaspoon grated nutmeg

¼ teaspoon ground cinnamon

For the yogurt layer:

6 pounds plain full-fat yogurt

10 cloves garlic, mashed, plus more to taste

1 tablespoon salt, plus more to taste

For the croutons:

1 cup vegetable oil

1 French baguette, cut into 1-inch-thick slices

For the lemon-garlic sauce:

1 cup fresh lemon juice

10 cloves garlic, mashed

1 teaspoon salt

*T*his is one of my mother's special party dishes. We always knew that a gathering was extra special if she made Fatet Lamice, a layered extravaganza fit for royalty. Crispy croutons, creamy rice, cool yogurt, and both ground beef and succulent lamb shanks are crowned with fragrant golden pine nuts and almonds. Though it takes a bit of time to prepare, you need to serve little more than a Simple Salad and an appetizer of Stuffed Grape Leaves to make this a full-course meal.

Fry the almonds in the same oil you use to fry the pine nuts, and then use the oil again when cooking the ground beef. Similarly, you can make the basmati rice with the reserved lamb stock. *Serves 8 to 10*

Cook the lamb shanks and make the stock: Rinse the lamb and pat it dry.

Heat the vegetable oil in a large pot over medium heat. Add the onions and sauté until they are soft, about 5 minutes. Add the lamb (you may have to do this in batches) and sear on all sides, about 10 minutes total. Then add the cinnamon sticks, allspice berries, peppercorns, cardamom, 1 teaspoon of the ground allspice, the pepper, bay leaves, and boiling water. Bring to a boil, skimming off the foam that forms on the surface. Reduce the heat to medium, cover the pot, and simmer until the meat is tender, about 2 hours.

Using a slotted spoon, transfer the meat to another large pot. Strain the stock.

Stir the salt, nutmeg, cinnamon, and remaining ¼ teaspoon ground allspice into 1 cup of the strained lamb stock. Add this to the lamb and set it aside. Reserve the remaining stock for another use.

Make the yogurt layer: While the lamb shanks are cooking, spoon the yogurt into a large bowl and place two layers of paper towels directly on the surface to absorb the excess liquid. Set aside for 10 minutes, replacing the towels as necessary. (This step is not necessary if using Greek Total brand yogurt.)

For the ground beef:

¼ cup oil from frying the pine nuts (see below) *or* ¼ cup vegetable oil

2 pounds ground beef

1 tablespoon ground allspice

½ teaspoon ground cardamom

½ teaspoon ground cinnamon

½ teaspoon grated nutmeg

1 teaspoon salt

1 teaspoon black pepper

For the rice:

Basmati Rice (page 164), hot or reheated

For the garnish:

½ cup fried pine nuts (see page 43)

½ cup fried peeled almonds (see pages 12, 43)

Combine the yogurt, garlic, and salt in a large bowl and stir to mix thoroughly. Taste, and add more garlic or salt if desired. Set aside.

Make the croutons: Heat the vegetable oil in a small skillet over high heat (the oil should be about 1 inch deep). Slide the bread slices into the hot oil and fry on both sides until golden. Using a slotted spoon, transfer the croutons to a paper towel–lined baking sheet and set them aside. (Alternatively, brush both sides of the bread slices with oil and spread them out on a baking sheet. Toast in a preheated 350°F oven, turning once, until both sides are golden.)

Make the lemon-garlic sauce: Whisk the lemon juice, garlic, and salt together in a bowl, and set it aside.

Cook the ground beef: Heat the oil in a skillet over high heat. Add the ground beef, breaking it up with the back of a wooden spoon, and cook until it loses its pink color, about 5 minutes. Add the allspice, cardamom, cinnamon, nutmeg, salt, and pepper, and stir to combine. Reduce the heat to medium and cook the mixture, breaking it up with the back of a spoon, until the beef is dark— almost black—about 20 minutes. Set it aside and keep warm.

Assemble the Fatet Lamice: Set the pot containing the lamb shanks over high heat to rewarm. Stir occasionally, and remove from the heat as soon as the meat is heated through.

Arrange the croutons on the bottom of a 4-quart baking dish or a large rimmed platter. Drizzle the lemon-garlic sauce over them. Give the rice a good stir, and then spoon it over the croutons. Spread the yogurt on top of the rice, covering it entirely. Arrange the lamb shanks on top of the yogurt. Spoon the ground beef on top, and sprinkle the pine nuts and almonds over the beef. Serve hot, using a large spoon to reach down through all of the layers.

Saudi Arabian Slow-Cooked Lamb

KABSA

For the lamb:

½ cup vegetable oil

4 pounds boneless lamb from the shoulder or shank, rinsed, patted dry, and cut into 5-inch pieces

2¾ pounds onions, finely chopped

1 tablespoon Saudi Spice Mix (page 40)

1 tablespoon salt

10 cups boiling water

For the rice mixture:

4 tablespoon butter

1 pound carrots, finely chopped

1¼ pounds yellow bell peppers, seeded and finely chopped

1 pound frozen peas

2 pounds tomatoes, peeled and finely chopped

12 cloves garlic, mashed

1 teaspoon ground saffron

½ teaspoon ground cardamom

1 teaspoon ground cinnamon

1 teaspoon ground allspice

2 teaspoons salt, plus more if needed

½ teaspoon white pepper

3 cups basmati rice, picked over, rinsed (see page 165), soaked, and drained

*T*hough today most Saudis enjoy all of the conveniences of a modern society, their loyalty to the food and hospitality traditions of their Bedouin culture is all but unchanged. They still slaughter a sheep to make a banquet-style feast for visiting guests. This centuries-old dish has all of the features of typical Saudi food: It is plentiful, made from simple ingredients, and employs a limited number of vegetables (though it features more here than it did fifty years ago, when the country was closed to foreigners—and to imported vegetables), and it is made in one pot. Though not officially declared as such, Kabsa could be considered the national dish of Saudi Arabia, where it is so beloved and so frequently served that it is always prepared for expat Saudis on visits home. This practice mimics the old days, when the tribes of Saudi Arabia, known for their courtesy and selfless hospitality, showed their warmth and generosity by serving guests huge platters piled high with rice and lamb.

The lamb is slow-cooked in a broth seasoned with cinnamon, cloves, cumin, and cardamom, and then the same broth is used to cook the rice. The water-to-rice ratio for basmati is typically one to one, but here I call for a bit less liquid because the vegetables release some juices.   *Serves 8*

Heat ¼ cup of the vegetable oil in a large pot over high heat. Add the lamb, a third of the onions, the Saudi spices, and 2 teaspoons of the salt. Sauté until the meat loses its pink color and the onions are soft, about 15 minutes. Then add the boiling water and bring to a boil. Skim the foam that forms on the surface, reduce the heat to medium, and cover the pot. Simmer until the meat is fork-tender, about 2½ hours.

Preheat the oven to 250°F.

Using a slotted spoon, transfer the meat to a baking dish. Season it with the remaining 1 teaspoon salt, cover with foil, and keep warm in the oven. Reserve the stock.

Heat the remaining ¼ cup vegetable oil and the butter in a large pot over high heat. Add the carrots, peppers, peas, tomatoes, remaining onions, garlic, saffron, cardamom, cinnamon, allspice, salt, and

For the garnish:

½ cup fried pine nuts (see page 43)

½ cup fried peeled almonds, (see pages 12, 43)

½ cup golden raisins

Spicy Tomato Sauce (page 35), for serving

white pepper. Cook, stirring, until the vegetables are soft and come together, about 20 minutes.

Heat 2 cups of the reserved stock over high heat. Add the rice to the vegetables and stir for about 3 minutes, until it is well incorporated. Then add the hot stock to the rice mixture, cover, and bring to a boil. Reduce the heat to medium and simmer for 15 minutes.

Give the rice mixture a quick stir. Taste, and add more salt if needed. Reduce the heat to low and slide a heat diffuser under the pot. Cook until the rice is fluffy, about 15 minutes. Remove the pot from the heat and wrap it in a fleece blanket to keep the rice mixture warm.

To serve, use a dessert plate to scoop the rice mixture onto a serving dish (it's quicker than using a spoon), piling it high in the center. Arrange the warm meat on top, and garnish with the pine nuts, almonds, and raisins. Serve the Kabsa with the Spicy Tomato Sauce on the side.

Lamb Kebabs

SHISH KABAB

For the marinade:
8 cloves garlic, mashed
½ cup extra virgin olive oil
¼ cup red wine vinegar
¼ cup fresh lemon juice
1 tablespoon tomato paste
½ teaspoon ground allspice
½ teaspoon ground cardamom
¼ teaspoon ground cinnamon
½ teaspoon salt
½ teaspoon black pepper

2 pounds boneless lamb, cut
   from the leg, trimmed of fat
   and cut into 1-inch cubes
12 pearl onions, unpeeled, root
   ends trimmed
2 green bell peppers, seeded and
   cut into 1-inch pieces
12 cherry tomatoes, stemmed
1 loaf *markouk* (see page 22) *or*
   other paper-thin flatbread

*T*he aroma of grilled lamb permeates the spring and summer air in cities and villages all over the Arab world, where it is offered from carts on bustling city streets and is cooking in what seems like every home. When I make this at home in Kentucky, it reminds me of our Friday lunches in Jordan, where the neighborhood was filled with the fragrance of char-grilled lamb. On those mornings I would hear my mother talking to the butcher, admonishing him to prepare her some top-quality lamb. "God have mercy on you," she would say. "I need fetayel," which means "the best and most tender part of the lamb." Back home, the kebabs were threaded with just the lamb chunks seasoned with salt and pepper, pieces of lamb fat, and shallots. They were the essence of simplicity and a perfect example of the cuisine of the Levant: tender, fresh meat grilled quickly and directly over hot charcoal.

Here in the States, I marinate the lamb to make it extra tender and juicy. While I always cook these on an outdoor grill, I know some people who char them under the broiler and try to impart the flavor and smell of the grill by lighting a piece of charcoal and putting it in the oven.

Shish Kebab goes well with almost all of the mezza dishes. Classic accompaniments include Cucumber and Yogurt, Garlic Paste, Hummus, or Roasted Eggplant Spread. You will need 8-inch-long metal skewers for these kebabs.   ***Makes about 8 skewers***

Prepare the marinade: Combine all the ingredients in a shallow glass or ceramic dish, and stir to combine. Add the meat and turn to coat it all over with the marinade. Refrigerate, covered, for at least 2 hours or as long as overnight.

Prepare a charcoal grill. Remove the lamb from the marinade.

Thread the meat, onions, green peppers, and tomatoes onto 8-inch metal skewers, alternating vegetables with pieces of meat. Each skewer should have at least 4 pieces of meat on it. (Alternatively, thread each skewer with a single ingredient: meat on one, tomatoes on another, onions on another, etc.) Grill until the meat is cooked through, 8 to 10 minutes in all.

Unfold the loaf of *markouk* on a large platter. As you remove the skewers from the grill, lay them on one half of the bread. Before serving, fold the other half over the kebabs.

To serve, tear a piece of bread from the top of the loaf and use it to pull the meat and vegetables off the skewer and onto each dinner plate.

Lamb Beryani

BERYANI LAHIM

For the meat:

3 tablespoons vegetable oil

4 pounds boneless lamb shoulder, rinsed, patted dry, and cut into 2- to 3-inch pieces

2 teaspoons Kuwaiti Spice Mix (page 41)

2 bay leaves

6 cardamom pods, crushed

7 cups boiling water

1 teaspoon salt

For the rice:

4 cups basmati rice, rinsed (see page 165), soaked, and drained

Three 3-inch cinnamon sticks

1 tablespoon whole cloves

1 teaspoon ground allspice

2 tablespoons salt

For the Al Masala sauce:

1 cup vegetable oil

2 pounds onions, halved and thinly sliced

1 pound potatoes, cut into 2-inch cubes

¼ cup grated fresh ginger

2 serrano chiles, seeded and finely chopped

¼ cup Kuwaiti Spice Mix (page 41)

2 heads garlic, cloves separated and mashed (see page 32)

½ cup tomato paste

2 teaspoons ground cinnamon

This elaborate layered Indian dish is one of many that were adopted by the countries in the Arabian Gulf region, which were stops on the Indian spice trade route. It is one of the most popular dishes in Kuwait, for example, where a large expatriate Indian community now lives. There are several steps to making Beryani Lahim—the lamb is cooked slowly over very low heat (this method is called taskeer *in Kuwait) and then baked in a saffron-scented yogurt sauce with basmati rice, potatoes, and onions. The Iraqis make beryani slightly differently; they add boiled eggs to the yogurt sauce.* *Serves 6 to 8*

Cook the meat: Heat the vegetable oil in a large pot over high heat. Add the meat and cook, stirring, until it loses its pink color, 10 minutes. Add the Kuwaiti spices, bay leaves, and cardamom pods. Sauté the meat in the spices until it is coated, about 3 minutes. Add the boiling water, reduce the heat to medium, cover the pot, and simmer until the meat is fork-tender, 1½ to 2 hours. As the lamb cooks, skim off the foam that forms on the surface. Season with the salt.

Drain the meat and set it aside.

Make the rice: Meanwhile, partially cook the rice: Put the rice in a large pot and add water to cover by 2 inches. Add the cinnamon sticks, cloves, allspice, and salt. Bring to a boil over high heat; then reduce the heat to medium-low, cover, and cook for 5 minutes. Strain the rice and set it aside.

Make the Al Masala Sauce: In a large skillet, heat ½ cup of the vegetable oil over high heat. Add the onions and sauté until they are soft and caramelized, 10 to 15 minutes. Using a slotted spoon, transfer the onions to a paper towel–lined plate.

Add the remaining ½ cup vegetable oil to the same skillet and heat until hot. Add the potatoes and fry, turning occasionally, until golden, 8 to 10 minutes. Use a slotted spoon to transfer them to a paper towel–lined plate.

Lamb Beryani *(continued)*

2 packed cups chopped fresh cilantro

2 teaspoons dried mint, preferably peppermint

2 cups plain full-fat yogurt

½ cup white vinegar

6 tablespoons (¾ stick) butter, cut into pieces

1 teaspoons saffron threads soaked in ½ cup water

Fresh mint leaves, for garnish

Spicy Tomato Sauce (page 35), for serving

In the same skillet, combine the ginger, peppers, Kuwaiti spices, garlic, tomato paste, cinnamon, cilantro, and mint. Stir, and cook over medium heat until the cilantro wilts, 10 minutes. Add the yogurt and vinegar, and cook until the mixture is heated through. Then add the meat, onions, and potatoes, and stir to coat them with the sauce.

Assemble and bake: Preheat the oven to 350°F, with a rack in the lower third of the oven. Spread one fourth of the rice on the bottom of a Dutch oven or other heavy-bottomed ovenproof pot. Ladle all the lamb and potato mixture over the rice. Spread the remaining rice over that, smoothing it with the back of a spoon. Scatter the butter and the saffron water over the rice. Cover, and bake until the rice is tender, about 2 hours.

Set the Beryani aside to rest, covered, for at least 30 minutes. If you are not serving it right after the meat rests, wrap the pot in a fleece blanket; it will stay warm for up to 3 hours.

To serve: Pushing a small plate down to the bottom of the pot, gently scoop up portions of the layers and transfer them to a serving platter. (A metal spoon will break up the meat. The blunt edge and the width of a saucer makes it easier to remove the meat from the pot in large portions without breaking it up.) Garnish with mint leaves, and serve with the Spicy Tomato Sauce alongside.

Eggplant Upside Down

MAKLOBIT BETINJAN

2 pounds eggplant, partially
    peeled and cut into
    1-inch-thick rounds

2½ teaspoons salt

3 medium onions

2 cups vegetable oil

1 pound stew beef *or* lamb
    pieces trimmed from the leg,
    in 2-inch chunks

1 teaspoon black pepper

1 teaspoon ground allspice

½ teaspoon ground cinnamon

6 cups boiling water

2 cups basmati rice

2½ teaspoons salt

Fried pine nuts (see page 43),
    for garnish

This soothing one-pot eggplant dish is a much-loved comfort food throughout the Arab world. It is one of the most-requested recipes from my sons' Arab friends living in the U.S. In fact, I once taught my best friend's son, Tariq, how to make Maklobit Betinjan over the phone! He was craving this layered dish of fried eggplant, cinnamon-flavored beef and onions, and basmati. The onions that line the bottom of the cooking pot are meant to prevent the eggplant from scorching. I like to leave a bit of the eggplant skin on—it helps to hold the pieces together.

The dish is loosely molded in the shape of the pot. It may fall apart slightly when you lift the pot off, but just patch it back together with a spoon. It shouldn't be too stiff and formal-looking. Serve this with Cucumber and Yogurt and a Simple Salad. ***Serves 6 to 8***

Place the eggplant in a colander and sprinkle it with ½ teaspoon of the salt. Set the colander in a bowl, and set it aside.

Meanwhile, dice two of the onions. Pour enough of the vegetable oil into a large pot to coat the bottom, and place it over high heat. Add the diced onions, beef, pepper, allspice, and cinnamon, and stir. Cook, stirring, until the onions are tender, about 5 minutes. Then add the boiling water, cover, and cook until the meat is fork-tender, about 1 hour.

Meanwhile, rinse the rice (see page 165) and let it soak in water to cover for 30 minutes.

Heat the remaining vegetable oil in a large skillet over high heat. Pat the eggplant slices dry with paper towels, and sauté until golden, about 10 minutes on each side, adding more oil to the pan if necessary. Place them on a paper towel–lined plate to drain.

Strain the beef, reserving the broth and discarding the diced onions.

Slice the remaining onion into 1-inch-thick rings, and arrange them on the bottom of a large heavy pot. Place the eggplant on top of the onions. Spoon the beef over the eggplant. Drain the rice well and spoon it over the beef. Pour 2½ cups of the reserved beef broth into the pot, season with the remaining 2 teaspoons salt, cover, and bring to a boil over high heat. Stir the rice layer lightly with a fork. Reduce the heat to medium and cook until the liquid absorbed, 15 minutes. Then reduce the heat to low, slide a heat diffuser under the pot, and simmer until the rice is tender and fluffy, about 30 minutes. If the rice on the top is not cooked but the grains underneath it are, place a damp paper towel directly over the rice, cover, and cook for 15 minutes more. Remove the pot from the stove and wrap it in a fleece blanket for at least 10 minutes before serving. Keep the blanket wrapped around the pot until ready to serve.

To serve, uncover the pot and invert a platter over it. Holding the two together, flip the pot over onto the platter. Do not remove the pot—let it sit for 10 minutes. Then carefully lift it off; the eggplant will be on top. If some of the onions fall onto the eggplant, remove and discard them. Garnish with the fried pine nuts, and serve.

Variation: In Jordan, this dish is made with carrots spiced with nutmeg and cinnamon instead of the eggplant. Slice the carrots into 1-inch-thick rounds and sauté them in olive oil. Place them in the pot on top of the onions. Add an additional 1 teaspoon cinnamon and 1 teaspoon nutmeg to the beef mixture.

You can also substitute large pieces of chicken, bone in and skin on, for the beef.

Beef with White Beans

FASOULIA

12 ounces dried cannellini, Great Northern, or lima beans (see Note)

1 teaspoon baking soda

1½ pounds boneless beef or veal from the shank, cut into 2-inch cubes

2 tablespoons canola oil

1 large onion, chopped

1 teaspoon ground allspice

½ teaspoon black pepper

6 cups boiling water

One 6-ounce can tomato paste

2 tablespoons ghee

5 cloves garlic, mashed

1 cup chopped fresh cilantro

2½ teaspoons salt, plus more if needed

Fresh lemon juice (optional)

3 cups Basmati Rice (page 164), warm

Chopped fresh cilantro, for garnish

Lemon wedges, for serving

Taqliya, the popular mix of garlic and cilantro that is favored by Egyptians, Lebanese, Syrians, Jordanians, and Palestinians, flavors this typical family supper dish of tender beef and creamy beans. Lamb can be substituted here; use a shoulder cut and cut it into 2-inch cubes. Serve Fasoulia over Basmati Rice, with Baby Arugula Salad alongside. *Serves 6*

Place the beans in a bowl, and add water to cover by 2 inches. Stir the baking soda into the water and set aside to soak overnight.

Rinse the meat under cold running water, pat it dry, and place it in a colander.

Heat the canola oil in a large pot over medium heat, and sauté the onions until soft, about 10 minutes. Add the beef, allspice, and pepper. Cook, stirring to coat the beef with the spices, until the meat loses its pink color, about 10 minutes. Add the boiling water, cover, reduce the heat, and cook for 30 minutes, skimming all the foam that forms on the surface.

Meanwhile, drain the beans and rinse them under cold water.

Add the beans and the tomato paste to the pot, give it a good stir, and bring to a boil. Cover, reduce the heat to medium, and cook until the meat is fork-tender and the beans are soft, about 45 minutes. (Depending on the variety of beans you use, you may need to add water to keep them covered.)

Meanwhile, heat the ghee in a small skillet over high heat. Add the garlic, cilantro, and salt, and sauté until the mixture is fragrant and the cilantro has brightened, about 10 minutes.

About 15 minutes before you take them off the heat, stir the garlic-cilantro mixture into the beans. Taste, and season with more salt and a squeeze of lemon if desired.

Serve over the rice in shallow bowls, and garnish with the cilantro and lemons.

Note: If you don't have time for the overnight soaking, use three 15-ounce cans of beans. Rinse and drain them, and add them to the pot after the meat is fully cooked, just before adding the garlic-cilantro mixture.

Marinated Spiced Beef

SHAWARMA

2½ pounds beef filet, trimmed of fat and membrane

1 orange, sliced into thin rounds

1 lemon, sliced into thin rounds

1 tablespoon plain yogurt

2 teaspoons white vinegar

1 teaspoon ground allspice

½ teaspoon grated nutmeg

½ teaspoon cardamom seeds

4 pieces crushed mastic, each about the size of a lentil (optional; see page 22)

1 teaspoon salt

Pinch of black pepper

2 teaspoons corn oil

Arab flatbread

Chopped fresh parsley, for garnish

Thinly sliced onion, for garnish

Ground sumac, for garnish

Tahini (page 32), for serving

*W*hatever street you walk down in a big city, small town, or tiny village in the Arab world, you are almost guaranteed to find shawarma, *marinated beef or lamb turning slowly on a spit over an open fire. The vendor serves the succulent meat to order by slicing away thin shavings while the skewers are still turning, revealing another layer of meat to be seared by the flames. The paper-thin shavings are wrapped in a split piece of Arab flatbread and garnished with Tahini, tomato slices, and pickles to create the ultimate fast food. Here is my version of shawarma—made at home without a spit or an open fire. The trick is to marinate the meat for at least a day (two is best) in order for it to be as tender as the street vendors'. Serve it with pickled cucumber and turnips.*

I often include a miniature sandwich version on a buffet table by tucking a few slices of meat into halved small loaves of Arab flatbread. I put the garnishes—Tahini, tomatoes, onions, pickled cucumbers or pickled turnip—in small bowls so that guests can dress their sandwiches as they please.

Although mastic is used primarily in sweet dishes, I like to add it to the spice mixture to give it a special flavor.   *Serves 6*

Cut the filet into ¼-inch-thick slices, and then cut the slices into ½-inch-wide pieces.

Combine the orange slices, lemon slices, yogurt, vinegar, allspice, nutmeg, cardamom, mastic, salt, and pepper in a shallow 3-quart baking dish and stir together. Crush the orange and lemon slices with a fork to release their juices. Add the beef, cover the dish, and marinate overnight in the refrigerator, turning the beef once.

Preheat the oven to 375°F, with a rack in the lower third of the oven.

Remove the beef slices from the marinade with your hands, squeezing out the excess liquid. Separate the slices and place them in a shallow roasting pan. Drizzle the corn oil over the meat, cover the pan with aluminum foil, and roast in the oven for 20 to 25 minutes, turning the slices twice.

Remove the foil from the pan, pour off the juices, and cook, uncovered, until the beef is tender, 15 minutes. Transfer the beef to a serving platter lined with Arab flatbread, and garnish with the parsley, onion slices, and sumac. Serve the Tahini on the side. (Or to serve the beef rolled into a sandwich, split the pieces of Arab flatbread in half, scoop some Shawarma onto one half, and top with the onions, parsley, and sumac. Drizzle the Tahini over it, and roll it up. Repeat with the remaining halves of Arab flatbread. To make bite-size appetizers, insert toothpicks into the roll every ½ inch or so, then slice the rolled sandwich between the toothpicks.)

MAKING KIBEH: ONLY THE FRESHEST MEAT WILL DO!

Ask any Arab-American what they crave when they are homesick, and chances are most of them will name some kind of *kibeh* dish. The odds are pretty good, too, that they each name a different preparation, since the variations are endless. *Kibeh* can be eaten raw or cooked, hot or cold; shaped into balls or patties, rolled into sheets, stuffed, broiled, grilled, baked, fried, or poached. What's more, it doesn't always include beef or lamb, but can be made with chicken, fish, pumpkins, potatoes, or rice!

Preparing and enjoying *kibeh* is a revered tradition all over the Arab world. It is particularly beloved in Lebanon and Syria, which both claim it as their national dish. *Kibeh* is also especially popular in Iraq, Jordan, and Armenia. Whatever form it takes, *kibeh* is always made with the finest cuts of meat (or chicken or fish). It is not prepared with leftovers or employed as a way to stretch meat!

In the old days, housewives in the mountain villages of Lebanon used to pound the meat with a large wooden pestle called a *madaq* in a large, stone mortar called a *jurn*. Strong arms and long fingers were needed for making *kibeh* this way, which is why, until recently, only certain members of a family were given the important job of making it. In mine, it was Auntie Nina. She made perfect *kibeh*. When she was around, no one else even tried! When Arab cooks were introduced to the food processor, the job became far less time-consuming and accessible. It's easier, quicker, and quieter—though I do miss the music coming from the *jurn*—and it makes quite delicious *kibeh*.

Here in the United States, I often use beef filet, while in the Middle East, lamb or goat meat is preferred. To make authentic *kibeh,* it's important to use the freshest ingredients.

MEAT: Use the leanest, finest cut of lamb or beef, from a young animal whenever possible. Ask your butcher for cuts from the upper part of the thigh of the lamb or from the thin layer that covers the ribs. Emphasize that the meat be free of blood vessels, muscle, or fat. "Only the freshest meat will do," Auntie Nina used to say. The exception is when making grilled *kibeh,* in which case you want some fat in the meat so it will hold together. Do not use frozen meat from the meat case at the local supermarket.

BULGUR: Use small-grain white or brown bulgur. Pick it over to get rid of any dirt and debris, and wash it well. Squeeze the moisture from the soaked bulgur before adding it to the meat.

FLAVORINGS: The juices from the mashed onions not only infuse the mixture with flavor but also help to bind the "dough" together. My basic *kibeh* recipe calls for allspice, cinnamon, and marjoram, but you can use whatever suits your taste, including ground black pepper, crushed red pepper, rose spices (see page 26), or Seven Spice Mix (page 73).

WATER: Every *kibeh* cook knows that it is essential to have a bowl of ice water at his or her fingertips. Ice water does two jobs: it helps to keep the raw meat cold as it is whirring around in the food processor, and the gradual addition of it to the "dough" helps to achieve just the right consistency. If you find that you have added too much water to the dough, refrigerate it until the bulgur has absorbed it. If resting the dough does not do it, add a little more bulgur to absorb the extra water.

Just as the Arab dialects differ slightly from country to country, so does the ratio of meat to bulgur and the combination of spices for making *kibeh.* In Palestine, more bulgur than meat is used in the basic dough. The recipe for Kibeh Balls, in which the dough is shaped into oblong torpedoes and filled with ground meat and pine nuts, hails from Palestine. The Iraqis use *jereesh,* a variety of cracked wheat, to make *kibeh* dough for the pride of their table, Kibeh al Mousel—palm-sized patties filled with a sautéed mixture of ground lamb, onions, and raisins. The cuisine in the Gulf States and North Africa includes most kinds of *kibeh,* but *jereesh* is added to the basic dough and saffron, ground *loumi,* cardamom, cinnamon, coriander, and cloves are added to some of the stuffings.

The *kibeh* recipes here are but a few of the dozens that are enjoyed all over the Arab world. These are the dishes my family enjoys the most—and that I love to prepare. Perhaps their favorite way to eat kibeh is filled and fried, as in Kibeh Balls, which are always on my mezza table. They show up in myriad ways—with dips, cooked in yogurt, or baked with onions and pomegranate. Grilled *kibeh,* or Kibeh Mashwi, is a typical dinner and casual entertaining offering during the summer months. Baked *kibeh,* Kibeh in the Tray, is a weeknight supper staple, just as it was during my childhood. Raw *kibeh,* or Kibeh Nayeh, is the steak tartare of Middle Eastern cuisine.

Kibeh

1 pound fine bulgur, picked over

1 tablespoon ground allspice

1 teaspoon dried marjoram (optional)

1 teaspoon ground cinnamon

1 tablespoon salt, plus more if needed

½ teaspoon white pepper

1 small yellow onion, cut into wedges

1 pound boneless lean lamb from the leg, *or* beef tenderloin, cut into small cubes

This basic recipe is used for making several different Kibeh *dishes, including Kibeh Balls, Kibeh in the Tray, and Grilled Kibeh. All* kibeh *dishes, with the exception of Kibeh Nayeh, can be frozen, either cooked or uncooked, for up to 4 months. For the best results, chill the meat in the refrigerator for 1 hour before you grind it in the processor.*

Makes 2 pounds of dough

Wash the bulgur in a bowl of cold water, wading through it with your fingers. Repeat, changing the water three times. Then use your hands to lift the bulgur out of the water and transfer it to a bowl. Squeeze the bulgur to extract as much water as possible.

Prepare an ice water bath in a large bowl and set it on a damp kitchen towel. Combine the allspice, marjoram, if using, cinnamon, salt, and pepper in a small bowl and set it aside.

Place the onions in a food processor and pulse to form a paste. Add the bulgur and ½ teaspoon of the spice mixture, and process until the mixture returns to a paste. Transfer the bulgur paste to a medium bowl and set it in the ice water bath.

Place the meat in the food processor, in batches if necessary, and pulse, scraping down the sides of the bowl, until it forms a very smooth paste, about 1 minute. The meat should maintain its pinkish tone; avoid overprocessing, or the heat of the machine will "cook" it.

Fill a small bowl with ½ cup ice water, and place it near your work area. Add the meat to the bulgur mixture and knead them together in the bowl. Add the remaining spice mixture 1 tablespoon at a time, dipping your hands into the ice water as you work, and knead until the mixture is silky smooth, 7 to 10 minutes. Add ice to the larger bowl if necessary, to keep it cold. Taste, and add more salt if needed.

Return the mixture to the food processor, working in batches if necessary, and pulse a few more times. Cover, and refrigerate until ready to use.

Kibeh in the Tray

KIBEH BI SENIYEH

½ cup oil from the pine nuts (below) *or* ½ cup vegetable oil

2½ cups chopped onions

2 pounds ground beef or lamb

2 teaspoons salt

1 teaspoon black pepper

2 teaspoons ground allspice

3 tablespoons butter

½ cup olive oil

Kibeh (page 226)

⅔ cup fried pine nuts (see page 43)

Radishes, for garnish

Fresh parsley leaves, for garnish

Throughout my childhood we enjoyed this kibeh *at least once every two weeks, always with hummus and a bowl of fresh yogurt next to the tray. Lebanese and Syrians like to prepare* kibeh *this way, layered in a large round baking tray—hence the name of the dish. A fragrant filling of ground meat and golden pine nuts is spread between two layers of* kibeh, *which are rolled out with a rolling pin to fit the baking dish. Fry the pine nuts first, and reserve the oil for sautéing the onions.*

Serve Kibeh bi Seniyeh for lunch or dinner with Shredded Cabbage Salad, Eggplant Salad, and Chickpeas with Yogurt or Hummus.

This can be assembled in advance, double-wrapped in plastic wrap, and frozen for up to 6 months. Defrost it in the refrigerator and bake as directed in the recipe. Leftovers freeze well, also. Defrost them and re-heat in a 300°F oven.

Serves 6

Heat the oil in a large pot over medium heat. Add the onions and sauté until they are soft and translucent, about 10 minutes. Add the beef, salt, pepper, and allspice. Sauté, breaking up the beef with the back of a spoon, until the spices are incorporated, 5 minutes. Cover the pot, reduce the heat to low, and cook for 15 minutes. Then remove from the heat and set aside.

Preheat the oven to 400°F, with one rack in the center and a second rack in the upper third of the oven.

Heat the butter and olive oil in a small pan until the butter has melted. Stir, and remove from the heat. Brush a 15-inch-wide round baking tray or a 4-quart baking dish with some of the butter mixture.

Divide the Kibeh in half. Place one piece of the dough between two sheets of wax paper and roll it out to the shape of the baking dish, extending it so that it is large enough to cover the sides of the dish as well. Remove the top layer of wax paper and flip the dough over into the baking tray. Press it onto the bottom and up the sides, and then remove the top sheet of wax paper. Spread the beef mixture evenly over the surface of the Kibeh, and sprinkle the pine nuts over it.

Roll out the remaining dough as before, making this layer slightly smaller so that it will fit inside the pan. Flip over the sheets of wax paper as above and lay the dough on top of the filling. Seal the edges of the two layers of dough together, pressing them against the sides of the pan. Wet your hands with cold water and smooth the rim of the dough, making sure it is sealed.

Score the surface of the dough into four triangles, and then score smaller triangles within the large ones. Drizzle the remaining butter mixture over the dough. Bake on the center rack for 30 minutes. Then transfer the pan to the upper rack, and bake for 20 minutes.

Remove the baking tray from the oven, and invert a large plate over it. Slowly tilt the tray at an angle, holding the Kibeh in place with the plate, to pour off the extra liquid. Then remove the plate and pat the Kibeh with paper towels to remove any extra oil. Cut along the score lines and lift the Kibeh out to your serving plate.

Serve, garnished with the radishes and parsley.

Grilled Kibeh on Skewers

KIBEH MASHWI

1 pound finely ground beef

½ cup bulgur, picked over and washed (see page 281)

½ cup fresh mint leaves, rinsed, patted dry, chilled, and finely chopped *or* ⅛ cup dried mint

1 medium onion, finely chopped

2 teaspoons salt

½ teaspoon ground cinnamon

¼ teaspoon ground allspice

¼ teaspoon ground coriander

¼ teaspoon ground cardamom

¼ teaspoon black pepper

2 ice cubes

Markouk (see page 22) *or* other thin flatbread, torn into 4-inch pieces

This simplified version of delicious Kibeh Mashwi is popular in Aleppo, Syria, and in Tripoli and the south of Lebanon. It tastes best when made with ground beef that is well streaked with fat. The original, more elaborate version is shaped like a tennis ball and stuffed with lamb fat (to hold it together), dried mint, onions, crushed walnuts, and hot green and red chiles. My Kibeh Mashwi are shaped like index fingers, with all of the seasonings mixed right into the dough. If you prefer to use lean meat, you'll need to add at least 2 tablespoons softened butter to the dough (or brush the skewers with clarified butter or olive oil frequently as they cook). Sometimes I add ½ teaspoon rose spices (see page 26) to the dough, which perfumes it ever so slightly. Serve Kibeh Mashwi with Roasted Eggplant Spread and Eggplant Salad. **Serves 6**

Place the beef in a food processor and pulse to form a rough paste. Add the bulgur, mint, onions, salt, cinnamon, allspice, coriander, cardamom, pepper, and ice cubes. Pulse until the ingredients are incorporated and the mixture is smooth, about 3 minutes. Wrap the meat in plastic wrap and refrigerate it for 10 minutes.

Meanwhile, soak 24 bamboo skewers in water. Prepare a charcoal grill or preheat the broiler. Line a broiler pan with aluminum foil.

Divide the chilled *kibeh* mixture into 2-tablespoon portions. With wet hands, press a portion onto a skewer, working it along the skewer until it is 2½ inches long. Place the skewer on the prepared broiler pan, and repeat with the remaining mixture.

Place the skewers on the hot grill rack (oil it first), or place the pan under the broiler. Grill, turning the skewers once, until both sides are deep brown, about 10 minutes.

Meanwhile, line the edges of a platter with the torn pieces of *markouk*.

Lay the skewers on the platter, and invite your guests to slide the *kibeh* off them, using the bread pieces to do so.

Kibeh Balls

⅓ cup vegetable oil

1 large onion, minced

½ pound lean beef or lamb, minced

1 teaspoon ground allspice

½ teaspoon ground cinnamon

1 teaspoon salt

½ teaspoon black pepper

⅔ cup fried pine nuts or walnuts (see page 43)

1 teaspoon ground sumac

Kibeh (page 226)

4 cups vegetable oil (if frying)

*T*hese torpedo-shaped savories are filled with spiced beef and fried pine nuts. They are typically offered on a formal mezza spread and make especially delicious scoops for Cucumber and Yogurt and Hummus. If you are serving the Kibeh Balls with yogurt sauce (see the variation on page 194), omit the sumac in the filling; the combination will be too tart. Authentic Kibeh Balls are fried, but I prefer the baked version when I'm adding them to Chicken Soup with Vermicelli.

If you plan to freeze Kibeh Balls, prepare them to the frying stage. Then, rather than cooking them in oil, drizzle them with oil and bake in a 400°F oven for 10 to 15 minutes, shaking the baking sheet twice during the cooking. Let cool, and store in freezer bags for up to 3 months. To complete the cooking, fry as directed below. ***Makes about 50 balls***

Heat the ⅓ cup vegetable oil in a heavy skillet over medium heat. Add the onions and sauté, stirring occasionally, until they are soft and translucent, about 5 minutes. Raise the heat to high, add the beef, and cook, breaking it up with the back of a spoon, until it loses its pink color, about 5 minutes. Add the allspice, cinnamon, salt, and pepper, and stir to incorporate. Continue cooking the meat, breaking it up with the spoon so that it resembles coarse crumbs, until it is cooked through and deeply browned, 10 to 15 minutes. Drain off the fat, transfer the filling to a bowl, and allow it to cool. Then add the fried pine nuts and sumac, and mix well. Taste, and adjust the seasonings to your liking.

Prepare a bowl of ice water and place it near your work area. Since it's easier to work with the *kibeh* when it is chilled, remove only a portion at a time from the refrigerator. Wet your hands in the ice water and scoop a heaping tablespoon of the paste into the palm of your hand. Roll the paste into a ball between the palms of your hands. Holding the ball in one hand, poke the index finger of your other hand into it. Then roll and spread the paste down to the middle knuckle of your finger, making a "cast" of even thickness; you are creating a tunnel for the filling. If the paste begins to break, wet your fingers and smooth it back together.

Remove the cast from your finger and fill it with about 1 teaspoon of the filling. Wet your fingers and close the opening by pinching the end together to form a point. Pinch the opposite end in the same manner. The *kibeh* ball should resemble a milkweed pod. Repeat with the remaining paste and filling.

To fry the balls, heat the 4 cups vegetable oil in a deep pot over high heat. Working in batches and using a slotted spoon, slide the balls into the hot oil. Fry, turning the balls occasionally, until they float to the surface, about 4 minutes. The balls will be chestnut brown. Cook them just a few seconds more, then remove them from the pot with the slotted spoon and transfer them to paper towels.

To bake the balls, preheat the oven to 400°F. Arrange the balls on an oiled rimmed baking sheet, and drizzle enough olive oil over each ball so that it is lightly but entirely coated. Bake for 15 minutes, shaking the baking sheet twice during the baking time.

Arrange the Kibeh Balls on a platter and serve hot, with one or more dips.

Potato Kibeh

KIBEH BATATA

2½ pounds baking potatoes, scrubbed

2 tablespoons corn oil

2 large onions, chopped

1 pound ground beef

½ cup pine nuts

2 tablespoons butter

¼ teaspoon grated nutmeg

2 teaspoons salt

½ teaspoon white pepper

2 tablespoons dry bread crumbs

*T*his is the Arab equivalent of Shepherd's Pie. Many Arab Americans substitute this for beef or lamb Kibeh, the traditional entertaining staple. Serve Kibeh Batata with a Mixed Vegetable Salad.

Serves 6

Place the potatoes in a large pot and add water to cover by 1 inch. Cover and bring to a boil over high heat. Reduce the heat to medium and cook until the potatoes are fork-tender, about 30 minutes. Drain the potatoes and set them aside to cool.

While the potatoes are cooling, heat the corn oil in a large skillet over medium heat. Add the onions and sauté until soft and translucent, about 7 minutes. Add the beef and cook, stirring to break the meat into coarse crumbs, until it is dark—almost black—and fragrant, about 5 minutes. Stir in the pine nuts and set aside.

Preheat the oven to 350°F.

When the potatoes are cool enough to handle, peel them and place them in a large bowl. Mash with the back of a fork or a potato masher, adding the butter, nutmeg, 1 teaspoon of the salt, and the white pepper as you mash them to a creamy consistency.

Spread half of the potato mixture over the bottom of an 8 by 12-inch baking dish. Spread the meat mixture evenly over the potatoes. Using the remaining potatoes, spoon about 2 tablespoons into the palm of your hand and flatten the mixture to form a patty. Lay it on top of the meat and repeat with the remaining potatoes. Using damp hands, smooth the patties together until none of the beef layer is showing. Sprinkle the bread crumbs on top, and season with the remaining 1 teaspoon salt. Using a sharp knife, score the surface to make 2½-inch squares. Prick the middle of each square with the tines of a fork. Bake until the potatoes are crisp and golden, about 20 minutes. Serve hot.

Note: This dish can be reheated, covered, in a 350°F oven for 20 minutes.

KAFTA

The foods of the many Arab countries have much in common, but nothing more so than *kafta*, which is enjoyed in every country in a multiplicity of ways. In fact, Arab cooks take pride in the variety of ways they prepare *kafta*, a basic mixture of minced lamb or beef flavored with simple ingredients such as parsley and onions and seasoned with a mix of spices. Like *kibeh*, *kafta* can be fried, baked, or grilled; shaped into burgers, pressed onto skewers for grilling, or layered and baked.

In Lebanon, Syria, Palestine, and Jordan, *kafta* is most popular grilled on skewers, as in Kafta Mashwi, or baked with potatoes, tomato, and pomegranate juice, as in Kafta bi Tahini. In the Gulf States cooks replace the meat with fish and flavor it with cilantro and orange zest, as in Kibeh Samak. Most Middle Eastern countries tend to use the basic *kafta* mixture of lamb, parsley, and onions mixed with allspice, black pepper, and salt. In Egypt, fewer spices are used and eggs enrich the mix, which is shaped into round balls, rolled in bread crumbs, and deep-fried. Other North African countries use various spices to season the meat—saffron, cinnamon, cloves, nutmeg, turmeric, cumin, cardamom.

Back home in Lebanon, *kafta* is prepared right on the butcher's block—he chops the meat together with the parsley, onion, and the spices for you. I fondly remember many trips to the local meat counter, where my mother would ask for "three times minced" meat, which meant that we were having *kafta* for lunch that day. She used to watch the butcher with eagle eyes, making sure he used the exact piece of meat she requested (which was always leg of lamb) with just the right amount of fat. When I was old enough to visit the butcher myself, I insisted he trim away lots of the fat, to which he always replied, "It's not *kafta* anymore!" Of course the butcher knew best, and now, here in the States, I ask for finely minced meat from a fairly well-marbled leg of lamb or loin cut.

Though it is a staple for novices in the kitchen, accomplished Arab cooks love the ease with which these dishes can be prepared. They are perfect for serving a small group of friends on short notice or, in the case of the Grilled Kafta, for satisfying a crowd of hungry guests on a summer evening.

Kafta

1 packed cup fincly chopped
   fresh parsley

2 pounds lean ground beef *or*
   ground leg of lamb

1 pound yellow onions, minced

1 tablespoon salt

1 teaspoon ground allspice

½ teaspoon black pepper

½ teaspoon ground coriander

¼ teaspoon ground cardamom

¼ teaspoon ground cinnamon

This is the basic recipe for all the Kafta recipes that follow. You can roll this mixture into small balls to use in soup, or pat it into small patties to fry for appetizers. This wonderful recipe actually has many delicious uses.
                                        Makes 3 pounds

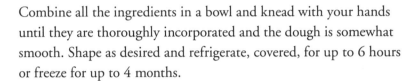

Combine all the ingredients in a bowl and knead with your hands until they are thoroughly incorporated and the dough is somewhat smooth. Shape as desired and refrigerate, covered, for up to 6 hours or freeze for up to 4 months.

Baked Kafta with Tahini Sauce

KAFTA BI TAHINI

2 medium potatoes (about 2 pounds), thinly sliced

2 teaspoons salt

Kafta (page 233)

Tahini (page 32), thinned with ½ cup water

Arab flatbread, cut into triangles

*A*rabs like to eat these baked beef patties for lunch, the largest meal of their day, because they are quite filling. Kafta prepared this way is popular in Palestine and Jordan, where I learned how to make it just after I was married. Many years later, I still make it for an easy weeknight dinner and serve it with Mixed Vegetable Salad or a Simple Salad, Arab flatbread, pickles, and olives. Jalapeños are sometimes served on the side, too (they are never left off my table since my husband enjoys this only if he can eat a whole chile with the meat!)

Serves 6 to 8

Preheat the oven to 350°F.

Spread the potatoes out in a 10 by 13-inch baking dish and season with the salt. Spread the Kafta over the potatoes, pushing it out to the edges of the dish. Smooth the meat with the back of spoon. Bake, uncovered, for 45 minutes.

Remove the dish from the oven and pour off the liquid that has accumulated. Spoon the Tahini over the meat, spreading it out evenly. Return the Kafta to the oven and bake until the sauce has thickened to the consistency of heavy cream, about 30 minutes.

Cut the Kafta (including the potato layer) into 6 or 8 squares and serve, spooning the Tahini Sauce over it. Serve with the Arab flatbread alongside.

To reheat: Pour ½ cup water into the baking dish to thin the sauce, which will have thickened as the dish cooled. Incorporate the water into the sauce, using the back of a spoon. Heat in a preheated 350°F oven until the meat is warmed through, 10 to 15 minutes.

Baked Kafta with Potato

KAFTA BI SENIYAH

3 tablespoons vegetable oil

4 pounds potatoes, cut into
½-inch-thick slices

½ pound onions, thinly sliced

¼ cup tomato paste

5 cloves garlic, thinly sliced

Salt and black pepper, to taste

Kafta (page 233)

2 pounds tomatoes, cut into
½-inch-thick slices

Essentially a layered lamb casserole, this is very easy to assemble—Kafta, tomatoes, sautéed potatoes and onions, all baked in a tomato sauce. Serve it with a Simple Salad and Arab flatbread for a satisfying weeknight dinner.   *Serves 6 to 8*

Preheat the oven to 350°F.

Heat 2 tablespoons of the vegetable oil in a large skillet over high heat. Add the potatoes and sauté, turning once, until they are lightly golden, about 10 minutes. Using a slotted spoon, transfer the potatoes to paper towels to drain.

Add the remaining 1 tablespoon vegetable oil to the skillet and let it get hot. Add the onions and sauté until they are soft and translucent, about 5 minutes.

Dissolve the tomato paste in ½ cup water, and pour it over the onions. Add the garlic and stir the mixture to completely coat the onions. Season with salt and pepper. Cook the onion mixture for 15 minutes, until they have melted slightly into the sauce.

Meanwhile, spread the Kafta in a 9 by 12-inch shallow baking dish. Arrange the potatoes over the Kafta, overlapping them if necessary. Layer the tomatoes on top of the potatoes. Then spread the onion mixture evenly over the tomatoes. Bake until the tomato sauce has thickened, the meat is a deep brown, and the potatoes are fork-tender, about 1 hour.

To serve, cut the Kafta into squares and serve directly from the baking dish. Spoon some of the tomato sauce over each square.

Variation: My Aunt Haleema used to shape the Kafta into patties and place a slice of potato on each one, then wrap the whole thing in two layers of grape leaves and cook it in the tomato sauce.

Kafta Burgers

AKRAS KAFTA

Kafta (page 233)
½ cup canola oil (for frying)
Ground sumac
Lettuce, for serving
Sliced tomatoes, for serving
Tahini (page 32)
Arab flatbread, for serving
Pickles, for serving

These ground lamb patties seasoned with allspice, coriander, and cardamom are the Arab equivalent of hamburgers. They can be cooked like hamburgers, too—grilled or fried—and taste delicious tucked into Arab pocket bread and dressed with Tahini, sliced tomatoes, shredded lettuce, sliced pickles, and a dusting of sumac. Almost any Arab dip tastes great with these: Hummus, Spicy Tomato Sauce, Cucumber and Yogurt. When my boys were in high school here in the States, I prepared them like hamburgers, with ketchup, relish, mustard, lettuce, tomatoes, and pickles between split hamburger buns. **Makes 12 patties**

Divide the Kafta into 12 equal portions. Roll each portion into a ball, then flatten it to form ½-inch-thick patties.

To fry: Heat the canola oil in a heavy, shallow skillet over high heat. Working in batches, gently slide the patties into the skillet and cook, turning them only once, until they are deep brown, about 5 minutes on each side.

To grill: Prepare a gas or charcoal grill, or preheat the broiler. Grill or broil the patties, turning them only once, until they are seared, about 3 minutes on each side.

To serve: Remove the patties from the skillet or the grill, and sprinkle with the ground sumac. Serve the Kafta Burgers topped with lettuce and sliced tomatoes, with the Tahini, flatbread, and pickles on the side.

Kafta Fingers

KAFTA ASABEH

1 tablespoon curry powder

½ teaspoon ground ginger

2 recipes Kafta (page 233)

2 pounds onions, halved and thinly sliced

Four 15-ounce cans tomato sauce

8 cloves garlic, mashed

Fresh parsley or mint leaves, for garnish

Kafta fingers are usually reserved for casual family dinners, but with the addition of curry powder and ginger, two spices that are commonly used in the Gulf States, where the Indian influence is strong, they become elegant enough to serve to company. Serve them with Roasted Eggplant Salad and rice. **Makes about 24 "fingers"**

Preheat the oven to 350°F.

Stir the curry powder and ginger together in a small bowl. Place the Kafta in a large bowl and using your hands, mix the spices into it.

Place a bowl of ice water nearby. Pull off a walnut-size piece of the meat mixture, and shape it into a 3 by 1-inch "finger," dipping your hands in the ice water to smooth the finger. Repeat with the remaining mixture, placing the "fingers" about ¼ inch apart in a shallow baking dish. Scatter the onions on top. Whisk the tomato sauce and garlic together, and pour this over the onions. Bake until the sauce has thickened and the meat is fork-tender, about 45 minutes.

To serve, transfer the Kafta Fingers from the baking dish to a serving platter. Drizzle the onions and tomato sauce over them, and garnish with the parsley leaves.

Grilled Kafta

KAFTA MASHURI

Kafta (page 233), made with
85% lean beef (any less fatty
and the meat will fall off the
skewers)

2 loaves *markouk* (page 22) or
other paper-thin flatbread

Ground sumac, for dusting the
onions

½ pound onions, thinly sliced

The traditional way to grill Kafta is on skewers placed as close to the charcoal as possible. To mimic the traditional method as closely as I can, I remove the grill rack and rest the tip and the neck of the skewers on the front and back of the grill itself.

I always use 20-inch long, 1-inch-wide flat skewers to make Kafta this way. They tend to hold the meat better than the slimmer kind, since the mixture is spread along the length and around the width of the skewer rather than pierced as in kebabs. You can find the flat skewers at ethnic grocery stores and kitchen specialty shops.

Serve Grilled Kafta with Tomato and Dill Seed Salad and Eggplant in Pomegranate Syrup. **Makes 8 skewers**

Prepare a charcoal grill, with the rack removed. Place a small bowl of ice water near your work area.

Divide the Kafta into 8 equal portions. Working with 1 portion at a time, press the meat onto the middle of the skewer. Wetting your hands, spread the meat along the length and around the blade until it's about 5 inches long. Make sure there is a thickness of meat along the sides of the skewers; this prevents it from falling off during cooking. Wet your hands again and press the meat between your thumb and forefinger along the length of the skewer, making dimples in it. These indentations prevent the meat from falling off the skewer as it cooks. Repeat with the remaining Kafta and skewers.

Set the skewers as close to the hot coals as possible without touching them. Grill, turning at least twice, for 3 minutes on each side.

To serve, unfold the *markouk,* tear it in half, and spread one half on a platter. Lay the skewers on top, sprinkle with sumac, and cover with the other half of the *markouk.* Set the platter on the table, accompanied by the onions and the remaining loaf of *markouk.* Traditionally, the hostess serves the meat by tearing a piece of the markouk from the top layer and using it to slide the meat onto each guest's plate, leaving the bread on the plate too. The onions may be tucked into the bread and eaten with each bite of meat, or eaten on their own after each bite of Kafta.

Fried Fish

6 cloves garlic, mashed

2 tablespoons Kuwaiti Spice Mix (page 41) *or* 1 tablespoon each ground cumin, ground coriander, and black pepper

1 cup fresh lemon juice

2 teaspoons salt

3 pounds fillet of cod, grouper, snapper, or any firm whitefish, skinned and cut into 8 pieces, cleaned (see below) and patted dry

1 cup all-purpose flour

1 cup vegetable oil

1 loaf Arab flatbread

1 lemon, sliced, for garnish

Parsley Sauce (page 36), for serving

Fried fish is very popular everywhere in the Arab world, from the Mediterranean to the Arabian Gulf, from the Tigris River to the Gulf of Oman. It is typically served with a squeeze of lemon, fried Arab flatbread, and Tahini. The frying time will vary depending on the thickness of the fish; it's cooked properly if the flesh flashes easily when lifted with a fork. Serve Samak Makli with Onion Rice and Roasted Eggplant Spread.

Serves 6

Combine the garlic, Kuwaiti Spice Mix, lemon juice, and salt in a 4-quart baking dish and stir to combine. Add the fish pieces and turn to coat them with the marinade. Cover the dish with plastic wrap and refrigerate for 4 to 6 hours or as long as overnight.

Spread the flour out on a piece of wax paper. Dredge the fish, 1 piece at a time, in the flour, turning to coat it all over, and transfer it to a plate.

Heat the vegetable oil in a deep skillet over high heat. While it is heating, cut the bread into triangles with kitchen shears. Split each triangle into single layers.

CLEANING FISH THE TRADITIONAL WAY

This is a tried and true method for cleaning fish, performed in the Arab world by housewives and chefs alike. It is effective in eliminating any "fishy" smell and results in cleaner, more delicious fish.

Combine 1 cup bottled lemon juice and 1 cup white vinegar in a shallow glass or ceramic bowl. Rinse the fish under running water, and then rub all-purpose flour all over the surface of the fish. Lay the floured fish in the bowl and rub it well with the lemon juice mixture. Rinse the fish again with clean water, and pat it dry with paper towels.

240 *The Arab Table*

Slide the bread triangles into the hot oil and fry until golden, about 4 minutes on each side. Using a slotted spoon, transfer the fried bread to paper towels to drain.

Reduce the heat to medium (385°F), and add 2 or 3 pieces of the fish to the skillet. Fry until deep gold on both sides, 4 to 5 minutes per side. Do not crowd the skillet. Transfer the fish to a paper towel–lined plate with the slotted spoon.

Repeat with the remaining fish, straining the oil between batches if necessary and bringing it back to 385°F before continuing to fry.

Serve with the fried Arab flatbread, lemon slices, and Parsley Sauce on the side.

Baked Sea Bass with Rice and Caramelized Onions

SAYADIAH

Six 8-ounce fillets of sea bass or any firm whitefish, cut into 4-ounce pieces, cleaned (see page 240) and patted dry

½ cup fresh lemon juice

3 cloves garlic, mashed

2 tablespoons ground cumin

1½ teaspoons salt

½ teaspoon black pepper

1¾ cups canola oil

5 pounds onions: 3½ pounds halved and thinly sliced, 1½ pounds cut into ¼-inch-thick slices

All-purpose flour, for dusting

2 cups basmati rice, rinsed (see page 165), soaked, and drained

½ cup fried pine nuts (see page 43)

½ teaspoon ground turmeric

½ teaspoon white pepper

2½ cups boiling water

Chopped fresh parsley, for garnish

Tahini (page 32)

*S*ayadiah *means "what belongs to the fisherman" (sayad means "fisherman") and indeed, whatever fish from the day's catch went unsold, the fishermen brought home to their wives to cook for dinner. Sayadiah varies from region to region in the Arab world. Only one version comes from the Eastern Mediterranean, where the rice and onions are cooked separately from the fish, which is fried. In the Gulf States, rice and fish dishes are very common; among my favorites is a preparation of broiled whole baby sea bass stuffed with cooked onions flavored with cilantro and tomatoes. It is served on top of rice cooked with onions, tomatoes, cilantro, and saffron. Some Lebanese cooks dredge the fish in flour seasoned with salt, pepper, and cumin, fry it, and serve it on top of rice topped with fried onions. In Tripoli, in northern Lebanon, the rice is seasoned with cinnamon.*

This is my mother's recipe—I don't think there's a better one—and it features the rice, onions, and fish layered in a pot. Once cooked, the dish is allowed to rest a bit, then the whole thing is inverted onto a serving platter, resulting in a loosely molded fish dish. The beauty of this dish is that the components can be made ahead: fry the onions 2 days before serving, and the fish 1 day ahead, then assemble it on the day you want to serve it.

Serves 6

Place the fish in a baking dish that is large enough to hold the pieces in a single layer. Mix the lemon juice, garlic, 1 tablespoon of the cumin, ½ teaspoon of the salt, and the black pepper together, and pour the mixture over the fish, turning to coat each piece. Cover with plastic wrap and marinate in the refrigerator for 4 hours or as long as overnight.

Heat ¾ cup of the canola oil in a large nonstick skillet over high heat. Add the thinly sliced onions and sauté until soft and golden, about 15 minutes. Using a slotted spoon, transfer them to a paper towel–lined plate to drain.

Remove the fish from the marinade, and dust the pieces with a light coating of flour. Add the remaining 1 cup canola oil to the oil left in the skillet, and heat over high heat. Sauté the fish until golden, about 3 minutes per side. Transfer the fish to a paper towel–lined plate, using the slotted spoon.

Arrange the thick onion slices on the bottom of a 4-quart pot. Spread the fried onions over the sliced onions. Scatter half the pine nuts over the onions. Arrange the fish on top. Combine the rice, remaining 1 tablespoon cumin, the turmeric, remaining 1 teaspoon salt, and the white pepper in a bowl; toss to mix well. Spread the rice mixture over the fish. Add the boiling water and place the pot over high heat. (The rice should be covered by ½ inch of water; add more if necessary.) Cover the pot and bring to a boil. Then reduce the heat to medium and cook until most of the water has been absorbed, about 15 minutes.

Slide a heat diffuser under the pot and reduce the heat to low. Cook until the rice is soft, about 20 minutes. Remove the pot from the heat and wrap it in a fleece blanket to keep it warm and to give the layers time to settle.

To serve, invert a rimmed platter (one that is at least 2 inches wider than the pot) over the pot. Holding the two together, turn the pot over. Let it sit for 5 to 10 minutes. Then gently lift off the pot to reveal the layered dish. If the rice and fish fall away, simply spoon them back into place. If any fried onions have adhered to the bottom bed of onions (which you do not serve), pull them away with a fork and arrange them on top. Garnish with the remaining pine nuts and the parsley, and serve with Tahini.

Baked Sea Bass with Tahini-Walnut Sauce

SAMAKEH HARRA BI TAHINI

For the fish:

One 4- to 6-pound sea bass fillet (a whole side), skin on, scaled, deboned, and cleaned (see page 240)

½ lemon

8 cloves garlic

1½ teaspoons salt, plus more for sprinkling

1 small jalapeño or other hot chile pepper, thinly sliced crosswise

1 teaspoon red pepper flakes

1¼ cups chopped fresh cilantro

1 teaspoon black pepper, plus more for sprinkling

1 tablespoon ground cumin

1½ teaspoons ground coriander

½ teaspoon ground cardamom

½ cup fresh lemon juice (squeezed-out lemon halves reserved)

¼ cup extra virgin olive oil

For the Tahini-Walnut Sauce:

12 cloves garlic

2 teaspoons salt, plus more if needed

1 small fresh hot red chile, thinly sliced crosswise

½ cup extra virgin olive oil

3 cups finely chopped fresh cilantro

2 cups walnut halves or pieces

2 cups sesame paste (tahini)

1 cup fresh lemon juice, plus more if needed

In Arabic, samakeh harra *means "spicy fish," and the name can refer to a variety of delicious preparations, including the Baked Whole Red Snapper on page 250. But of all of these, Samakeh Harra bi Tahini is perhaps the best known and the most elaborate version. Certainly it is my favorite to serve at Eid al Adha or any other big celebration. It's as beautiful as it is flavorful: succulent sea bass stuffed with herbs and spices, totally encased in a sparkling sauce of tahini and ground walnuts.*

Back home in the Middle East, when we lived near the Mediterranean or the Arabian Gulf, it was easy to find the perfect fish for this dish—a local variety of sea bass known as lukhos. *It was baked whole, with the spices inside the cavity, and looked impressive with the head and tail poking out from the blanket of sauce. Here in America, it is nearly impossible to buy a whole sea bass that's the right size. Most markets sell only fillets cut from much larger fish, and of course these pieces don't have a head or tail. To make a traditional presentation, I recently devised the method I give here: two layers of sea bass fillet with the spices between them, baked in a long fish-shaped assembly. I coat it from "head" to "tail" with the tahini sauce and decorate it with fish motifs. And for important occasions like the Eid, I display my creation on a long silver platter made espressly for serving whole fish.*

True sea bass is best for this dish. "Chilean sea bass," which is really a different kind of fish, is easier to find and also delicious, as is grouper. Of course you can follow this procedure with a smaller piece of fish to make a delicious dinner anytime—just divide the ingredients proportionally.

Whether you are making Samakeh Harra bi Tahini as part of a larger menu or alone as a main course, you can prepare and bake the fish a day ahead: open the foil, let the fish cool, and then refrigerate it until an hour or so before serving. Transfer the chilled fish to a platter and let it sit at room temperature. Make the tahini sauce and coat the fish just before serving. **Serves 10**

Prepare and bake the fish: Preheat the oven to 400°F, with a rack in the lower third of the oven. Tear off a sheet of heavy-duty aluminum foil that's twice as long as the fish fillet and lay it in the bottom of a sturdy roasting pan or baking dish that is at least 3

2 or more lemons, cut into
    wedges or slices

10 walnut halves

At least ¼ cup chopped fresh
    parsley

inches deep and big enough to hold the whole fillet. Tear another
sheet of foil, just a bit shorter, and lay it on top of the first sheet at
a right angle; you want a double layer of foil on the bottom and the
ends of the foil sheets extending over the sides of the pan all
around.

Rub the fish all over with the cut surface of the lemon half.
Carefully slice the fillet lengthwise down the middle, forming 2
long pieces that are almost exactly the same shape. Lay them, skin
side down, in the foil-lined pan and sprinkle them liberally with salt
and pepper.

Mash the garlic cloves in a large mortar with the 1½ teaspoons salt,
the sliced jalapeño (with all its seeds), and the red pepper flakes;
pound vigorously with the pestle to form a rough paste.
(Alternatively, pulse into a paste in a food processor.) Put the
chopped cilantro in a medium bowl, scrape the garlic paste on top,
add the pepper, cumin, coriander, and cardamom, and stir
everything together until well blended.

Spread the cilantro mixture evenly over one of the fillet halves, then
drizzle half of the lemon juice over it. Flip the other fillet half on
top of the filling, skin side up, to form a neat, long, fish-shaped
"sandwich" about 3 inches thick, with the cilantro mixture inside.
Pour the rest of the lemon juice and all the olive oil over the top
fillet. Cut the squeezed lemon halves into large pieces and scatter
them around the fish.

Bring the ends of the top sheet of foil together (crosswise), covering
the fish, and pinch and fold them together to make a sealed package
that holds the layers in a neat shape. Do the same with the bottom
sheet, folding the edges together over and over, forming a tight
double enclosure for the fish.

Place the roasting pan in the oven, with the thick end of the
wrapped fish at the back of the oven if possible (the rear area is
hotter). Carefully pour hot (not boiling) water into the pan to a
depth of 1 inch, and close the oven door. Bake the fish for 1 hour
(or longer if the layered fish is thicker than 3 inches).

Make the sauce: While the fish is baking, mash the garlic cloves, salt, and the sliced chile, with its seeds, to form a rough paste, using a mortar and pestle or a food processor.

Pour the olive oil into a large sauté pan and set it over high heat. When the oil is hot, stir in the cilantro and the garlic paste. Cook for about 5 minutes, stirring continuously until the moisture has evaporated and the seasonings are concentrated; make sure the garlic does not burn. Remove from the heat.

Put the walnut pieces in a food processor and pulse to form a gritty powder (don't overprocess).

Scrape the sesame paste into a large, heavy-bottomed saucepan and stir in the lemon juice thoroughly. The tahini will thin and may turn white. Very gradually stir in 2 to 3 cups water, ¼ cup at a time, until the sauce reaches the consistency of light cream; the amount of water will vary with different brands of tahini.

Stir the cooked cilantro mixture, with all the oil from the pan, into the tahini liquid and set the saucepan over high heat. Stirring constantly, heat the sauce; it will thicken and begin to bubble and boil. Reduce the heat and cook briefly at the boil until you see oil appear on the surface of the sauce. Immediately remove the pan from the heat and stir in the ground walnuts until well blended. Taste the sauce, and add more salt or lemon juice if needed. Set it aside.

Finish and serve: Remove the roasting pan from the oven, and carefully unwrap the foil at the thick end of the fish. Check the middle of the "sandwich": the flesh should be opaque and should flake easily. If it is not fully cooked, seal the foil, return the pan to the oven, and bake for another 15 minutes; then check again. When it is done, leave the fish in the foil until you are ready to sauce and serve it.

To transfer the layered fish in one piece, place the serving platter alongside the roasting pan and spread open all the foil wrapping. Place the edge of a thin flat plate under each long side of the fish— you'll have a plate in each of your hands—and slide them under the bottom fillet. Carefully lift the entire fish (have someone peel away the foil if necessary) and lower it onto the platter. Remove the skin from the top fillet—it should come off easily.

Saucing the fish is like icing a cake: Spoon about half of the sauce on top of the fish, and using a scraper or other flat utensil, spread it out so it drapes down the sides of the layers. Smooth the sides and top, pressing the sauce against the fish (and taking more from the pan as needed) so it is neatly and completely coated.

Clean the platter of any drips, and arrange the lemon wedges decoratively around the fish. Place the walnut halves on top of the fish in a nice pattern. Finally, sprinkle the chopped parsley all around and over, creating a head, tail, fins, or other fish features if you like. Present the platter at the table, with the remaining sauce in a serving bowl.

To serve the fish (or to show guests how to serve themselves): At the "head" end, slide a cake server or similar implement into the middle of the layers, under the top fillet, and lift off a single portion of fish with some of the spicy filling and sauce. Continue to slide the server under the top fillet and lift off portions until all the top fillet has been portioned out. Serve the bottom fillet in a similar manner, lifting portions off the bottom skin, which remains in the platter.

Baked Cod with Tahini Sauce

TAGEN AL-SAMAK

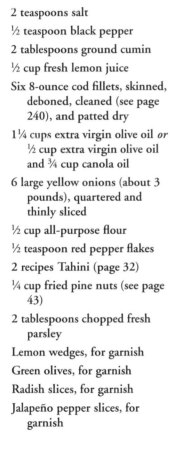

2 teaspoons salt

½ teaspoon black pepper

2 tablespoons ground cumin

½ cup fresh lemon juice

Six 8-ounce cod fillets, skinned, deboned, cleaned (see page 240), and patted dry

1¼ cups extra virgin olive oil *or* ½ cup extra virgin olive oil and ¾ cup canola oil

6 large yellow onions (about 3 pounds), quartered and thinly sliced

½ cup all-purpose flour

½ teaspoon red pepper flakes

2 recipes Tahini (page 32)

¼ cup fried pine nuts (see page 43)

2 tablespoons chopped fresh parsley

Lemon wedges, for garnish

Green olives, for garnish

Radish slices, for garnish

Jalapeño pepper slices, for garnish

*T*agen, *as this dish is referred to in my house, is a dish you build, layering flavors beginning with sautéed onions and golden pine nuts, then succulent fried cod, and tahini sauce on top of that, then bake it to a bubbling golden brown. (Tagen al-Samak is a traditional Moroccan dish that bears little resemblance to this, my mother's version, which she always referred to as* her *Tagen.) You can use any kind of firm, flaky fish; I typically use cod because good-quality pieces are available to me year-round, and occasionally I use grouper, which is equally delicious. Serve Tagen with Mixed Vegetable Salad, Arab flatbread, and small plates of green olives, pickled wild cucumbers, scallions, and lemon wedges.* Serves 6

Combine the salt, pepper, cumin, and lemon juice in a deep baking dish and stir to combine. Place the fish in the marinade and turn it once to coat it. Cover with plastic wrap and refrigerate for at least 4 hours or as long as overnight.

Heat ¼ cup of the olive oil in a large skillet over medium heat. Add the onions and sauté until they are soft and translucent, about 10 minutes. Reduce the heat to medium and cook, stirring, until the onions are golden and tender, about 20 minutes. Using a slotted spoon, transfer the onions to a paper towel–lined plate. Set it aside.

Add the remaining 1 cup olive oil to the oil in the skillet and heat it over high heat. While the oil is heating, spread the flour on a large plate. Remove the fish from the marinade and dredge the pieces in the flour, turning to coat both sides evenly.

Slide the fish into the hot oil, working in batches if necessary, and fry until golden, about 3 minutes per side. Use the slotted spoon to transfer the fish to a paper towel–lined plate. Set it aside.

Preheat the oven to 350°F.

Combine the red pepper flakes and the tahini in a bowl, and mix together until smooth. Gradually add water to achieve the desired consistency. Set the sauce aside.

Spread the onions evenly over the bottom of a 3-quart baking dish. Scatter all but 1 teaspoon of the pine nuts over the onions. Lay the fish over the onions and spoon the tahini sauce over the fish. Bake until the sauce is golden brown and has thickened to the consistency of heavy cream, 20 to 30 minutes. The dish will look somewhat like baked lasagna.

Remove the dish from the oven, sprinkle the parsley and the remaining 1 teaspoon pine nuts on top, and garnish with the lemons, olives, radishes and jalapeño slices. When you serve the Tagen, make sure to dig the spoon down to the bottom of the dish to get a bit of the onions and pine nuts; place a lemon wedge on each plate.

Baked Whole Red Snapper

SAMAKEH BI BANDORA

This is a very simple way of preparing fish. In the old days, home cooks in the Middle East used to carry this stuffed fish to the local baker to cook in his wood oven, and then return within the hour to pick up a fragrant and piping hot whole fish. The stuffing, or hashweh *(the generic term for almost any combination of herbs, garlic, and onions used to stuff fish, chicken, or lamb), is sautéed before it is spooned into the fish. Serve this with Lentils with Caramelized Onions or Bulgur and Broad Beans, and Tabouleh.* Serves 6

For the stuffing:

¼ cup extra virgin olive oil

½ pound onions, finely chopped

15 cloves garlic, mashed

1 green bell pepper, seeded and finely chopped

½ teaspoon minced jalapeño pepper

2 cups chopped fresh cilantro

¼ cup fresh lemon juice

1 teaspoon salt

For the fish:

1 large onion, cut into ½-inch-thick slices

½ teaspoon ground cardamom

1 tablespoon ground coriander

2 tablespoons ground cumin

¼ teaspoon ground cinnamon

2 teaspoons salt

½ teaspoon black pepper

15 cloves garlic, mashed

½ cup fresh lemon juice

One 8-pound whole red snapper, sea bass, or halibut, head on, gutted, scaled, and rinsed cleaned (see page 240)

½ cup olive oil

1 pound tomatoes, cut into ½-inch-thick slices

10 sprigs fresh cilantro

1 lemon, cut into ½-inch-thick slices

Prepare the stuffing: Heat the olive oil in a large skillet over medium high heat. Add the onions and sauté until soft and tender, about 7 minutes. Add the garlic, green peppers, and jalapeño, and continue to cook until the garlic is fragrant and the peppers are soft, about 15 minutes. Add the cilantro and cook, stirring, until it brightens and wilts, 5 minutes. Then stir in the lemon juice, season with the salt, and remove from the heat. Set aside to cool.

Prepare the fish: Preheat the oven to 375°F. Line a 4-quart baking dish with foil running both the length and the width of the pan, with excess hanging over the sides. Spread the onion slices in a single layer on the bottom. Set the dish aside.

Combine the cardamom, coriander, cumin, cinnamon, salt, pepper, garlic, and lemon juice in a small bowl and mix together to make a paste.

Pierce the skin of the fish by making 4 or 5 small slits along the length of one side with a sharp knife. Lay the fish on its side, slit side up, over the onions in the baking dish. Rub the spice mix all over the inside and outside of the fish. Spoon the stuffing into the cavity, spreading it evenly from head to tail. Pack some into the slits, too. Drizzle with the olive oil.

Arrange the tomatoes, cilantro sprigs, and lemon slices over and around the fish. Fold the excess foil loosely around it, and bake until it flakes when pierced with a fork, about 30 minutes.

Fried pine nuts (see page 43), for garnish

Fresh parsley leaves, for garnish

Lemon wedges, for garnish

Parsley Sauce (page 36), for serving

To serve: Transfer the fish, in the foil, to a large platter. Open the foil and slide it out from underneath the fish. Use a knife to remove the skin from the fish to make it easier to serve (it also looks better). Garnish with the pine nuts, parsley, and lemon wedges. When serving your guests, spoon the stuffing out of the cavity and place it alongside each serving of fish. Serve warm or at room temperature, with the Parsley Sauce alongside.

Tibsi Red Snapper in Pomegranate Syrup

TIBSI SAMAK BI SHARAB RUMAN

1 tablespoon salt

1 tablespoon ground allspice

1 teaspoon ground cumin

1 teaspoon red pepper flakes

4 pounds red snapper fillet, skinned, cleaned (see page 240), patted dry, and cut into 3-inch pieces

4 tablespoons butter or glee

6 medium onions, halved and thickly sliced

4 dried limes *(loumi),* slit in several places

4 green Thai chile peppers, seeded and diced

10 cloves garlic, mashed

2 pounds tomatoes, cut into ¼-inch-thick slices

2 tablespoons pomegranate syrup

4 ribs celery, finely chopped

Tibsi is the name of the clay pot that Iraqis use to cook this and other baked dishes. Loumi, the dried limes that give this dish its distinctive tang, are grown in Iraq, as is the celery that garnishes the fish. If you can't find loumi, use a tablespoon of fresh lime juice. The Kuwaitis make Samak Matfi, a skillet version of this dish that calls for cilantro instead of celery because the herb grows abundantly in that country. It is traditionally served with Sweet Rice. I use red snapper fillets here, but you can use salmon or any other fatty fish with excellent results. If you don't have pomegranate syrup, substitute lemon juice.

Serves 6

Preheat the oven to 400°F.

Combine the salt, allspice, cumin, and red pepper flakes in a small bowl and stir well. Rub all but 1 tablespoon and ½ teaspoon of the mixture onto both sides of the fish.

Butter a 3½-quart baking dish, and arrange half of the onions on the bottom of the dish. Sprinkle ½ teaspoon of the reserved spice mixture over the onions. Lay the fish on the bed of onions, and tuck the dried limes between the pieces. Combine the remaining onions with the chile peppers, garlic, and remaining 1 tablespoon of the spice mixture. Scatter the onion mixture over the fish; then cover it with the tomato slices.

Dissolve the pomegranate syrup in 1 cup of water, and pour this into the dish. Bake until the tops of the tomatoes are toasted and the sauce has thickened enough to coat the back of a spoon, 40 to 50 minutes. Remove the dish from the oven, scatter the celery on top, and serve.

Kuwaiti Grilled Snapper

SABOUR MASHWI

2 pounds Golden Zahady dates, soaked for 2 hours, soaking liquid reserved

One 6-pound whole red snapper, head and tail on, scaled, fins trimmed, and cleaned (see page 240)

1 tablespoon Kuwaiti Spice Mix (page 41)

2 packed cups chopped fresh cilantro

½ pound onions, coarsely chopped

12 cloves garlic, mashed

¼ cup chopped fresh dill

1 tablespoon plus 2 teaspoons salt

1 teaspoon black pepper

2 tablespoons ground turmeric

1 dried lime (loumi), broken into pieces and ground in a spice grinder or grated zest and juice of 1 fresh Mexican lime

2 tablespoons olive oil

Flat-leaf parsley sprigs, for garnish

This classic Kuwaiti dish features a whole fish, swathed in a sweet paste of pureed dates, grilled directly over hot coals. The date coating, probably used this way because dates are so plentiful in Kuwait, seals in the fish juices, resulting in a remarkably succulent dish. Use Golden Zahady dates if you can find them; they make the best paste. The Iraqis prepare an encased fish, too, though they use a paste of salt and water. Ask your fishmonger to clean, scale, and remove the fins from the fish. Serve Sabour Mashwi with Onion Rice, Spicy Tomato Sauce, and a plate of wild chicory. Serves 6

Place the dates and their soaking liquid in a food processor and pulse to form a smooth paste. If the paste is too thick, gradually add a little water. Set the paste aside.

Split the fish open on its belly side from head to tail, to create a pouch for the filling. Rub the Kuwaiti Spice Mix over the inside and outside of the fish.

Combine the cilantro, onions, garlic, dill, salt, pepper, turmeric, and dried lime in a large bowl. Add ¼ cup of the date paste and the olive oil, and mix together with a wooden spoon. Pack this mixture inside the fish. Using kitchen string, tie the fish every 2 inches or so across its length. Spread the remaining date paste over the fish, covering the entire body except the head and tail, patting it onto the fish with your hands as you spread it.

Line a V-shaped roasting rack with enough foil to hang generously over the sides. Make a clamshell shape with a second piece of foil, to use as a cradle for the fish. Set the fish in the clamshell, belly side up, and place the whole rack in the refrigerator for 3 to 4 hours.

Prepare a charcoal grill or preheat the oven to 400°F.

Place the rack directly over the coals and grill until the fish flakes when pricked with a fork, about 1½ hours. (Alternately, set the roasting rack in a roasting pan and bake in the oven until the fish flakes when pricked with a fork, about 1 hour.)

To serve, cut away the trussing string and transfer the fish, in the foil, to a serving platter. Trim as much foil away as possible, and garnish the platter with parsley. Break away the hardened outer shell. Cut a piece of fish for each guest, and spoon some of the filling onto each plate. Use a spoon to scoop a bit of the soft inner part of the date coating (only a thin exterior layer of the paste will harden) onto each plate as well.

Shrimp with Garlic and Cilantro

MAHMOUS RUBYAN

In the Gulf States, succulent shrimp sautéed in a potent garlic-cilantro mixture is a classic combination. The cilantro mixture, known as taqliya in Egypt, Lebanon, Syria, Jordan, and Palestine, is found in many Middle Eastern dishes including Fried Potatoes with Cilantro, and flavors many stews including Okra Stew and Fish Soup. This dish is always served with soft Arab flatbread and wedges of lemon for squeezing all over the shrimp. Serve it with Sweet Rice, Spiced Bulgur with Tomatoes, or Eggplant and Pomegranate Stew. **Serves 6**

3 tablespoons olive oil

2 pounds onions, finely chopped

10 cloves garlic, mashed

½ teaspoon ground cardamom

1 teaspoon Kuwaiti Spice Mix (page 41)

1 packed cup chopped fresh cilantro

¼ cup chopped fresh dill

1 tablespoon salt

½ teaspoon white pepper

2 pounds shrimp, peeled and deveined

1 lemon, cut into 6 wedges

Fresh cilantro sprigs, for garnish

Heat the olive oil in a large nonstick skillet over low heat and add the onions—don't let them overlap too much. Cook, stirring frequently, until they release their juices and are tender, about 10 minutes. Add the garlic, cardamom, Kuwaiti Spice Mix, cilantro, dill, salt, and pepper. Stir until the onions are coated. Raise the heat to high, add the shrimp, and cook, stirring, until the shrimp turn pink, 8 to 10 minutes.

Transfer the shrimp and onions to a serving platter, and garnish with the lemon wedges and cilantro sprigs.

Fish Kibeh

KIBEH SAMAK

For the kibeh "dough":

1½ cups fine bulgur, washed (see page 281)

½ pound onions, coarsely chopped

1 pound grouper, skinned, cleaned (see page 240), patted dry, and coarsely chopped

1 teaspoon salt

¼ teaspoon black pepper

½ teaspoon ground allspice

1 tablespoon grated orange zest

2 cups chopped fresh cilantro

1 ice cube

For the stuffing:

½ cup plus ½ tablespoon olive oil, plus extra if needed

¼ cup pine nuts

3 pounds onions, halved and thinly sliced

¼ teaspoon ground osfour (see page 24) or ground turmeric

½ teaspoon salt

½ teaspoon black pepper

For the garnish:

1 lemon, sliced into thin rounds

2 tablespoons chopped fresh cilantro

This dish reminds me of spring in Sidon, a city my mother's family is from, two hours south of Beirut. Sidon is one of Lebanon's principal fishing centers, and it is also the citrus capital of the country. The first stop on our arrival in Sidon was always at my great-aunt Khalti Latifa's house for Kibeh Samak, which she would proudly declare was made with fish plucked from the sea only hours before our arrival. After lunch we would walk out to her orange and lemon orchards to have coffee and fruit we picked right off the trees.

This recipe is for Kibeh Samak made the traditional way—sautéed onions spread between two layers of a smooth paste of ground fish and bulgur and then baked. But I also make an unconventional version in which I bake a single layer of fish dough, cut it into diamond-shaped pieces, and top each piece with the onion filling. If you want to prepare it this way, halve the fish dough recipe. Serve Kibeh Samak with Tahini Onion Sauce or tartar sauce on the side. Eggplant in Pomegranate Syrup or Fried Potatoes with Cilantro will complete a casual meal.

Serves 6 to 8

Preheat the oven to 425°F, with a rack in the upper third of the oven. Coat a 13 by 15-inch baking dish with butter or ghee. Prepare an ice water bath.

Prepare the kibeh "dough": Combine the bulgur, onions, fish, salt, pepper, allspice, orange zest, and cilantro in a food processor. Process until the mixture is smooth, about 1 minute, adding the ice cube through the feed tube to keep the processor blade cool. Transfer the mixture to a bowl, and place it in the ice water bath. Knead the "dough" by hand in the bowl until it forms a smooth, thick paste, about 3 minutes. Add up to ¼ cup ice water if it is too thick. Cover the bowl with plastic wrap and refrigerate it.

Make the stuffing: Heat the ½ cup olive oil in a large skillet over high heat. Add the pine nuts and fry until golden, about 45 seconds. Using a slotted spoon, transfer the pine nuts to a paper towel–lined plate and set it aside.

Add the onions to the skillet and sauté over medium heat, stirring occasionally, until they are soft and translucent, about 10 minutes. Reduce the heat and add the osfour, salt, and pepper. Cook for 3 minutes. Pour the onion mixture into a strainer placed over a bowl, and drain. Reserve the strained oil.

Spread a large sheet of wax paper on a clean surface, and drizzle the remaining ½ tablespoon olive oil over it. Rub it all over to coat the paper. Remove the kibeh "dough" from the refrigerator and divide it in half. Place one portion on the prepared wax paper, and fold the paper over it so the kibeh is sandwiched between the two layers. Roll the kibeh out with a rolling pin, forming a ½-inch-thick rectangle. Lift off the top half of the wax paper, and flip the kibeh into the baking dish. Wet your hands with cold water, and smooth it out in the dish. Combine the onions and pine nuts in a medium bowl, and spread the mixture evenly over the kibeh.

Roll out the remaining kibeh in the same fashion, and lay it over the onion filling. Smooth the surface, including the edges, with wet hands. Clean the edges of the dish with a damp paper towel.

Score the surface of the kibeh with a kitchen knife, creating 3-inch-long diamonds. Add enough olive oil to the reserved onion cooking oil to make ¼ cup (if necessary). Pour it over the kibeh and spread it all over the surface with the back of a spoon. Bake until the surface of the kibeh is browned and crisp, about 25 minutes.

Remove the pan from the oven, let it cool slightly, and then cut out diamond-shaped pieces along the score marks. Place them on a platter, garnish with the lemons and cilantro, and serve.

RAMADAN
A MONTH OF FASTING AND FAMILY MEALS

The one tradition of the Islamic faith that non-Muslims are most curious about is Ramadan, the monthlong observance that includes fasting. The first thing people ask me is "How can you fast for a whole month?" The simple answer is that Ramadan's fasting is required only during daylight hours; we take our meals at night, once the sun has set.

More and more, I find that Americans want to understand the meaning and customs of Ramadan. With so much media reporting on the Middle East and other parts of the Islamic world, many people are aware of Ramadan and sense its impact on daily life in Muslim countries. More gratifying, they're learning that Ramadan is widely observed here in the United States. I'm delighted that so many friends now call to wish us "Happy Ramadan!" every year.

This section is a brief explanation of Ramadan and its many traditions, both religious and social. There's much more to this holy month than going without food—and although it is a solemn time, with much prayer and reflection, it is also a happy time of visiting with family and friends and exchanging good wishes.

As always in the Arab world, though, food is a big part of Ramadan: while the month is defined by the daytime fast, the evenings are filled with memorable meals and traditional treats. And the observance ends with one of the great celebrations of the Muslim year, Eid al-Fiter, the "Feast for Breaking the Fast."

The Religious Significance of Ramadan

Ramadan is the ninth month of the Islamic calendar, revered as the month in which God revealed the holy book of Islam, the Qur'an, to the Prophet Muhammad. The Qur'an prescribes that all Muslims should fast during the daylight hours, from daybreak until sunset, on every day of Ramadan. A proper fast means abstaining from food, drink, and all other sensual pleasures, and from intemperate language and bad behavior as well.

The monthlong fast is so important that it is one of the Five Pillars of Islam—the five acts that are basic to our faith. Though fasting can be difficult, it is also the source of many blessings: it brings us closer to God and his graces; it teaches patience and piety. The fast also makes all people equal for a time, as even the wealthy feel the same pangs of hunger and thirst as the poor. This deprivation reminds Muslims of the obligation to share with those less fortunate. Indeed, the giving of alms, called *zakat,* on a regular basis and according to a prescribed formula, is another of the Five Pillars of Islam. Paying *zakat* during Ramadan is especially important and worthy.

Muslims are also called upon to focus on spiritual matters all month long, to read the Qur'an with great concentration and to gather for special lengthy prayer services every night at the mosque. During the last ten days of the month, the solemnity heightens. One of the final nights of Ramadan is the most sacred of all, commemorating the Night of Power (Laylat Al-Qadr), when God revealed the very first verses of the Qur'an to the Prophet.

Fasting—and Eating—During Ramadan

Does everyone have to fast during Ramadan?

All Muslim adults, including adolescents who have reached puberty, are supposed to fast from dawn to sundown each day of Ramadan. Islamic law recognizes a variety of circumstances, however, that exempt an individual from fasting for all or part of Ramadan, most notably if the fast will in any way injure their health. Pregnant and nursing women are excused from fasting, as are travelers on long journeys. Such exemptions can be made up for by fasting at other times of the year. And a family can make a charitable payment to help feed a poor person, in payment for a family member who cannot fast.

How does it feel to fast every day for thirty days? What do you do to make it easier?

In my own experience, only the first couple of days are difficult, until I adjust to the changed routine. But this is a welcome change, and when it comes, we have been preparing for Ramadan and looking forward to the fast and other rituals. After these first days of adjustment, the feeling I have while fasting is serene. And with work, prayer, and reading the Qur'an, the day goes by quickly, until sunset when we can break the fast.

If you can eat only at night, what meals do you have?

Customarily we have two formal meals each night of Ramadan. The first and largest meal, taken immediately or shortly after sunset, is called *iftar;* it is a typically bountiful dinner with many courses and dishes. The second, called *suhur,* is a lighter meal that is traditionally eaten just before sunrise, after which no food or drink can be taken. In addition to the meals, an abundance of fruits and sweets are offered during the many social gatherings each evening.

Mealtime practices vary a bit from one household to another. For instance, many people break their fast by sitting down to the full *iftar* meal as soon as the sun has officially set. Others choose to break the fast more gradually, perhaps eating two or three dates with a drink or water; then they'll perform the evening prayer, after which they will sit down to enjoy their *iftar.* Many Muslims believe this is exactly what Prophet Mohammed used to do, and that emulating the Prophet brings one closer to him and to God.

Interestingly, scientific studies have found that this modest meal is a healthier way to end many hours of fasting. For both these reasons, Aref and I take this gradual approach. We eat a few dates (as the Prophet did) with a little water or soup, wait for a bit, and then enjoy a big meal.

Traditional meal patterns are changing over time, as well. For centuries, Muslims awoke before dawn to eat the *suhur* meal just before the day's fast commenced. But in recent times (and in our own lives), people are more frequently staying up late and eating *suhur* before bed. Often, at a social gathering that lasts into the early hours, the host will serve *suhur* to the guests—who then go home and go to sleep, with their fast already started.

How do you know when the sun has set or risen and it is permissible (or forbidden) to eat?

In the holy month, the exact moments of daybreak and sunset are determined by Islamic authorities; they are publicly announced and strictly observed by all Muslims. Each mosque publishes a prayer and fasting schedule for its locality, and the information is available on many websites, too.

Before the Internet, of course, more traditional methods were used to tell the faithful when they could break the fast. One of the greatest traditions, dating from the fifteenth century, was the cannon of Ramadan. In cities and towns all across the Muslim world, a cannon would be fired twice each day, signaling the precise start and end of the hours of the fast. As children, my sisters and I would wait outdoors to hear the cannon's boom and then run inside as fast as we could to announce the breaking of fast. All the grownups were delighted to hear our news, and we would then gather at the table for *iftar.*

Another precious tradition that is disappearing from our modern Muslim world is the figure of the *musaharatee,* a kind of town crier who would walk through his neighborhood in the darkness two hours before sunrise, beating on a small drum and singing songs. The music would wake people, giving them enough time to eat the *suhur* before the appearance of daylight and to pray the morning prayer.

Why Does Ramadan Seem to Come at a Different Time Every Year?

The month of Ramadan and the eleven other months of the Islamic calendar do not coincide with the familiar January to December of the Gregorian calendar because the Islamic calendar is lunar: each month is exactly the same length (about 29.5 days), the time it takes for the moon to go through its phases. Counting up this way, the year on the Islamic calendar is about 354 days long—11 days shorter than the Gregorian year, which follows the 365-day cycle of the sun. Because of this, Ramadan starts eleven days earlier each solar year.

As a result, fasting can be more or less difficult, depending on the season when Ramadan occurs. In midwinter, when the daylight hours are short, we might eat *suhur* shortly before 8 a.m. and break the fast a little after 5 p.m. But in the height of summer, *suhur* must be taken well before 6 a.m. and *iftar* will not come until after 9 in the evening. Because no liquids can be consumed, the effect of summer's heat and thirst add to the rigors of the long day. In the countries of the Middle East, the blistering heat of summer makes the fast a greater test of self-discipline.

The effect of the calendar on Ramadan was brought home to our family in a very American way just a few years ago. My three sons are wonderful athletes, and all played on their high school varsity football team. They also observe their Muslim faith and started to fast Ramadan when they were old enough.

This was no problem for Wasfi, my eldest. During his seasons as a football player, Ramadan took place in late fall. Since the days were relatively short, he was able to keep to his fast on the days when the football season and the holy month overlapped. When my middle son, Basil, and Naji, the youngest, were both on the team, however, Ramadan came in the late summer. The days were long, hot, and humid, and the hours of practice and games were very demanding. They were ready to fast, but this possibility raised serious concerns for their health and their ability to perform. Aref discussed this with the coach, then with both boys. He explained to them that instead of fasting—and possibly harming themselves—God could be served by their contribution to a charity or performance of some good deeds.

In the end, the boys decided not to fast that year; they both did an excellent job on the field, and they contributed part of their savings to charity. Basil and Naji resumed fasting Ramadan in later years, and to our delight, some of their football teammates joined them in the fast and came to our house to enjoy *iftar* with the family.

What Else Happens During Ramadan?

In the Arab world, life changes completely during Ramadan as daily routines shift to accommodate the observance of the fast. Throughout government and in the business sector, offices and workplaces open later and close earlier. Food markets and bakeries are closed until the late afternoon; restaurants open only in the evening. When Ramadan occurs in the heat of the summer and the hours without food or drink are long and draining, the pace of life slows noticeably.

At sunset, however, when it is time to break the fast, a happy hustle and bustle returns to society. Families and friends gather for *iftar*—

having guests in, or going to someone else's house, to break the fast together almost every night. After *iftar,* people are out and about until late in the night. Both men and women go to the mosque for extended evening prayers and then drop in on friends; or they'll spend their whole evening in a round of visits. Many people stay up into the early morning hours reading the Qur'an. Young people gather at friends' houses and play games until it is time to eat the *suhur.*

For Muslims observing Ramadan in the United States, Canada, and other non-Muslim countries, the shift in work and social life is less dramatic than it is in Arab and other Islamic societies, yet the essential spirit of the month is the same. It is very important to share good wishes with all your family and friends, and although we can't do it in person—as we would in the Middle East—people call each other from all over town, all over the country, and all around the world. On the first day of Ramadan, our phone never stops ringing.

The social customs of visiting, hospitality, and sharing find different expression here. In most places around the U.S., people don't drop in at someone's home unannounced; instead, weekends are the main time for visiting and gift-giving. Mosques are a particularly important social center for American Muslims during Ramadan. At our mosque in Cincinnati, everyone shares *iftar* on Saturdays: dishes are assigned and the feast is enjoyed in a big community room, just like a church supper.

In places like Detroit and Los Angeles, where there are large populations of Arab Americans, it is easier for friends to get together to chat or play cards until late in the evening, when the host will serve the *suhur.* And young people will head for Arab cafes, listen to music, and smoke the *argila*—the traditional water pipe often called a hookah. During Ramadan the *argila* is filled with "tobacco" made from fruit.

At our home, Aref and I still enjoy inviting guests to *iftar* as often as possible. We don't have family nearby, as we did in years past, but we have many friends (mostly non-Muslim) who join us; some have been coming for years. We started doing this soon after we moved to the area in 1990. We found that our new acquaintances and neighbors were curious about Ramadan, and so we asked them to come over for *iftar.* At first we were worried that they wouldn't enjoy the customs of a Ramadan meal, such as gathering before sunset, hearing us say the traditional sunset prayers, and abstaining from alcohol. Everyone had a great time, though, and they stayed late into the evening, just the way our Arab friends do.

On the other hand, we have adapted our observance of Ramadan to our social life in a non-Muslim country. For instance, we still go out to dinner at restaurants and the homes of friends—we simply do not drink any alcohol. And we break our fast at home first, at sunset, in the traditional way, with a date and a cup of soup.

What About Children and Ramadan?

Children do not fast during Ramadan, though they naturally want to do what the big kids and the grownups are doing and are often eager to fast. Only as they approach adolescence are they allowed to experience fasting, and then only on a limited basis. One year they might fast for part of the day for several days; the next year for more hours and more days; and so on, until they are old enough to fast the entire month. Children go to school as usual during Ramadan.

The daytimes during Ramadan, then, are not much changed for kids, but the nighttimes are quite special. They participate in all the activities: the breaking of the fast, the big *iftar* dinners with guests every night, and paying visits to family and friends.

They get to stay up later, as everyone else does, and they enjoy the nonstop sweets and treats that are always offered. They also receive gifts from relatives and friends—all month long!

One of my favorite parts of Ramadan as a little girl was to be wakened in the very early morning hours and join my parents for the *suhur* meal. We would come to the table in our pajamas and sleepily enjoy the food, then go back to sleep until it was time to have our regular breakfast and go to school.

In the Arab world, there's a custom in the evenings called Fawaneese Ramadan. Portable lanterns, or *fawaneese,* are hung from buildings in all the streets and around the mosques to light the way for people heading toward the mosques for the evening prayers. In Egypt in particular, groups of children carrying their own *fawaneese* walk through their neighborhoods singing songs and playing in the darkness. They visit all the houses of family and neighbors and receive candy and sweets along the way.

Children in the Gulf States enjoy a similar custom on the fourteenth, fifteenth, and sixteenth days of Ramadan. On these days, called *gergeoan,* the children put on traditional clothing—fancy *dishdasha* (a floor-length Arab dress) *kofia* (head cover), and *beshit* (a robe embroidered with gold threads to cover the *dishdasha*). At sunset they walk through the neighborhood knocking on doors and singing songs so people will give them *gergeoan*, a selection of chocolate, nuts, and candy that they collect in large bags, just as American kids do at Halloween.

How Can I Share in the Spirit of Ramadan?

Many Americans with Muslim friends want to send a greeting or gift for Ramadan but are unsure of the proper thing to do. It's easy—as you will see from the tips that follow. Any small gesture of acknowledgment means a great deal and will bring pleasure to both the receiver and the giver.

Whether delivered on the phone, in person, or in a card, here are some appropriate expressions of good wishes:

Happy Ramadan!—no translation necessary!

Mabrook alaykum al Shahar—"Congratulations on the arrival of the month"

Kul Ramadan wa antum bi khair—"Hope you are well and in good health every Ramadan"

If someone wishes you well during Ramadan, say to them:

Yenad a laik—"May it came back to you," meaning "May you experience the month with the same wishes you wish for me."

On Eid al-Fiter, the festival at the end of Ramadan, you can say:

Eid saeed—"Happy Eid!"

Eid Mubarak—"Blessed Eid!"

Traditionally it was customary to give food to family and close friends, in particular something you made for them because you knew it was a favorite dish or treat. It was also nice to share a particular delicacy if you had it, such as the finest dates from Iraq or Saudi Arabia. Today food is no longer the only kind of gift presented at Ramadan. In America and the Arab world, the custom has become more like Christmas, where gifts of every sort are exchanged. Here are some simple and suitable gift suggestions:

A pretty basket with a selection of dried fruits. Dates are important to Ramadan; raisins and nuts are also nice.

For a Muslim friend, it is appropriate to send a copy of the Qur'an, the holy book, or a prayer carpet.

A lovely gift for a woman or an older girl is a *dishdasha,* the long embroidered Arab-style dress. Look for the Nattouri label—it is one of my favorites!

If you are invited by a Muslim friend for *iftar,* here are some tips to please your host.

No gift is expected, but flowers or sweets—such as a basket of dried fruit or a box of chocolates—are welcome. Do not bring a gift of wine or other alcoholic beverage. Make sure the chocolates have no alcohol in them.

Be on time—well before sunset! Breaking the fast at the proper time is an important part of Ramadan observance.

Dress for *iftar* should be modest though not necessarily formal, befitting its significance as part of the holy month.

The longer you stay and the more you eat, the better!

Are There Special Foods for Ramadan?

Across the Arab world—and well beyond it, wherever Muslims live—certain foods and dishes are deeply associated with Ramadan and are served frequently or even daily during the month.

More than any other time of the whole year, Ramadan is when we make, serve, and indulge in desserts and sweet snacks.

In keeping with the oldest custom of breaking the fast—begun by the Prophet himself, it is said—the first morsel of food for many Muslims, every night of Ramadan, is a bite of sweet dates, or *tamr*. Dates are native to the desert regions of the Middle East and North Africa and have been a dietary staple of Arab peoples for many thousands of years. Today they're used extensively in Arab cuisine year-round, in a multitude of forms: fresh and dried, whole and ground, raw and cooked, in savory dishes and desserts. And with hundreds of varieties cultivated in Arab countries, dates are a subject of discriminating connoisseurship. The finest dates (usually from Iraq or Saudi Arabia) are prized delicacies: these are the dates we want to serve or give as gifts during Ramadan.

Dried fruits of many varieties, such as apricots, prunes, raisins, and cherries, are also a favorite for Ramadan snacking and gift-giving. Fragrant *khoshaf*—dried fruits marinated in rose water or orange-blossom water—are often part of the break-fast meal.

Another sweet staple of Ramadan is *qatayef*, dessert pancakes, or crêpes, stuffed with sweet cheese, cream, or nuts.

Soup is one of the first foods eaten after fasting and is part of every *iftar*, even when Ramadan comes in the summertime.

Special beverages for Ramadan include a variety of juices, also an important component of breaking the fast. At our home we always have *jalap*, made from dates and grape molasses, served with crushed ice, sweet raisins, and pine nuts—a children's favorite; *kamar al deen*, a luscious apricot drink that Aref and I love (but it is packed with calories so we try to be moderate); and *erik al souse*, a refreshing licorice-flavored drink. My aunt always made this from scratch for Ramadan: She wrapped ground licorice root in cheesecloth and dripped filtered water over it all night long, slowly collecting the liquid in a bowl. One of my earliest memories of Ramadan is entering her house and seeing the cheesecloth with water dripping over it.

If You Are Fasting, When Do You Have Time to Prepare All This Food?

If you think that a month of fasting means that there is less work in the kitchen, you are mistaken! Every evening of the holy month is likely to present several calls for delicious food—and plenty of it. First, the *iftar* meal must satisfy the anticipation of a table full of very hungry people. Then there might be informal get-togethers for cards and conversation, energized by hours of snacking. Finally, either late at night or early in the morning, we must present a nourishing, tasty *suhur* that will help people get through the daytime fast.

The wise cook therefore spends the weeks and days before Ramadan in food shopping and cooking. Freezers must be stocked with sweet and savory pas-

tries, *kibeh,* breads, and main-course casseroles; refrigerators filled to bursting with fresh fruits and vegetables, eggs, cheeses, and yogurt; and pantry shelves loaded with staples, especially the dried fruits and other sweets that are so central to the month. In addition to food for serving, some of us also find time to make food as gifts for relatives and friends, choosing the special dishes that we know each person loves.

Eid al-Fiter: A Feast and Holiday at the End of Ramadan

On the day after the month of Ramadan ends, Muslims mark the conclusion of the fast with a celebratory holiday called Eid al-Fiter. In the Arab world and in many other Islamic societies, the Eid is a three-day festival—in some countries it is a national holiday—with schools and businesses closed.

Eid al-Fiter is a joyous celebration, one of the two great holidays of the Muslim year (along with Eid al-Adha, described on page 90). The festivities commence with a bountiful feast on the first day. Customarily, the close family circle gathers at the home of a grandparent or other family elder around noontime, eager to eat. The Eid feast is always magnificent, and having it at midday is a special pleasure after the month of only nighttime meals. After the feast, the rest of the day and the two that follow are spent in a whirl of visiting, hosting, and gift-giving. It is a time of universal good cheer, like Christmas: everyone is happy that the rigors and restrictions of Ramadan are over, yet also grateful for the many spiritual and personal benefits of the fast.

In the United States, Eid al-Fiter is a time of special celebration too, though businesses, government, and schools don't stop as they do in the Middle East. We frequently invite friends for a grand midday meal on the first day. Sometimes we join friends at the home of an elder in our local Muslim community. The custom of visiting, gift-giving, and well-wishing among friends and family is also followed here, but

since everyone works midweek, we mostly do it at night or on the weekend.

Part of the excitement about Eid al-Fiter—especially for those who cook the first-day feast—is that you can't be certain when the month of Ramadan will end. According to Islamic law, a new month begins, and the fast ends, only if the new crescent moon is actually seen by an official observer during the night that follows the thirty days of Ramadan. Then, if the moon is sighted, Ramadan has ended and the Eid festivities begin the next day. But if the moon is not seen, everyone must fast Ramadan one more day and the Eid is postponed—which is why we women who prepare the feast may be up all night. Let's say I am going to roast a whole baby lamb, which needs hours of cooking, to serve at noon for the Eid feast. I may have to wait until the middle of the night to know if the moon was sighted and the Eid has arrived. If it has, I must start the roasting immediately in order to be ready for lunch. If the moon was not seen? All the food goes back into the fridge and we cooks go to bed, knowing we will fast another day and cook another night.

Sample Menus

Iftar

I hope you will have an opportunity to make these bountiful meals and enjoy an authentic taste of Ramadan. And since *iftar* also is an important part of the daily observance of the breaking of the fast, let me tell you how I serve *iftar* here in America.

First, I invite our guests to arrive about half an hour before the official sunset time. (And if they are not Muslim, I explain the ritual of breaking the fast exactly when the sun sets.) I have the dining room set up well in advance. On the main dining table, I have laid place settings for everyone, making sure that everyone can be seated comfortably together to share this special occasion. On a side table, I put a large platter of dates and the beverages with which we break our fast. There's a small bowl of pine nuts, one of raisins marinated in rose water, and a bowl of crushed ice to add to the *jalap*.

As guests and family gather, we explain (whenever necessary) that *iftar* is not a rushed meal: after abstaining from food for a long time, the body needs to adjust gradually. When sunset occurs, guests have juice and dates to break the fast, and I bring the soup and salad to the side table. Then we take a break as some of us perform the *magrib,* or sunset prayers. After that, the meal resumes in a relaxed manner.

Dessert comes after everyone has finished eating and the table is cleared. Guests enjoy a fresh fruit platter or *khoshaf,* marinated dried fruit, while I fill and fry the *qatayef*—the essential Ramadan dessert—and serve the crêpes hot from the stove. Our *iftar* ends with coffee and tea served in the living room.

Iftar Menu # 1

- Beef and Freka Soup
- Oregano and Cheese Crescents
- Hummus
- Mixed Vegetable Salad
- Okra with Tomatoes
- Cucumber and Yogurt
- Baked Lamb with Rice and Chickpeas

- Arab Flatbread
- Dates
- Olives and pickles

- Fresh fruit platter
- Baklava with almonds
- Arab Pancakes

- *Jalap*
- Apricot Juice

- Coffee
- Tea with Rose Water

Iftar Menu #2

- Tomato Soup with Vermicelli
- Tomato Spread
- Baby Arugula Salad
- Chicken and Rice with Creamy Yogurt Sauce
- Eggplant with Ground Beef
- Basmati Rice

- Arab Flatbread
- Dates
- Olives and pickles

- Ladies' Arms
- Dried Marinated Fruits
- Broad Pudding with Syrup

- Tamarind drink (store-bought)
- Apricot Juice
- Coffee
- Mint tea

Suhur

Suhur is a late-night meal, served during Ramadan after friends have been together for several hours, enjoying cards and each other's company. It doesn't have to be Ramadan for you to enjoy this assortment of dishes—serve it as a delightful refreshment after an evening of cards or other games, or after a movie or similar shared entertainment. If you have an *argila*—a water pipe—give your guests a choice of fruit tobaccos, such as apple and apricot.

Suhur Menu #1

- Dressed Chickpeas
- Pull-Away Cheese Rolls
- Zucchini-Egg Cakes

- A plate of mixed nuts
- A plate of sliced tomatoes and cucumbers
- Arab Flatbread
- Olives

- Almond Cookies
- Date Fingers
- Apricot Pudding with Almonds and Pistachios

- Yogurt Drink
- Mulberry juice (store-bought)

Suhur Menu #2

- Pull-Away Cheese Rolls
- Oregano Cakes
- Fava Beans
- Yogurt Cheese Balls

- Arab Flatbread
- Olives and pickles

- Shredded Pastry with Cheese
- Date Cake

- White Coffee
- *Jalap*
- Apricot Juice

Eid al-Fiter

The following menu is typical of the feast I serve on the first day of Eid al-Fiter. In the Middle East, we expect such a banquet on this most special day, but here, our American guests are sometimes astounded by the variety and bounty of dishes—they can't quite believe what they are getting for "lunch"!

On the Savory Table:

- Baby Arugula Salad
- Meat Pies
- Cucumber and Yogurt
- Zucchini with Bread and Mint
- Green beans in Tomato Sauce
- Tibsi Red Snapper in Pomegranate Syrup
- Grape Leaves Stuffed with Lamb and Rice
- Poached Chicken with Garlic-Chile Relish
- Olives
- A plate of scallions, radishes, green chiles, and pickles

On the Dessert Table:

- Fresh fruits
- Milk Pudding
- Semolina Pistachio Layer Cake
- Semolina Purses
- Baklava with pistachios or almonds
- Assorted store-bought desserts

Beverages:

- White Coffee
- Mint tea
- Sweet coffee (hot water infused with rose water)

Side Dishes

SIDE DISHES ARE SIMPLY A SELECTION of small dishes that feature vegetables, pulses, pasta, or grains. They complement and enhance the main course and the salads that are being served. I always like to keep in my pantry a variety of dried beans, lentils, bulgur, chickpeas, and similar ingredients. These provide a wealth of nutrition and delicious dishes that are the backbone of the Arab table. Side dishes also feature different vegetable preparations. Fresh, frozen, or canned vegetables can be used to prepare these dishes, but use fresh ones whenever possible.

Side dishes are essential to make any meal complete and make any table look good. As with salads, side dishes should be chosen with care to fit in with the main course that is being served. For instance, if I am serving a fish dish as a main course, I would choose to serve a side dish such as Eggplant in Pomegranate Syrup or a simple vegetable side dish like Green Beans in Tomato Sauce. If I am serving grilled meat, I may choose to serve with it a cooked lentils side dish such as Pasta with Lentils. Pasta, too, is a favorite Arab side dish, especially when it is layered with cooling yogurt and a bit of spiced beef like Pasta with Ground Beef and Yogurt. For a table that is featuring meat and rice, I always add a couple of vegetable side dishes like Sautéed Greens with Crispy Onions.

In this chapter, you will also find a range of side dishes that can easily stand in for that sole vegetable dish you want to put on the table every night. But a selection of them, arrayed on a buffet table and served with a main course of rice, meat, or fish, is perfectly suited for a regular family dinner or a special or festive occasion for a vegetarian crowd. These dishes give you great flexibility in preparing a great meal. But be careful, side dishes are known to compete with the main course that you so carefully prepared for the attention of your family and guests.

Pureed Split Lentils

MUJADARA SAFRA

1 cup split orange lentils, picked over and rinsed

¼ cup short-grain rice, picked over

¼ cup extra virgin olive oil

2 medium onions, chopped

1 teaspoon salt

Fresh mint leaves, for garnish

Olives, for garnish

This is a family favorite, one that I always serve with Tomato Salad. We eat it the same way every time, too, by scooping up some of the salad in soft Arab flatbread and then following it with a taste of Mujadara. For a vegetarian Lenten feast, include Fried Eggplant with Hot Chiles, Broad Bean Salad, and Fried Halloumi Cheese.

My grandmother always advised against adding any salt to the lentils until they were at least halfway cooked—she claimed that seasoning them early would increase their cooking time. The age and type of lentils you use may have an impact on how long they take to cook, but I follow grandmother's rule anyway. If the lentils turn thick like mashed potatoes, stir in ¼ cup water to bring them back to the consistency of porridge. Mujadara is traditionally served with Arab flatbread, a bowl of olives, and a plate of quartered white onions. *Serves 6*

Combine the lentils, rice, olive oil, onions, and 2½ cups water in a medium saucepan, and bring to a boil over high heat. Skim off the foam that forms on the surface. Cover the pan, reduce the heat, and simmer, stirring occasionally, for 20 minutes. Then add the salt and stir. The lentils should have the consistency of pudding and be tender to the bite.

Transfer the lentils to a serving dish, garnish with the mint leaves and olives, and serve at room temperature. (Alternatively, chill them in the refrigerator and serve cold.)

Sautéed Greens with Crispy Onions

HINDBA BI ZEIT

3 pounds wild chicory, dandelion greens, Italian chicory, curly endive, *or* other mildly bitter leafy green

1 tablespoon plus ½ teaspoon salt

1 pound large onions

⅓ cup plus ½ cup extra virgin olive oil

1 pound medium onions, finely diced

3 tablespoons fresh lemon juice, plus more to taste

¼ teaspoon black pepper

2 or 3 lemons, cut into wedges or slices

2 tablespoons chopped fresh parsley

An essential component of all of my holiday menus is a platter of fresh, flavorful cooked greens, equally wonderful as an appetizer with Kibeh and Spinach Triangles or as an accompaniment to a main course of lamb, fish, or chicken.

Of the many varieties of tangy, leafy greens used in Arab cooking, one of my favorites is hindba, *the wild chicory that grows all over the Eastern Mediterranean region. It is cultivated here in the U.S. and is sold at Middle Eastern markets in larger cities. But other greens with a slightly bitter flavor—such as dandelion greens, radicchio, curly endive, and mature frisée—are perfect alternatives and are probably easier to find. Any of these can be prepared just like* hindba: *briefly blanched and then sautéed slowly in olive oil with onions and seasoned with lemon juice. A generous topping of crisp fried onions—a typical Arab garnish for greens and lentils—provides a delicious counterpoint of taste and texture.*

Hindba bi Zeit is best served at room temperature, so you can make it well ahead of the meal—even the day before—including decorating the serving platter. Cover and seal the platter with plastic wrap and refrigerate it. Remove it an hour or two before serving to allow the greens to come to room temperature.   ***Serves 6 to 8***

To prepare the greens, cut or pull out the thick central rib from each leaf and discard it. Pile the leaves together and slice them crosswise into 1-inch pieces. (You should have almost 8 quarts of leafy pieces, loosely packed.)

Fill a large stockpot with water (8 to 10 quarts), add the 1 tablespoon salt, cover, and bring to a boil.

While the water is heating, wash the greens: fill a large bowl or the sink with cold water, dump in the leaves, and swish to rinse them. Lift them out into a colander; empty the bowl and refill it with clean water; and rinse the greens again. Repeat the rinsing and draining until the rinse water is completely clean.

Stir the greens into the boiling water until they're all submerged. Then bring the water to a steady boil and cook for 3 minutes.

Drain the greens and set them aside in the colander until they are cool enough to handle comfortably.

While the greens are cooling, make the onion garnish: Peel the large onions and cut them in half lengthwise. Then slice each half crosswise into ⅛-inch-thick half-moons (you'll have about 4 cups). Cover a large plate with several layers of paper towels. Heat the ⅓ cup olive oil in a large, deep heavy-bottomed saucepan over high heat. Add the onions and cook, stirring very frequently, until they begin to brown, about 5 minutes. Stir almost constantly as the onions darken. Cook until they are deep golden brown, lowering the heat as necessary so they don't burn, another 5 to 10 minutes. Then immediately remove the pan from the heat and spoon the onions onto the paper towels. Discard the oil in the pan and wipe out the pan.

When the greens are cool, squeeze them firmly to remove all excess liquid. Heat the ½ cup olive oil in the same heavy saucepan over medium-high heat. Add the diced onions and cook, stirring, until they are soft and translucent, about 4 minutes. Lower the heat and mix the greens into the onions. Add the lemon juice, ¼ cup water, the remaining ½ teaspoon salt, and the pepper. Stir well, then cover the pan with a tight-fitting lid. Reduce the heat to the lowest possible setting and let the greens cook until the visible liquid has just cooked away (lift the lid occasionally to check), about 15 minutes. Taste the greens and add more lemon juice if needed. Turn them out onto a large serving platter, smooth them into an even layer, and allow to cool.

To serve, spread the browned onions over the cooled greens. Surround the greens with the lemon wedges, and decorate the rim of the platter with the chopped parsley, sprinkled all around or in a pattern of small dots.

Green Beans in Tomato Sauce

LOBIEH BI ZIET

⅓ cup olive oil

½ pound onions, coarsely chopped

6 cloves garlic

2 pounds fresh Italian green beans, ends trimmed, string removed, and cut in half *or* three 9-ounce packages frozen wide beans, thawed

2 pounds tomatoes, peeled and chopped

3 cloves garlic, crushed

⅓ cup canned tomato sauce

1½ teaspoons salt

½ teaspoon black pepper

¼ cup fresh lemon juice

Lemon slices, for garnish

Arab flatbread, for serving

I learned to cook this dish over the telephone, with my grandmother on one end and me on the other, standing at the stove. I had been married for two months, and up until that time (and before Aref discovered it!), my grandmother had cooked all our meals at her home and sent them over while Aref was working.

In this room-temperature side dish, the beans are cooked in a garlicky tomato sauce that will vary in thickness depending on the tomatoes you use; some release more liquid than others. If the sauce is soupy, drain some from the beans so that there is just enough to coat them and a little more for drizzling over each serving. Serve these with Arab flatbread for soaking up the sauce and whole scallions or white onions to eat between bites.

The Italian wide beans, called Romano beans, have a very short season; use them if you can find them. Otherwise, the frozen version, which is available year-round, is fine. Serves 6

Heat the olive oil in a medium pot over medium heat. Add the onions and garlic cloves, and sauté until the onions are soft and translucent, about 5 minutes. Reduce the heat to medium, add the beans, and cover the pot. Cook, stirring occasionally, until the beans brighten, about 10 minutes. Then reduce the heat to medium-low and add the tomatoes, crushed garlic, tomato sauce, salt, and pepper. Cook, covered, until the beans are tender and the sauce has thickened, 35 to 40 minutes. Slide a heat diffuser under the pot for the last 20 minutes.

Remove the cover and cook for 5 minutes more. Then remove the pot from the heat, stir in the lemon juice, and set it aside to cool. Transfer the beans to a serving plate, using a slotted spoon. Then pour a bit of the sauce over them and garnish with the lemon slices. Serve the Arab flatbread alongside.

Okra with Tomatoes

BAMYEH BI ZIET

1 cup extra virgin olive oil

1 pound fresh okra, caps trimmed, stem left intact *or* 2 pounds frozen okra, partially thawed, rinsed, and patted dry (see headnote)

8 shallots, left whole, or 4 to 6 small onions, sliced

6 cloves garlic, mashed

1 pound ripe tomatoes, peeled and cut into ½-inch-thick slices

1 tablespoon tomato paste dissolved in 1 cup water

1 teaspoon ground allspice

1 teaspoon salt

¼ teaspoon black pepper

⅓ cup fresh lemon juice

Lemon slices, for garnish

This vegetable layer cake is refrigerated overnight in order for the succulent tiers of onions, okra, and tomatoes to settle together; then it is served cold or at room temperature. The vegetables are cooked slowly over low heat—with the layers compressed by a plate placed directly on top of them—which results in melt-in-your-mouth okra. If you use frozen okra, it's not necessary to sauté it in the olive oil first. Whether you use frozen or fresh, the okra should be small—no longer than your thumb. If I use frozen, I look for the Egyptian variety. If you prefer a looser presentation, put all of the vegetables in the pot in a mélange rather than layering them, and proceed with the recipe. Serves 8

Heat the olive oil in a large pot over high heat. Add the okra and sauté until the flesh around the trimmed cap end is golden, about 15 minutes. Using a slotted spoon, transfer them to a paper towel–lined plate.

Add the shallots to the pot and sauté until they are soft and golden, about 5 minutes. Add the garlic and sauté until fragrant, about 1 minute. Remove the pot from the heat. Arrange half of the tomato slices over the shallots and garlic. Arrange the okra neatly in layers on top of the tomatoes, followed by a layer of the remaining tomatoes. Combine the tomato paste mixture with the allspice, salt, and pepper, and drizzle this over the tomatoes.

Place a small heatproof plate directly on top of the tomatoes to compress the layers. Cover the pot and bring the liquid to a boil over high heat. Reduce the heat to low, and add the lemon juice by pouring it directly over the plate. Cover the pot and simmer until the sauce is reduced by a third, about 50 minutes; slide a heat diffuser under the pot after the mixture has cooked for 20 minutes. Set the pot aside to cool. Refrigerate overnight.

To unmold, remove the plate. Invert a shallow rimmed platter over the pot, and holding them together, flip the pot over. Do not remove the pot—let it sit for 10 minutes. Then gently lift off the pot. Mop up any excess sauce with a paper towel. Garnish with the lemon slices, and serve.

Eggplant in Pomegranate Syrup

MUSAKA BETINJAN

½ cup dried chickpeas, soaked overnight (see page 52), rinsed, and drained or one 15-ounce can chickpeas, drained and rinsed three times

3 pounds eggplant

Salt

¾ cup extra virgin olive oil

2 large onions, halved and thinly sliced

15 cloves garlic, thinly sliced

1 pound tomatoes, peeled and finely chopped

1 jalapeño pepper, seeded and minced

1½ tablespoons pomegranate syrup

½ teaspoon ground allspice

¼ teaspoon black pepper

Fresh mint leaves, for garnish

This recipe is the Arab version of Greek moussaka, without the white sauce or the cheese topping. Rather, it is flavored with pomegranate syrup, a staple in the Arab pantry. Traditionally Musaka is made with meat, but I prefer the vegetarian version made with eggplant—the most adaptable, and highly honored, vegetable in the Syrian kitchen. Serve Musaka warm or at room temperature, with Arab flatbread alongside. Serves 6

Put the chickpeas in a large pot and add water to cover by 1 inch. Bring to a boil over high heat. If using canned chickpeas, drain them, rinse them under hot water, and set them aside. If using dried, chickpeas, cook, skimming the foam from the surface until no more appears, about 15 minutes. Then reduce the heat, cover the pot, and simmer until they are tender, about 1½ hours. Drain, and rinse under hot water.

Meanwhile, peel the eggplant in strips, leaving some of the skin on (this prevents the pieces from falling apart during cooking) Cut the eggplant into ½-inch by 3-inch-long matchstick strips. Place them in a colander, sprinkle liberally with about 1 teaspoon salt, and set aside to drain for 1 hour.

Heat the olive oil in a 3-quart pot over high heat. Pat the eggplant dry with paper towels. Working in batches, slide the eggplant strips into the hot oil and sauté, turning them once, until they are golden brown and the edges are crisp, 6 to 8 minutes per side. Use a slotted spoon to transfer the strips to a paper towel–lined plate.

Add the onions to the oil in the pot and sauté over medium heat until they are soft, about 15 minutes. Stir in the garlic. Add the chickpeas, tomatoes, jalapeño, and pomegranate syrup. Cook, stirring frequently, until the sauce has thickened, about 5 minutes. They add the eggplant, 2 teaspoons salt, the allspice, and the pepper, and sir gently with a wooden spoon (to prevent the eggplant from breaking apart). Bring to a boil. Reduce the heat to medium, and taste; adjust the seasonings if necessary. Cover the pot and cook the eggplant until the liquid has reduced to the consistency of a sauce, 20 to 30 minutes. Using a slotted spoon, spoon the eggplant mixture into a serving bowl. Garnish with the mint leaves, and serve.

Braised Fava Beans

FUL BI ZIET

2 pounds fresh or frozen fava
    beans (see headnote)

⅓ cup extra virgin olive oil

1½ pounds onions, diced

1½ cups Spiced Chicken Stock
    (page 125), low-sodium
    canned chicken broth, *or*
    water

1½ teaspoons salt

2¼ teaspoons black pepper

6 cloves garlic, mashed

1 packed cup chopped fresh
    cilantro

¼ cup fresh lemon juice

Lemon slices, for garnish

Arab flatbread cut into triangles

My grandmother used to make this dish in the spring, when the fava beans were fresh and tender. When choosing the beans, make sure the skin is soft. If you are using frozen beans, rinse them under cold water and then submerge them in a bowl of water to which ½ teaspoon baking soda has been added; soak for a few minutes, and then rinse well. Serve this with grilled meats such as Shish Kebab.

Serves 6

Stem the fava beans and break each pod in half with your hands. Place the beans in a colander and rinse under cold water. Set aside.

Heat the olive oil in a medium pot over medium heat. Add the onions and sauté, stirring occasionally, until they are soft and translucent, about 10 minutes. Add the beans and sauté until they brighten, about 5 minutes more. Reduce the heat to low and cook the onions and beans, partially covered, for 10 minutes. Then add the chicken stock, salt, pepper, garlic, and cilantro. Simmer, partially covered, until the beans are tender and the liquid has been absorbed, about 1 hour. (If using frozen beans, reduce the cooking time to 30 minutes.)

Remove the pot from the heat and let the beans rest for 30 minutes to allow the flavors to develop. Then add the lemon juice and stir it into the beans. Transfer them to a serving platter, and garnish with the lemon slices. Serve with the Arab flatbread.

Fried Potatoes with Cilantro

BATATA MA KUZBARAH

1 cup extra virgin olive oil

3½ pounds yellow-fleshed
    potatoes, cut into
    1-inch dice

2 cups chopped fresh cilantro

10 cloves garlic, mashed

2 teaspoons salt

1 teaspoon black pepper

Arab flatbread, for serving

Lemon wedges, for serving

*M*ost of what grows in and around the tiny villages that dot the Lebanese and Syrian landscape is anything but exotic, but home cooks there learn to make the most of what nature gives them. Potatoes, for example, show up on their tables fried, boiled in kibeh and in stews, and cut into chunks and tossed into salads. This dish is a fond favorite of mine because it reminds me of my friend Wafa, who always squeezes a lot of lemon on the potatoes and then scoops them up with Arab flatbread.

I sauté the potatoes in a good amount of oil, but if you would rather, you can bake the diced potatoes, and while they're in the oven, sauté the garlic and cilantro on the stove, then toss it all together and cover for 5 minutes to allow the flavors to come together. Serve Batata ma Kuzbarah hot or at room temperature, with Grilled Kafta on skewers, Kafta Burgers, or Chicken Kibeh.

Serves 6

Heat the olive oil in a large skillet over high heat. Add the potatoes and sauté, stirring occasionally, until they are golden and parts of the edges are crisp, 8 to 10 minutes. Add the cilantro, garlic, salt, pepper, and ¼ cup water. Reduce the heat to low, cover, and simmer for 10 minutes. Then uncover and simmer until all of the water has evaporated, about 5 minutes more. Serve hot, with Arab flatbread and lemon wedges.

Chickpeas with Yogurt

FATTEH HUMMUS BI LABAN

1 cup dried chickpeas, soaked
  overnight (see page 52),
  rinsed, and drained *or* two
  19-ounce cans chickpeas,
  drained and rinsed three
  times

2 loaves Arab flatbread

8 cloves garlic, mashed, plus
  more to taste

¼ cup fresh lemon juice

4 cups plain full-fat yogurt

1 teaspoon salt, plus more if
  needed

¼ cup sesame paste (tahini)

Chopped fresh parsley, for
  garnish

Red pepper flakes, for garnish

Fried pine nuts (see page 43),
  for garnish

This layered dish tastes best when the chickpeas are warm; they sit on garlic-and-lemon-soaked croutons and are cloaked in a tangy yogurt-tahini sauce. Make sure to scoop up a little bit of each layer for the full effect: crispy, smoky, pungent, creamy, and cool. This makes an excellent side dish at brunch.   *Serves 8 to 10*

If using dried chickpeas, place them in a 5-quart pot. Add water to cover by several inches and bring to a boil over high heat. Cook, skimming the foam from the surface until no more appears, about 15 minutes. Then reduce the heat, cover the pot, and simmer until the beans are tender and break easily when pressed with the back of a spoon, about 1½ hours. Drain and set aside.

If using canned chickpeas, place them in a pot and add water to cover by 2 inches. Bring to a boil over high heat. Cover, reduce the heat to medium, and simmer for 5 minutes. Drain and set aside.

Meanwhile, preheat the oven to 350°F.

Cut the flatbread into bite-size pieces and spread them out on a foil-lined baking sheet. Bake until golden and crisp, 7 minutes.

Using a fork, blend two thirds of the mashed garlic with the lemon juice in a small bowl. In another bowl, combine the remaining mashed garlic with the yogurt, salt and the sesame paste, and mix well. Taste, and add more salt and garlic if desired.

Spread the toasted croutons on the bottom of a 4-quart baking dish, and pour the garlic-lemon mixture over them. Spoon the chickpeas on top of the croutons, and top with the yogurt mixture. Garnish with the parsley, red pepper flakes, and pine nuts, and serve immediately.

Variation: Chickpeas with Yogurt and Ground Beef

Prepare the dish as described, up to the point of adding the garnishes.

Chickpeas with Yogurt (continued)

Heat 2 tablespoons olive oil in a small skillet over high heat. Add ½ pound ground beef, a dash of allspice, and salt and pepper to taste. Cook, breaking up the beef into coarse crumbs, until it is dark and a bit dry-looking, 15 to 20 minutes. Spoon the meat over the yogurt and garnish with the parsley, red pepper flakes, and pine nuts.

Cooked Bulgur

BURGUL MUFALFAL

⅓ cup olive oil

1 large onion, minced

2 cups coarse bulgur, soaked (see page 281) and drained

1 teaspoon salt

3 cups boiling water

Bulgur, or cracked wheat, has a distinctly nutty flavor that makes it an excellent companion to many Arab dishes. The best bulgur comes from northern Syria and the mountains of Lebanon, particularly the Bekaa Valley. Famous for the Roman temple at Baalbek, which boasts one of the tallest columns in the world, this fertile valley is considered the country's breadbasket.

Bulgur is available in either coarse or fine grains, and each has specific uses. Fine bulgur is used in delicate dishes like Tabouleh and Kibeh, while the coarse variety is used in heartier preparations such as Spiced Bulgur with Tomatoes and Bulgur and Fava Beans.

Bulgur is rarely served plain; like pasta, it is always flavored with a vegetable, meat, poultry, or a sauce. In this recipe, sautéed onions gently flavor it, making it an excellent side dish for Eggplant with Ground Beef.

Serves 6

Heat the olive oil in a medium pot over high heat. Add the onions and sauté until soft, about 3 minutes. Add the bulgur and salt, and stir until the grains of bulgur are well coated. Then add the boiling water, cover, and bring to a boil. Reduce the heat to low, slide a heat diffuser under the pot, and cook until the bulgur is soft and fluffy when poked with a fork, about 30 minutes. Serve hot.

SOAK BULGUR BEFORE COOKING

Spread the bulgur on a plate and pick over it, removing any debris. Then place it in a bowl, add cold water to cover, and soak for about 10 minutes. Scoop the soaked bulgur out of the water by the handful, squeezing it to extract as much water as possible, and transfer it to a clean bowl.

THE BEKAA VALLEY HARVEST

My brother-in-law Wael grew up in the Bekaa Valley in Lebanon, where wheat fields stretch as far as the eye can see. Wael's mother used to oversee the wheat harvest in their hometown each June. To make bulgur, the wheat is boiled in huge cauldrons for hours and is then carried to rooftops all over the village and spread out to dry for several days. Once dry, it is collected, husked, and cracked between millstones into various sizes (the most common in the U.S. being coarse and fine). To separate the coarse grains from the fine and very fine, the bulgur is passed through a series of sieves with screens of ever finer mesh. Whatever is left in the top sieve—the one with the biggest holes—is gathered and fed to the animals. Some of the coarse bulgur is fermented in yogurt, then dried in the sun and ground to a powder called *kishik,* which is used in meat and rice soups in the same way that dried sheep's milk (*jameed)* is used in the Jordanian specialty Mansaf.

The entire village participates in the harvest. Men, women, and children work, play, and sing songs together, and it is often the occasion during which courtships begin. As part of her role as the head of the family, Wael's mother would present each family in the village with a portion of the bulgur harvest as a gift, which is the custom in the Arab world.

Bulgur and Fava Beans

FUL BI BURGUL

One 14-ounce package frozen
 fava beans

½ teaspoon baking soda

2 tablespoons canola oil

3 cloves garlic, mashed

1 packed cup chopped fresh
 cilantro

2 cups Spiced Chicken Stock
 (page 125), low-sodium
 canned chicken broth, *or*
 water

1 cup coarse bulgur, soaked (see
 pages 15 and 225) and
 drained

1 teaspoon salt

¼ teaspoon black pepper

Olive oil, for serving

Fava beans are among the most ancient vegetables in the Arab pantry. The fresh beans are commonly eaten raw as a snack, offered on the mezza table, or served as an hors d'oeuvre with a glass of arak. Because the season is so short (one month in the summer, at best) and because they must be prepared soon after they are picked—they turn black quickly—I've written this recipe using the frozen variety. Serve Ful bi Burgul with Cucumber and Yogurt.   ***Serves 8***

To thaw the beans, put them in a medium bowl and fill with water to cover. Add the baking soda (to preserve their color) and soak for 30 minutes. Then drain and pat dry.

Heat the canola oil in a medium pot over medium heat. Add the garlic, beans, and cilantro, and sauté until the garlic is soft and the cilantro has brightened, about 5 minutes. Add the stock, cover, and bring to a boil. Cook over medium heat until the beans are tender, about 15 minutes. Then reduce the heat to low, add the bulgur, and cook, covered, for 20 minutes. Season with the salt and pepper, and serve hot. Pass a cruet of olive oil for drizzling over the dish.

Spiced Bulgur with Tomatoes

BURGUL BI BANDOURA

¼ cup olive oil

1 medium onion, chopped

1½ pounds very ripe tomatoes, peeled and chopped, juices reserved

1 cup coarse bulgur, soaked (see pages 15 and 225) and drained

1½ teaspoons ground allspice

¼ teaspoon ground cinnamon

¼ teaspoon finely ground black pepper

½ cup boiling water

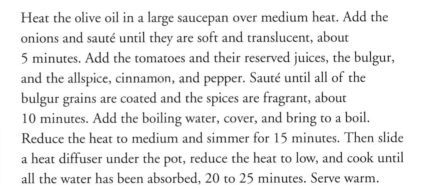

This hearty side dish is typical of everyday cooking in the Lebanese and Syrian mountains, where cracked wheat, or bulgur, is far more abundant and less expensive than rice, which is reserved for special-occasion dishes. Serve Burgul bi Bandoura with Lamb Kebabs, page 215, Cucumber and Yogurt, and grilled vegetables.

Serves 6

Heat the olive oil in a large saucepan over medium heat. Add the onions and sauté until they are soft and translucent, about 5 minutes. Add the tomatoes and their reserved juices, the bulgur, and the allspice, cinnamon, and pepper. Sauté until all of the bulgur grains are coated and the spices are fragrant, about 10 minutes. Add the boiling water, cover, and bring to a boil. Reduce the heat to medium and simmer for 15 minutes. Then slide a heat diffuser under the pot, reduce the heat to low, and cook until all the water has been absorbed, 20 to 25 minutes. Serve warm.

Pasta with Ground Beef and Yogurt

MACARONA BI LABAN

3 tablespoons olive oil

1 pound ground beef

¼ teaspoon grated nutmeg

¼ teaspoon black pepper

1 teaspoon ground allspice

4 pounds plain full-fat yogurt, preferably Greek Total brand (see Note)

1 tablespoon salt

3 cloves garlic, mashed

1 pound elbow macaroni, cooked and cooled

¼ cup fried pine nuts (see page 43)

1 tablespoon crumbled dried mint, preferably spearmint

In the Arab world, pasta is typically combined with ingredients like yogurt, cinnamon, mint, and/or pine nuts, giving it a simultaneously cool and warm flavor. I always make Macarona bi Laban in the summer—it's my version of the American pasta salad—and accompany it with Beet Salad, Shredded Cabbage Salad, and Fried Cauliflower with Tahini. Serves 6

Heat the olive oil in a large skillet over high heat. Add the beef and sauté, breaking it up with the back of a spoon, until it has lost its pink color, 5 minutes. Then add the nutmeg, pepper, and allspice, and reduce the heat to low. Cook, continuing to break up the beef until it resembles coarse, dark crumbs, 10 minutes. Taste, and adjust the spices if needed. Set it aside.

Mix the yogurt, salt, and garlic together in a large bowl until evenly incorporated. Add the pasta and mix well. Transfer the pasta mixture to a deep serving dish. Spoon the ground beef on top, and garnish with the pine nuts and mint. Serve at room temperature.

Note: If you use low-fat yogurt, soak up some of the liquid by putting the yogurt in a bowl and placing several layers of paper towels directly on top of it. Set it aside for 30 minutes or so, replacing the wet paper towels as necessary.

Baked Pasta

MACARONA BI FOURN

For the tomato-beef sauce:

2 tablespoons vegetable oil

1 pound ground beef

1 pound onions, coarsely chopped

1 clove garlic, mashed

1 bay leaf

¼ teaspoon black pepper

½ teaspoon ground allspice

½ teaspoon salt

One 15-ounce can tomato sauce

½ cup chopped fresh basil

For the béchamel:

4 cups whole milk

4 tablespoons butter

¼ cup all-purpose flour

2 teaspoons salt

1 teaspoon white pepper

For the pasta:

3 tablespoons salt

1 pound spaghetti

For the topping:

½ cup grated kashkawan *or* Gruyère cheese

*P*asta is beloved in Egypt, where it is often found in rice dishes and soups. Here, spaghetti is baked in an allspice-seasoned tomato-beef sauce and crowned with a layer of rich béchamel and kaskawan, *a popular grating cheese made from sheep's milk. Serve it straight from the baking dish with Mixed Vegetable Salad, Simple Salad, or Tabouleh.*

Makarona bi Fourn can be prepared up to the point of baking and then frozen, tightly wrapped, for up to 1 month. Thaw it in the refrigerator and then bake as directed. Serves 6

Prepare the tomato-beef sauce: Heat the vegetable oil in a large pot (one that has a tight-fitting lid) over high heat. Add the beef and cook, uncovered, until it loses its pink color, about 5 minutes. Add the onions, garlic, and bay leaf, and cook, stirring, until the onions have softened, 5 minutes. Reduce the heat to medium, cover the pot, and cook for 10 minutes. Then add the pepper, allspice, and salt, and give the mixture a good stir. Stir in the tomato sauce, basil, and 2 cups water, and cook, uncovered, until the mixture has the consistency of spaghetti sauce, 20 minutes.

Meanwhile, make the béchamel: Warm the milk in a saucepan over medium heat. Keep it warm without letting it boil. Meanwhile, put the butter in a heavy saucepan over high heat. Add the flour and salt, and stir as the butter melts and the flour begins to absorb the butter. Once the butter has completely melted, cook, stirring constantly, until the mixture has darkened slightly, about 5 minutes. Reduce the heat to low and slowly whisk in the warm milk, breaking up any lumps as you whisk. Add the white pepper and continue to simmer for 10 minutes. Set the béchamel aside.

Preheat the oven to 350°F.

Bring 6 quarts water to a boil in a large saucepan. Add the salt and the spaghetti, and cook until it is al dente, about 8 minutes. Drain off the cooking water and transfer half of the spaghetti to an 8 by 11-inch baking dish. Spoon the tomato-beef sauce over the spaghetti, then top with the remaining spaghetti. Spoon the béchamel over the spaghetti, and then sprinkle the cheese over the béchamel. Bake until the top is bubbling and golden brown, about 30 minutes. Let the dish set for a few minutes; serve hot.

Pasta with Lentils

KUSHARI

2 cups dried brown lentils,
    picked over and rinsed

2 teaspoons salt, plus more for
    the pasta water and to taste

1 cup elbow macaroni

2 cups medium-grain rice,
    picked over and rinsed

½ cup olive oil

3 pounds onions, halved and
    thinly sliced

1½ teaspoons ground cumin

1 teaspoon black pepper

Stewed Tomato Sauce (page 34)

Egyptian food has the reputation for being bland, but any home cook there will tell you that this criticism should be reserved for the country's restaurant food. This macaroni and lentil dish—comfort food Egyptian-style—is liberally seasoned with warming cumin and served with flavorful Daama' (Stewed Tomato Sauce).   **Serves 8**

Place the lentils in a large pot and add water to cover by 2 inches. Add 1 teaspoon of the salt and bring to a boil over high heat. Then reduce the heat to medium-low and simmer until tender, about 8 minutes. Drain the lentils and set them aside.

Bring a large pot of salted water to a boil, add the macaroni, and cook until firm to the bite, about 7 minutes. Drain, and set aside.

Meanwhile, place the rice in a saucepan and add water to cover by 2 inches. Add the remaining 1 teaspoon salt and bring to a boil over high heat. Reduce the heat to medium and cook, uncovered, until the rice is fluffy, about 7 minutes. Drain, and set aside.

Heat the olive oil in a large skillet over high heat. Add the onions and fry until crisp, about 10 minutes. Using a slotted spoon, transfer the onions to a paper towel–lined plate. Reserve the cooking oil.

Combine the lentils, rice, macaroni, cumin, and pepper in a large pot and stir until the ingredients are thoroughly mixed together. Add the reserved cooking oil and one fourth of the onions, and stir until the oil is absorbed. Place the pot over low heat and cook, stirring, for 10 minutes. Season with salt to taste.

Spoon the macaroni mixture onto a large serving platter and scatter the remaining fried onions on top. Serve with Stewed Tomato Sauce on the side.

Beverages

OR ARABS THE DAY BEGINS WITH tea—never coffee, which is enjoyed throughout the rest of the day. Coffee or tea is invariably offered to guests as soon as they arrive at an Arab home, a restaurant, or a business meeting. Not only does the host or hostess have an obligation to serve coffee or tea, but guests are required to accept a cup when it is served. To decline an invitation to share a cup of coffee or tea is an insult to the host.

Included in this chapter are recipes for the coffees and teas that are among the most widely enjoyed—Arab Coffee and Turkish Coffee. "Tea" refers to drinks made with loose black tea leaves and to those that are made with spices steeped in hot water. Black tea is typically infused with rose water, cardamom, and dried lime. Other teas include a sweetened cinnamon brew with crushed walnuts and a soothing licorice drink made with anise seeds.

Coffee and tea are enjoyed year-round, and there are seasonal drinks as well. During the hot summer months, one of the most popular refreshers, especially in the Gulf region, is the cooling beverage *Ayran,* made from diluted goat's or sheep's-milk yogurt. Lemonade lightly flavored with orange water is a favorite. Pomegranate, mulberry, and tamarind are among the most popular fruit juices; they are packaged in concentrated form, to be diluted with water and poured over crushed ice. You can buy these in many supermarkets and Middle Eastern markets.

High-quality, ready-to-drink vegetable juices are widely available all over the Arab world. A wise Arab wife keeps carrot juice on hand, keeping in mind the saying "If your husband is not in a good mood, give him a glass of carrot juice and he will become like butter."

Wine, beer, and spirits are enjoyed by many Arabs, but fruit juices, yogurt drinks, and water are the choice of observant Muslims, since alcohol is forbidden by the Qur'an. All Muslims, however, avoid alcohol during Ramadan and Hajj, the pilgrimage to Mecca. Arak, the anise-flavored aperitif of Syria, Lebanon, and Jordan, is traditionally served with mezza.

Perhaps the most cherished drink of all in the Arab world is water, which is revered as a purifier and a gift from God. When I was a young girl, water was scarce and we had to buy it, making it one of the most expensive drinks available. While this is no longer the case, water is still held in high regard by those who live there. It is often flavored with a bit of rose water.

Apricot Juice

KAMAR EL DEEN

One 12-ounce sheet apricot
  leather

2 tablespoons sugar, or to taste

2 tablespoons orange-blossom
  water, or to taste

2 tablespoons rose water, or to
  taste

½ cup pine nuts and ½ cup
  raisins, soaked in water until
  soft

Delicious eaten as a snack, apricot fruit leather also makes a very refreshing—and exquisitely colored—fruit drink. During the month of Ramadan, Kamar el Deen is one of the fruit drinks offered to guests at sundown to break the fast. It is always served in a big glass pitcher filled with crushed ice, accompanied by a small plate of pine nuts and raisins. Guests spoon a bit of the nuts and raisins into their glass, then fill it with the apricot juice. **Makes 5 cups**

Tear the apricot sheet into 2-inch pieces and soak them in 3 to 4 cups water (the more water you use, the more diluted the drink) overnight. The sheet will turn to liquid.

Transfer the apricot liquid to a blender and process until smooth, about 2 minutes. Then pour it through a fine-mesh strainer into a jug or pitcher. Thin the juice with a little water if it is too thick for your taste.

Add the sugar and fragrant waters, and give the juice a good stir. Taste, and adjust the flavors if needed. Chill the juice in the refrigerator, or pour it over ice in juice glasses. Serve, passing the pine nuts and raisins on a small plate.

Lemonade

LAMONADA

4 lemons, scrubbed, seeded, and cut into 8 wedges each

¼ cup sugar

4 teaspoons orange-blossom water

Mint leaves, for garnish

2 lemon slices, quartered, for garnish

This brings back memories of the Brumana mountains in Lebanon, where I spent my childhood summers. When the heat set in, my sisters Maha, Ikram, and Haifa and I could be found in the kitchen sitting around a big bucket full of quartered lemons. We would dig in, squeezing every bit of juice and pulp from them—and some pungent oils from the rinds, too—then add a bit of water and orange-blossom water to the bucket. Then we would pour the cooling drink into crystal glasses, set them on a silver tray, and sip the lemonade in the living room, as if we were very important ladies. We talked and sipped and talked and sipped for hours.   **Serves 6 (makes about 1½ quarts)**

Combine the lemon wedges and the sugar in a large bowl and stir until the lemons are coated. Cover the bowl with plastic wrap and set it aside at room temperature for 3 hours or as long as overnight. The mixture will form a thick syrup at the bottom of the bowl.

Using your hands, squeeze the lemons until all of the juice has been extracted. Add 4 cups water and stir to dissolve the sugar. Remove the lemons (and any stray seeds) with a slotted spoon. Pour the juice into a pitcher (through a strainer and if you prefer lemonade with no pulp), and stir in the orange-blossom water. Taste, and adjust the sweetness as desired. Serve in tall glasses filled with crushed ice. Garnish each glass with mint leaves and a quartered slice of lemon.

Salep

SAHLAP

6 cups whole milk

2 tablespoons *salep* (see page 27)

2 pea-size pieces mastic, crushed (see page 22)

6 tablespoons sugar

1 tablespoon butter

Ground cinnamon, for garnish

My boys used to call this "Mama's magical medicine" because whenever they complained of a sore throat and pleaded to stay home from school, I would make them sip this sweetened milk and then put them on the bus. Sahlap is named for the powdered thickening agent it contains, which is made from the roots of wild orchids. The powder is thought to have health-giving properties, which is why it is common to find coffeehouses in Lebanon and Egypt full of late-night revelers sipping Sahlap before they turn in. I make Sahlap the way it is made in Lebanon, Syria, Palestine, and Jordan: with a dash of cinnamon and a pat of butter floating on top. In Egypt it is garnished with pine nuts, almonds, and raisins. Sahlap thickens as it cools; eat the chilled version with a spoon. **Serves 6**

Combine ½ cup of the milk with the *salep* in a small bowl and stir to dissolve.

Combine the remaining 5½ cups milk with the *salep* mixture in a large saucepan and bring to a boil over medium heat, stirring constantly. Add the mastic and stir for 5 minutes. Then add the sugar and stir until it dissolves. Taste, and add more sugar if needed.

Ladle the Salep into mugs, and garnish with a pat of butter and a pinch of cinnamon. Serve hot.

Yogurt Drink

AYRAN

This refreshing summer drink is as popular in the Gulf region as Coca-Cola is in the U.S. It is enjoyed, too, in other parts of the Arab world during Ramadan. Ayran has the consistency of a milkshake, though it is more savory than sweet. When I first arrived in Kentucky, I tried dozens of brands of yogurt before I decided that Willow Hills Farm sheep's-milk yogurt and Greek Total yogurt make the best drinks. If you can't find these brands, look for any thick Mediterranean or Greek sheep's- or cow's-milk yogurt. **Serves 4**

1 cup plain yogurt
Salt, to taste
Mint leaves, for garnish

Combine the yogurt with 2½ cups cold water in a 2-quart pitcher, and whisk until the water is incorporated. Season to taste with salt. Add crushed ice to fill the pitcher. Pour into tall glasses, and garnish each one with a few mint leaves.

White Coffee

KAHWA BYDA

White coffee isn't coffee at all—it is simply what we call this fragrant warm drink, which I often offer guests when a gathering goes into the late hours of the evening. Kahwa Byda is a nice alternative to caffeinated beverages; the orange-blossom water aids in digestion, which will promote a good night's sleep after a big meal. **Makes 6 demitasse cups**

1½ cups water
2 tablespoons orange-blossom
   water

Combine the water and orange-blossom water in a small saucepan and bring to a boil over high heat. Pour into demitasse cups and serve on a tray, with a bowl of sugar for guests to sweeten the "coffee" as they please.

Variation: Substitute ¼ teaspoon saffron threads for the orange-blossom water.

Arab Coffee

KAHWA ARABIA

10 cardamom pods, coarsely ground

½ cup ground dark-roast coffee beans (ground on espresso grind)

Coffee is a sign of welcome in an Arab home, and it plays a big role in social life all over the Arab world. This brew is especially common in the Gulf States, Palestine, and Jordan, where Kahwa Arabia is offered to you the minute you set foot in a hotel or restaurant. It is sipped at all times of the day except first thing in the morning—Arabs take tea for breakfast rather than coffee—and is always offered to guests visiting an Arab home as a symbol of hospitality. If coffee is not offered, the host is intentionally sending a message that a guest is not welcome. By the same token, visitors should never refuse a first cup of coffee unless they absolutely cannot have it, in which case mulberry or apricot juice is offered. Declining this welcoming gesture is insulting to the host—and in fact, it is customary to accept at least three cups of coffee from an Arab host, who will press a very important person to drink even more. When a guest has had enough, he or she rapidly shakes the empty cup a half dozen times to alert the host to clear the glass from the table.

Outside of the home, cup after cup of Arab coffee is served in coffeehouses, which are most popular in Yemen, where the best coffee grows in the Al Mokha region. In small villages and towns, the coffeehouses are unchanged from the old days, with a men-only policy and a lot of political and social discussion taking place. In larger cities, however, both women and men make the coffeehouse part of their social life. In Lebanon and Syria, Arab coffee is reserved for big feasts, weddings, funerals, and for the month of Ramadan.

Arab coffee is never made with sugar, and unlike traditional coffee, it tastes better when it is simmered on low heat for 3 to 4 hours. Kahwa is traditionally poured into a silver or brass dallah, or small pot, for serv-

ONE FOR TOMORROW'S POT

In Kuwait it is customary to reserve one cup of coffee from the day's brew to add to the following day's pot. When the day-old coffee is added to the fresh pot, the host murmurs *"ye khamer,"* or "make it like wine."

ing. By custom, the oldest son or daughter in the family is responsible for pouring a small amount—just two or three sips—into a tiny handleless cup for each guest. **Serves 8 to 10 (makes 4½ cups)**

Combine 7 cups water, the cardamom, and the ground coffee in a saucepan and bring to a boil over high heat. Stir, reduce the heat to medium-low, and cook at a constant low simmer for at least 3 hours. The coffee in the pot should be gently bubbling; adjust the heat accordingly.

Remove the coffee from the heat and let it sit until the sediment settles to the bottom, about 30 minutes. Then pour the coffee—minus the sediment—into a second saucepan, reheat it, and transfer it to a serving pot, or a *dallah* if you have one. Serve hot.

My father was not only the olive oil taster in our home, he also bought the coffee to ensure that it was just the way he liked it: The ratio of dark to light roasted beans was 2 to 1, and he always had the roast master add 1 ounce of cardamon to the coffee grinder.

Turkish Coffee

KALWA TURKY

6 teaspoon sugar

7 heaping teaspoons ground
coffee (a mix of dark and
light roasts)

Ground cardamom, to taste
(optional)

*I*n mountain villages, valley towns, and big cities in Lebanon, Syria, Jordan, Palestine, and Morocco, Turkish coffee is sipped after every meal at home and in restaurants, in coffeehouses, for celebrations and solemn occasions of every kind, and always to welcome guests into an Arab home. It is typically made with sugar, although at gatherings to mourn the loss of a loved one, it is never sweetened.

To make authentic Turkish coffee, you must use a rakwi, a long-handled, narrow-necked coffee pot made of brass or enamelware. They are available in various sizes—this recipe requires a 6-cup model—and are used to both make and serve the coffee. Demitasse cups are customary, and small glasses of water always accompany the coffee cups.

This recipe is for medium coffee. I like mine without sugar, but Aref likes it sweet, so I make the coffee without sugar, then put sweetener in his cup for him rather than adding it to the pot. He also likes it with a bit of foam, which I skim from the top of the pot into his cup. Arrange your cups and glasses of water on a tray, along with some napkins, before you begin to make the coffee so that you can pour it when it is piping hot—the best way to enjoy Turkish coffee. **Makes 6 demitasse cups**

Fill a *rakwi* or a small pot with 2½ cups water and bring to a gentle boil over high heat. Add the sugar and stir until it dissolves. Add the coffee and cardamom, if using, and stir to dissolve. Reduce the

YOUR FUTURE'S IN THE CUP

*A*rabs believe that the sediment that falls to the bottom of a cup of Turkish coffee can predict the future. To find out what's in yours, spin your coffee cup while you make a wish. Overturn the cup onto a plate to release the sediment, which will nat-urally fall into a telltale design. If the grains are shaped like a bird, you'll get good news; a river, you will travel; a snake, you're in harm's way; a fish or a baby, you will enjoy good fortune.

heat to low. When the coffee boils up to the rim of the pot, remove it from the heat, stir just the top third of the coffee—do not let the spoon touch the bottom of the pot—and return the pot to the heat. Allow the coffee to boil four times this way, removing it from the heat and stirring each time.

Spoon the foam off the top into the cups for those who like it, fill the demitasse cups with the coffee, and serve it very hot.

Cinnamon Tea

SHAY DARSEEN

*T*his warm winter beverage is not a tea at all, but a lightly sweet-ened spice drink that is especially popular during the Christmas season, when Arabs visit each other for the Christmas Eid.

Makes 6 cups

8 teaspoons ground Ceylon cinnamon

10 teaspoons sugar, or more to taste

6 tablespoons ground walnuts

Combine 6 cups water and the cinnamon in a saucepan and bring to a boil over high heat. Reduce the heat to medium and simmer for 15 minutes. Then add the sugar and cook, stirring, for 2 minutes. Taste, and add more sugar if you like. Pour the tea into mugs, and add 1 tablespoon of the walnuts to each mug. Serve piping hot.

Sage Tea

MERAMIEH

2 teaspoons loose black tea
8 dried sage leaves
Sugar, for serving

Flavored teas such as Meramieh are served mainly in the afternoon when friends come to visit. The tea is presented on a tray, surrounded by small colored or clear delicate glasses or tiny cups and saucers. Sugar and spoons are placed on the tray for each guest to add as much sugar as he or she likes.   *Serves 6*

Bring 6 cups water to a boil in a medium saucepan. Remove the pan from the heat, add the tea and sage leaves, and cover the pan. Wrap a kitchen towel around the pan and set it aside for 10 minutes to allow the tea to steep. Then strain the liquid into a teapot and serve hot, with a bowl of sugar on the side.

Variations

Loumi and Thyme Tea: Pierce *loumi* (dried limes) in several places with a knife. Add the *loumi* and 4 sprigs fresh thyme to the boiling water, and steep as above.

Tea with Rose Water—A Special Drink for Ramadan: Pierce 1 *loumi* (dried lime) in several places with a knife. Add the *loumi,* 1 teaspoon rose water, 6 partially cracked cardamom pods, and either a few sprigs of fresh mint or 1 teaspoon dried to the boiling water, and steep as above.

Anise Seed Tea

SHAY YANSOON

2 tablespoons anise seeds

This tea is a natural relaxant—it settles the stomach and promotes sound sleep. It certainly saved me from many sleepless nights when I was a new mother. My middle boy, Basil, was a colicky baby and rarely slept for more than half an hour at a time. I used to make this tea for both of us, because it is known to soothe the stomach (Basil's) and relax the mind (mine). When my boys were teething, I would strain the seeds from the steeping liquid and pack them in cheesecloth, for them to suck on to soothe their gums. Shay Yansoon is delicious hot or cold; Arab adults take it hot, while children drink it cold. Add a bit of honey to sweeten it if you like. **Serves 6**

Place 6 cups water in a saucepan, cover, and bring to a boil over high heat. Meanwhile, place the anise seeds in a small bowl and add cold water to cover. Let them sit until the seeds float to the surface; this allows any impurities to collect on the bottom of the bowl. Skim the surface with a spoon to collect the seeds, and set them aside.

Remove the boiling water from the heat, add the seeds, cover, and steep for 2 minutes. Then strain and serve hot, or refrigerate and serve cold.

TEA TRADITIONS

Throughout the Arab world, tea is always served black, with a small bowl of either granulated or lump sugar served on the side. Tea, not coffee, is the preferred morning drink, and it is the only time that milk is added to the cup. In some countries, including Iraq and those that make up the Gulf States, tea is flavored with cardamom or cinnamon and is served throughout the day.

Ceylon, Indian, and Assam tea are the preferred leaves in the Gulf and in my house, where we choose a brew depending on the mood. Assam tea is a rather sophisticated tea, while Ceylon and Indian are easy-going, everyday varieties.

Arabs always warm the teapot and teacups by running them under hot water before pouring the steaming hot liquid into them.

Desserts

T HE ARAB FONDNESS FOR SWEETS MAY be surpassed only by their love of bread, but unlike that daily mealtime staple, the vast repertoire of pastries, cakes, cookies, puddings, and ice creams on the Arab dessert table are reserved for holidays, celebrations, and guests. Fresh seasonal fruit is the typical conclusion to most family meals, with watermelon, oranges, and apricots among the most popular desserts. During the winter months, a few dates—or any combination of dried fruits—and a cup of coffee is a perfect way to end a meal, as is enjoying a piece of the sweetmeat known as *halawah,* either plain or studded with nuts. *Dibsi,* a carob molasses available in Middle Eastern grocery stores, is mixed with tahini for a casual dessert.

When an Arab cook makes pastries for special occasions, she usually prepares large quantities, either because she is expecting a crowd or so that some can be frozen to have on hand for unexpected guests. For this reason, many of the recipes in this chapter yield several dozen treats. A proper dessert table always features several different kinds of pastries—many cloaked in sugar syrup—and cookies, mounded high on individual platters or in an assortment to suggest abundance. Some, such as Almond Cookies, are traditionally presented for social obligations, such as greeting a new neighbor, while others are reserved for marking special religious celebrations. Pastries with Walnuts, Pistachios, and Dates are always on the Easter and Eid tables, while Date Fingers are a customary Ramadan sweet. There is also at least one pudding—rice, milk, or semolina—on every lavish dessert spread (though pudding also is often eaten as a snack between meals), as well as some kind of semolina-based cake.

Arabs love ice cream, especially their native version, which is made with *salep,* a powdered thickener that gives it its characteristic elastic, chewy texture, and *mastic,* a licorice-flavored resin that infuses it with subtle anise flavor.

Many of the desserts here are gently flavored with either orange-blossom water or rose water, or a combination of both. These two scented waters are staples in the Arab pantry, imparting a distinctive taste to pastries and puddings when just a few tiny drops are used. Use these fragrant waters sparingly if you are cooking with them for the first time, adding them gradually to the recipes as your appreciation for their flavors and aromas grows.

Almond Cookies

KAAK LUZ

3 cups (about 1 pound) whole
almonds, peeled and finely
ground in a food processor

2 cups powdered sugar

2 cups dried unsweetened
coconut

1 teaspoon grated lemon or
orange zest

4 egg whites

This is the first cookie I learned to make as a newlywed. They were my contribution to an elaborate celebratory spread my mother prepared for guests who came to congratulate Aref and me after our wedding. I chose Kaak Luz because they are essentially foolproof and are as appropriate on a formal dessert table as they are with a casual cup of coffee. You can vary the kind of nut you use; Lebanese cooks use pine nuts rather than almonds.

Bake these one cookie sheet at a time; if you bake two sheets at a time, the cookies on the lower rack will bake unevenly. Do not use oil to prepare the pan, or the bottoms of the cookies will bake faster than the top. The cookies can be refrigerated in a rigid container, with wax paper between the layers, for up to 1 month. Bring them to room temperature before serving.

Makes 9 dozen bite-size or 3 dozen half-dollar-size cookies

Preheat the oven to 375°F, with a rack in the upper third of the oven. Line a baking sheet with parchment or a baking mat.

Stir the ground almonds, powdered sugar, coconut, and lemon zest together in a large bowl.

Beat the egg whites with an electric mixer on high speed until stiff peaks form. Using a rubber spatula, gently fold the egg whites into the almond mixture until the whites are combined. Drop the mixture by teaspoonfuls (for bite-size cookies) or tablespoonfuls (for the larger version) onto the prepared baking sheet, leaving about 1 inch between them.

Bake until golden brown, 8 minutes for the bite-size cookies and 10 to 12 minutes for the larger ones. Leave the cookies on the baking sheet to cool; then transfer them to a serving platter.

Repeat, baking one sheet of cookies at a time.

Date Fingers

ASSABEH TAMR

For the dough:

3 cups all-purpose flour

1½ teaspoons baking powder

½ teaspoon ground cinnamon

½ teaspoon ground anise seeds

¼ teaspoon salt

½ teaspoon mahlab (see page 22)

½ cup clarified unsalted butter (see page 45), melted

1 cup whole milk

For the filling:

1 pound pitted Medjool dates

3 tablespoons unsalted butter, softened

1 teaspoon ground cardamom

½ teaspoon ground cinnamon

Vegetable oil, for the baking sheet

Egg wash: 1 egg beaten with 1 saffron thread

These tiny cookies—somewhat similar to a miniature Fig Newton—are beloved by the Iraqi people, who always have some in the refrigerator during Ramadan. They are popular in the Gulf States and in North Africa too, and are a fixture on the dessert table for any celebration or social event. In some countries, you will find them made with semolina dough, while in others they are fried rather than baked. In Algeria the dough is filled with walnuts, cardamom, and a hint of rose water. My recipe is the classic Iraqi version. Date Fingers are traditionally presented to new families in the neighborhood, along with Spiced Beef with Rice and a Simple Salad. **Makes about 70 cookies**

Combine the flour, baking powder, cinnamon, anise, salt, and mahlab in the bowl of a food processor fitted with the plastic blade. Pulse to combine. In a separate bowl, whisk together the clarified butter and milk. With the processor on medium speed, gradually add the milk mixture to the flour mixture, and process until the dough comes together. Transfer the dough to a bowl, cover it with plastic wrap, and let it rest for 2 hours.

Meanwhile, make the filling: Combine the dates, butter, cardamom, and cinnamon in the bowl of the food processor fitted with the steel blade, and pulse until the mixture forms a smooth paste.

Preheat the oven to 400°F. Coat a baking sheet with vegetable oil.

Divide the dough and the filling into thirds. On a lightly floured surface, use your hands to roll one piece of the dough into a ¾-inch-thick rope. Flatten it with the tips of your fingers until it is 2 inches wide. On a clean surface, roll one piece of the date filling into a ¼-inch-thick rope. Place the date rope down the middle of the dough, and pinch the dough together to conceal it. Roll the filled dough under your hands to seal and smooth the rope. Using the back of a fork, make a decorative pattern along the length of the dough. Cut the dough into 1-inch "fingers" and place them close together, but without touching, on the prepared baking sheet.

Brush each cookie with the egg wash, and bake until golden, about 25 minutes. Repeat with the remaining dough and filling. Cool on wire racks.

The cookies will keep in the refrigerator, tightly covered, for up to 2 weeks or in the freezer for up to 1 month. Bring them to room temperature before serving.

Pastries with Walnuts, Pistachios, and Dates

MAAMOUL

For the dough:

1 pound (about 4 cups) fine semolina

1½ cup (3 sticks) unsalted butter, melted

¼ cup orange-blossom water

¼ cup rose water

Date Filling:

1 pound Medjool dates, pitted

1½ teaspoons unsalted butter

¼ teaspoon grated nutmeg

Walnut Filling:

2 cups walnuts

2 tablespoon sugar

2 tablespoons unsalted butter, melted

1 tablespoon orange-blossom water

Pistachio Filling:

¾ cup shelled unsalted pistachios

2 tablespoons sugar

2 tablespoons unsalted butter, melted

1 tablespoon orange-blossom water

Powdered sugar, for dusting

These festive delicacies originated in Jerusalem, where traditionally they were made only for Eid al Adha, the celebration for the end of the pilgrimage, and for Easter. The date-filled pastries are round, to resemble Jesus' crown of thorns and the stones that were thrown at Him, while the pistachio- and walnut-filled versions are oval, to symbolize His tomb. It is a tradition in the Middle East for Christian families to gather in a different home each day of Holy Week to make maamoul *and sing hymns. It was always a special time for me and my Aunt Nadia, who would also press her two young boys into service to help make dozens of these cookies, assembly-line-style. I still make a huge batch once a year and freeze them. Mine are a bit smaller than the traditional pastries, but I always make them the old way, shaping them by hand. However, there are molds for sale in Middle Eastern groceries and speciality stores here in the States (just ask for the* maamoul *molds), and they do make the process go a bit quicker.*

The dough must chill in the refrigerator overnight to give the semolina time to absorb the clarified butter, which in turn results in an elastic dough. Each filling recipe is enough for a full batch of dough, so if you want to make a variety of fillings, reduce the filling recipes by half or two thirds. You can make the fillings a day ahead.

To make the traditional decorative pattern on the surface, use the small brass clips with pinked edges, called Malkat, *that are available at Middle Eastern grocery and speciality stores.* **Makes 7 dozen pastries**

Prepare the dough: Combine the semolina flour, melted butter, and orange-blossom and rose waters in a large bowl. Work the dough with your fingers until the flour has absorbed all of the butter. Cover the dough with plastic wrap and let it rest in the refrigerator overnight.

Make the filling: *To make the date filling,* combine the dates, butter, and nutmeg in a food processor and pulse until it forms a smooth, thick paste.

To make a nut filling, pick over the nuts and remove any bits of shell. Place the nuts in a food processor and pulse until they form coarse crumbs. Add the sugar, melted butter, and orange-blossom water, and pulse to form a thick paste.

Bake the cookies: Bring the dough to room temperature, 2 to 4 hours. Preheat the oven to 400°F. Line a baking sheet with parchment or a baking mat.

Work the dough with your fingers until it is smooth. Divide it into walnut-size balls and set them on a tray. Cover the tray with plastic wrap (to prevent the dough from drying out) while you form the cookies. Place a ball of dough in the palm of your hand and flatten it with your other palm. Place 1 teaspoon of the filling in the center, and gather the dough up around it. Using the traditional brass clips, or the tip of a knife, pinch the edges. Make decorative patterns all over the surface by lightly pinching the dough with the clips. Avoid puncturing the dough, or the filling will ooze out during baking.

Place the pastries on the prepared baking sheet and bake until they are pale blond, 10 to 15 minutes. Transfer the pastries to a rack to cool. (The pastries can be stored at this point in a rigid airtight container in the refrigerator for 2 weeks or in the freezer for 3 months. Thaw, and serve at room temperature.) Before serving, dust the pastries liberally with powdered sugar by tapping it through a fine-mesh sieve.

Ladies' Arms

ZNOOD AL SIT

One 16-ounce box frozen phyllo dough, thawed

1 cup clarified butter (see page 45), melted

2 recipes Kashta (page 317)

Simple Syrup (recipe follows)

3 cups vegetable oil

¼ cup ground unsalted pistachios

¼ cup rose petal jam

Arab poets are famous for metaphors relating women and food, and I suspect this wonderful pastry may have gotten its name that way. In fact, it wouldn't surprise me if these were described to be "as delicious as a lady's arm." You won't find a Lebanese cook making these pastries at home—they are readily found in every sweet shop in my homeland. But I have not been able to find anything resembling these filled phyllo treats in the U.S. so, I re-created them in my kitchen. This is a nice dessert to present at a large gathering or to bring to someone else's celebration, since the yield is fairly large and they are best eaten the day they are made. **Makes about 40 pastries**

Unroll the phyllo onto a lightly floured work surface with a short side facing you. Using a sharp knife, cut the dough lengthwise into two rectangles, slicing through all the layers. Place a single layer on a work surface with a short side facing you. Cover the remaining phyllo with a lightly dampened kitchen towel. Brush the dough with some of the clarified butter and fold it in half lengthwise. Place a heaping tablespoon of Kashta at the bottom center of the rectangle. Roll the dough up over the Kashta, and continue rolling, pressing the ends together as you go, until you reach the top. Place the pastry, seam side down, on a tray. Repeat with the remaining phyllo and Kashta.

Place the Simple Syrup in a shallow bowl and set it near the stove.

Heat the vegetable oil in a deep skillet over high heat. It is hot enough when a few drops of water sprinkled over it spit back at you. Using a slotted spoon, carefully slide the pastries, in batches, into the hot oil and fry, turning once, until the phyllo is golden, about 3 minutes. Remove each batch of Ladies' Arms with the slotted spoon, and submerge them in the simple syrup. Let them soak up the syrup while you return to the stove to fry more pieces. Just before the next batch is cooked, lift the pastries out of the syrup and transfer them to a serving plate. Repeat with the remaining pastries.

Sprinkle pistachios over each pastry—I always decorate just the ends of the pastries with them—and dot the centers with a bit of rose petal jam.

Simple Syrup

QATER

3 cups sugar

¼ teaspoon fresh lemon juice

1 teaspoon rose water

1 teaspoon orange-blossom
water

Qater is as ubiquitous as zaatar, the thyme spice mixture, in the Arab kitchen. Few Middle Eastern desserts are ever presented without the sheen of this glistening, delicately flavored sugar syrup. Pastries are dunked, and often soaked, in it; it may be drizzled over a whole platter of pastries just before serving; and sometimes it is served on the side. There is one rule of thumb when using this syrup: If the dessert is hot, the Qater should be cold when you use it; if the dessert is cold, the Qater should be hot. Store any leftover syrup in a glass jar with a tight-fitting lid and use it over pancakes. It will keep for 1 week. **Makes 2½ cups**

Combine the sugar and 1½ cups water in a saucepan and heat over high heat, stirring until the sugar dissolves. Bring to a boil and continue to boil for 3 minutes. Reduce the heat to medium, stir in the lemon juice, and cook for 10 minutes. Then remove the pan from the heat and stir in the rose water and orange-blossom water. Set aside to cool.

Shredded Pastry with Cheese

KUNAFA BI JIBIN

For the Pastry:

1 pound *kunafa or kataifi* (shredded phyllo), thawed in the refrigerator overnight if frozen

1 cup clarified butter (page 45)

For the Cheese Filling:

1½ pounds akawi cheese, desalted (see page 310)

½ pound fresh mozzarella cheese, unsalted, shredded or desalted (see page 310)

2 tablespoons sugar

2 teaspoons orange-blossom water

2 teaspoons rose water

For the Pan:

2 tablespoons unsalted butter, softened

2 drops red food coloring

For the Syrup:

3 cups sugar

½ teaspoon fresh lemon juice

2 tablespoons orange-blossom water

For the garnish:

½ cup unsalted pistachios, coarsely ground

*K*unafa bi Jibin *is the special-occasion dessert of the Arab world, a dish that marks moments to remember, both happy and sad. It's what you serve when someone beloved comes to visit from far away, or when someone dear has died. It's what you serve when a suitor asks for your daughter's hand in marriage (if you accept him) and what you'll serve at the wedding, too. Indeed, it is a fitting finale to an Eid al Kibeer feast: a splendid ruby-gold pastry, its top crisscrossed with chopped pistachios and gleaming with syrup. Present it steaming from the oven, filling the air with the fragrance of buttery baked phyllo, sweet cheese, orange, and roses. For me, Kunafa is personally special as well, because it is the dessert that my father loves best and one he would prepare in the traditional manner when I was a very little girl.*

These days, almost no one makes Kunafa the old, time-consuming way. In fact, even in the Middle East, most people just purchase the dessert from a bakery. But the streamlined version I give here is quick and easy, making good use of the food processor, microwave, and freezer—and it tastes better than anything you can buy. You'll need raw kunafa—*shredded phyllo dough usually sold frozen and labeled* "kataifi."

For the hidden layer of cheese, I like to use akawi, which I mix with fresh mozzarella. The combination is delicious and melts beautifully inside the pastry. You can usually find kataifi and akawi cheese at Middle Eastern markets. Otherwise, purchase them by mail order (see Sources) and store them in the freezer.

Kunafa bi Jibin is made in stages, conveniently. You will need to soak the akawi (and maybe the mozzarella too) in water overnight to remove the salt, so plan ahead. Once the pastry is assembled in the cake pan, you can freeze it for a week or two. Thaw it on the day you plan to serve it, and bake it while your guests are eating dinner, so it will be hot and fragrant when it's time for dessert. **Serves 10**

Prepare the Pastry: Spread the raw strands of *kunafa* on a tray and separate them into three roughly equal bunches. Place one bunch in a food processor and pulse in three very short bursts to cut the strands into ½-inch lengths. Transfer the pieces to a large bowl. Process the remaining two bunches of *kunafa* in the same way and add them to the bowl.

Place the clarified butter in a heatproof measuring cup, cover it with plastic wrap, and heat it in a microwave oven until it boils. Carefully pour the hot butter over the dough in the bowl while turning and tossing the pieces with a fork, so they are all moistened. When the butter is cool enough to handle, mix and rub the pieces of dough with your fingers to make sure every bit of *kunafa* is coated with butter.

Prepare the cheese filling: Spread the cheese on paper towels and blot dry. Put the pieces in a bowl and crumble them into small bits with your fingertips. Sprinkle the sugar, orange-blossom water, and rose water over the cheese and toss well. Set the filling aside.

Assemble the dish: Press the 2 tablespoons soft butter in the bottom of a 12-inch round pan. Drop the red food coloring on top. With your fingertips—or with a wad of plastic wrap if you don't want them to get pink—mix the color and butter together. Then spread it all over the bottom and sides of the pan, coating the pan thoroughly.

Put about three quarters of the buttered *kunafa* in the pan and spread it out evenly, covering the bottom and coming about halfway up the sides. Press the dough firmly against the pan,

SAVE SOME FOR LATER!

It's worth making a big pan of Kunafa bi Jibin even for a small party, just to enjoy the leftovers. You can warm it in a double-boiler or microwave, or for a real Arab treat, put a piece of cold Kunafa inside a fresh pocket bread and heat it in the oven. At home, this "sandwich" is made with a special sesame-flavored bread called *kunafa kaak*. But from my mother-in-law (who had an insatiable sweet tooth) I learned that there's no better way to start the day than with a bite of last night's Kunafa, enjoyed cold straight from the refrigerator!

forming a smooth, slightly concave layer. Then spread the cheese filling evenly over the dough and press it in place. Spread the remaining *kunafa* over the cheese layer and press it smooth.

(At this point you can seal the entire pan, wrapping it first in plastic wrap and then in aluminum foil, and refrigerate it for a day or freeze it for up to 2 weeks. Transfer the frozen *kunafa* to the refrigerator several hours before baking.)

Bake and Serve: Preheat the oven to 400°F, with a rack in the lower center of the oven.

Just before baking the *kunafa,* make the syrup: Stir the sugar and 1½ cups water together in a deep, heavy-bottomed saucepan. Bring it to a boil over high heat, and add the lemon juice. Let the syrup boil, without stirring, until it has reached the thread stage (about 225°F on a candy thermometer), when it will spill slowly from a teaspoon, forming a thin thread. Pour the syrup into a heatproof container, stir in the orange-blossom water, and set it aside at room temperature.

Place the *kunafa* on the middle lower oven rack. Bake for 40 minutes, or until the sides of the pastry are golden brown (check by gently pulling an edge away from the pan with a flat knife or a spatula).

Lay a large flat serving platter over the hot pan. Holding them together tightly with oven mitts or thick towels, invert the platter

KUNAFA THE AMERICAN WAY

To make Kunafa the way my Arab American friends do, don't bother making the traditional cheese filling but rather mix together 32 ounces ricotta, 2 tablespoons whole milk, and 3 heaping tablespoons powdered sugar. Spread this over the first layer of dough and cover it with the second layer. Cover the pan with foil and bake in a preheated 350°F oven for 25 minutes; then remove the foil and bake for 5 minutes more. Place a large inverted serving platter over the pan and flip the pan and platter together. Drizzle ½ cup of the sugar syrup over the unmolded Kunafa. Cut the Kunafa into squares and serve with the remaining syrup on the side.

and pan, unmolding the *kunafa*. Pour 2 cups of the syrup all over the top of the pastry; put the remainder (a cup or so) in a serving pitcher. Sprinkle the coarsely ground pistachios over the top in a crosshatch pattern (marking squares for serving portions) or other decorative design.

After presenting it to your guests, slice the hot *kunafa* into squares, pour a bit of the remaining syrup over each portion if desired, and serve immediately.

DESALTING AKAWI CHEESE

Cut the block of akawi cheese into ¼-inch-thick slices and then into sticks about 1 inch long and ¼ inch thick. Place them in a bowl and add cold water to cover. (If the recipe calls for mozzarella and it is salted, shred it on a hand grater and add to the bowl.) Soak overnight, or for at least 12 hours, in the refrigerator, twice pouring off the salty water and covering the cheese with fresh water. (To desalt the cheese more quickly, soak it for about 3 hours, changing the water every 30 minutes.) When the cheese has no salty taste, pour off the water, pick it up by the handful and squeeze out the excess moisture, and put it in a strainer to drain and dry.

Desalt mozzarella by shredding it on a hand grater and soaking it in cold water for 2 hours.

THE KING OF KUNAFA

In so many ways, my appreciation for good food comes from my father, Abdul Aziz Shakhashir. A hardworking businessman, he has never cooked but has always observed and advised whoever was in the kitchen—he tasted everything and offered expert opinions. He also made it his business to buy all our meat and fish: I remember him at the market, instructing the butcher on the exact cuts of beef or lamb he wanted, or examining every fish, opening it up, sniffing and touching it to be sure it was absolutely fresh and perfect.

Of all the foods my father loves, one of his great passions is Kunafa bi Jibin. His expertise comes from long experience, since he is originally from Nablus, a city known throughout the region as a center of great sweets, expert pastry makers, and fine cheese. The best cheese for Kunafa, indeed, is *jibneh Nabulsy,* a white table cheese you may find in a Middle Eastern grocery, but it bears little resemblance to the kind my father grew up eating. To this day, my father is a connoisseur of the dessert: If he says a Kunafa is good, you know it is good. And if he say's it's not good, that's the final word. In our family, he is the unquestioned "king of Kunafa."

This is a title he truly deserves, I think. When I was a little girl in Jordan, on a few unforgettable occasions my father prepared authentic Kunafa bi Jibin, by hand in the traditional way. It was a long labor of love just for the family, I realized now. He sat on a little stool in the living room, with an enormous round pan before him, set over an open heater (an old-fashioned type of room heater). He spread several pounds of raw kunafa dough in the pan, poured the hot butter over it, and patiently rubbed it into hundreds of fine long strands of dough. He worked the butter and the kunafa this way for over an hour—while we children watched him, fascinated—as the dough slowly heated up and "cooked" in the butter. Then he formed the dessert right in the pan, pressing the kunafa to form a bottom pastry layer, then spreading a layer of sweetened jibneh Nabulsy over it, then a top layer of pastry. And the pan remained right on the heater to bake—it took almost 2 hours for the Kunafa to become crisp all over and for the cheese to melt. It seemed like an endless wait for us, but it was worth it when he served us the pastry, doused in syrup.

Appreciation for the traditional techniques and fine ingredients that go into a great Kunafa certainly adds to my love for this dessert. And whenever I make it, I am reminded of my father, skillfully manipulating buttery shreds of phyllo in his fingers—attired, as always, in a business suit and dress shoes.

Baklava

BAKLAWA

3 cups walnuts

3 cups pecans

3 tablespoons sugar

2 cups clarified butter (see page 45), melted

2 pounds 9 by 14-inch sheets frozen phyllo dough (about 40 sheets), thawed

2 cups Simple Syrup (page 306)

½ cup finely ground unsalted pistachios

If Kunafa is the king of Middle Eastern desserts, then Baklava is the queen. These delicate layers of phyllo filled with crushed nuts and drenched in sugar syrup are beloved everywhere in the Arab world, and are as welcome on a formal dessert table as they are on a casual dessert plate. Authentic baklava is made with crushed walnuts; a refined version is made with almonds; and when a cook really wants to impress her guests, she'll make it with pistachios. This recipe, however, features pecans, which I came up with when we were asked to bring a dessert to a friend's house for our first American Thanksgiving gathering.

There are a few tips for making this baklava, which is a less sweet version of the frozen or commercial bake-shop variety: First, butter the sheets of phyllo liberally and evenly; the layers will separate if they are too dry. Second, to prevent the top layer of dough from separating from the nuts, make sure to butter both sides of the layer that tops the nuts and then press it down gently. Third, use only 2 cups of the syrup and no more. You don't want your baklava to be soggy or too sweet.

The baklava can be prepared up to the point just before baking, cut into diamond shapes, then covered tightly and frozen for up to 2 weeks. Defrost it for a couple of hours and then bake as directed. Baked baklava can be stored in the refrigerator, in a rigid container with a tight-fitting lid, for up to 2 weeks, or frozen for up to 2 months.

Makes about 65 pieces

Preheat the oven to 350°F.

Combine the nuts and sugar in a food processor and pulse until they form fine crumbs. Transfer the nuts to a large bowl and add ¼ cup of the clarified butter. Use your hands to moisten the nuts with the butter, and set aside.

Brush the bottom of a 9 by 14-inch baking dish with clarified butter. Remove 7 sheets of the phyllo dough, wrap them in plastic wrap, cover them with a damp towel, and set them aside.

Place 1 sheet of the remaining phyllo in the prepared baking dish and smooth it with the palm of your hand to deflate any air bubbles. Brush it with clarified butter. Repeat with 12 more sheets of dough.

Spread all the nut mixture evenly over the stack of dough, pressing down on the dough with the back of a spoon as you distribute it.

Place one of the seven sheets of dough on a clean work surface and brush it liberally with clarified butter. Gently transfer it to the baking dish, placing it butter side down on the nuts. Press down on the dough with the palm of your hand so that the nuts stick to the sheet of dough. Brush the top of the sheet with clarified butter. Layer all the remaining sheets on top, brushing each one with clarified butter. There should be 27 layers on top of the nuts. Brush the top layer with clarified butter.

To make the traditional diamond-shaped pieces, slice through all the layers of the dough across the width of the pan, making the cuts about 1 inch apart. Then make diagonal cuts across the pan. Next, wet your hands with water and gently smooth the dough with your wet palms (you may need to wet them twice). Bake in the middle of the oven until the edges of the dough take on color, about 45 minutes. Raise the temperature to 450°F and bake 5 minutes more, or until the top is lightly golden (watch carefully, as it can burn easily).

While the baklava is hot, ladle the cold Simple Syrup along the cut lines in the surface of the dough. Let it cool completely in the baking dish. Then retrace the cuts with a sharp knife, and lift the pieces out of the dish with an offset spatula. Transfer the pieces of baklava to a serving platter, and sprinkle the ground pistachios all over. Serve at room temperature.

Variations: During Ramadan we make a finer version, known as *hadif,* with ground almonds. If you prefer to make it this way, use ½ pound almonds, preferably the Spanish Marcona variety, 20 sheets of phyllo, and half of the remaining ingredients; reduce the baking time by about 10 minutes. To make baklava with walnuts or pistachios, substitute 1 pound of the nuts for the walnuts and pecans.

Date Cake

KAKAT AL TAMR

½ pound Medjool dates, pitted and coarsely chopped

7 tablespoons unsalted butter, softened, plus extra for the dish

1 cup sugar

1¾ cups all-purpose flour

1 teaspoon baking powder

1 teaspoon baking soda

1 teaspoon vanilla extract

1 egg, lightly beaten

For the topping:

¾ cup light brown sugar

6 tablespoons unsalted butter

5 tablespoons heavy cream

My boys' grade school in London celebrated the diversity of the student body with an annual International Day. The children wore their country's traditional dress, performed dances, and taught their friends about their customs. One Saudi Arabian girl, Rania Al Husseini, always brought this snack cake, which is delicious warm from the oven and moist enough to be enjoyed at room temperature with a cold glass of milk.

When you are chopping the dates, dust them with a bit of flour to prevent them from sticking to the knife.　　　　　*Serves 8*

Place the dates in a heatproof bowl. Bring 1 cup water to a boil in a small saucepan, pour it over the dates, and let them soak until plumped, 10 minutes. Do not drain.

Preheat the oven to 375°F. Coat a 7 by 11-inch baking dish with butter.

Cream the butter and sugar together in a standing mixer fitted with the whisk attachment (or with a handheld electric mixer). Sift the flour and baking powder together in a bowl, and set aside. Combine the dates and their soaking liquid, the baking soda, and the vanilla in a small bowl.

With the mixer on medium speed, add the egg and one third of the flour mixture to the creamed butter and beat until incorporated, about 2 minutes. Gradually add the remaining flour and beat until it is mixed into the batter. Add the date mixture and beat until well blended.

Pour the batter into the prepared baking dish, and bake until the cake springs back when tapped with a finger, or when a cake tester inserted in the middle comes out clean, about 30 minutes. Using a fork, poke holes all over the surface of the cake.

Preheat the broiler.

Prepare the topping: Combine the butter, brown sugar, and cream in a saucepan and cook over medium heat, stirring, until it bubbles slightly, about 3 minutes. Pour this caramel syrup over the baked cake, and slide it under the broiler until the surface begins to bubble, about 30 seconds. Immediately remove the dish from the oven. Let the cake cool a bit; then cut it into squares. Serve warm or at room temperature.

Semolina Pistachio Layer Cake

BOHSALINI

1 cup (2 sticks) unsalted butter, melted

1½ cups coarse semolina

½ cup sugar

2½ cups unsalted pistachios

1 tablespoon rose water

3 cups Kashta (recipe follows)

½ cup powdered sugar

1 cup fried pine nuts and/or fried peeled almonds (see pages 43, 12)

This no-bake dessert features alternating layers of savory pistachio-studded semolina and cooked cream set into a springform cake pan and chilled in the refrigerator overnight. If you are feeding a crowd, double the recipe and forgo the cake shape for a looser presentation: Spread all the semolina mixture on a large platter, spoon the kashta over it, and garnish with the nuts and powdered sugar; then spoon it into dessert bowls. **Serves 8 to 10**

Mix the melted butter and semolina in a medium bowl, and set aside at room temperature for at least 6 hours or as long as overnight.

Combine the sugar, pistachios, and rose water in a food processor and pulse until the mixture has the consistency of coarse sand. Add the pistachio mixture to the flour mixture, and using your hands, mix them together, breaking up the lumps until the mixture feels like damp sand.

Line a 9-inch springform cake pan with wax paper, using two pieces crossing at right angles and allowing lengths of paper to hang over the sides of the pan. Spoon half of the semolina mixture into the pan and smooth it out to the edges with the back of the spoon. Follow with all of the Kashta, spreading it over the semolina in an even layer. Spoon the remaining semolina mixture on top and spread it out in an even layer. Fold the overhanging wax paper over the top, and press to smooth the semolina. Cover with plastic wrap and refrigerate overnight.

One hour before serving, remove the cake from the refrigerator, invert it onto a serving plate, and release it from the pan. Sprinkle the powdered sugar on top: Hold a fine-mesh sieve over the cake, pour the powdered sugar into it, and gently tap the rim to release the sugar. Garnish with the nuts, and serve in wedges.

Kashta

1 gallon whole milk

¼ cup fresh lemon juice

2 tablespoons rose water

2 tablespoons orange-blossom water

There is no English translation for kashta, *pronounced "ahshta," but it is often described as the Arab equivalent of clotted cream. This fragrant cake filling is also delicious as a breakfast treat, drizzled with honey or swabbed on a piece of toast. Kashta will keep, covered and refrigerated, for up to 3 days.* **Makes 3 cups**

Pour the milk into a large pot and bring it to a boil over high heat, stirring occasionally. When the milk rises to the top of the pot, stir in the lemon juice and remove the pot from the heat. Set it aside to cool until the milk separates, 10 to 15 minutes.

Pour the milk through a fine-mesh strainer into a bowl, stirring to release the whey. Discard the whey. Transfer the curds in the strainer to a large bowl. Stir in the rose water and the orange-blossom water with a wooden spoon. The Kashta should look like small-curd cottage cheese. Cover and refrigerate until ready to use.

Semolina Fingers

ASABEH ZEINAB

¼ cup plus 2 teaspoons anise
   seeds, picked over and rinsed
2 cups fine semolina
2 cups all-purpose flour
¼ teaspoon ground mahlab (see
   page 22)
1 teaspoon baking powder
⅔ cup olive oil
¼ cup sesame seeds
½ cup sugar
Simple Syrup (page 306), cold
3 cups vegetable oil

These traditional Ramadan sweets, traditionally made by the older women in the family, have enjoyed something of a revival on modern dinner tables because they can be made in advance. They get their sweet, spicy flavor from mahlab, *a spice made from the ground kernels of black cherries. The seemingly intricate pattern on the surface of these cookies is actually very easy to make by pressing the dough on the holes of a plastic colander (the dough will stick to a metal one). The tiny nodules are meant to catch the sugar syrup. Semolina Fingers will keep, tightly covered, in the refrigerator for up to 1 week.*

Makes about 40 cookies

Combine the ¼ cup anise seeds with 1½ cups water in a small saucepan and bring to a boil over high heat. Boil for 2 minutes, and then set aside to cool. Grind the remaining 2 teaspoons anise seeds in a spice grinder or a mortar and pestle and set aside.

Combine the semolina, flour, ground anise, mahlab, and baking powder in a large bowl. Add the olive oil and rub the mixture between the palms of your hands to moisten the dough. Then add the sesame seeds, sugar, and the boiled anise seeds with their soaking water. Mix well with your hands. The dough should be wet and somewhat elastic. Cover with plastic wrap and let rest for 1 hour.

Working with 1 tablespoon of the dough at a time, roll each piece into a 2-inch-long log. Press the log on the back of a plastic colander, creating tiny modules all over it. Set it aside on a tray and repeat with the remaining dough.

Place the Simple Syrup in a bowl, and set it near the stove.

Heat the vegetable oil in a medium pot over medium heat. It is ready when it reaches 300°F (test by dropping a piece of dough in the oil; if the oil bubbles, it's hot enough). Working in batches, slide the semolina "fingers" into the oil one at a time, using a slotted spoon. Do not overcrowd the pot. Using the slotted spoon to move the cookies around in the pot so they fry evenly, cook until they are golden brown, about 10 minutes. Transfer the cookies to the bowl of Simple Syrup, using the slotted spoon. Repeat with remaining dough, transferring those soaking in the syrup to a serving plate just before the next batch is fried. Serve at room temperature.

Semolina Cake

NAMOURA

2 cups Simple Syrup (page 306)

1 tablespoon unsalted butter

3 tablespoons sesame paste (tahini)

3 cups coarse semolina

2 cups sugar

1 cup finely grated dried unsweetened coconut (grated fine in a food processor)

1 cup whole milk, heated

1 cup (2 sticks) unsalted butter, melted

¼ cup orange-blossom water

½ cup almonds, peeled (see page 12)

A batter of semolina, coconut, milk, and rose water bakes in a pan sliced with tahini in this wonderfully fragrant cake. I always swirl a bit of butter into the sugar syrup the minute I take if off the stove to give the topping a nice sheen. Namoura will keep in a tightly sealed container for 4 days at room temperature. **Serves 8 to 10**

Preheat the oven to 400°F, with a rack in the center.

Prepare the Simple Syrup. In the final step, remove the pan from the heat and stir in the 1 tablespoon butter. (If you already have the Simple Syrup on hand, heat it gently in a small saucepan. Then remove it from the heat and stir in the butter.) Set it aside to cool completely.

Coat a 13-inch round cake pan with the sesame paste, and set it aside.

Combine the semolina, sugar, and coconut in a large bowl. Add the hot milk, melted butter, and orange-blossom water, and mix until the ingredients are well incorporated. Pour the batter into the prepared cake pan and bake until the edges begin to brown, about 10 minutes. Remove the pan from the oven and reduce the heat to 350°F.

Using a sharp kitchen knife, score the cake in squares or diamond shapes, and place an almond in the center of each. Return the pan to the oven and bake until the almonds are toasted, 40 to 50 minutes.

Using a soup ladle, pour the Simple Syrup along the scored lines in the cake, filling them in and repeating until the entire surface of the cake is covered. (If you prefer a less sweet cake, drizzle a very thin layer of Simple Syrup over the entire cake.) Set the cake aside to cool completely.

Cut the cake into pieces along the score marks, arrange the pieces on a platter, and serve.

Yellow Diamonds

SFOOF

2 cups all-purpose flour

2 cups semolina flour

2 tablespoons ground turmeric

1 teaspoon vanilla powder or
  vanilla extract

1 tablespoon baking powder

1½ cups sugar

1½ cups whole milk

¾ cup vegetable oil

¼ cup sesame paste (tahini)

½ cup pine nuts

Standing on busy street corners and in front of schools in Syria and Lebanon, street vendors sell these little cakes out of huge round trays that they cradle in a specially folded towel on top of their head. To serve up a slice of the diamond-shaped confection, they set the tray on a folding stand, make the transaction, and reposition the tray on their head. The pan is coated with tahini, which imparts a subtle nutty flavor to this moist cake, while turmeric, which tinges it a delightful orange hue, gives it a slightly spicy flavor. Sfoof will keep in a sealed container at room temperature for up to 1 week. ***Makes about 40 pieces***

Preheat the oven to 350°F, with a rack in the center.

Combine the all-purpose flour, semolina flour, turmeric, vanilla powder, if using, and baking powder in a large bowl and stir well. Combine the sugar, milk, vanilla extract, if using, and vegetable oil in the bowl of a standing mixer fitted with the whisk attachment, and mix on medium speed until combined. Gradually add the semolina mixture and continue to beat until the batter is smooth. Set it aside.

Using a pastry brush, spread the sesame paste over the bottom and up the sides of a 16-inch round cake pan or a 12 by 16-inch rectangular pan. Pour the batter into the prepared pan and smooth the surface with the back of a spoon. Sprinkle the pine nuts evenly over the batter. Bake until the cake springs back when you touch it, about 30 minutes.

Transfer the pan to a wire rack and let it cool. Then cut the cake into squares or diamonds, and serve warm or at room temperature.

Milk Pudding

MOHALABIA

6 heaping tablespoons
   cornstarch, dissolved in ½
   cup water

6 cups whole or 2% milk

6 tablespoons sugar

6 pieces mastic, each the size of
   a grain of coarse salt,
   crushed (see page 22)

1 tablespoon orange-blossom
   water

1 tablespoon rose water

½ cup heavy cream

Crushed unsalted pistachios,
   soaked in water for 30
   minutes, then drained, for
   garnish

We eat this creamy white custard on almost any occasion, and always on New Year's Day because it is a symbol of prosperity and happiness. It is a fragrant trio of traditional Arab flavors: rose water, orange-blossom water, and mastic, a rather sweet anise-flavored resin from the tree of the same name. On its own, this pudding is pure silkenness. But if you like, garnish it with a drizzle of honey (halve the sugar if you add honey) and toasted nuts of any kind. If you are making this for a dinner party, make it extra-special by pouring the custard into individual custard cups. When it's time to serve them, invert the cups onto individual dessert plates and pour a little thickened Apricot Juice onto each plate around the custard. Garnish with a few crushed pistachios.

Serves 6 to 8

Combine the cornstarch, milk, and sugar in a medium saucepan and cook over high heat, stirring constantly, until the mixture begins to bubble. Lower the heat to medium, and stirring frequently as the milk simmers, add the mastic. Then reduce the heat to low and simmer, continuing to stir frequently until the mixture coats a wooden spoon, 20 to 30 minutes.

Stir in the orange-blossom and rose waters. Whisk in the cream and continue to cook on low heat, stirring frequently, until the mixture resembles heavy cream, about 30 minutes.

If there are tiny dark lumps floating in the mixture (they're from scraping the cooked milk and cream from the bottom of the pot), strain it. Pour the mixture into a 1½-quart baking dish and set it aside to cool. Then cover it with plastic wrap and refrigerate it until the pudding has a custard-like consistency, at least 2 hours or as long as overnight.

Garnish with the pistachios, and serve.

VARIATIONS ON MOHALABIA

- Layali Lubnan, or "Nights of Lebanon," is among my favorite variations on versatile Mohalabiah. To make it, spread a layer of Kashta (page 317) over the cooled pudding, then cover the Kashta with a layer of thinly sliced bananas. Scatter crushed pistachios over the bananas. Drizzle a bit of honey on each plate just before serving the pudding to your guests.

- In Morocco, the surface of Mohalabia is paved with fried, peeled almonds and dusted with cinnamon.

- In the Gulf States, 5 crushed cardamom pods are cooked with the milk, and the rose water is flavored with saffron threads before it is added to the hot milk. The cardamom pods are strained from the liquid before it is poured into the serving dish and set aside to cool.

- Some Lebanese and Syrian families substitute 6 tablespoons rice flour for the cornstarch.

Apricot Pudding with Almonds and Pistachios

MOHALABIA KAMAR AL DEEN

Two 12-ounce sheets apricot leather

½ cup pine nuts

½ cup almonds, peeled (see page 12)

½ cup unsalted pistachios

6 tablespoons sugar

3 tablespoons cornstarch

2 tablespoons rose water

2 tablespoons orange-blossom water

This rich custard is named for one of the many varieties of apricot trees that grow in Damascus, where the apricots are among the most aromatic and flavorful in all the Middle East. The Syrian capital is especially well known for its apricot fruit leather, which is made by mashing the golden flesh of the apricot and then spreading it out on long wooden tables and leaving it to dry in the sun. Once the juices have evaporated, the sheets are brushed with sesame oil to give them a glistening sheen and a soft texture. The leather is then folded several times and stored so that it can be enjoyed all year long—but most widely during Ramadan, since it is believed that apricots do the best job of quenching the thirst after a day of fasting.   ***Serves 6 to 8***

Using kitchen scissors, cut the apricot sheets into bite-size pieces and place them in a bowl. Add 4 cups water and set aside to soak for at least 5 hours at room temperature or overnight in the refrigerator.

Meanwhile, soak the pine nuts, almonds, and pistachios in separate bowls of cold water for at least 3 hours or overnight.

Place the apricot liquid (in batches if necessary) and any remaining pieces of the leather in a blender and process until smooth. Strain the mixture through a fine-mesh sieve into large bowl, and add enough water to make 6 cups.

Combine the apricot juice, sugar, and cornstarch in a saucepan and bring to a boil, stirring constantly. Reduce the heat to medium and cook for 5 minutes. Then remove the saucepan from the heat and stir in the rose water and orange-blossom water. Pour the mixture into a 1½-quart serving dish or four individual pudding molds. Let cool, uncovered. Avoid moving the dish, to allow the pudding to set.

Preparing nuts to garnish sweet dishes: Soak the pine nuts, peeled unsalted pistachios, and walnuts separately in small bowls filled with fresh water for 3 to 4 hours or overnight.

To finish the pine nuts, simply drain and dry them on paper towels.

To peel the membrane off pistachios and walnuts, rub your fingers against the soaked nuts until the skins come off, then soak them again in fresh cold water. Drain and dry the nuts on paper towels.

To prepare the almonds, place them in a small bowl, pour some boiling water over them, and let them sit for 5 to 10 minutes. Then remove the skins by rubbing your fingers against the nuts. When all the nuts are peeled, combine them in a small bowl, submerge them in fresh water, then drain and dry them on paper towels.

Once the pudding is set, scatter the nuts on top. Serve at room temperature, or refrigerate for 2 hours and serve chilled.

Variation: To make a beautiful layered pudding, pour the apricot pudding over cooled Milk Pudding (page 322) and refrigerate for up to 2 hours, or until the pudding sets. Garnish with the pistachios, pine nuts, and almonds, and serve.

Caraway and Anise Seed Pudding

MUGHLI

1 tablespoon anise seeds

1 cup rice flour

1 tablespoon plus 2 teaspoons
  ground cinnamon

2 tablespoons ground caraway
  seeds

1¼ cups sugar

½ cup unsalted pistachios

½ cup walnuts

½ cup pine nuts

½ cup almonds, peeled (see
  page 12)

½ cup finely shredded dried
  unsweetened coconut
  (shredded fine in a food
  processor)

*T*he secret to preparing this traditional celebratory pudding is in the stirring: the longer you stir, the creamier it will be. You might want to have a book or a magazine close by while you prepare it, because you will be vigorously stirring for almost 2 hours. The result, however, after this creamy custard has absorbed all the aromatic spices and is topped with mixed nuts, is worth it.

To make this dessert, you'll need to plan ahead because Mughli must be cooled for several hours before serving. The nuts also require a minimum of 3 hours soaking time, so be sure to begin prepping them while the pudding is cooling. Both the Mughli and the nuts will keep in the refrigerator for up to 4 days.
Serves 8

Place the anise seeds in a small bowl, add water to cover, and let sit until the seeds rise to the surface. Then scoop the seeds from the surface with a spoon, and discard the water. Combine the seeds with 1 cup water in a small pot and bring to a boil over high heat. Boil for 3 minutes. Then strain the mixture through a fine-mesh strainer into a bowl, reserving the liquid and discarding the seeds. Measure the liquid and add water, if necessary, to make 1 cup.

Combine the rice flour, cinnamon, caraway, sugar, anise seed liquid, and 7 cups water in a large heavy-bottomed pot over high heat, and whisk together until well blended. Using a wooden spoon, stir the mixture vigorously until it begins to boil, about 30 minutes. Continue to boil over high heat for 20 minutes, continuously stirring and scraping the bottom of the pot to prevent the rice flour from sticking.

MUGHLI THE FAST WAY

Though I always make Mughli the slow way, there is a quicker method: you can prepare it in a pressure cooker from the very first step. When the mixture starts to boil, stir it for 15 minutes on low heat, then cover the pressure cooker and cook for 45 minutes. Cool the pot under running water for a few minutes, remove the lid, and bring the mixture to a boil again, stirring for 15 minutes until it is creamy and smooth.

Reduce the heat to low and simmer, scraping and stirring vigorously every 10 minutes, for 1 hour. Then remove the Mughli from the heat and pour it into a 9 by 12-inch serving dish or divide it among 8 small ramekins. Wipe away any drips on the serving dish(es) with a damp paper towel, and set aside to cool completely. Then cover with plastic wrap (do not let the wrap touch the pudding) and refrigerate for 3 to 4 hours or as long as overnight.

Meanwhile, peel the pistachios and walnuts by rubbing them between your palms until the skins come off. Combine the pine nuts, pistachios, walnuts, and almonds in a bowl, add water to cover, and refrigerate for 3 to 4 hours or overnight. Transfer them to a paper towel–lined plate to drain.

To serve the pudding, remove it from the refrigerator and sprinkle a thin layer of shredded coconut on top. Garnish with the nuts, and serve.

MUGHLI FOR MUBARAKEH
A DELICIOUS BIRTH ANNOUNCEMENT

The world is changing rapidly everywhere, and many of the time-honored traditions that I grew up with are changing too. And occasionally I discover that a tradition has been altogether forgotten or ignored.

A friend of mine called with the good news that a young Arab American woman in our area had given birth to her first child. But there was something missing, she told me with great concern.

"May! She does not have *mughli!* The new mother does not know how to prepare *mughli!* The grandmother is there and *she* does not make *mughli!* May, you have to bring her some *mugli*," my friend insisted.

I was amazed. I thought that every Arab and Arab American woman (and man!) knew that you must make a huge batch of *mughli*—our aromatic, delicately spiced, and delicious rice pudding—when a baby is born.

It has always been the custom that we make *mughli* for forty days after the baby is born. We serve *mughli* to everyone who visits the home to see the baby. We serve *mughli* at Mubarakeh, the celebration and baby shower that is given after baby is born. And we don't just wait for people to come: I was taught that everyone you know—relatives, friends, neighbors—should eat *mughli* to announce the birth of the baby!

Of course, things are never like they "used to be." While *mughli* is still prepared to mark the birth of a child throughout the Arab world, it is not always according to the strictest tradition. For instance, some families will make *mughli* for the full forty-day period for their firstborn child, especially if it is a son. Should they have a daughter, though, or it is a second or third child, they might cook

mughli for only a week or two. Some families will cook it for only a week or so for any child. And nowadays, just serving *mughli* at Mubarakeh is often considered adequate. It is also less common, especially in America, to distribute *mughli* to the neighbors.

My own experience reflects this changing tradition. When my first child, Wasfi, was born, we made *mughli* even longer than forty days, because this was such a notable occasion: He was not only my first child but the first grandson to my parents. Also, I was the first grandchild to my grandparents and the first girl to get married among my cousins on my mother's side. On Aref's side, Wasfi was the "crown prince" in the Bsisu family, as he carries his grandfather's name. On the other hand, when Basil and Naji were born, we were thrilled—but we cooked *mughli* for only four weeks, as our lives had already changed.

When I heard about the new mother in Cincinnati who didn't have *mughli*, I sprang into action and cooked enough for her to serve to thirty guests. Cooking and serving *mughli* is a wonderful way to share the joy in having a healthy, happy baby with family, friends, and community, even if you make it for only one celebration or a few days. And when I have a granddaughter or a grandson (I'm hoping for a girl), I intend to cook *mughli* for forty days!

Forty Days of Rest: A Disappearing Tradition

The forty days following the birth of a baby is an important period in Arab tradition—and not just for cooking *mughli*. If the baby is a boy, he is circumcised after forty days, according to Islamic law. And it

is an old custom that the mother is to rest and stay in the house for forty days after childbirth—even to remain in bed, in the strictest observance—and to be cared for by her own mother, grandmother, or older sister.

Certainly this is old-fashioned. Yet in many ways, I believe this custom is rooted in wisdom, as the nurturing and support can help a young mother at a time that is often stressful. Without this help, taking care of a new baby on top of all of one's regular responsibilities, is not easy—and for some women it can be totally overwhelming.

As a first-time mother, I let myself be pampered by my mother and grandmother, though I did not stay inside for the full forty days. However, when our second son, Basil, was a week old, Aref came into our house and suggested we take a walk. My grandmother, who was there to take care of me, all day every day, was horrified when she saw me dressed, getting ready to go out so soon after the baby's birth.

I was sorry to upset her but I certainly enjoyed our walk around the block, and when Naji was born three years later, neither my mother nor my grandmother tried to keep me in the house.

Mubarakeh: A Party for the Birth of a Child

Here's a menu for a festive Mubarakeh that I hope you will prepare in celebration of a newborn—or for any happy occasion. The *mughli* takes some time and attention but the other dishes—savory and sweet finger foods—are easy to make and can be prepared ahead and frozen. An ancillary part of the celebration is the giving of souvenirs in honor of the newborn. These can be either silver or porcelain, with the baby's name and date of birth engraved on them, for the guests to take home with them.

Mubarakeh Menu

- Oregano Cakes
- Pull-Away Cheese Rolls
- Caraway and Anise Seed Pudding (Mughli)
- Date Fingers
- Almond Cookies
- Jordan almonds (store-bought)

- Assorted chocolates (store-bought)
- Lemonade
- Sage Tea

Rice Pudding

RUZ BI HALEEB

¼ cup short-grain rice, rinsed
  and drained
6 cups whole milk
½ cup sugar
1 tablespoon orange-blossom
  water

*T*his is my favorite Arab dessert, no doubt because it was my grandmother's specialty. I remember her standing at the stove, stirring and stirring—it is crucial to stir it constantly for the first hour to achieve a creamy consistency—and telling us stories that were endlessly fascinating. To this day, Ruz bi Haleeb comforts me. I think it tastes best when it is made a day in advance. Any short-grain rice will make a fine rice pudding, but avoid using instant rice. Putting the rice pudding in the oven to bake is called ye jamer, *which means "to catch the aroma of the coals."*

Serves 6 to 8

Combine the rice, milk, and sugar in a large saucepan and bring to a boil over medium heat, stirring constantly, about 1 hour. Reduce the heat to low, slide a heat diffuser under the pot, and continue to cook, stirring frequently, until the mixture becomes thick and creamy and turns slightly yellow, about 45 minutes.

Meanwhile, preheat the oven to 400°F.

Stir the orange-blossom water into the mixture, and pour it into a 2-quart baking dish. Bake until the top is golden brown, about 15 minutes.

Remove the dish from the oven and allow it to cool. Serve, or refrigerate overnight and bring back to room temperature before serving.

Bread Pudding with Syrup

UM KHALID

One 1½-pound loaf challah, brioche, Hawaiian sweet bread, *or* other sweet bread

¼ cup raisins, golden or dark

4 cups heavy cream

10 ounces mozzarella cheese, shredded on the large holes of a box grater, desalted if necessary (see page 310)

Pine nuts, for garnish

¾ to 1 cup Simple Syrup (page 306), cold

*M*ost Arab food is named for its shape, or for the acidic ingredient in it (as in Sumakiyah, page 207), or after the person who is known for making the best version. This comforting dessert, which almost every Arab home cook knows how to make, is named for Um Khalid, or "mother of Khalid," the Syrian Queen of Sweets, who, legend has it, invented it. It likely came to be out of necessity—it is often made with leftover bread and cheese. Um Khalid is best eaten hot, so slide it into the oven just as your guests sit down for the main course and it will be ready when the dinner plates are cleared. If you can't find unsalted mozzarella, be sure to soak the salted variety well before adding it to the dish.

Serves 8

Tear the bread into bite-size pieces. Line a 2-quart baking dish with half of the bread. Sprinkle the raisins evenly over the bread, and drizzle 2 cups of the cream over it. Sprinkle half the mozzarella over the cream, then top with the remaining bread. Drizzle the remaining 2 cups cream over the bread. Flatten the moistened bread with the palm of your hand or the back of a spoon, and then scatter the remaining mozzarella over the bread. Strew the pine nuts on top. Cover with plastic wrap and refrigerate for at least 30 minutes, or until the bread has soaked up the cream.

Bring the bread pudding to room temperature. Preheat the oven to 350°F.

Bake the bread pudding until the top is golden, 30 to 40 minutes. Remove it from the oven, drizzle the Simple Syrup over the top, and serve immediately.

Semolina Purses

TAMRIYEH

2 cups granulated sugar

1½ cups fine semolina

2 quarts 2% milk

5 tablespoons rose water

¼ cup all-purpose flour

One 12-ounce package 8-inch square spring roll wrappers

3 cups vegetable oil, plus more if needed

1 cup powdered sugar

These sweetened semolina-filled pouches are occasionally offered at Ramadan instead of Arab Pancakes. Some of the best Tamriyeh I have ever tasted came from a little place in the Lebanese mountains, where the purses were made to order so that they could be enjoyed as they should be—pipping hot. Because making the authentic dough is a challenge—even for a longtime cook like me—I improvise with spring roll wrappers, which work exceptionally well. Bring them to room temperature on the kitchen counter and cover them with a damp towel while you are working with them. Tamriyeh can be made a day in advance, covered with plastic wrap, and refrigerated. **Makes 24 pastries**

Place the granulated sugar, semolina, milk, and rose water in a large pot and stir vigorously over high heat until the liquid thickens, 5 to 6 minutes. Reduce the heat to medium and cook for 5 minutes more. The mixture will resemble grits.

Pour the semolina mixture into a shallow 4-quart dish and smooth it with the back of a spoon. Allow it to cool completely.

Mix the flour and ¼ cup water together in a small bowl, stirring to smooth any lumps. This will be the paste that helps seal the rolls shut.

Place the spring roll wrappers on a clean work surface and cover them with a damp cloth. Working with one wrapper at a time, place 1 tablespoon of the cooled filling in the middle of the lower third of the square. Fold the bottom of the wrapper over the filling, then fold the sides over it. Brush a bit of the flour paste across the top of the wrapper, and roll up to seal the "purse." Repeat with the remaining wrappers and filling.

Pour the vegetable oil into a pot. It should be about 1 inch deep; add more if necessary. Heat it over high heat. Then gently slide the purses into the hot oil, using a slotted spoon and working in batches so as not to crowd the pot. Fry, turning once, until golden brown, about 2 minutes. Use the slotted spoon to transfer the Tamriyeh to a paper towel–lined plate. Put the powdered sugar in a fine-mesh sieve and tap it over the Tamriyeh to give the purses a fine dusting. Serve hot.

Variation: If you want to offer a few different fillings in the spring roll wrappers, try shredded halloumi cheese mixed with chopped parsley, or a combination of 2 parts mozzarella, 2 parts halloumi, and 1 part sharp cheddar cheese, all shredded. These fillings can be made 1 day in advance, tightly covered, and refrigerated.

Semolina Rolls

HALAWAT EL JIBIN

4 tablespoons rose water

4 tablespoons orange-blossom water

4 cups Simple Syrup (page 306)

1 pound mozzarella cheese, desalted (see page 310)

½ cup fine semolina

1½ cups Kashta (page 317)

Ground unsalted pistachios, for garnish

Rose petal jam, for garnish

These sweetened cheese-filled semolina pastries are bakery specialties, so they will take a bit of practice to perfect at home. In fact, most accomplished Middle Eastern cooks have to make them several times before they master rolling out the dough, which is very wet and elastic due to the presence of melted mozzarella cheese. There is an easy alternative to rolling it out: many home cooks spoon the dough like drop cookies onto a serving platter, then put a dollop of the cheese filling on top of each and drizzle the Simple Syrup all over the platter. Another common presentation is to tear the rolled dough into 3-inch pieces, scatter them onto a serving platter, drizzle the syrup over them, and then spoon the Kashta on top.

If you don't have a heavy-bottomed cooking pot to melt the cheese in, use a double-boiler to prevent it from burning. I have made these sweets with both packaged and fresh mozzarella, and curiously, I find the packaged variety results in a nicer dough. Halawat el Jibin will keep in the refrigerator for 3 to 4 days. The Kashta can be made 2 days in advance, covered, and refrigerated. **Makes about 50 rolls**

In a heavy-bottomed nonstick pot, combine 2 tablespoons of the rose water, 2 tablespoons of the orange-blossom water, and ½ cup of the Simple Syrup. Add the cheese and melt it, stirring, over medium heat, about 10 minutes. The cheese will have a consistency similar to melted marshmallows. Gradually add the semolina and the remaining 2 tablespoons rose water and 2 tablespoons orange-blossom water, stirring with a wooden spoon after each addition until the liquid is absorbed. The cheese "dough" will be stiff and may be somewhat difficult to stir; work it up against the sides of the pot to incorporate the ingredients. The mixture should be soft and smooth.

Working very quickly, pour 1 cup of the Simple Syrup directly onto a large, clean work surface (marble works well). Place the dough on the syrup. Pour another ½ cup of the syrup over the dough and roll it out as thin as possible with a rolling pin. The dough will not spread perfectly or entirely smoothly. Let it cool completely.

Cut the dough into 2 by 3-inch pieces, stacking them as you cut them. (The pieces can now be stored in the refrigerator.) Working with one piece at a time, with a short end facing you, spoon 1 teaspoon of the Kashta along the short side of the rectangle. Roll the dough up like a cigar, and place it on a serving platter. Repeat with the remaining dough and Kashta. Drizzle the remaining syrup over the rolls, garnish with the ground pistachios and rose petal jam, and serve.

Arab Pancakes

QATAYEF

1 teaspoon active dry yeast

½ teaspoon sugar

1½ cups warm water (110°F)

1½ cups all-purpose flour

½ cup fine semolina

1 tablespoon powdered whole milk

½ teaspoon baking soda

Dash of salt

1 egg, beaten

Semolina pancakes, whether filled and dried or left open-face, announce the arrival of Ramadan. They are traditionally prepared every day of the holy month and served after the iftar (breaking of the fast) meal or later in the evening when friends, relatives, and neighbors visit. The Qatayef are usually offered in one of three ways: filled with sweetened cheese or walnuts, fried, and dipped in sugar syrup (see page 338); filled with Kashta, formed into "horns" left open on one end, and garnished with crushed pistachios; or left open-face, spread with ghee, and sprinkled with cinnamon sugar.

Makes twelve 6-inch pancakes or forty-five 3-inch pancakes

Combine the yeast with the sugar and ¼ cup of the warm water in a small bowl, stir, and set aside until foamy, about 5 minutes.

Meanwhile, combine the flour, semolina, powdered milk, baking soda, and salt in a medium bowl. Gradually add the remaining 1¼ cups warm water and the egg to the dry ingredients, using a handheld electric mixer to combine them. When the batter begins to resemble thickened milk, add the yeast mixture and mix well. Cover, and set aside to rest for 3 hours.

Heat a heavy-bottomed nonstick skillet over medium heat, or heat an electric griddle to 350°F. Holding the measuring cup at least 8 inches above the skillet (this makes for perfectly round pancakes), pour the batter into the skillet: ¼ cup for each Cheese- or Walnut-Filled Pancake, 1 tablespoon each for the Kashta-filled version, which traditionally are very small. The pancakes will begin to form tiny bubbles. When the entire surface is covered with bubbles and the pancakes no longer have a sheen (a sign of uncooked batter) yet remain pale, they are cooked. (Do not flip them over.) Transfer them to a plate, arrange them in a single layer, and cover with a kitchen towel. Repeat with the remaining batter. Stack the cooled pancakes on a plate, with wax paper between them, as the warm pancakes come out of the pan.

Fill the Qatayef as desired (see headnote). Serve within 2 hours.

Cheese and Walnut Crescents

JIBNEH WA JOZ HASHWEH

*T*hese twice-cooked filled pancakes are a staple of the Ramadan sea-son. I've developed two filling recipes: cheese for my boys and wal-nut for Aref. The filled pancakes can be prepared a few hours before you plan to fry them, but they should be served immediately after frying.

Each filling makes enough for 1 recipe Arab Pancakes

For the cheese filling:

1 pound akawi, mozzarella, or ricotta cheese

2 tablespoons sugar

1 teaspoon rose water

1 teaspoon orange-blossom water

1 teaspoon nigella seeds (optional)

For the walnut filling:

2 cups walnuts, finely crushed

¼ cup sugar

1 teaspoon rose water

½ teaspoon ground cinnamon

Arab Pancakes (page 336)
Simple Syrup (page 306), cold
1 cup solid vegetable shortening

For the cheese filling: Cut the akawi into bite-size pieces, place them in a bowl, and add water to cover. Let the cheese soak for about 6 hours or overnight, changing the water every hour to remove the salt.

Transfer the cheese to a colander to drain. Release the water by squeezing handfuls of the cheese or by pressing down firmly on it in the colander. The cheese will crumble and resemble damp curds. Transfer the drained cheese to a bowl, and add the sugar, rose water, orange-blossom water, and nigella seeds, if using. Mix until just incorporated. Cover and refrigerate until ready to use; it will keep for 1 day.

For the walnut filling: Combine the walnuts, sugar, rose water, and cinnamon in a medium bowl and stir to combine. The filling will keep for 1 day.

To fill the pancakes: Place a pancake in the palm of your hand and spoon 1 tablespoon of the filling into the middle. Fold the pancake in half to form a crescent shape. Pinch it closed, using your thumb and index finger to form a good seal. Repeat with the remaining pancakes and filling, covering them with a kitchen towel as you fill them. If you are going to hold them before frying, cover and refrigerate.

To fry the filled crescents: Put the Simple Syrup in a bowl and place it near the stove.

Melt the shortening in a deep pot over high heat. When it has completely melted, reduce the heat to medium. Working with 1 filled crescent at a time, pinch the edges tightly closed and then slide the crescent into the hot shortening. Repeat with several more crescents, but do not crowd the pot. Fry, turning them once with a slotted spoon, until they are golden brown, about 4 minutes.

As they are cooked, use the slotted spoon to transfer the crescents to the bowl of Simple Syrup. Then use another slotted spoon to place them on a serving platter. Offer the crescents to your guests immediately.

Marinated Dried Fruits

KHOSHAF

½ cup unsalted pistachios

½ cup walnuts

½ cup pine nuts

½ cup sugar

2 tablespoons rose water

2 tablespoons orange-blossom
water

½ cup dark raisins

½ cup golden raisins

1 cup dried apricots

1 cup dried figs

1 cup dried prunes

½ cup almonds, peeled (see
page 12)

*T*his traditional Ramadan dessert was a fixture in my mother's refrigerator during the entire fasting month. You can use whatever
combination of dried fruits and nuts you like—for festive occasions, add
a bit of Apricot Juice to the sugar syrup.   *Serves 6 to 8*

Soak the pistachios, walnuts, and pine nuts in separate bowls of
cold water for at least 3 hours or as long as overnight.

Remove the pistachios and walnuts, peel off their fine skins by
rubbing them between your palms, and return them to the cold
water.

Combine the sugar and 1 cup water in a small saucepan over high
heat, stirring until the sugar has dissolved. Bring to a boil and cook
for 2 minutes. Then remove the pan from the heat and stir in the
rose and orange-blossom waters. Set the syrup aside.

Rinse the raisins, apricots, figs, and prunes under cold water and
place them in a large serving bowl. Drain the pistachios, walnuts,
and pine nuts and add them, along with the almonds, to the fruit
mixture. Pour the syrup over the mixture and stir well. Refrigerate
for at least 3 hours or as long as overnight.

Serve in dessert bowls.

Fruit Salad with Rose Water

FAWAKEH MUSHAKAL

*T*he Arab version of fruit salad is liberally perfumed with rose water. Adjust the amount to suit your taste.   ***Serves 4***

2 tablespoons unsalted
    pistachios

1 orange

1 grapefruit

2 pears, peeled, cored, and cut
    lengthwise into 8 pieces each

1 pound strawberries, hulled

For the syrup:

½ cup sugar

¼ cup rose water

Soak the pistachios in warm water for 20 minutes.

Peel the orange and grapefruit with a sharp knife, removing all the white pith, and cut out the segments.

Combine the orange and grapefruit segments, pears, and strawberries in a large bowl. Drain the pistachios and add them to the fruit. Set the bowl aside.

Make the syrup: Combine the sugar and 1 cup water in a small saucepan over high heat, stirring until the sugar has dissolved. Bring to a boil and add the rose water. Then remove the pan from the heat and let the syrup cool completely.

Add the cooled syrup to the bowl and toss to coat the fruit in the syrup. Serve cold.

Arab Ice Cream

BOZZA BI HALLEEB

16 pebble-size pieces of mastic (see page 22)

3 cups sugar, plus extra for crushing the mastic

2 quarts 2% milk

1 tablespoon salep (see page 27)

1 tablespoon rose water

2 tablespoons orange-blossom water

Unsalted pistachios *or* seasonal berries, for garnish

This recipe comes from Yumna Assaily, a wonderful friend who began to make her own ice cream when she moved with her family from Lebanon to London in the 1980s. Yumna's ice cream was always anticipated at our dinner parties, where fellow expatriates declared it second only to the beloved Bozza bi Halleeb they enjoyed in the Middle East. Arab Ice Cream features the subtle licorice flavor of mastic and gets its smooth consistency from sahlap, the same powder used to make Salep, the hot winter drink flavored with rose and orange-blossom waters. It will keep in the freezer up to 1 month. **Makes ½ gallon**

Place a few pieces of mastic and some sugar on a spoon, top with a second spoon facing the other way, and press together to crush the mastic.

In a large pot, combine 1 quart of the milk, the mastic, and the 3 cups sugar. Bring to a boil, stirring occasionally. Reduce the heat to low to keep warm.

Combine 1 tablespoon of the warm milk mixture with the salep in a small bowl, and stir to dissolve the salep.

Pour the remaining 1 quart milk into a large bowl, add the salep mixture, and mix with a handheld electric mixer until the milk is foamy, about 1 minute. Pour this cold mixture into the hot milk in the pot, and stir with a wooden spoon. Raise the heat to high and continue to stir until the mixture returns to a boil. Then reduce the heat to medium and cook for 10 minutes. Return the heat to high, add the rose water and orange-blossom water, and bring to a boil. Cook over high heat for 5 minutes.

Remove the pot from the heat. Strain the liquid through a fine-mesh sieve into a 3-quart glass or ceramic dish, and set it aside to cool. Then cover it with plastic wrap and refrigerate overnight.

Pour the chilled mixture into the canister of an ice cream machine and process, following the manufacturer's instructions. Transfer the ice cream to a mold (I use a glass bowl), cover it with plastic wrap, and freeze for at least 6 hours or overnight.

Two hours before serving, transfer the ice cream from the freezer to the refrigerator (this promotes the "chewy," somewhat elastic texture that makes this ice cream so special).

When you are ready to serve the ice cream, wrap a hot towel around the mold, set an inverted serving plate over the bowl, and holding the two together, flip the whole thing over so the mold rests on the plate. Remove the bowl, garnish the ice cream with the pistachios or seasonal berries, and serve.

Halvah Ice Cream

BOZZA HALAWA

2 cups whole milk

1 egg

2 egg yolks

½ cup sugar

2 teaspoons chestnut flour dissolved in ¼ cup water

¾ teaspoon vanilla extract

½ pound halvah

1½ teaspoons rose water

½ teaspoon ground cardamom

½ cup heavy cream

½ cup pistachios, soaked in warm water for 20 minutes and drained

¼ cup carob molasses (see page 15)

*H*alvah, a sesame-rich sweetmeat, rose water, and cardamom flavor this rich frozen treat, which is enjoyed year-round in the Gulf States, where the winter season is very short. The secret to making the most authentic version of Halvah Ice Cream is to use the finest halvah you can find. Look for brands that are creamy beige, flaky, and don't taste too intensely of tahini. The best variety comes from Saudi Arabia, but I can get that only when my friends visit. Here in the States, I have found that the Ghandour and Cortas brands of halvah, carried by my local Middle Eastern grocer, make excellent ice cream. Chestnut flour gives the ice cream a subtle nutty flavor; if you can't find it, use whole-wheat, almond, or all-purpose flour.   ***Makes 1 quart***

Heat the milk in a medium saucepan over medium heat until it is warm to the touch, about 140°F. Set it aside.

Bring 3 cups water to a boil in the bottom of a double-boiler over high heat. Remove the pan from the heat. Combine the egg, yolks, and sugar in the top of the double-boiler, set it over the hot water, and beat with a handheld electric mixer on high speed until the sugar dissolves and the mixture is foamy. With the mixer running, gradually add the flour mixture and the warmed milk, and mix until thoroughly combined. Return the double-boiler to high-heat. Cook, stirring with a wooden spoon, until the mixture thickens enough to coat the back of the spoon, about 10 minutes.

Remove the double-boiler from the heat and stir in the vanilla. Then strain the liquid through a fine-mesh sieve into a large bowl. Set it aside to cool. Then cover it with plastic wrap and refrigerate for 3 to 4 hours.

Combine the halvah, rose water, cardamom, and chilled milk mixture in a blender and process until frothy.

Pour the cream into a bowl and beat it with a handheld electric mixer until stiff peaks form. Fold the whipped cream into the milk mixture. Pour the mixture into the canister of an ice cream maker and process, following the manufacturer's instructions.

Halvah Ice Cream (continued)

Spoon the ice cream into a serving bowl, sprinkle the pistachios on top, cover tightly in two layers of plastic wrap, and freeze overnight.

About 2 hours before serving, place the ice cream in the refrigerator to soften. Serve with a little carob molasses drizzled on top.

CHRISTMAS AT AUNTIE NINA'S

Our close family friends, Nina and Hanna Ayoub, who lived at the time in Lebanon, introduced me and my sisters to all of the Christmas traditions and rituals: the thrilling novelty of midnight mass, the solemn and moving ringing of the church bells, the Christmas tree, and of course the giving and receiving of gifts.

Auntie Nina and Uncle Hanna, as I called them, are Christians and I often celebrated Christmas with them, both when I was growing up and later when Aref and I lived in Kuwait. Christmas in the Arab world is celebrated by the majority of Christians on the twenty-fifth of December, as it is in the West. Orthodox Christians, who follow the Julian calendar, consider the seventh of January a more accurate date for the birth of Christ, and celebrate that day.

The season would start with a visit to Auntie Nina to help her decorate the tree and the manger that symbolized Christ's birthplace. On the tree we'd hang beautiful ornaments and small embroidered bags filled with raisins, almonds, and pine nuts. She would serve delicious sweets such as Ladies' Arms, Semolina Pouches, and Pastries with Walnuts, Pistachios, and Dates. Auntie Nina usually started her preparations for Christmas a good month in advance. She got us all involved in decorating the Christmas tree—under which, when finished, she would place all the carefully wrapped presents. We children looked on and tingled with anticipation.

On Christmas Eve we gathered at their house again, for a wonderful dinner followed by presents. My favorite time, though, was going to the midnight church service with Auntie Nina and Uncle Hanna.

As I grew up, I came to appreciate how hard Auntie Nina worked. Her preparations for Christmas were like ours for Ramadan—for a month or more she was busy shopping, cooking, and freezing food for the holiday. And getting gifts for everyone. I especially admired how she served enormous back-to-back meals for Christmas Eve and Christmas Day: her grown daughters brought their husbands and kids for Christmas Eve, and on Christmas Day, her sons came with their families.

On Christmas Eve, Auntie Nina would prepare a stuffed chicken or stuffed lamb shoulder, several vegetable dishes, and always Khoshaf (Marinated Dried Fruits) for dessert.

Christmas Day was a more elaborate feast. The centerpiece at the Ayoubs' table was always a big turkey stuffed with rice and chestnuts. Another favorite of mine was chicken soup with Kibeh Balls. Following tradition, Auntie Nina stuffed just one of the balls with a pitted olive: whoever found it in his soup would have good luck in the New Year. Christmas desserts always included Mughli (Caraway and Anise Seed Pudding) and a big array of pastries.

In our home, we've always enjoyed many Christmas customs. During the years when our children were growing up, we decorated a tree, and a friend dressed as Santa Claus always came to our house on Christmas Eve to give our children and their friends their presents. Since we've lived in the United States, we've happily shared in the social events and spirit of goodwill of the Christmas season. I of course always like to prepare a holiday meal with some of Auntie Nina's specialties, as in the menu here.

Christmas Menu

- Stuffed Grape Leaves
- Meat Pies
- Parsley Salad
- Kibeh in the Tray
- Stuffed Leg of Lamb

- Eggplant in Pomegranate Syrup
- Chicken Soup with Vermicelli and Kibeh Balls
- Chicken Stuffed with Spiced Beef and Rice

- Arab Flatbread
- Cucumber and Yogurt
- Olives
- A plate of white onions and mint leaves
- Pickled cucumbers and turnips

- Pastries with Walnuts, Pistachios, and Dates
- Marinated Dried Fruits
- Ladies' Arms
- Caraway and Anise Seed Pudding

- Wine
- Fruit juices
- White Coffee
- Cinnamon Tea

Sources

Athens Pastries and Frozen Food
13600 Snow Road
Cleveland, OH 44142
800-837-5683
www.athens.com

   Frozen phyllo.

Bob's Red Mill
5209 Southeast International Way
Milwaukee, OR 97222
800-553-2258
www.bobsredmill.com

   Spices, flours, Turkish bay leaves.

Buy Lebanese
www.buylebanese.com

   A website shop that ships from Lebanon.

Dean & Deluca
560 Broadway
New York, NY 10012
800-221-7714
www.deandeluca.com

   In-store shopping: pomegranate molasses, rose water, dried roses, green almonds, and much more.

Farahat Pita Bread
10391-7 Old Street
Augustine Road
Jacksonville, FL 32257
904-262-1787

   Arab flatbread.

Ideal Cheese Shop
942 First Avenue
New York, NY 10022
800-382-0109
www.Idealcheese.com

   Halloumi cheese, Greek Total yogurt, kashkawal cheese, Marcona almonds.

I gourmet.com
Internet shop
www.iGourmet.com

   Feta cheese.

Jamison Farm
171 Jamison Lane
Latrobe, PA 15650
800-237-5262
www.jamisonfarm.com

   Best lamb in America.

Jerusalem Food Market
Khalid Dager
Old Gate Plaza
300 North Blvd.
Springdale, OH 45246
513-771-8888

    All your needs in the Cincinnati area.

Kalustyan's
123 Lexington Ave.
New York, NY 10016
212-685-3416
www.kalustyan.com

    Dried rose petals, and much more.

Melissa's
P.O. Box 21127
Los Angeles, CA 90021
800-588-0151
www.melissas.com

    Baby cucumbers, quince, Mejdool dates.

Mission Liquors
1801 E. Washington Blvd.
Pasadena, CA 91104
626-797-0500
877-772-0500
www.missionliquors.com

    Arak.

Oasis Date Gardens
59-111 Highway 111
P.O. Box 757
Thermal, CA 92274
800-827-8017
www.oasisdategardens.com

    Best dates of all kinds.

Peet's Coffee & Tea
P.O. Box 12509
Berkeley, CA 94712-9901
800-999-2132
www.peets.com

    Adani coffee beans.

Penzeys, Ltd.
P.O. Box 1448
Waukesha, WI 53187
800-741-7787
www.penzeys.com

    A great selection of spices and dried herbs.

    Catalogue available.

Shatila Food Products
14300 W. Warren
Dearborn, MI 48126
313-934-1520
www.shatila.com

    Large selection of Arab sweets; rose petal preserves.

Star Hill Dairy, LLC
P.O. Box 295
South Woodstock, VT 05071
802-457-4540
www.woodstockwaterbuffalo.com

    Buffalo mozzarella and yogurt.

Stewart and Jasper Orchards
3500 Shiells Road
Newman, CA 95360
www.stewartandjasper.com

    Almonds and green almonds.

Sur la Table
410 Terry Avenue North
Seattle, WA 98109
800-243-0852
www.surlatable.com

    Kitchenware, including heat diffusers.

Willow Hill Farm
For sheep yogurt and cheese, available through
distributors, check their website: *www.sheepcheese.com.*
Or for mail order: Formaggio Kitchen, in Boston,
888-212-3224.

Zenobia Company
5774 Mosholu Avenue
Bronx, NY 10471
718-796-7700
www.nutsonthenet.com

    Pistachios from Turkey.

Ziyad Brothers
5400 W. 35th Street
Cicero, IL 60804
708-22-8330
www.ziyadbrothers.com

    Olives, pickles, beans, semolina, zaatar, and more.

Index

A

aijeh arabia, 115

aish, 12

ajet bayd bi koossa, 120

akawi cheese, 16

    in cheese and walnut crescents, 337–38

    desalting of, 310

    in shredded pastry with cheese, 307–10

akras kafta, 237

akras kibeh makli, 230–31

akrass zaatar, 86–87

aleb falafel (shaping tool), 109

allspice, 12

    in spinach and ground lamb stew, 141

    in stuffed leg of lamb, 209–10

almonds, 12–13

    apricot pudding with pistachios and, 324–25

    cookies, 300

    in semolina cake, 320

anise seeds, 13

    and caraway pudding, 326–27

    in semolina fingers, 318–19

    tea, 298

appetizers, *see* mezza

apricot(s), 13

    juice, 288

    pudding with almonds and pistachios, 324–25

Arab coffee, 13

    basic, 292–93

Arab culinary history and customs, 2–11

Arab flatbread, 14

    basic, 94–95

    for fried fish, 240–41

    for fried kafta triangles, 78

    for grilled halloumi cheese triangles, 75

    for spicy Lebanese cheese dip, 54

    toasted, eggplant with pomegranate syrup and, 65

    for yogurt cheese wraps, 113

Arab ice cream, 341–42

Arab omelet, 115

Arab pancakes, 336

Arab pantry (ingredients), 12–30

Arab-style rice, basics of, 165

Arab yogurt cheese, 110–11

arak, 14

ardichokeh mahshi, 195–96

caraway seeds, 15
    and anise seed pudding, 326–27
    in Yemeni spice mix, 41
cardamom, 15
    in Arab coffee, 292–93
    in beef and freka soup, 134
    in beef stock, 131
    in chicken soup with vermicelli, 126–27
    in lamb beryani, 217–18
    in lamb in creamy sheep's-milk yogurt, 205–6
    in rice and ground beef in phyllo pockets, 200–201
carob molasses, 15–16
    in halvah ice cream, 343–44
carrots:
    in eggplant and pomegranate stew, 137
    in lamb and pea stew, 140
    in stuffed leg of lamb, 209–10
cauliflower, fried, 77
cayenne pepper, 16
chat masala, 16
    in Saudi spice mix, 40
cheese(s), 16
    Arab yogurt, 110–11
    and oregano crescents, 84–85
    phyllo, pie, 114
    pull-away, rolls, 102–3
    shredded pastry with, 307–11
    spicy Lebanese, dip, 54
    and walnut crescents, 337–38
    yogurt, balls, 112
    yogurt, wraps, 113
    see also specific cheeses
chicken:
    freka with ground beef, 184
    gizzards, sautéed, 80
    kebabs, 189
    kibeh, 191–92

    in Lebanese couscous, 179–81
    poached, with garlic-chile relish, 188
    and rice with creamy yogurt sauce, 185
    rose water–scented, with saffron rice, 186–87
    shawarma, 190
    soup, Moroccan, 128
    soup with vermicelli, 126–27
    stock, spiced, 125
    stuffed with spiced beef and rice, 182 83
    traditional cleaning of, 181
chickpea(s), 17
    baked lamb with rice and, 203–4
    canned vs. dried, 52
    in deep-fried fava bean patties, 107–9
    dip, 51–52
    dip with meat, 53
    dressed, 60
    for eggplant in pomegranate syrup, 273–74
    freezing of, 61
    lamb with sumac and, 207–8
    in Lebanese couscous, 179–81
    in Moroccan chicken soup, 128
    in Moroccan couscous, 177–78
    toasted, flour and spice mix, 39
    with yogurt, 277–78
chiles, *see* jalapeño peppers
chips, Arab, 42
Christmas, 345–46
cilantro, 17, 46
    in baked sea bass with tahini-walnut sauce, 244–47
    in baked whole red snapper, 250–51
    in beef with white beans, 221–22
    in braised fava beans, 275
    in bulgur and fava beans, 281
    in deep-fried fava bean patties, 107–9
    in fish kibeh, 256–57

in fish soup, 135

fried potatoes with, 276

in Kuwaiti grilled snapper, 253–54

in lamb beryani, 217–18

in lamb and pea stew, 140

in lentil soup with chard leaves, 130

in okra stew, 142–43

in potato salad, 154

shrimp with garlic and, 255

cinnamon, 17

in caraway and anise seed pudding, 326–27

in chicken soup with vermicelli, 126–27

in chicken stuffed with spiced beef and rice, 182–83

in lamb beryani, 217–18

in lamb with rice and yogurt, 211–12

in Lebanese couscous, 179–81

in Moroccan couscous, 177–78

in rose water–scented chicken with saffron rice, 186–87

in spiced chicken stock, 125

tea, 296

cloves, 17

coconut:

in almond cookies, 300

in caraway and anise seed pudding, 326–27

in semolina cake, 320

cookies:

almond, 300

date fingers, 301–2

semolina fingers, 318–19

coriander seeds, 17

Cornish hens, in Moroccan couscous, 177–78

couscous:

Lebanese, 179–81

Moroccan, 177–78

in Moroccan chicken soup, 128

couscous bi khodra wa dajaj, 177–78

cucumbers, 18

in Jerusalem salad, 147

in mixed vegetable salad, 148

in simple salad, 146

and yogurt, 57–58

cumin seeds, 18

in baked sea bass with rice and caramelized onions, 242–43

in dressed chickpeas, 60–61

in Kuwaiti spice mix, 41

in Saudi spice mix, 40

D

dajaj bi freka, 184

dajaj mahshe, 182–83

dakka, 162

dakous, 35

damaa', 34

dandelion, 18

date(s), 18–19

cake, 314–15

fingers, 301–2

in Kuwaiti grilled snapper, 253–54

pastries with walnuts, pistachios and, 303–4

desserts, 299–346

almond cookies, 300

apricot pudding with almonds and pistachios, 324–25

Arab ice cream, 341–42

Arab pancakes, 336

baklava, 312–13

bread pudding with syrup, 331

caraway and anise seed pudding, 326–27

cheese and walnut crescents, 337–38

date cake, 314–15

greens (*continued*)

in mixed vegetable salad, 148

sautéed, with crispy onions, 269–70

see also romaine lettuce

Gulf States, 9–10

H

halawat el jibin, 334–35

halloumi cheese, 16

desalting of, 75

fried, 74

grilled, triangles, 75

in oregano and cheese crescents, 84–85

in pull-away cheese rolls, 102–3

topping, for mountain bread, 100

halloumi kulage, 75

halloumi makli, 74

halvah, 21

ice cream, 343–44

harissa, 21

in Moroccan chicken soup, 128

hashweh, 173–74

herbs:

dried, 45–46

fresh, 46

see also specific herbs

hindba bi zeit, 269–70

holidays and special occasions, 10

Christmas, 345–46

Easter, 122–23

Eid al Adha, 90–91, 210

Eid al-Fiter, 90–91, 264–66

iftar, sample menus for, 264–65

istikbal, 143

Lent and fasting, 121

Mubarakeh, 328–29

Ramadan, 258–66

Suhur, sample menus for, 265–66

hummus, 51

I

ice cream:

Arab, 341–42

halvah, 343–44

ingredients, 4–5, 12–30

sources for, 347–49

Iraq, 6

J

jalapeño peppers:

in fried eggplant with hot chiles, 76

in garlic-chile relish, poached chicken with, 188

in okra stew, 142–43

in spicy Lebanese cheese dip, 54

in spicy tomato sauce, 35

in tomato and dill seed salad, 162

in tomato spread, 50

jameed, 21, 206

in lamb in creamy sheep's-milk yogurt, 205–6

jereesh, 21

Jerusalem salad, 147

jibneh malfofeh, 114

jibneh wa joz hashweh, 337–38

Jordan, 7–8

K

kaak luz, 300

kabsa, 213–14

milk, 23

   in Arab ice cream, 341–42

   in date fingers, 301–2

   in halvah ice cream, 343–44

   in holy bread, 96–97

   in *kashta,* 317

   in phyllo cheese pie, 114

   pudding, 322–23

   in rice pudding, 330

   in *salep,* 290

   in semolina cake, 320

   in semolina purses, 332–33

   in yellow diamonds, 321

mint, 23

   in grilled kibeh on skewers, 229

   in mixed vegetable salad, 148

   in stuffed grape leaves, 68–70

   in stuffed leg of lamb, 209–10

   zucchini with bread and, 64

mohalabia, 322–23

mohalabia kamar al deen, 324–25

monazallet bi aswad, 138

Moroccan chicken soup, 128

Moroccan couscous, 177–78

Morocco, 5–6

mortar and pestle, 72

mountain bread, 98–101

mozzarella cheese:

   in bread pudding with syrup, 331

   in oregano and cheese crescents, 84–85

   in pull-away cheese rolls, 102–3

   in semolina rolls, 334–35

   in shredded pastry with cheese, 307–10

Mubarakeh, 328–29

mudardara, 172

mufarakat batata bi bayid, 118

mufarakat betinjan, 119

mufarakat kossa, 202

mughli, 326–27

mugrabieh, 179–81

muhamar, 166–67

mujadara, 170–71

mujadara safra, 268

musaka betinjan, 273–74

N

namoura, 320

nigella seeds, 23

   in halloumi topping for mountain bread, 100

   in pull-away cheese rolls, 102–3

nutmeg, 23

nuts, 23

   in baklava, 312–13

   in caraway and anise seed pudding, 326–27

   fried, 43

   for marinated dried fruits, 339

O

okra, 23–24

   stew, 142–43

   with tomatoes, 272

olive oil, 24, 48

olives, 24, 49

   green, in tomato salad, 161

   hot green, 48

onions:

   caramelized, baked sea bass with rice and, 242–43

   in chicken kibeh, 191–92

   in fish kibeh, 256–57

P

salads (continued)

   simple, 146

   tomato, 161

   tomato and dill seed, 162

salatat al rahib, 159–60

salatat arabi, 146

salatat bandora, 161

salatat batata, 154

salatat el malfoof, 153

salatat ful akhdar, 156–57

salatat jarjeer, 152

salatat kudsiyeh, 147

salatat shamandar, 155

salatat zaatar, 151

salep, 27

   basic, 290

samakeh bi bandora, 250–51

samakeh harra bi tahini, 244–47

samak makli, 240–41

samna, 45

sauces:

   Al Masala, for lamb beryani, 217–18

   béchamel, for baked pasta, 284–85

   creamy yogurt, chicken and rice with, 185

   parsley, 36

   spicy tomato, 35

   stewed tomato, 34

   tahini onion, 33

   tahini-walnut, baked sea bass with, 244–47

   tomato, for rose water–scented chicken with saffron rice, 186–87

   tomato-beef, for baked pasta, 284–85

   yogurt, stuffed zucchini in, 193–94

Saudi Arabian slow-cooked lamb, 213–14

Saudi spice mix, 40

sayadiah, 242–43

scallions:

   in eggplant salad, 158

   in Jerusalem salad, 147

   in oregano salad, 151

   in simple salad, 146

   in spicy Lebanese cheese dip, 54

semolina, 27

   in Arab pancakes, 336

   cake, 320

   fingers, 318–19

   in oregano cakes, 86–87

   in pastries with walnuts, pistachios, and dates, 303–4

   pistachio layer cake, 316

   purses, 332–33

   rolls, 334–35

   in yellow diamonds, 321

sesame seed paste, *see* tahini

sesame seeds, 28

   in deep-fried fava bean patties, 107–9

   in semolina fingers, 318–19

   in toasted chickpea flour and spice mix, 39

   in zaatar, 38

sfoof, 321

shallots:

   in chicken stuffed with spiced beef and rice, 182–83

   in okra with tomatoes, 272

shamandar mutabal, 62–63

shankleesh cheese, 16

   in spicy Lebanese cheese dip, 54

shankleesh mutabal, 54

shawarma, 223–24

shawarma dajaj, 190

shay darseen, 296

shay yansoon, 298

shish kabob, 215–16

shish tawook, 189

shorabat adas, 129

shorabat adas bi hamod, 130

shorabat al samak, 135

T